BRAZIL

BRAZIL

Five Centuries of Change

SECOND EDITION

Thomas E. Skidmore

Professor Emeritus, Brown University

New York   Oxford
OXFORD UNIVERSITY PRESS
2010

Oxford University Press, Inc., publishes works that further Oxford University's
objective of excellence in research, scholarship, and education.

Oxford   New York
Auckland   Cape Town   Dar es Salaam   Hong Kong   Karachi
Kuala Lumpur   Madrid   Melbourne   Mexico City   Nairobi
New Delhi   Shanghai   Taipei   Toronto

With offices in
Argentina   Austria   Brazil   Chile   Czech Republic   France   Greece
Guatemala   Hungary   Italy   Japan   Poland   Portugal   Singapore
South Korea   Switzerland   Thailand   Turkey   Ukraine   Vietnam

Published by Oxford University Press, Inc.
198 Madison Avenue, New York, New York 10016
http://www.oup.com

Oxford is a registered trademark of Oxford University Press

Library of Congress Cataloging-in-Publication Data

Skidmore, Thomas E.
    Brazil: five centuries of change / Thomas E. Skidmore.—2nd ed.
      p. cm.
    Includes bibliographical references and index.
    ISBN 978-0-19-537455-1 (pbk.)
    1. Brazil—History.   I. Title.
    F2521.S54 2010
                                                    2009011669

CONTENTS

LIST OF EXHIBITS AND FIGURES

Exhibits

Figures

PREFACE

Writing a one-volume history of any well-established country is inevitably a collective enterprise, no matter what the title page may say. My greatest debt is to the many Brazilians who over the past four decades have been unfailingly generous with their historical knowledge and their hospitality. Alberto Venancio Filho and Paulo Sérgio Pinheiro, both friends of many years, read a draft manuscript of the first edition and made valuable suggestions, although neither saw the final version before publication. A number of American colleagues gave similar help; they include Dain Borges, Todd Diacon, Frank McCann, Steve Topik, and Joel Wolfe. For the second edition, in addition to Paulo Sérgio Pinheiro once again, my heartfelt thanks go especially to James N. Green and David Fleischer, good friends as well as esteemed colleagues in the world of Brazilianistas. David kept me straight on events, people, and places during the Cardoso and Lula years. Jim gave a critical and most helpful read of the entire manuscript, with particularly sharp focus on the "Suggestions for Further Reading."

The major changes in the second edition are several. First, I have updated my analysis by adding the second term of Fernando Henrique Cardoso, the first term and reelection of Luiz Inácio Lula da Silva, and some remarks about how Lula's second term seems to be going, what accounts for his relative success as this book goes to press, and the ongoing problems that are bound to confront Lula's successor as president. Second, I have revamped my "Suggestions for Further Reading." In the previous edition, this was a list of books that had been particularly valuable in helping me learn about Brazil. In this edition, in response to reviewer comments, the conception of the list has been changed to be a vehicle for student learning and teaching. Third, I have added several images to the text to relieve reading fatigue. Finally, in response to withering criticism of my sloppy, incomplete, and sometimes flat wrong treatment of the colonial era, I have made major revisions to what used to be chapters 1 through 3 (rearranged as this edition's chapters 1 and 3), and added a completely new chapter (this edition's chapter 2).

As anyone who knows my work understands, I specialize in the study of Brazil's modern period. The reviewer comments made me acutely aware of my insufficient knowledge of recent bibliography on Brazil's colonial era. Boris Fausto's excellent volume, *A Concise History of Brazil* (Cambridge University Press, 1999), helped me correct numerous factual errors in my first edition. In addition, my new chapter 2, in particular, owes a great deal to the anonymous reviewers' extended and often detailed comments, including valuable guidance to recent research. Since the text of chapter 2 is based heavily and directly on several recent research articles by historians of colonial Brazil, I wish to acknowledge these scholars specifically. The articles I used most heavily are the following, in alphabetical order by author:

B. J. Barickman, "Reading the 1835 Parish Censuses from Bahia: Citizenship, Kinship, Slavery, and Household in Early Nineteenth Century Brazil," *The Americas* 59:3 (2004).

B. J. Barickman, "Revisiting the *Casa-grande*: Plantation and Cane-Farming Households in Early Nineteenth-century Bahia," *Hispanic American Historical Review* 84:4 (2003).

Flavio dos Santos Gomes, "A 'Safe Haven': Runaway Slaves, *Mocambos*, and Borders, in Colonial Amazonia, Brazil," *Hispanic American Historical Review* 82:3 (2002).

Herbert S. Klein and Francisco Vidal Luna, "Free Colored in a Slave Society: São Paulo and Minas Gerais in the Early Nineteenth Century," *Hispanic American Historical Review* 80:4 (2002).

Hendrik Kraay, "Transatlantic Ties: Recent Works on the Slave Trade, Slavery, and Abolition," *Latin American Research Review* 39:2 (2004).

Hal Langfur, "The Return of the *Bandeira*: Economic Calamity, Historical Memory, and Armed Expeditions to the Sertão in Minas Gerais, Brazil, 1750–1808," *The Americas* 61:3 (2005).

Alida C. Metcalf, "The *Entradas* of Bahia of the Sixteenth Century," *The Americas* 61:3 (2005).

John H. Monteiro, "The Heathen Castes of Sixteenth-century Portuguese America: Unity, Diversity, and the Invention of the Brazilian Indians," *Hispanic American Historical Review* 80:4 (2000).

Muriel Nazzari, "Vanishing Indians: The Social Construction of Race in Colonial São Paulo," *The Americas* 57:4 (2001).

Jorge M. Pedreira, "Contraband, Crisis, and the Collapse of the Old Colonial System," *Hispanic American Historical Review* 81:3 (2001).

Jorge M. Pedreira, "From Growth to Collapse: Portugal, Brazil, and the Breakdown of the Old Colonial System (1760–1830)," *Hispanic American Historical Review* 80:4 (2000).

A. J. R. Russell-Wood, "New Directions in *Bandeirismo* Studies in Colonial Brazil," *The Americas* 61:3 (2005).

Stuart B. Schwartz, "Brazil: Ironies of the Colonial Past," *Hispanic American Historical Review* 80:4 (2000).

Patrick Wilcken, "'A Colony of a Colony': The Portuguese Royal Court in Brazil," *Common Knowledge* 11:2 (2005).

I am extremely grateful for the insights into the colonial period provided by these specialists. Wherever I use their material directly, I include a direct quote from their work as a signal of my debt. Any errors that remain are, of course, my own.

A series of excellent research assistants through the years includes Joel Karlin, Helan Gaston, Nelly Letjer, Lisbeth Pimentel, Chi Watts, Telia Anderson, Barbara Martinez, and Nicole Bush. Sheldon Meyer, formerly senior editor at Oxford University Press, furnished the knowing encouragement for all my work that has been so important to many American historians. Sheldon died as I began working on the new edition. I shall continue to miss him, not only as an inspired editor but also as a mentor and close family friend.

As always, I owe a special debt to my wife, Felicity, who once again demonstrated her formidable skills as a book midwife. With her left hand she edits, and with her right hand she tends the heart. What more could a spouse ask for?

Spring, 2009

BRAZIL

A Brief Sketch of Brazil and Its Place in the World

Brazil is not only by far the largest country in Latin America. It also is one of the largest in the world, exceeded only by Canada, the People's Republic of China, Russia, and the United States (if Alaska and Hawaii are included). Covering over 3.3 million square miles (8.5 million square kilometers) and spanning some 2,700 miles from north to south and roughly the same distance from east to west, it stretches from slightly north of the equator to well south of the Tropic of Capricorn. (See exhibit I-1.) At the equator there are no seasons. In the rest of Brazil, as is true throughout the Southern Hemisphere, the seasons are the reverse of ours—with the coolest period from May to September (our summer) and the hottest from December to March (our winter).

Brazil's enormous expanse from north to south encompasses a wide range of climates. The Amazon Basin in the far north, which covers about 40 percent of South America's total area and is the largest tropical rain forest in the world, lies mostly in Brazil. It has a hot, wet, tropical climate, with rainfall well over one hundred inches a year in some places. The narrow coastal plain bordering the Atlantic, where the majority of Brazilians live, goes from tropical in the north (in the cities of Belém, Fortaleza, and Recife, for example) to temperate in the south (in cities such as São Paulo, Curitiba, and Porto Alegre). Rio de Janeiro, perhaps Brazil's best-known city, is between the two extremes—subtropical, with summer temperatures averaging upwards of eighty degrees Fahrenheit and very humid and winter lows in the range of sixty degrees. Hurricanes and earthquakes are unknown in Brazil, although floods and drought are relatively common threats.

EXHIBIT |-1

Comparative size of Brazil. Updated from E. Bradford Burns, *A History of Brazil*, 3rd ed. (New York, 1993), p. 14.

Brazil's topography is dramatic. In the far north of the Amazon Basin a series of mountain ranges includes Brazil's highest mountain, Pico da Neblina at 9,888 feet. South of the Amazon Basin lie the Brazilian Highlands, which meet the Atlantic Ocean in a vast, almost vertical escarpment that includes mountains ranging from 7,000 to 8,000 feet above sea level at its southeastern end. Brazil's major rivers, which flow largely from west to east, include the Amazon River in the north, the world's second longest (after the Nile) at 4,000 miles and the one that carries the largest volume of water of any river in the world; the Tocantins River, which flows more than 1,500 miles into the Atlantic Ocean south of the Amazon proper; the São Francisco River, which flows almost 2,000 miles through northeastern and central Brazil; and the Paraná, Paraguay, and Uruguay Rivers, which flow through southern Brazil.

Brazil's plant life is justly famous, with about a quarter of the world's known plant species found in Brazil. The Amazon Basin, for example, includes Brazil nut trees, brazilwood, multiple kinds of palm trees, and rosewood, all intertwined with creepers and vines, plus orchids, water lilies, and endless tropical flowers. Some people even speculate that a final cure for cancer lies somewhere in Amazon plant life. The rain forest also includes hundreds of types of macaws, toucans, and parrots; splendid butterflies; many species of monkeys; and a wide range of snakes, crocodiles, and alligators, as well armadillo and sloth, among many other species. Brazil's rivers are filled with more than two thousand species of fish, of which the people-eating piranha is one of the more common.

Brazil can also boast:

- A history of long and amicable relationships with the United States, unlike any other major South American or Central American country;
- A society of enormous creative energy, as expressed in Brazil's world champion soccer teams, its internationally admired supermodels, its infectiously captivating popular music, and its widely read novelists;
- An economy that is at last realizing its vast potential, emerging as a major trader on the world scene that exports everything from soybeans to jet aircraft and is self-sufficient in fuel, thanks in good measure to Brazil's decades-long program of producing ethanol from sugarcane;
- The type of international muscle that has waged a successful fight to break the HIV drug patents held by pharmaceutical companies in the United States and western Europe and helped bring generic drugs to the many AIDS sufferers in Brazil and other parts of the developing world;
- The election and reelection of its first working-class president, who has confounded his critics by turning from a career of espousing economic socialism to the pursuit of conventional economic policies that have brought the country into unprecedented prosperity—while retaining his wide popularity along the whole political spectrum of Brazilians.

Present-day Brazil covers five major regions: North, Northeast, Center-West, Southeast, and South. (See exhibit I-2.) The North includes the states of Rondônia, Acre, Amazonas, Roraima, Pará, and Amapá. By far the largest region, the North accounts for 42 percent of the national territory. Enthusiasts, both Brazilian and foreign, have nourished illusions through the years about the potential of the greater Amazon Basin for commercial agriculture—from Henry Ford's disastrous effort in the 1930s to grow rubber on a massive scale by clearing the forest to the Brazilian military dictatorship's building of the Trans-Amazon highway in the 1970s (now so totally grown over in places that it is not visible even from the air). The great barrier to agricultural development of

EXHIBIT 1-2

The five regions of Brazil. From E. Bradford Burns, *A History of Brazil*, 3rd ed. (New York, 1993), p. 11.

the Amazon Basin is and always has been the vast tropical rain forest, glorious though it is to naturalists and conservationists. It makes overland travel impossible, which before air travel left the rivers the only mode of transportation (not very effective for communicating with the rest of Brazil, given that the rivers flow from west to east rather than north to south). More fundamentally, the omnipresent rain leaches the soil if the vegetable cover is cut down, preventing the use of conventional agriculture and leaving the area with insufficient carrying capacity for intense human settlement.

The Northeast includes the states of Maranhão, Piauí, Ceará, Rio Grande do Norte, Paraíba, Pernambuco, Alagoas, Sergipe, and Bahia. This region, which covers 18 percent of the national territory, was the heart of Brazil's early settlement. Since the nineteenth century, however, it has been in economic decline, with its once-flourishing export agriculture no longer competitive in world markets. The result has been continuing poverty for the population, which now constitutes the largest pocket of misery in the Americas. Much of the coast is a humid strip (*zona da mata*) that has lent itself to plantation agriculture, especially cane sugar and cotton. Behind this narrow humid zone lie two other zones that are less hospitable to agriculture: the *zona de agreste*, a semiarid region, and the *sertão*, a larger region subject to periodic drought. Both were famous in the 1920s and 1930s as the areas of the Brazilian bandits, such as Lampião, immortalized in verse, song, and film. The Northeast is also notable for the effectiveness with which its politicians have represented the region's interests (historically synonymous with the interests of the wealthy landowners).

The Center-West includes the states of Mato Grosso, Tocantins, Mato Grosso do Sul, Goiás, and the Federal District (Greater Brasilia). Traditionally underpopulated, this has become one of Brazil's fastest-growing areas. It covers 22 percent of the national territory, including much of the interior farmland (*cerrado*), which has become highly productive since the 1970s, especially for soybeans. The building of Brasilia (a modernistic city built from scratch and inaugurated as Brazil's capital in 1960) was a great stimulus to this growth, bringing modern transportation for the first time and with it the capacity to market products to the rest of Brazil and the world.

The Southeast comprises the states of Minas Gerais, Espirito Santo, Rio de Janeiro, and São Paulo. This is the heartland of Brazilian industrialization, occupying 11 percent of the national territory. The state of Minas Gerais is growing particularly rapidly, successfully combining commercial agriculture with industry. Espirito Santo still relies primarily on agriculture, particularly coffee and cacao. Since it lost its status as the country's capital, Rio has been losing industry to surrounding states. São Paulo, in contrast, has grown from an economic backwater until the second half of the nineteenth century, when it became the world's primary coffee-producing area, to become the industrial giant of Brazil—at the same time that it remains the champion producer of noncoffee foodstuffs.

The population of Brazil is approaching 190 million inhabitants, and some analysts project it will approach a quarter of a billion by midcentury. What is the racial/ethnic makeup of the population? The answer to this question begins to illustrate how the attitudes of Brazil to racial and ethnic identification differ from those of the United States. More than 50 percent of Brazilians are of African ancestry—the largest population of African descent outside Nigeria, due to Brazil's large-scale importation of slaves (nine times more than were brought to mainland North America). Given this fact, it may sound odd to American ears that only about 5–6 percent of Brazilians say they are black (*preto* or *negro*). This is because Brazilians do not view race as an issue of ancestry but rather of individual skin color. Somewhat over 40 percent self-identify as "brown" (*pardo*).

There is no official category called "Asian;" instead, the Brazilian Census introduced the category "yellow" (*amarelo*) in 1940; less than 1 percent of Brazilians say they are in this category. Less than 1 percent say they are "Indian" (*Índio*). Slightly over 50 percent say they are "white."

What questions should we ask as we proceed through Brazil's five centuries of change? One important question is how Brazilian society has proved to be remarkably integrated through the years, given that it is organized on hierarchical (class) terms rather than on any sense of equal status. In the United States, when we are asked what class we belong to, 90 percent of us say we are middle class. We do not typically identify ourselves within a social hierarchy (either below an "elite" or above a "lower" class). This is very different from the situation in Brazil, where the culture inculcates a sense of social distance as well as one of intimacy. Our task is to ask how this society emerged and what has kept it, at least until now, from becoming more open and egalitarian—which has been the declared aim of national leaders at least since the proclamation of Brazil as a republic in 1889.

One must marvel at how a relatively small political elite has been able to defuse and deflect popular unrest. Again and again, the threat of government overthrow through violent means has been averted by shrewd conciliatory or co-optive moves by those in power (which does not at all mean that Brazil has no violent bloodiness in its past). The result has been a remarkable continuity in the hierarchical social structure and in the distribution of power. The 2006 reelection of Luiz Inácio Lula da Silva as president of Brazil—a genuine member of Brazil's working class—may possibly signal that the lower classes in Brazil are beginning to vote for their economic interests on a national scale as never before. Will this threaten the social cohesion of the country? Time will tell.

There are many other questions to explore as well. One is how leaders in post-independence Brazil held together such a huge territory while Spanish South America after independence (1810–24) fragmented into many different nations, as the map of South America makes clear (see exhibit I-3). Brazil's consolidation of national identity owes much to the Brazilian sense of uniqueness in Latin America—one of the stunning accomplishments of nation building in the modern world.

Brazil has had a vocation for democracy but only at historical intervals. The nineteenth century saw a monarchical system that steadily evolved toward a more inclusive franchise and the final overthrow of the monarchy in 1889 that brought Brazil its first experiment in republican democracy. But the republic that resulted bogged down in sporadic regional violence and endless political battles among different factions representing diverse interests. It collapsed in 1930 in the face of a coordinated regionalist revolt. The subsequent resistance to national leadership led eventually to another coup, the authoritarian takeover by Getúlio Vargas in 1937. Vargas fell in 1945, with the end of World

EXHIBIT 1-3

The countries of South America.

War II. This ushered in a new attempt at participatory government and included Vargas's 1950 victory as a democratically elected president. That experiment in democracy wrecked on the shoals of the Cold War in 1964, whipped by the fury of both left and right, bringing another dose of authoritarian government and years of political repression. In the aftermath of military rule, political forces developed a new constitution and new framework for democratic government.

We are now in the midst of Brazil's newest experiment in democracy. Thus far, the Brazilians seem to be learning the lessons of the past—the need to honor majority rule, recognize the validity of the rule of law, and act in the spirit of compromise needed for any democratic system to work. These are the lessons that every society bent on freedom, old or new, on whatever continent, must keep clearly in focus.

1

The Birth and Growth
of Colonial Brazil

Portuguese Arrival in the New World

Any explanation of Portugal's historic role in the Americas must begin with the relationship between the crown and overseas exploration. The discovery of Brazil fits squarely into that relationship. The series of events leading directly to the discovery of Brazil began in early March 1500, when King Manuel of Portugal attended a solemn mass in his capital city of Lisbon to celebrate the launching of a new ocean fleet. Less than a year earlier, the great Portuguese navigator Vasco da Gama had returned to Lisbon from the epic voyage (1497–99) that opened the sea route to India. His success, with its promise of future trading riches, stimulated the Portuguese court to sponsor and organize a new voyage. Larger than any of its predecessors, it was to include thirteen ships carrying a total of 1,200 crew and passengers. The commander of the expedition was Pedro Alvares Cabral, a nobleman (unlike da Gama) who, though young, may have given the new expedition a social distinction the earlier one had lacked.

The stated intent of this expedition was the same as earlier ones: to head for the southern tip of Africa, sail around the Cape of Good Hope, and head north toward India through the Indian Ocean. Almost as soon as the fleet had set out to sea, however, disaster appeared to strike. The lead ship, commanded by Cabral, swung off course into the Atlantic, sailing due west. Cabral and his fleet eventually reached the coast of what is now the Brazilian state of Bahia, anchoring at Porto Seguro on April 22, 1500.

They had stumbled onto what turned out to be a vast continent. Or was it more than stumbling? There has been considerable scholarly debate about whether the Portuguese navigators had in fact planned this "accident" to

9

SPECIAL V-83861

REPUBLICA DOS ESTADOS UNIDOS DO BRASIL

AMERICAN BANK NOTE COMPANY

Pedro Alvares Cabral, the sailor who found Brazil after suffering a terrible storm in the Atlantic. Whether he knew what he was doing is still a matter of controversy.

outflank the Spanish, and whether they were really following the route of previous secret voyages to Brazil. Historians have failed to uncover any evidence in the Portuguese archives or elsewhere to support this version of Cabral's intent. This does not, however, disprove what some historians think—that previous Portuguese (and/or other European) navigators may have reached the coast of present-day Brazil before 1500.

What Cabral and his men thought about the people they encountered when they first landed is captured in an official account written for King Manuel by Pero Vaz de Caminha, the fleet's scribe. His "Carta" (letter) demonstrated a typical late-Renaissance perception of the new land, naturally emphasizing what was exotic to European eyes—some of it wishful thinking, no doubt, since the Europeans of the time had vivid imaginations of what they expected to see in their travels—including kingdoms more beautiful than any before encountered and monsters more hideously frightening than any yet known. Vaz de Caminha depicted Brazil as a realm where human and environmental resources were there for the taking. The native women were described as comely, naked, and without shame, and the soil as endlessly fertile. This image of endless fertility, a romanticization of the Portuguese later shared by the Brazilians, has led to a variety of overoptimistic estimates of Brazil's agricultural potential. It was no accident that Vaz de Caminha's description of the new continent sounded seductively different from the hardscrabble life facing most Portuguese at home. It was designed to encourage the monarch to send follow-up expeditions as well as to attract would-be explorers.

The continent was not, in any case, new to the millions of indigenous peoples who already lived there. Many of these tried to resist or flee the Portuguese, although some became allies. As with all groups who live in close proximity, their mutual contacts resulted in the birth of a mixed population, called *mamelucos*, who feature quite prominently in the history of colonial Brazil. (See chapter 2 for more on the *mamelucos* and on race mixing more generally in Brazil.)

Historians have had difficulty describing the indigenous people and their society because the chroniclers, travelers, and priests who wrote about them at the time tailored their descriptions to fit their prejudices about which were "good" Indians (i.e., potential allies) and which were "bad" (i.e., anti-Portuguese). The Tupí Indians, who were considered relatively benign, for example, were described as living in a human fashion (which meant they lived in houses); the Aimoré, who were considered unfriendly, were described as living like animals (which meant in the forest). The attitudes of the tribes toward cannibalism were described by contemporaneous observers in a way designed to further differentiate between good and bad. Since both groups were believed to eat their enemies, this was a somewhat delicate matter. The Portuguese resolved it by coming up with the following distinction about motive: The Tupí ate their enemies only out of vengeance (thus "culturing" the act because vengeance is a recognized human motive); the Aimoré ate them simply as food (i.e., they were bestial).

It is unknown how many Indians there were when Cabral landed; estimates range from two to five million. What is certain is that the subsequent fate of the Amerindian population in Brazil was largely death by disease or brutality (see further discussion in chapter 2). The current indigenous population of Brazil numbers less than 300,000.

Factors Leading Up to Cabral's Voyage

Cabral's feat, though dramatic, was in fact part of the continuing success of the Portuguese at overseas exploration. Despite their relatively meager resources (the Portuguese population was about 1 million, compared with Holland's 1.5 million, England's 3 million, Spain's 7 million, and France's 15 million), the Portuguese had been in the process of creating a trading empire reaching all the way to Asia for almost a century. This overseas expansion began in the early fifteenth century in the Mediterranean and northern Africa and then stretched south, concentrated mainly along the western African coast. In this region the Portuguese focused on trading various goods and, beginning in the 1440s, slaves, who were sent to work in Portugal. In addition to exploring the African coast, the Portuguese extended their reach to the Atlantic islands (Madeira, the Azores, Cape Verde, and São Tomé), where they used slave labor to establish and work farms, the most successful crop being sugar.

The factors contributing to the success of such a small kingdom in becoming a major international player in fifteenth-century Europe are several.

Early Consolidation of the Monarchy

Like Spain, Portugal had to fight a long war against the Muslims, who had occupied the Iberian Peninsula since the eighth century. But the Portuguese had liberated their kingdom from its Arabic-speaking occupiers by the thirteenth century, two hundred years earlier than the Spanish. In addition, they were able to resist repeated attempts by the kingdom of Castile (the bureaucratic and military core of modern Spain) to manipulate the succession to the Portuguese throne. To strengthen its position against Castile, Portugal forged an alliance with the English crown in 1386. This alliance, which remained the bedrock of Portuguese foreign policy for the following five centuries, was to lay the basis for England's later involvement—especially its economic involvement—in Brazil. The marriage of Portuguese King João I to the granddaughter of England's Edward III consolidated the Portuguese dynasty, known as the "House of Avis" (1385–1580), which facilitated the concentration of economic resources necessary to finance Portugal's forays into world exploration and trade.

Social Structure with a Merchant Class

Portugal's economy in the fifteenth century combined commercial agriculture, subsistence agriculture, and trade. The merchants were the key to trade and had the support of their sovereign as they maneuvered on the world stage, pursuing trade and gaining the cooperation of foreign merchants, especially the Genoese in what is modern-day Italy. Exploration also had the support of the common people in Portugal, for whom going to sea meant the possibility of a better life—a way out of the hopelessness of daily living in the home country. Only the large landowners in Portugal failed to benefit since exploration abroad, by draining off potential workers, raised the cost of labor at home.

The interests of the merchants combined with those of the crown to produce the resources necessary to make Portugal a leader in perfecting the technology necessary for traveling long distances by sea. One of Portugal's relative advantages in maritime skills was in shipbuilding, about which the Portuguese had learned much from their Basque neighbors in northern Spain. Portugal produced the caravel, for example, the first ship that was reliable on the high seas yet had a shallow enough draft to facilitate coastal sailing. Previous European ships were designed for use in the relatively calm inland sea of the Mediterranean. When sailed on an open ocean, they were apt to be swamped and often capsized. The Portuguese also excelled at navigation. This included development of the astrolabe, the first instrument capable of using the sun and stars to determine position at sea. Finally, they were skilled at drawing maps, which were based on the increasingly detailed geographical knowledge accumulated on their voyages. Such maps made possible systematic repeat trips—giving some credence to the speculation that explorers before Cabral may already have reached Brazil.

Long-standing Involvement in Trade Routes

Over the preceding centuries, Lisbon had been a regular stop for Genoese traders traveling from the Mediterranean to European Atlantic ports. By 1450, as a consequence, Portugal was already integrated into the most advanced trading network of the time. Its location on the Atlantic also stimulated a natural focus west, as compared with fleets that had set out from ports inside the Mediterranean.

Too Small to Send Nationals to Settle Abroad

Portugal's small population made it impossible to settle nationals in colonies on the scale soon to be launched by the English and the Spanish. Rather, the Portuguese established a worldwide network of trading posts—militarily fortified and minimally staffed—in order to exchange goods with the local population. Between 1450 and 1600, the Portuguese established the most viable worldwide network of trading forts. Greatest competition came from the English, the Dutch, the French, and especially the Spanish—competition that soon made soldiers and naval gunners as vital to the Portuguese kingdom as were its navigators and traders. The Portuguese negotiated to obtain local products, which would be produced for export by local labor with minimal Portuguese involvement. Such trading was established in Africa and Asia in the fifteenth and sixteenth centuries to obtain spices (black pepper, ginger, cinnamon, cloves, nutmeg) and other foods. The spices were particularly important because food preservation was done by very primitive methods or not at all, making it practically impossible to tolerate without strong seasoning. The Portuguese also hoped to find gold or other precious metals.

The catalyst that brought all these factors together was a combination of individual characteristics that led the Portuguese people to excel in exploration and trade. First, they believed in the religious mission to convert the heathen. The importance of this commitment to evangelize for the holy faith was advertised by the cross emblazoned on the sails of their ships. But their zeal was more pragmatic than that of the Puritans who settled New England. Unlike the Puritans, for example, they stressed their economic rather than their theological mission in the reports of success they sent back to their homeland. Second, they saw their primary mission as solidifying trade rather than imposing formal political authority over the indigenous people they encountered. This contrasted with the overseas mission as seen by Spanish explorers, whose first order of business in the Valley of Mexico, for example, was to claim legal dominion over the millions of indigenous inhabitants of the region. Finally, and perhaps most important, the Portuguese had a collective thirst to discover the new and exotic, which drove them to travel the high seas in spite of the obvious and frequently confirmed dangers. Of Cabral's original fleet of thirteen, for example, six went down at sea (even though they were the caravels that were best suited to ocean sailing). This drive to succeed in spite of the odds was captured by the fifteenth-century Portuguese poet Camões in his epic poem *The Lusiads,* which remains the literary document of Portugal: "We must sail!" (*Navegar é preciso!*).

Securing the Frontiers

Running through the story of colonial Brazil is Portugal's continuing struggle to expand its hold on the new continent, even as it warded off efforts by other countries to encroach on the land it called its own. The first efforts at exploiting Brazil used the same approach that Portugal had become accustomed to with its earlier explorations abroad. Brazil was treated as a trading post, appearing in the documents of the time as a port of call on the way to India. This did not stop intense competition with Spain, however, about which country owned which part of the New World. As early as 1493, the year after Columbus's first voyage, the Portuguese contested Columbus's claim of ownership of the new land, wherever it was (Columbus thought it was in the China Sea). Negotiations between the two parties led to an agreement in 1494, called the "Treaty of Tordesilhas," which drew a north-south line through the New World. The line was supposed to be drawn 370 leagues west of the Cape Verde Islands. The Spanish were to get everything west of the line, the Portuguese everything east of it. The line was more fantasy than real, however, because it was not until about two centuries later that longitude could actually be calculated.

The treaty was, in any case, disregarded by both sides. Early settlement efforts by the Spanish were on the coast south of São Paulo (in the 1520s to 1530s) and on the coast of modern Santa Catarina (1540–60), both unsuccessful. Thereafter, Spanish settlements were mostly in the Rio de la Plata Basin, where the Spanish and Portuguese collided head-on. Brazilians, in their turn, freely traded (and smuggled) in Spanish America, especially in Upper Peru (present-day Bolivia). The dividing line became somewhat ambiguous between 1580 and 1640, insofar as Portugal (and therefore Brazil) was under Spanish Hapsburg sovereigns. It was not until 1828 that the modern boundaries between Brazil and its Spanish American southern neighbors emerged after an inconclusive war and British pressure forced the creation of an independent Uruguay.

The French turned out to be at least as much of a menace to the Portuguese hold on Brazil as the Spanish, refusing (though Catholic) to honor the papal bulls or the treaty. They began their own exploration of the Brazilian coast as early as 1504 and continued their incursions into the early seventeenth century. In addition to outright piracy, the French controlled the area of Rio de Janeiro in the 1550s, which was to be the base of what the French saw as a future refuge for French Protestants, called "Antarctic France." They were driven out by a column of Portuguese and indigenous troops in 1560. The French also fiercely contested parts of the Amazon Basin, managing to settle at São Luís, located on the northeast Atlantic coast in present-day Maranhão, from which they were finally driven out by the Portuguese only in 1615.

Portuguese de facto expansion to the west did not encounter resistance from other colonial powers. Exploration of the interior lay in the hands of the colonists themselves. Known as *bandeirantes*, these primary explorers of inland Brazil became the heroes of much folklore and mythification later on in Brazil. The myth and the facts of their story, including their attitudes toward and interaction with Brazil's indigenous peoples, are told in chapter 2.

From Trading to Colonizing

In the first three decades after Cabral's voyage, the Portuguese crown relied on its earlier overseas experiences, which had returned a handsome profit to the crown for minimal outlay in resources and personnel. By the early 1530s, however, the incursions by the French and Spanish, and the need for more trade to replace declining activity in the Indian Ocean, forced the Portuguese crown to reconsider its position. As it came increasingly to realize the massive task it had in South America, as opposed to its tiny ocean holdings, it resorted to a semifeudal system of land grants, or captaincies, to help settle Portuguese America. The recipients of these grants all had some connection to the crown but were otherwise a rather diverse group. Some were petty nobility; others were merchants, soldiers and sailors, and home-country bureaucrats. None was high nobility, who had access to more lucrative pursuits in Portugal and elsewhere in its overseas territories.

The captaincies were hereditary, but they were not outright gifts—only the crown could divide or sell them. Grantees (donateries) could establish towns, form militias, institute systems of justice, and levy fees for use of the lands. They could also allocate tracts of land (*sesmarias*) to individuals. But the crown retained substantial rights, among them the right to collect part of the fees levied by the captaincy and the right to intervene in certain laws if members of the high nobility were involved. Exhibit 1-1 shows the captaincies that had been granted by the late sixteenth century. Unfortunately for the crown, the risks were too great and the rewards too uncertain to persuade most of the grantees to make the investment required to be successful. All but two of the original

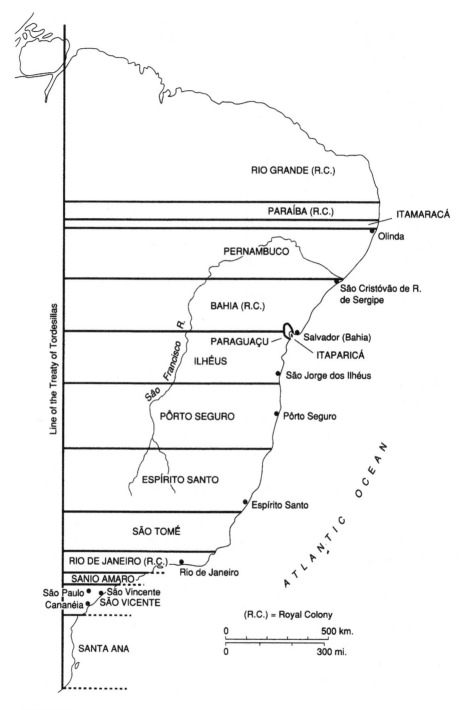

RIO GRANDE (R.C.)

PARAÍBA (R.C.)

ITAMARACÁ

• Olinda

PERNAMBUCO

• São Cristóvão de R.
de Sergipe

BAHIA (R.C.)

PARAGUAÇU

Salvador (Bahia)

ITAPARICÁ

ILHÉUS

• São Jorge dos Ilhéus

PÔRTO SEGURO

• Pôrto Seguro

ESPÍRITO SANTO

• Espírito Santo

SÃO TOMÉ

RIO DE JANEIRO (R.C.)

• Rio de Janeiro

SANIO AMARO

São Paulo • • São Vincente
Cananéia • SÃO VICENTE

SANTA ANA

Line of the Treaty of Tordesillas

São Francisco R.

ATLANTIC OCEAN

(R.C.) = Royal Colony

0   500 km.
0   300 mi.

EXHIBIT 1-1

The captaincies of Brazil in the late sixteenth century. From James Lockhart and Stuart B. Schwartz, *Early Latin America* (Cambridge, 1983), p. 185.

captaincies failed as economic endeavors. In addition to inadequate resources and internal squabbles, the causes for failure included attacks by hostile indigenous people. The two captaincies that were successful—São Vicente, south of the present-day city of São Paulo, and Pernambuco, in the northeast—were both sugar economies situated in areas with relatively friendly indigenous inhabitants. The crown finally repurchased these captaincies, and the whole captaincy system, including captaincies created later on, was transferred from the private to the public domain in the mid- to late 1700s.

In 1549, in a new sign of royal commitment—the need for which was highlighted by the already struggling early captaincies—Dom João III created a governor-generalship in Bahia. Governor Tomé de Souza arrived in that year, bringing with him instructions from Lisbon to colonize the land and administer the crown's income from it, as well as more than one thousand people from the home country and the first Jesuits to reach Brazil. He also founded the city of Salvador, which was to remain the capital of the whole colony for more than two centuries.

The Portuguese Jesuits helped the colonization effort immeasurably. This aggressive religious order established mission networks in many parts of Brazil, including the Amazon Valley, harnessing vast supplies of indigenous labor to live in Jesuit-run villages (*aldeias*) and work the Jesuit-run ranches and vineyards. In so doing, the Jesuits helped "pacify" (read: subjugate) the local Indian peoples and establish the Christian religion. They also played an important role as cultural brokers. Jesuit linguists, for example, were the persons who established a standard form of Tupi, the principal native language. As late as the end of the seventeenth century, this lingua franca was more widely spoken in Brazil than Portuguese, and its standardization eventually facilitated the spread of the Portuguese language. (The Jesuits' attitudes toward, and competition with, settlers for, Indians are discussed in chapter 2.)

In 1572, the threats of French and Spanish penetration near Rio and the south persuaded the Portuguese government to divide its administration between Salvador and Rio de Janeiro, a brief dual governorship that ended after only six years. In 1580, Portugal entered a sixty-year "union" with Spain, as lack of a royal heir in Portugal led to the sharing of a single monarch (initially Philip II of Spain, Philip I of Portugal). The Crown Union did not involve an actual joining of countries. Rather, the two kingdoms maintained separate, independent identities—including distinct overseas empires and imperial bureaucracies. The Portuguese continued to fly their own flag both at home and abroad, and the separation of the two empires was considered so vital that Philip actually forbade Spaniards from encroaching on Portuguese overseas interests (and vice versa). It was, of course, impossible to enforce such prohibitions in practice. In the case of Brazil, Spanish Jesuits frequently complained to the Spanish crown about Paulista incursions into what is today southern Brazil and Uruguay, while the Paulistas did precisely the same thing—except that they were writing to the Portuguese crown (in the person of the Spanish king!) about Spanish Jesuits. The Spaniards' major constructive activity in Brazil was the regularizing of administrative and judicial procedures, including development of new civil and penal codes in 1603. Otherwise, Spain's energies were engaged mainly in fighting to retain its possessions elsewhere in the New World.

The Crown Union ended when a suitable successor to the Portuguese throne was found, who led a successful coup that installed him as Dom João IV of Portugal, the founder of the Bragança dynasty. It must also be said that the coup that brought an end to the Crown Union was precipitated at least in part by the (joint) crown's attempts to establish more Spanish rather than Portuguese administration of the Portuguese Empire, especially to finance wars (the *union de armas* of the count-duke of Olivares).

In Portugal's struggles to keep its territories intact in the American hemisphere, the Dutch, in particular, took advantage of the Crown Union to attack the new outpost of "Spanish" imperialism by invading Brazil's northeastern coast in 1624. These Dutch invaders (sponsored by the Dutch West India Company) managed to maintain control for thirty years, occupying Recife and taking over the lucrative sugar trade. During the Dutch occupation of Recife, under Governor Maurice of Nassau (1637–44), scores of distinguished and mostly Dutch scientists and artists—including the naturalist Jorge Marcgrave and the painter Frans Post—descended on the area to document its flora and fauna. In 1654, a coalition of Brazilians of all social classes, supported by the local planters' desire to escape their debts to the Dutch, finally drove the Dutch off the coast. Brazilian patriots often point to this resistance campaign as the birth of Brazilian nationalism. In fact, it was not entirely local. The Portuguese crown was sympathetic to the resistance movements within Brazil and secretly provided aid to the local insurgents.

The seventeenth century saw a dramatic expansion of territorial control (north, west, and south) by the Portuguese. The administration in Lisbon accommodated this expansion through a codification and extension of the existing authority to newly secured locations, rather than changing the administrative structure. There were two exceptions to this continuity. The first was creation of the position of *juiz de fora*, a regional judgeship that was intended to reduce the power of the colony's rural landowners. The second was creation in 1620 of a new state in Brazil—Maranhão, which included the upper Northeast and the entire Amazon Basin. Maranhão was divided into six hereditary captaincies, following the precedent set by the earlier, largely unsuccessful, captaincies.

The impetus for the establishment of Maranhão was Portugal's need to consolidate its control of the North after the expulsion of the French. The action was also explicit recognition of the geographic separateness of Maranhão—a consequence of the prevailing southeasterly winds, which often made travel up the coast from Salvador impossible. Land travel was not a realistic alternative, given hostile indigenous peoples and jungle terrain. It was common at that time for overland journeys in Brazil to take months. Rivers were used where possible. But the Amazon flows from west to east, cutting across many logical travel routes, and the most important river in the northeast, the São Francisco, is broken by falls so vast as to be impassable.

The eighteenth century was dominated by the rise and decline of the mining industry, following the discovery of gold (which the Portuguese had been vainly seeking for almost two centuries). The resulting shift in population southward to those regions led the crown to create a new captaincy of São Paulo and Minas de Ouro in 1709. Then, in 1720, the captaincy of Minas Gerais was created, separate from São Paulo, and in 1748 captaincies were established for Mato Grosso and Goias. The capital of the colony was moved from Salvador to Rio de Janeiro in 1763 to keep closer administrative control over the lucrative mining areas and to fend off Spanish incursions in the south.

Brazil's Colonial Economy and Its Nexus with Portugal

Colonial Brazil's economy began, as already discussed, as a series of crudely constructed trading posts (known as *feitorias* or factories) scattered along the coast from Pernambuco in the north to São Vicente (modern-day São Paulo) in the south. Brazilwood, prized for its rich, red, dye-making qualities, was the first main export from Brazil, giving the colony its permanent name. More exotic items such as parrots and animal skins were also exported. The main beneficiary of these exports was the mother country, Portugal. In return, Portugal delivered necessities to the colony such as clothing and tools.

This trading structure, which typified the international economy of the time, is known as "mercantilism." A doctrine as well as a policy, mercantilism holds that the economic purpose of a colony is to enable its mother country to be economically self-sufficient. To this end, mother countries worked to maintain a trading monopoly with their colonies that enabled them to keep low the prices the mother countries paid for their colonies' products while selling the same products on the international market at prices that returned the mother countries a handsome profit. Although Portugal was not always consistent or successful in maintaining this type of monopoly with its colonies, it benefited substantially on balance from its trading activities with its colonies, particularly Brazil.

When the Portuguese crown increased its commitment to Brazilian settlement by creating the captaincies of the 1530s, Brazil's principal crop was sugar, grown largely within the humid zone on the northeastern coast and exported to the Dutch-dominated European trade. The sugar-growing plantations were the plots of land that donateries allocated within their captaincies—plots that were large enough to reap substantial economies of scale and formed the basis for what became the enormous estates (*latifundias*) that modern land reform

Sugar production in Brazil, as depicted in 1595. Brazil
was to become the world's greatest sugar producer later
in the colonial period. (Art Resource, NY)

efforts in Brazil are trying to break up. The cane was then processed and refined
in mills (*engenhos*) owned by the wealthier plantation owners in the area.

For more than a century, Brazil was the world's leading sugar exporter.
From 1600 to 1650, for example, sugar accounted for 90–95 percent of Brazil's
export earnings. Even in the period around 1700, when the sugar sector had
declined, it continued to represent 15 percent of Brazil's export earnings. Sugar
set Brazil on the course of being a primary-producing plantation economy for
the colonial era and well into the twentieth century. The intensive cultivation
involved also left for subsequent generations deep ecological damage.

Cane cultivation and processing required a labor force far beyond what
the colonists themselves could provide, a need that was filled by forced labor
(i.e., slavery). First the colonists went after the indigenous peoples to serve
their purposes. Later, for a variety of reasons, including the susceptibility of the
Indians to European-imported diseases such as smallpox, the settlers turned
to African slaves, brought initially from Portugal and from the Atlantic islands
and later from the African continent. (More on the colonists' justification for
slavery and for the circumstances of Indian as well as African slaves appears
in chapter 2.)

Brazil's land-extensive agriculture based on slave labor was an important part of the larger South Atlantic economy, which the Portuguese controlled on both sides of the ocean—one side the source of imported slaves (west and central Africa), the other side the location of their work (Brazil). Nor was sugar the only form of rural economy pursued by the colonists. One of the major additional endeavors, particularly in the northeastern interior, was the cattle culture, which furnished animal power, meat, natural fertilizer, and leather. In the sixteenth and seventeenth centuries, the cattle culture was an important counterpart to the sugar regions that consumed the cattle products.

By the seventeenth century, the Brazilian Northeast was one of the richest regions in the Americas, surpassing New England or Virginia. Disaster struck as the seventeenth century wore on, however, with international sugar prices falling in the 1670s and 1680s as increased production in the Antilles cut into Brazil's world market share—and therefore Portugal's trading profits. An epidemic of smallpox in Angola and of yellow fever in Bahia and Pernambuco, all in 1689, were further blows. Padre Antônio Vieira (1608–97), the great Jesuit missionary whose sermons became a classic of Portuguese and Brazilian culture, wrote from Bahia in 1684: "We shall shortly relapse into the savage state of the Indians, and become Brazilians instead of Portuguese." This gloomy forecast turned out to be premature, as gold was discovered in the early 1690s. By 1696, the discovery of gold in Brazil had become official news in Lisbon.

The Portuguese had always been interested in precious metals. They wanted above all to find gold, the ultimate currency in Europe's mercantilist trade, and never gave up the hope of equaling the Spanish luck in finding vast supplies of gold and silver. In 1500, Cabral had taken special care to interrogate the native population about the possible presence of gold, "because we wanted to know if there was any in that land." When there were few traces of these metals to be found near the coast, the colonists set out to penetrate the vast interior (see further discussion in chapter 2).

The first discovery of gold was in the region of modern-day Minas Gerais in the 1690s, followed by modern-day Cuiabá, Mato Grosso, in 1718, the modern-day state of Goias in 1725, and the region of Vila Bela, Mato Grosso, in 1734. The Goias find would be ultimately more lucrative than any of the discoveries made in Mato Grosso. By the 1760s, the government of Goias was actually subsidizing (i.e., sending gold to) its western counterpart because the captaincy of Mato Grosso did not extract enough to maintain the region's soldiers. This type of subsidization would continue into the early nineteenth century.

The discovery of gold triggered a gold rush of migrants from all over Brazil. There was also a sudden increase in new arrivals from Portugal, from Portuguese Africa and Asia, and even from non-Portuguese areas of the world. The drain on Portuguese youth became so large that the crown attempted to slow the flow. Taking the century as a whole, Brazil was the largest gold producer in the world. By the 1720s, Brazil was producing diamonds as well. This mineral wealth went to Portugal, which used much of it to cover Portuguese debts to England. Thus, Brazilian mining riches can be said to have helped capitalize the first industrial revolution.

Gold and diamond production also financed the flowering of a rich culture in south-central Brazil. The eighteenth-century mining towns in Minas Gerais, for example, saw the building of Christian churches in a unique Brazilian baroque style. Antônio Francisco Lisboa ("Aleijadinho") stood out for the churches he designed in Ouro Preto, Sabará, and São Paulo and for his full-size sculptures of the prophets in Congonhas do Campo. His is an astounding story. A mulatto leper—crippled from his leprosy, he moved himself around on a low wheeled cart—he became one of the giants of Brazilian art.

Not everyone considered the gold discoveries good news. As early as 1711, the noted Italian Jesuit chronicler Antonil gave his view that "no prudent person can fail to admit that God permitted the discovery of so much gold in the mines so that he could punish Brazil with it." Whatever the case for Brazil itself, it is generally agreed in retrospect that Portugal's gold and diamond windfall from Brazil was at least one factor implicated in Portugal's failure to participate in the industrial revolution of the nineteenth century.

In the early years of the eighteenth century, however, the Portuguese economic outlook seemed particularly bright. Everyone assumed Portugal could count on Brazil's gold and diamond riches to continue to increase the standard of living in the home country. Instead, the middle of the eighteenth century dealt Portugal three major economic blows. The first was a strong earthquake and related fire in 1755 that destroyed the city of Lisbon as well as a great deal of cargo from Brazil, which was unfortunately stored in Lisbon warehouses at the time.

To this was added a financial drain from massive military expenditures incurred in wars with Spain in the 1760s and 1770s over the borderlands of southern Brazil. The Treaty of Madrid in 1750, which was signed by both Portugal and Spain, accepted the principle of *uti possidetis*, or ownership by possession, by which Portugal retained most of the territory it was then occupying. This did not end the border differences, however. In 1761, the Treaty of El Pardo nullified that of Madrid. Intermittent wars continued, with the Treaty of San Ildefonso in 1777 once again renegotiating boundaries.

The third economic blow was declining gold production in Brazil, shrinking the gold remittances to Portugal from Brazil. Gold and diamond revenues from Minas Gerais, for example, dropped by 50 percent between 1750 and 1770. (See exhibit 1-2 for trends in Brazil's gold production during the eighteenth century.)

The resulting strain on the Portuguese economy reduced the supply of hard currency and, with it, the country's ability to settle its foreign debts.

EXHIBIT 1-2

Brazilian Gold Production in the Eighteenth Century

Five-Year Period	Total Production (kilograms)
1700–1705	1,470
1721–1725	7,600
1740–1744	17,147
1760–1764	10,499
1780–1784	6,204
1795–1799	4,399

Source: Leslie Bethell, ed., *The Cambridge History of Latin America vol.2* (Cambridge, 1984), p. 594.

During the same period when these disasters were occurring, the government in Portugal, through an important minister—Sebastião José de Carvalho, better known as the "Marquis de Pombal"—was engaged in efforts to make the Portuguese economy more efficient and to change its relationship to the colonies in a way that would benefit Portugal. Appointed by Dom José I, who ascended to the Portuguese throne in 1750, Pombal aimed to reorganize both the colonial trade and the main export sector in the home economy. This included regulating the sugar and tobacco trade in 1756 and creating three monopoly trading companies between 1755 and 1765. These were to exploit exports from Amazônia, the Pernambuco region, and the coastal whaling industry. Pombal was also promoting creation of industry in Portugal. One of the Pombal government's most dramatic acts was to expel the Jesuits from Portugal and all its territories and to expropriate their wealth (for more on the Jesuits in Brazil, see chapter 2). Obviously, the wealth itself was an incentive. But Pombal's primary concern was to centralize the authority of the Portuguese state and eliminate the power of the church, which he saw as "a state within a state" with separate goals.

By the mercantilist standards of the day, shared by generations of policymakers in all the major colonizing countries, the economic results of Pombal's efforts were favorable. Sugar production recovered, wheat cultivation was successfully introduced, and rice and indigo exports increased. All of this helped reduce Portugal's trade deficit by about 70 percent between 1751 and 1775, a trend that continued after Pombal's fall from power in 1777. By 1800, the colony's exports were thriving, aided especially by a revolt in Haiti that disrupted the competing Caribbean sugar trade. Between the 1770s and the early 1800s, Portuguese trade with Brazil and Brazil-based foreign trade grew fivefold. By 1807, Portugal was showing a healthy surplus in its trade balance and was even solidly in the black with England.

The Marquis de Pombal (1699–1782). Considered by many to have been the de facto head of government in Portugal from 1750 to 1777, he instituted far-reaching fiscal and economic reforms in both Portugal and its Brazilian colony. (Giraudon/Art Resource, NY)

Over 60 percent of the exports that earned this trade surplus were furnished by Brazil. This meant not only that Portugal's major colony had far surpassed it in economic importance but also that the mother country had become dramatically dependent on its colony rather than the other way around. Since mid-century, the Portuguese crown had been pressing hard to boost revenues from Brazil in the face of declining productivity in the mines, including the raising of taxes on colonial residents, which many of the most prominent Brazilian-born figures in Minas failed to pay. The reality of Portugal's economic dependence on (some might say "exploitation of") its colony did not go unnoticed by the Brazilian elite, who were already feeling restless under Portugal's yoke for non-economic reasons.

The Influence of Enlightenment Ideas

By the mid-eighteenth century, Portuguese America, like other European colonies in the Americas, was feeling the influence of new and disturbing ideas. Seventeenth-century Europe, especially France and England, had seen an intellectual revolution, known to historians as the "Enlightenment," which began to question the prevailing view of the world as governed by powerful mysteries that were beyond people's ability to fathom or control. Thinkers like René Descartes and Sir Isaac Newton were challenging established ideas and authority, arguing that human reason could and should use observation and experimentation to understand the environment and to solve problems. Aided by a newly developed type of mathematics, calculus, Enlightenment scientists were opening a whole new understanding of the physical world. This accumulating knowledge and the wider intellectual movement radiating from it put people at the center of the universe, displacing the realm of God and religion (some would say superstition and emotion) to a more marginal area of human thinking.

How did the new ideas reach the Brazilian colony? A major part of the answer is that young members of the Brazilian elite were sent to Portugal to study because, unlike in Spanish America, the crown did not establish universities in Brazil. Virtually all went to the University of Coimbra, the most famous and influential in Portugal, where some three hundred Brazilian-born students enrolled between 1772 and 1785. Once in Europe they were exposed directly or indirectly to an intellectual ferment in France, which was to spawn a violent revolution in that country in 1789.

Most of the Brazilian students going to Coimbra were the sons (no daughters invited!) of the wealthiest class—those who had benefited from the phenomenal prosperity stimulated by the gold mines. These young men brought Enlightenment ideas back to Brazil and spread them around. One of their favorite authors was the Frenchman Abbé Raynal, whose four-volume study of European commerce in the Indies criticized the economic policies of both Portugal and England and called for Brazil's ports to be thrown open to free international commerce.

In addition to the intellectual ferment coming from Europe, Brazil had the real-world example of England's North American colony rising up against its home country ("no taxes without representation" must have resonated with the delinquent taxpayers in Brazil). The Boston Tea Party, when more than fifty American "Sons of Liberty" disguised as Mohawks protested the British tea tax (three cents a pound) by dumping tea chests into Boston Harbor, happened in 1773. The formal start of the American War of Independence (the battles in Lexington and Concord) began in 1775. The American Declaration of Independence was signed in 1776, though the war did not end until the Treaty of Paris in 1783.

Conspiracies against the Portuguese

Enlightenment ideas fed the already-existing sense among elite Brazilians that, since they were now economically stronger than Portugal, they should be recognized as such. Open expressions of hostility toward the crown were, of course, dangerous. They could lead to denunciation, arrest, imprisonment, torture, and, in extreme cases, execution. So this resentment mostly simmered beneath the surface, occasionally appearing in disguised form, such as the *Cartas Chilenas*, published in the late 1770s. This was a very long satirical poem by Tomás Antônio Gonzaga (1744–1810) that purported to be a series of letters describing the popular chaos caused by the acts of a fictitious despotic governor. Gonzaga addressed his thinly disguised polemic to the authorities in Portugal (*aos Grandes do Portugal*), telling them he had translated these letters from the Spanish because of the lessons Portuguese speakers might learn from them.

Eventually, actual plots began to surface. The first serious anti-Portugal conspiracy (known as the Inconfidência Mineira) appeared in Minas Gerais. In 1788–89, a group of prominent citizens in Ouro Preto (full name: Vila Rica de Ouro Preto) developed a plan to assassinate the governor and proclaim an independent republic. One of the conspirators, José Joaquim da Maia (code name "Vendek"), exemplifies the impact of foreign contact. He had attended the University of Coimbra and attended medical school in Montpelier, France, in 1786. Vendek communicated with Thomas Jefferson, then the U.S. ambassador to France, first by letter and then in person on a visit to Nîmes, France, requesting U.S. support for the revolt. Portuguese rule, Vendek wrote to Jefferson, was "rendered each day more insupportable since the epoch of your glorious independence." Jefferson, otherwise noncommittal, did note that a successful revolution in Brazil would "not be uninteresting to the United States. . . . " Vendek's correspondence is one of the earliest instances of a long history of Brazilians looking to the United States for positive or negative inspiration. The U.S. example in this case was highly relevant for Brazilians because Jefferson had apparently seen no inconsistency between writing the Declaration of Independence and owning slaves.

These plotters were, with few exceptions, wealthy men with no wish to upset the socioeconomic order. They made no attempt to recruit slaves or poor freemen to their cause, although their program did call for the freeing of all native-born slaves. They saw themselves as remaining at the top of a slavocracy of new slaves from Africa, from which they would continue to profit. To quote historian Kenneth Maxwell, it was "a movement made by oligarchs in the interests of oligarchs, where the name of the people would be evoked merely in justification."

Unfortunately for the would-be rebels, the governor learned of their plot and ordered their movements monitored. The most dedicated conspirator was a jack-of-all-trades named "Joaquim José da Silva Xavier." One of his talents was amateur dentistry, a practice that gave him the nickname of "Tiradentes" (tooth-puller). He was also the one nonaristocrat among the leadership. After a show trial, during which Tiradentes took full responsibility for the conspiracy, six defendants were sentenced to be hanged. But Tiradentes became the fall guy. The other five were granted clemency and banished to prison in Angola. Tiradentes faced the gallows on April 21, 1792. After being hanged, he was decapitated, as happened often to those found guilty of treason, and his head displayed on a pole in the center of Ouro Preto. To further drive home the crown's message, the remainder of his body was quartered, with pieces displayed around the city; his house was demolished; and his grounds were salted to make sure the land would be barren.

This plot, though never a real threat on the ground, was significant for several reasons. First, it confirmed that the North American revolution had indeed influenced the colonial elite, despite the Portuguese crown's strenuous efforts to insulate its largest colony. Second, it showed the depth of some colonists' resentment against continuing Portuguese control. Third, it highlighted serious economic differences between the colony and Lisbon, especially now that Brazil had surpassed the mother country in total productive capacity. Fourth, it made clear that the crown would bring down the full force of the law on any active enemies, however socially prominent. Fifth, given the crown's official actions to increase tax revenues, it offered unusually favorable circumstances for revolt. Sixth, except for Tiradentes, the conspiracy operated entirely within elite society. Since the conspirators had no desire to upset the prevailing social order, they never considered mobilizing non-elite groups.

But the most important aspect of the revolt for Brazil's history became clear only a century later. During the waning years of the colony and throughout the monarchy, Tiradentes was not a favored figure among the Brazilian elite. But his reputation underwent a transformation when the country declared itself a republic in 1889. It turned out that Tiradentes, with his horrific death, had been seeping into the public consciousness over the years as a symbolic warrior against repression. The date of his death, April 21, was declared a national holiday, and Tiradentes was elevated from conspirator to martyr in the annals of Brazil. Graphic depictions of Tiradentes's savage death and severed head are still shown in Brazilian schools, and he is now revered throughout the political spectrum as a true Brazilian hero.

In August 1798, six years after Tiradentes was hanged, drawn, and literally quartered, a very different kind of plot was hatched in the port city of Salvador. Later described as Brazil's first social revolution, the so-called Tailors' Revolt (Conspiração dos Alfaiates) was organized by artisans, soldiers, sharecroppers, and schoolteachers. These plotters were overwhelmingly nonwhite (*pardo*), reflecting the predominant racial makeup of such economic groups. This revolt was very much influenced by the French Revolution and an ongoing revolution in Haiti against the French. The tailor after whom the revolt was named, João de Deus, was said to have proclaimed at the outset, "All [Brazilians] would become Frenchmen, in order to live in equality and abundance.... They would destroy the public officials, attack the monasteries, open the port...and reduce all to an entire revolution, so that all might be rich and taken out of poverty, and that the differences between white, black, and brown would be extinguished, and that all without discrimination would be admitted to positions and occupations." The plotters posted handwritten manifestos on walls and public places, demanding removal of the "detestable metropolitan yoke of Portugal," and that the government be "democratic, free, and independent."

This conspiracy also failed. Once again, the plot was discovered (the handwritten manifestos were an obvious clue), and forty-seven suspects were arrested, nine of them slaves. Three, all free mulattos, got the full Tiradentes treatment. Sixteen prisoners were released. The rest were banished to exile and left to fend for themselves on the coast of Africa.

The Bahian conspiracy highlights the social and political status of the mulatto in late colonial Brazil. Racial mixing had been occurring at a high rate since the Portuguese had first arrived. In addition, due to the relative lack of whites, especially for the size of the territory and the scale of African slave imports, there had been increasing "economic space" for those of mixed blood. Not least among the factors increasing awareness of the racial dimension in Bahia was news of the Haitian Revolution (1791–1804), an uprising that eventually expelled the French and put blacks in power. In fact, sporadic slave uprisings and collective slave runaways were not unknown in Brazil. But they had not undermined the social system as a whole. These and other dimensions of life in the Portuguese colony are discussed further in the next chapter.

2

Peoples and Dramas in the Making of the Colony

The story told in chapter 1 is a brief outline of the dates and events of Brazil's colonization. This chapter uses recent research by specialists studying colonial Brazil to enrich the narrative with glimpses into how people thought and how life was lived in the wild and often dangerous world of colonial Brazil. Since an important part of the story involves slavery, the story starts with the hunting of indigenous peoples, the first group to be enslaved in Brazil.[1]

Hunting Indigenous People for Enslavement and the Jesuit Role

Slavery did not begin in the Americas. The Portuguese had been bringing Africans to work as slaves in Portugal since at least the mid-fifteenth century. Given the tenets of the Christian faith—and the colonists, as we have seen, were true believers—they looked for and found two principles that could be used as legal justification for enslaving other human beings The first was the principle of the Just War, derived from the debates of classical philosophers and the writings of Christian theologians on how the killing inherent in war could be justified, given the Sixth Commandment (thou shalt not kill). Thomas Aquinas thought up the answer. He specified a war as just and not a sin when three conditions were met. The sovereign had to give authority for it; those who were attacked should deserve it; and the attackers should intend, by their actions, to advance

---

1. This chapter is based heavily on research guidance provided by anonymous reviewers and especially on the articles I acknowledge in the preface. The specific authors noted there will readily recognize their work, and I owe them many thanks.

One of the first representations of Brazil's Indian
population. Fascinated with the creatures their
explorers had discovered in the New World, European
artists were proud to depict what they perceived
"Indians" to be like. (Snark/Art Resource, NY)

good in the world. The second principle was used to justify slave trading (i.e.,
the purchase of slaves). This was the principle of ransoming (*resgate*)—that is,
buying back of—persons who had been taken as prisoners of war, presumably
by the "unjust" side. *Resgate* was a very useful rationalization in Brazil because
indigenous tribes were sometimes found to have captured members of other
tribes for cannibalism ceremonies—making it particularly "virtuous" for the
colonists to save them from such an "unjust" fate.

The Jesuits were just as comfortable with the principles used to justify the
legality of enslavement as were the colonists. Indeed, slave labor was considered necessary to run the mission villages (*aldeias*) that the Jesuits founded to
house the indigenous people they were striving to convert. Jesuits also needed
indigenous slaves to run the cattle ranches, cotton plantations, and sugar plantations they set up to finance their mission (and possibly enrich themselves in
the process).

But many Jesuits had considerable qualms about how the settlers were applying the slavery principles on the ground, including the fact that they sometimes raided the mission villages, capturing any Indians they could and causing thousands of others to flee (and thus be lost from the Jesuit sphere of influence). The leader of the Jesuits' first mission to Brazil, Manuel da Nóbrega, for example, assessed the colonists' motives this way: "their subjection of the Indians is not to save them nor to know Christ...but to rob them of their sons, their daughters, and their women." But Manuel da Nóbrega's sentiments about the indigenous peoples were not always noble. At another point, possibly after the first bishop of Brazil was killed and eaten by indigenous people after a shipwreck, he said, "Indians are dogs who kill and eat one another. And in their vices and dealings with one another, they are pigs." His story is, in fact, a good example of the Jesuits' powerful role in how the colony dealt with indigenous people and other matters.

Manuel da Nóbrega was born in Portugal in 1517, studied at universities in Spain and at the University of Coimbra, and entered the Jesuit novitiate in 1544. In 1549, he, with five other Jesuit missionaries, came to the New World with the first governor-general and helped found the captaincy of Bahia and the city of Salvador. He later helped establish the captaincy of São Vicente, in the present-day state of São Paulo, where he established a school for indigenous children—one of the many schools founded during his leadership of the Jesuit mission. He led the order's activities in Brazil until his death in 1570. During that period, among many other things, he was instrumental in the expulsion of the French colonists who took over Rio de Janeiro in 1555 and founded France Atlantique for French settlers (as described in chapter 1). He did this by persuading an indigenous tribe, the Tamoio, who had previously fought against the Portuguese, to come over from the French to the Portuguese side. In this he was helped immeasurably by a younger Jesuit, José de Anchieta, who was fluent in the indigenous Tupí language. Anchieta in fact wrote the first grammar of Tupí and made major contributions in describing indigenous people's ways of life, customs, folklore, and diseases.

In response to the pro-indigenous entreaties of Nóbrega and other religious, the Portuguese crown made several attempts to limit the colonists' enslavement activities. As early as 1548, the crown's instructions to the first governor of Bahia outlawed "illegal" raiding of indigenous peoples, but to little effect. In 1570, the Portuguese king signed a law outlawing the enslavement of native peoples in Brazil, although with several face-saving exemptions—authorizing their enslavement, for example, as long as there was crown verification of their "legal" status. Loopholes notwithstanding, the colonists still complained to the king about the restrictions on Indian enslavement and were rewarded with further concessions, including a requirement that the authorities come to an agreement with the Jesuits that allowed the colonists access to "necessary labor" while protecting the indigenous peoples in the mission villages. And this back-and-forth went on into the seventeenth century. In a law of 1609, for example, the king declared all Indians free. But in 1611, he signed yet another law reiterating the right to enslave indigenous peoples, as long as the governor of that region judged that a Just War or *resgate* had been involved.

The Portuguese Explorers and Their Expeditions

The colonists who went out to capture indigenous people are known as *bandeirantes*. The expeditions are known as *bandeiras* (also as *entradas* or *expedições*). The traditional picture of the *bandeirante*, as described by A. J. R. Russell-Wood, is an "image of swashbuckling males, invariably associated with São Paulo..., independent in thought and action, [with] superhuman courage, [with] a compulsive obsession to find mineral deposits, and struggling against the forces of nature and hostile Indians." This has been generally recognized as an idealized and distorted picture. Depending on the time and place, a wide spectrum of people joined such expeditions, including plantation owners, traders, people of mixed racial ancestry, and, particularly later on, members of the military. The expeditions also included many Indian slaves, presumably captured on earlier expeditions, who might well have found this a less demeaning way of life for tribal men than working in agriculture (the other forced alternative). One expedition in 1629 is reported to have included 69 whites, 900 people of mixed blood, and 2,000 indigenous people (mainly slaves).

The first bands of settlers to explore the hinterlands (*sertão*) did, indeed, have mineral riches on their mind. Some were searching directly for gold, others were interested more generally in learning about the geography and characteristics of the new land. But the forays quickly turned into expeditions explicitly to capture Indians and bring them down to the coastal regions, where most became slaves. Thousands of Indians (one estimate puts it at forty thousand) were brought to coastal Bahia and Pernambuco in this manner in the second half of the sixteenth century.

During the same period, African slavery became more common, at least in part because of the truly horrendous death rate among Indian slaves, from epidemics of diseases brought by the Europeans, including smallpox and measles. It has been claimed by some that Indian slavery declined as a result. But recent evidence indicates that this was not the case. Although the indigenous population in the coastal parts of Brazil shrank drastically, this was not true farther into the backlands. Enslaving of Indians went on during the seventeenth century, and even into the eighteenth century in the Amazon and inland mining regions of Minas Gerais. One reason was that Indian slaves were much less expensive than their African counterparts, and participating in an Indian-hunting expedition entitled someone to at least a few slaves without further payment.

Count Maurice's gate near a slave market in Pernambuco. This state was a key locale for selling and buying slaves in the heart of Brazil's sugar plantation country.

By the second half of the eighteenth century, however, economic hard times led *bandeirante* expeditions to change somewhat in location and focus. In Minas Gerais, in particular, the rounding up of Indians for slavery gave way to the conquest of lands still occupied by indigenous tribes who were not considered tractable enough for productive labor. These latter-day expeditions into areas both west and east of the settled inland mining district in Minas Gerais were more military than civilian—commanded by military officers, often consisting largely or wholly of soldiers, and encountering fierce Indian resistance.

The Role of the *Mameluco*

The primary story so far is Portuguese settlers capturing Indians for slavery and later fighting them for possession of their land. And this story is true. It is only a partial story, however, because it leaves out the fact that Portuguese settlers also met and had children with Indian women and the important role played by these mixed-blood children. Known as *mamelucos*, they played a major role in the Portuguese-Indian interactions over both slaves and territory.

Álvaro Rodrigues exemplifies the role of the *mameluco*. His grandfather was Diogo Alvares Correia (1475–1557), a Portuguese who was shipwrecked on the coast of Bahia in the early sixteenth century. He was befriended by the Tupinambá tribe, who gave him the name "Caramurú." He got on so harmoniously with tribal members that he founded a settlement and married and had children with the daughter of the tribal chief. In 1526, he traveled to France with his Indian wife, who was even baptized as a Christian by the queen of

France. Alvares Correia kept contact with Portuguese trading ships and used his influence with the local indigenous groups to help the Portuguese crown and missionaries during the early years of the new colony. He also helped found Salvador and the first royal governorship (Bahia) in the colony. In return for this help, the governor, Tomé de Sousa, conferred knighthoods on Correia's three (*mameluco*) sons.

Álvaro Rodrigues, Caramurú's grandson, was the leader of at least six *entradas*. He and many like him often acted as powerful mediators between the worlds of the indigenous peoples in the *sertão* and the Portuguese along the coast. As Alida Metcalf put it, they "used their familiarity with languages and customs to negotiate exchanges that on the surface benefited chiefs in the backlands, but served the long-term interest of the sugar planting colonists on the coast." To gain the trust of the Indian tribes, the *mamelucos* often spent long periods living as Indians in the *sertão*, including changing their names and tattooing their bodies. Indian men also gave these *mamelucos* their own daughters as wives, with the *mamelucos* often accepting more than one. Domingo Fernandes Nobre, for example, a *mameluco* who also led several *entradas*, lived, according to his own testimony, with two Indian women during one expedition, three during another, and seven during yet another. *Mamelucos* were so successful in their efforts to persuade whole tribes to come down to a "better" life on the coast that the Jesuits came to view them as rivals, competing directly for the same Indians with the same siren-song strategy of a better life. But the *mamelucos* often contrasted their own offer of relocation (as a chance to keep the Indian way of life) to the competing Jesuit offer (which would, according to the *mamelucos*, destroy that way of life).

It would be a mistake to assume from this account that the Indians always submitted passively to their capture. Although some tribes did respond relatively peacefully, others successfully resisted, sometimes for considerable periods. The Barbarians' War (Guerra dos Barbaros) is one example. This was a general uprising of non-Tupí-speaking indigenous peoples—also known as the "Confederation of Kariri"—that spread from Piauí along the frontiers of Rio Grande do Norte and into the backlands of Ceará. The cause of the revolt was the invasion of their grazing areas by settlers' herds of cattle, which were brought to the region to help feed the hordes of new explorers flooding in as part of the gold rush. The Indians were able to keep the colonists at bay for thirty years (1683–1713), in the process killing many colonists. The revolt finally ended after an unexpected invasion by the Indian Confederation of the Villa of Aquiraz, then a captaincy capital, in defense of which two hundred people were killed and the rest of the village inhabitants had to flee. After such an ignominious and bloody rout, it became an all-out war for the colonists, who brought in a famous Portuguese cavalry regiment. These men knew how to dress for, navigate, and fight in the *sertão* and finally ended the war.

Another revolt, slightly overlapping in time, further exemplifies indigenous resistance. This one was led by Mandu Ladino, an Indian baptized and educated by priests. The revolt, which lasted from 1712 to 1719, began with a plantation uprising on the plantation of one Antônio da Cunha Souto, during which he was murdered. Ladino was of the Kariri nation, but many Tupí-speakers joined in the revolt, which was able to destroy numerous plantations in the northeastern *sertão*. The end came when Jesuits, who were fluent Tupí speakers, were able to persuade a group of Tupí Indians to break away from Ladino's revolt. A large expedition was organized against Mandu Ladino and his remaining followers, who were killed in a battle that ended the revolt.

The Concept of Race as Applied to Indians in the Colony

The concept of race in a society involves differentiating groups considered as "other" from the groups who view themselves as society's insiders and therefore, in some sense, superior. In the case of Brazil, the concept of racial differences as an exclusionary mechanism evolved out of the Iberian practice of differentiating insiders from outsiders based on religion. After the expulsion or forced conversion of the infidels (i.e., Jews and Moors) in the thirteenth century and successive campaigns against Jews in Portugal in the fourteenth and fifteenth centuries, the Inquisition's preoccupation with stamping out surviving non-Christian practices led to a distinction between "new" Christians (i.e., possible nonbelievers) and "old" Christians (i.e., proven believers). Since all important privileges and titles were reserved for "old" Christians, it became important to prove purity of blood, since that was the criterion for separating the true Christians (who happened to be white) from the secret pagans (who were not considered "white"). This led directly to the confusion of religion with race, and a new distinction between white and nonwhite was introduced.

This racial distinction, when transferred to the New World, was readily applied to issues relating to Indians and Africans, both peoples with a pagan past. The royal government, naturally enough, wanted to keep power in the hands of Europeans. Thus, a 1725 law reserved positions on the Portuguese Overseas Council for the husbands or widowers of white women, with the explicit purpose of encouraging white men to marry white women. The fact that people, especially in areas where there were few white women, were able to get around this regulation does not negate it as an exemplar of how society at the time felt about race. There also seemed to be a gradation of races, with Africans seen as a lower race than Indians. In 1771, for example, the viceroy from Portugal removed a particular Indian from his post because he had married a black woman—showing both that blacks were barred from posts that Indians were able to hold and that marrying blacks was worse than marrying Indians.

As European men fathered mixed bloods with indigenous women— although they did not typically marry them since Portuguese law required joint property rights upon marriage—they often made their mixed-blood offspring property owners, which sometimes helped them "become" white. Analysis of the census lists in a rural São Paulo neighborhood between 1765 and 1825 confirms the view that property as well as marriage partners could indeed change the perceived race classification of people. Antônio Raposo Tavares is one example. He was counted as an Indian-white mixed blood in the 1770s, 1780s, and 1790s but became classified as white in 1802 and 1807. The main reason for his race change seems to have been his second marriage to the daughter of a couple consistently listed as white. In the later censuses she was documented as being the granddaughter of a slave owner and her father as owning a slave. Anna de Oliveira provides a similar example. In the 1770s and 1780s, though married to a white man, she was classified as Indian-white mixed blood. In 1802, one of her daughters was listed as a widow and white. Another daughter, who had been the mistress of a wealthy, white, married slave owner and had eight children by him, was listed as a white member of the white man's household in the 1780s and 1790s and as white, *married to a white man*, and a slaveholder herself in 1802. Anecdotes cannot prove how frequent such changes were, of course. But they may be a component of the answer, at least in colonial São Paulo, to why the so-called Indian race shrank so rapidly over time.

The Place of African Slaves and Free Coloreds

What about the African in colonial Brazil? As already mentioned, African slaves were not brought to Brazil in any great numbers before the mid-eighteenth century. By the early 1800s, however, the population included many people of African descent. Brazil received more African slaves in total than any other region in the Americas. As a result, present-day Brazil has the largest population of African descent of any country outside Nigeria. Central and west Africa were the origin of the largest number of slaves brought to Brazil. Indeed, it was said that the "Angola" language became the lingua franca of the Brazilian slave regions. As has been noted: "This shared language along with broadly shared understandings of religion and esthetics formed the basis for the 'Bantu Proto-Nation' that emerged in the slave population of colonial Brazil."

Africans, like the Indians before them, resisted their masters in multiple ways. Among other forms of sabotage, they broke equipment. They also escaped to the backlands. Some formed runaway slave communities called *quilombos*, much more possible in the wilds of Brazil than in the United States. The most famous was the fortified settlement at Palmares (in the present state of Alagoas), formed by the joining of several separate *quilombos*, which at its height numbered some twenty thousand inhabitants. It survived for more than sixty years before being wiped out by a large armed expedition of *bandeirantes* in 1694 after six failed attempts to conquer it during the 1680s. A colonial governor at the time declared the destruction of Palmares to be no less important than the expulsion of the Dutch. The leader of the Palmares *quilombo*, the chieftain Zumbi, escaped when the settlement was destroyed and briefly mounted a new line of resistance before he was caught and killed on November 20, 1695. Zumbi is now a hero and symbol of freedom to the modern-day Afro-Brazilian political movement. The date of his death is celebrated, primarily in Rio, as a day of black awareness (*consciência negra*).

In spite of continuing sparks of resistance, no slave uprising was ever major enough to threaten the colonists' way of life. So what do we know about that way of life and the place of Africans and Afro-Brazilians in it?

The traditional picture of the colonial Brazilian—famously painted by Gilberto Freyre (or at least attributed to him, the reality being that Freyre was not consistent in his descriptions of Brazilian society)—is that of the plantation household, dominated by a white male patriarch and including his wife and legitimate children plus his nonwhite mistress(es) and their illegitimate offspring, numerous extended kin, free retainers of various sorts, and many slaves. Freyre described this "domestic and conjugal life under a slaveholding and polygamous patriarchal regime" as "the intimate history of practically every Brazilian."

Analysis of several counties in Minas Gerais and São Paulo in the early nineteenth century reveals this to be a distorted view of colonial life, at least in those regions. A majority of the population consisted of free people, with a significant percentage of free people of color (defined in that study as blacks plus mulattos). By the 1835 census, free people of color made up about 43 percent of that population in these regions. At 21 percent of the total population, they made up a quarter of all heads of households and about a third of all households that owned no slaves. They constituted about 6 percent of all slave owners in São Paulo and about 14 percent in Minas Gerais, compared with 35 percent for whites in São Paulo and 47 percent in Minas Gerais. Note that less than half of the white households owned slaves.

Free people of color were found in all occupations, although predominantly at the lower end of the social and economic scale—due to the obvious factors of poorer backgrounds and the related disadvantages of less education and less money. Among Brazil's poor, color did not seem to discriminate much, with poor whites closer in occupation to their mixed-race compatriots than to their richer white ones. Mulattos were more numerous among the free people of color and did better than blacks, however, in part because people of mixed blood were more likely to be the beneficiaries of manumission (and thus the chance to get ahead). As Herbert S. Klein and Vidal Luna put it, "This social [and] economic mobility of the free colored before emancipation may go a long way towards explaining the relative willingness of the Brazilian non-white population to support the social order even after the abolition of slavery and despite the persistence of racial discrimination to the present day."

So Freyre's picture is not accurate for São Paulo and Minas Gerais. But is it accurate even for the plantation economy of northeastern Brazil? Analysis of the 1835 census of Santiago do Iguape, a major sugar parish in the province of Bahia, presents, as B. J. Barickman puts it, "a rare opportunity to examine planter households and revisit, so to speak, Gilberto Freyre's casa grande (plantation mansion)." Even in the northeast agrarian economy, the depiction attributed to Freyre does not stand up very well.

According to the 1835 records, Santiago do Iguape had 7,410 inhabitants. More than half were African- and Brazilian-born slaves. Whites accounted for about 8 percent of the parish population. The remainder were freeborn and freed blacks and people of mixed bloods of various types. This population was spread across 966 inhabited dwellings, over 95 percent of which belonged to small farmers, fishermen, seamstresses, poor cane farmers, and artisans, typically classified as mulatto or black in the census.

A look at thirty-seven of the wealthiest families in the parish provides suggestive evidence that Freyre's picture was oversimplified at best, even for those at the top of the social pyramid. Of the thirty-seven household heads of this economic top echelon, for example, one was a freeborn mulatto who owned fifteen slaves. The overall average for the thirty-seven households was about twenty-nine slaves, the average for the wealthiest (i.e., those who also owned mills) was about 125. Eight of the thirty-seven households were headed by women, including some of the largest slave owners in the parish. Of the twenty-nine men who headed households in this wealthy group, analysis of the detail in the census suggests that no more than seven could plausibly have had concubines as part of their households, and in only two cases (neither of which included a current wife) is the presence of a concubine likely. That does not mean monogamy was the rule, of course, only that mistresses typically lived apart from the household of their lover.

How slaves were counted in the censuses of the era deserves further comment. The census takers did not define "household" as a group living under one roof. Rather, they counted everyone beholden to the plantation owner as part of the household. Thus, the many slaves these families had were members of the household by definition—even though they are documented to have lived, often as separate families, in separate slave quarters. Without slaves, household size among the thirty-seven wealthy families was relatively small, with the number of non-nuclear-family members (i.e., extended family members and free retainers) averaging only about four for households that had any at all, with several of the households having none.

The Persistence of the African in Brazilian Culture

One of the best-known facts about Brazil is the multiracial nature of its population—a mixture of Portuguese, indigenous Indian, and African, with much later additions of Japanese, Middle Easterners, and non-Portuguese Europeans. Out of all these potential cultural legacies, the African takes first place. This is particularly remarkable given that Portuguese writers at times expressed extreme distaste of the physical characteristics of the Africans they saw. In 1505, for example, Duarte Pacheco, a Portuguese who traveled extensively, dismissed west Africans as "dog-faced, dog-toothed people." In addition, Brazilians of the late nineteenth and early twentieth centuries subscribed to eugenic principles (the whiter, the better)—with the unique Brazilian twist that interbreeding in the Brazilian context actually helped "whiten" the population. It is also well established that Brazilian society subtly discriminated against nonwhites—not by blood (the one-drop rule practiced in the United States) but literally by appearance—how black or kinky-haired someone looked. Thus, for most of the twentieth century, two siblings could have very different outcomes in Brazil—with the whiter-looking child in the family becoming a bank teller, for example, and the darker one a domestic servant.

Even so, the tradition with the most resonance in Brazil is the African tradition. Why? Recent research by many scholars, including James Sweet, has turned up rich evidence helping us understand the lasting African presence in Brazil. Slaves, Sweet finds, transferred numerous cultural practices from Africa to Brazil. These included kinship structure, divination rituals, judicial ordeals, ritual burials, dietary restrictions, and secret societies. Sweet notes that "as Africans of different ethnic stripes were thrown together in the various slave societies they began to create a body of rituals and beliefs that would resonate with all Africans, regardless of ethnic backgrounds."

Most interpretations of this legacy, however, have been distorted by the Christian impulse to explain African religion as little more than "savagery." Portuguese authorities, both religious and secular, devoted maximum effort to converting the Africans to "pure" Christianity. Where unsuccessful they called in the Inquisition and administered horrible punishment, sometimes even relegating the victims to years in the galleys (at sea). The Africans, mostly slaves, often adopted a strategy of feigned cooperation. They would apparently adopt Christian beliefs while really retaining their own core beliefs. This led the Portuguese to vastly overestimate the true extent of Christianization in Brazil and to underestimate the persistence of African religious belief in practice.

In more recent years, the picture has begun to be corrected. The religious beliefs of western and central Africa, which predominated among slaves transferred to Brazil, contrasted sharply to Christianity. First was Christianity's belief in a unitary, all-powerful God. For the Africans, in contrast, God was the creator of a specific people. For the Africans, religious belief was also closely linked to everyday life, in relations with all other persons, and in the struggle to resist the weight of slavery. Thus, the African deities were far less remote than the Christian God. African deities were also more intimate and helped their believers to control events in the immediate world. Finally, for the African, healing and rituals took the place of Western "science."

Thus, medicine was a realm where African religion played a key role. From central Africa came the use of spirit possession, which enabled the believer to communicate with the other world. The power of this religious practice to treat illness, as well as knowledge of the medical value of certain roots and herbs, greatly attracted European followers and began with masters using African healers to cure other slaves. This even went so far as whites buying slaves for the specific purpose of earning money from their cures. But some slaves turned their religion against their masters, hitting the masters where they felt most vulnerable—the fear that slave anger could visit malicious injury or illness on them. And sometimes it did, through either spells cast or (possibly more effective) poison from an earthly source.

The durability of African religious influence is exemplified in the group of Afro-Brazilian religious sects, such as Candomblé, Umbanda, Batuque, and Macumba. Defined by the *Encyclopedia Britannica* as "a marked syncretism of traditional African religions, European culture, Brazilian spiritualism, and Roman Catholicism," many of the Afro-Brazilian religions involve being possessed by African deities. Roman Catholic elements in Brazil include the worship of Christian saints, who are believed to intercede on behalf of individuals and are given African names. The Virgin Mary, for example, is called "Iemanja." Many followers of the Afro-Brazilian religions move easily between these beliefs and practices and those of Roman Catholicism.

Many other African legacies were also brought to Brazil during the slave trade and became transformed and adapted to a new environment. Music, dance, folk tales, public religious ceremonies, and culinary contributions are just some of the influences of African traditions in Brazilian culture and society. As African slaves interacted with captured people from other parts of the continent and were forced to adopt a new language and practices within the confines of slavery, new creole cultures emerged that borrowed from indigenous traditions, Portuguese influences, and African practices. African slaves not only provided the labor to make the Portuguese colony in the Americas so wealthy but also contributed to the forging of new cultural and social identities in the New World.

3

From Colony to Independence as a Monarchy

The Portuguese Court Comes to Brazil

As the eighteenth century drew to a close, the economic and political tensions between the Portuguese crown and its largest colony continued, but against the backdrop of a growing conflagration in Europe, sparked by the French Revolution of 1789 and continuing as the Napoleonic Wars (1803–15). Napoleon Bonaparte, who had seized power in 1799 and crowned himself emperor of France at the end of 1804, was determined to conquer the whole of Europe, including Great Britain. To this end, Napoleon declared the Continental Blockade in 1806, forbidding the importation of British goods into continental Europe. Britain was Portugal's trading partner, protector, and long-time ally (through a treaty that dated back to 1373). Given the strength and longevity of this alliance, Portugal refused to join the Continental System, in return for which Napoleon sent an army through Spain to invade Portugal.

Britain, locked in a continent-wide battle with Napoleon, was in no position to prevent the French army, helped by two Spanish divisions, from entering Portugal. As an alternative, not only to defy the French but also to open Brazil to British trade, Britain pressed the Portuguese court (headed by a prince regent, as discussed further below) to flee Portugal and establish a base of power in its New World colony. The Portuguese council of state agreed with this strategy, and on November 27, 1807, the entire court and more than ten thousand courtiers, military advisers, religious leaders, lawyers, and nine thousand sailors set sail in twenty-three Portuguese warships and thirty-one merchant ships, along with four Royal Navy warships to guard the entourage during its 4,500-mile voyage. The move was unprecedented, not only in the history of the Americas but also in the whole history of colonial exploitation. Never before had a European monarch even set foot in a New World colony, much less settled in one as the seat of power. Napoleon, writing his memoirs in eventual exile in Santa Helena, said he recognized it as a major setback, "C'est ca qui m'a perdu" (This is what defeated me).

The following day French troops entered Lisbon, to be greeted by a council of governors appointed by the Portuguese regent deliberately to let the French know that the court would return when circumstances allowed. But did the court really plan to return? Historian Patrick Wilcken argues that what the Portuguese brought with them on their ships suggests that they may have been already considering an indefinite stay. They brought masses of government files, some dating back hundreds of years, plus manuscripts, maps, detailed records of official correspondence, and the royal treasury, which contained as much as half the coinage circulating in Portugal at the time. The regent's early initiatives in Brazil added to the impression that the court may have intended more than a temporary stay by creating a full-scale European-type bureaucracy within a year of its arrival.

What may be most fascinating is that the idea of moving the court to Brazil had been in the air for half a century. First raised by the Jesuit priest Antônio Vieira, it was mentioned again in a secret memorandum to João V (1706–50) by Luiz da Cunha, a Portuguese career diplomat, who wrote, "... it is about time for Your Majesty to see that immense continent of Brazil as a resourceful and well-populated country.... [in which you could establish] your court, taking people...who wanted to follow you—and there would be many." Da Cunha did not, of course, foresee a foreign invasion of Portugal as the impetus. He saw such a move to the New World in longer-run terms—as the solution to Portugal's failing economy.

The royal party was a strange assemblage. The power of the crown rested with Prince Dom João (later João VI when he became king in 1816), who had formally assumed the role of regent in 1799 when his mother, Queen Maria I, had been declared mentally incompetent. He was accompanied in the lead ship by his mother and his two sons, Principe Real Dom Pedro (the future Pedro I) and Dom Miguel. Had this ship gone down, the whole Bragança dynasty would have gone down with it. The voyage also began inauspiciously, with the fleet soon running into a fierce storm that drove the ships apart. They survived the storm, but conditions aboard were abominable, including infestations of lice that attacked even the royal family.

The fleet arrived at Salvador on the northeastern coast in January 1808. The Bahian population, largely black and mulatto, greeted the court's arrival with celebrations. The Portuguese royalty were shocked at how primitive the city was—and how African. They lost no time commandeering Bahia's best houses for their own use. For the residents of Salvador, the sight must have been bizarre indeed: a mad queen, an obese regent, and thousands of disheveled courtiers aghast at the new world they saw before them.

In February 1808, the royal entourage sailed on to Rio, the real administrative center of the colony, where the prince regent was determined to settle. Again there were problems with housing. Prominent Rio residents offered their best mansions, which were quickly accepted. Others were less willingly evicted by royal decrees to provide housing for the many courtiers and officials who arrived as part of the royal entourage. Once more, the royal family and its retainers found themselves in a sea of nonwhite faces. At least two-thirds of the colony's population was now black, mulatto, or of other mixed blood. And at least one-third of Rio's population was enslaved. The court and its retinue settled in for an uncomfortable stay of unknown length.

Even before the court had moved to Rio, the regent opened Brazil's ports to "friendly" nations, meaning primarily Britain. This was in good part in settlement of a bargain with Britain by which privileged access to Brazilian trade would be given in return for safe passage to Brazil. Rio de Janeiro became the port of entry for British manufactured goods, bringing one hundred to two hundred British merchants and commercial agents to that city before the end of 1808. A treaty in 1810 set the tariff on British goods actually below the tariff on goods brought from Portugal. Shortly thereafter the two tariffs were made equal. Even so, Britain retained a tremendous competitive advantage in both price and variety of goods because Portugal was already behind in the industrial revolution that was transforming production elsewhere in Europe.

Creating a New Portuguese America

The prince regent lost no time in consolidating the royal presence in the colony. As noted, he opened the colony's ports, thus ending three centuries of Portuguese monopoly and jettisoning the mercantilist system that had governed Portuguese economic policy for much of the period since the era of discovery. He also founded a bevy of new institutions, including the National Library, the Botanical Garden, the Bank of Brazil, and medical faculties in Bahia and Rio de Janeiro; and he brought the first printing press to the colony. This was used, among other things, to print the official *Gazeta do Rio de Janeiro*, a virtual replica of the *Gazeta de Lisboa* of the old country.

Although this "Lusitanian" invasion irritated the local Brazilians—in particular through the assigning of key positions in the expanding state structure to the newly arrived Portuguese—the prince regent himself was popular with his Brazilian compatriots. He also grew rapidly fond of his new home city, which under his auspices acquired such European-style attractions as an orchestra, theater, and a lively, though censored, publishing scene. Between 1808 and 1822, as the presence of the Portuguese court attracted business and in-migrants, Rio's population doubled, from 50,000 to 100,000.

Back in Portugal, the mood was very different. With Napoleon defeated in 1814, the Portuguese were clamoring for the court to return to its rightful place in the home country. Instead, the prince regent, in December 1815, elevated the Estado do Brasil to the status of equal partner with Portugal by creating the United Kingdom of Portugal, Brazil, and the Algarves. The person who had originally advocated Brazil's elevation to a kingdom was none other than Talleyrand (Charles Maurice de Talleyrand Perigord), France's chief negotiator at the Congress of Vienna, a conference of European ambassadors to redraw the continent's political map after Napoleon's defeat. This suggests that it was not only the Portuguese who viewed the court's continued location in a supposedly subservient possession of the home country as highly inappropriate. With that act, the prince regent legitimized his continued residence outside Portugal while also giving Brazilians new grounds for pride. One year later, "Mad Maria," still formally the monarch, died. Her son became Dom João VI, a monarch in his own right after seventeen years as the prince regent.

As the royal presence was being consolidated in Brazil, the upheaval caused by the French invasion and occupation was turning Portuguese politics upside down. Pre-1807-style loyalty to an absolute monarch was gone. Portuguese liberal revolutionaries, who triumphed by arms in 1820, demanded a more limited monarchy and a liberal constitution, to be drawn up by a *Cortes*, a representative body in Lisbon to which members would be elected by the entire Portuguese Empire (Brazil was allocated 72 of 181 seats). The revolutionary junta, to which the Cortes was responsible and which was governing in the name of the king, called with increasing insistence for Dom João VI's return from Brazil.

Within Brazil, the king's return to Portugal was supported by the higher military and the merchants, who expected to profit from Brazil's renewed subordination to the home country. Opposed were the large landowners, along with the Brazilian-born royal bureaucrats and some Portuguese, who had come, through either business or marriage, to identify with Brazil. Dom João VI made the decision to return because he was afraid he would lose the throne if he stayed. Four thousand Portuguese, less than half the number who had left Lisbon for Brazil in 1807, accompanied the sovereign on his return. He left behind his son, Pedro, whom he now named the prince regent, to administer Brazil. Dom João VI warned his son that if it ever came to a break between the two kingdoms, he (the prince) should choose Brazil. We do not know his reasons for this advice. One explanation actually given by one of his senior ministers was that the Rio base gave the crown more independence from British pressures to abolish the slave trade (Brazil's all-important source of labor). The king may also have had extreme misgivings about the crown's long-term future in Portugal, given its political (and economic) instability.

The Cortes met in early 1821, well before the delegates from Brazil could get to Portugal, and adopted an aggressive stance toward Brazil, with the intent of restoring it to subservient colonial status. In a particularly offensive move it divided the Brazilian realm into separate units, each of which would report directly to Lisbon—thus at least implicitly revoking Brazil's status as a co-kingdom with Portugal. Later in the year, the Cortes decided to send more Portuguese troops to Brazil and also ordered Pedro to return to Portugal. On January 9, 1822 Dom Pedro received a petition from residents of Rio de Janeiro requesting that he remain in Brazil. His response was "Diga ao povo que fico!" (I say to the people that I am staying.) This date is known in Brazil as the *Dia do Fico*. On September 7 of the same year, along the Ipiranga River in São Paulo, he rejected a final Portuguese decree that he return to Portugal, proclaiming Brazilian independence, according to reports, with the cry, "Independência ou Morte!" (Independence or death.) The declaration is known as the *Grito do Ipiranga* (Cry of Ipiranga) and this date is celebrated as Brazilian Independence Day. On December 1, 1822, he was crowned Emperor Pedro I at the age of 24. Thus did Portuguese America assume a unique historical path. No other former colony has ever embraced independence with its own monarch a member of the ruling family of the very country against which it had rebelled.

Portuguese troops in Rio that refused to swear allegiance to Dom Pedro I were forced to leave. (Dom Pedro had already decreed in August 1822, while still regent, that any troops coming in from Portugal be treated as enemies.) The military that remained began to build a Brazilian army, which went on to defend the Empire against forces, both foreign and domestic, although Brazilian

Dom Pedro I upon his acclamation as first emperor of Brazil in 1822. This occasion asserted Brazil's separateness from the Portuguese and made Brazil the first and only durable monarchy in the New World. (Snark/Art Resource, NY)

military engagements never reached the epic battles fought over independence in Spanish America.

What was the significance of this path to Brazilian independence? First, it meant severing political and administrative ties to Portugal—ties that went back three centuries. Second, because there was never any question of challenging the existing socioeconomic order, it meant Brazil would continue to be dominated by the landholding elite, which was strongest in the Northeast, Rio de Janeiro, Minas Gerais, and São Paulo. Third, Brazil would be under the direct influence of England. This had begun when the English sponsored the transfer of the Portuguese court to Brazil and lent large sums to the Portuguese crown to help consolidate its hold. Brazilians now had to assume the large Portuguese debt to the British (incurred in part to fight *against* Brazil's independence from Portugal!) and to agree to continue giving British goods favored entry through low tariffs.

It was also true that important issues remained unsettled. Most important was slavery, with the British threatening to cut off the slave trade to Brazil, as they had already done in 1808 to the United States (where trading in African slaves was still going on, even though a legal ban against the African slave trade had been passed in all U.S. states and written into the U.S. Constitution years earlier). A second issue was how the monarchy could secure the loyalty of Brazil's scattered provinces, especially where republicanism was particularly strong, such as in Pernambuco and other parts of the Northeast. Still another issue was the future of the new country's elite, who were substantially outnumbered by nonwhites. In 1823, one aristocratic observer, discouraged by the liberal revolutions in Spanish America, made the (unfulfilled) prophecy that within three years the "white race will come to an end at the hands of other races and the province of Bahia will disappear from the civilized world."

Brazilian Hierarchies

As independence came, Brazil lacked even the beginnings of a bourgeoisie. The export economy was dominated by agriculture and mining. Local merchants might have formed a bourgeois nucleus, but Brazilians played virtually no role in the overseas marketing of Brazilian exports, which were shipped directly to Portugal. Portuguese merchants were then responsible for the re-exportation to trading centers such as Antwerp. Furthermore, since the crown had prohibited manufacturing in the colony (mercantilism at work again), there was no manufacturing class. However, Brazil had finally established some institutions of higher learning. In addition to the medical faculties established in Bahia and Rio de Janeiro by the prince regent in 1808, law faculties were established in São Paulo and Olinda (in the state of Pernambuco) in 1827. These faculties now began to produce the core of the future bourgeoisie.

The economic base of the newly independent Brazil, given the continued decline of the mining sector, was agriculture. Sugar, tobacco, cotton, and coffee were the prime commercial crops and earned most of Brazil's foreign exchange. Just as in the era before independence, slaves supplied most of the labor. The Brazilian non-elite encompassed the 95 percent of the population who had neither the income nor the family connections to rise very far. Society was a pyramid. At the bottom were the slaves, both African and of African-slave descent. Slightly above them were the free men, mostly of color (of indigenous and African descent), both free-born and emancipated slaves. But these existed in the interstices of the economy, as artisans and tradesmen with little or no political leverage. Women street vendors were part of the population. They were of much more concern to the authorities than their numbers would imply, as they were suspected of being smugglers of gold and precious stones out of Minas Gerais. Above them were the subsistence farmers and purveyors of services. Above them was a huge gap between the tiny elite at the top (1–2 percent of Brazil's population) and the rest of the population.

Did the huge non-elite pose any real threat to the elite? Not really. Slave uprisings did occur, as in Cachoeira, Bahia, in 1814, when rebels set fire to the city, and the Malé Revolt in 1835, when hundreds of black Africans rose up in Salvador. These were Muslims, known as "Malés," from which the revolt got its name. About seventy participants died in the uprising; more than five hundred Africans were sentenced (to death, prison, whiplash, or deportation). But Bahia was unusual, and even Bahia did not see any uprisings after 1835.

The brutality used to maintain slavery was unending, although occasional masters were exceptions. Whipping and mutilation were commonplace, and execution of slaves was not unknown. Physical punishments of ordinary criminals were also brutal. And the high crime of treason was still rewarded by hanging, decapitation, and display of the victim's head on a spike. But incarceration and physical punishment were only the most obvious forms of control in this society. More insidious was the socialization of the young into an automatic acceptance of the social hierarchy and their place in it. Monarchy combined with slavery created an atmosphere of deference that was powerfully transmitted to the non-elites. Inculcation of this attitude of subservience was by and large successful in convincing non-elites there was no way to change their world. Religion and folk culture combined to create a vocabulary that articulated deference in a thousand ways. Given the color stratification of the society, the Portuguese attitude of racial superiority reinforced this passive attitude.

The Tribulations of Brazil's First Emperor

The elite in the newly independent nation had a clear idea of how to run their economy. Their doctrine—a version of the Manchester liberalism emanating from England and already seen in action when the prince regent yielded to British pressure and opened Brazil's ports in 1808—held that every country should concentrate on producing what it could produce best and trade with other countries for goods it could buy more cheaply than it could produce them. This doctrine, impeccable in its logic, meant Brazil would continue to export primary products and import most of its finished goods. It was anti-protectionism and, for primary producers such as Brazil, anti-industrialization. Since tariffs, according to this doctrine, should only be levied for revenue, protecting nascent domestic industrialization efforts from foreign competition was out of the question.

The Brazilian elite also absorbed much of the political liberalism of Britain. The constituent assembly drafted a constitution under the direction of José Bonifácio de Andrada e Silva, a prominent landowner and jurist. It largely copied the English parliamentary system, with the objective of creating a government controlled by the elite through highly restrictive voting eligibility. Emperor Pedro I found it not to his liking. He dissolved the assembly and arbitrarily issued his own constitution. It was an ominous beginning for a colony that had justified its independence by claiming Portuguese authority had been too arbitrary.

The emperor described his Constitution of 1824 as "twice as liberal" as the assembly's version. It created a two-house parliament. The Senate consisted of lifetime members who were chosen by the emperor from a list of three nominated by each province. The Chamber of Deputies was to be elected directly by parliamentary districts. The franchise was limited to wealth holders but the minimum requirement was relatively low. Illiterates who met the property requirement were eligible to vote, although women (whether literate or not) were excluded. Restrictions on the franchise were not unlike those in Britain after the Great Reform Act of 1832 (although a higher percentage of Britons undoubtedly met the property requirement).

But the emperor left himself vast powers under his constitution, should he choose to assert them. He could dissolve the lower house, then call new elections. He also had the power to approve or veto any measure passed by the Chamber or the Senate. This inherent responsibility to act as the final judge and arbiter in vital matters of state was referred to by the Brazilians as the "moderating power" of the crown. Such an exalted idea of the monarch's role, which was fully shared by the elite, was borrowed in part from the French commentator Benjamin Constant, a favorite author among Brazil's political elite of the era.

The newly independent Brazilian empire was divided into eighteen provinces, each replacing a previous captaincy and each governed by a president appointed by the emperor. The elite's intent was to build a highly centralized structure. Reaction on the provincial level to this centralized design was strongly negative. The new imperial structure represented a far tighter administration than the local landowners had experienced during the colonial era. Some regions, such as Pará and Maranhão in the North, were used to communicating more often with Lisbon than with Bahia or Rio. They now nursed hopes of breaking away from their continental links, as had the viceroyalties and captaincies of

Spanish America. In the words of a visiting aristocrat, "Brazil is a country being born, a settlement inhabited by peoples of different colors who have a mutual dislike for each other.... The captaincies cannot help each other, as they are separated by enormous expanses so that the country does not yet constitute a single kingdom with unbroken territorial unity."

Revolts occurred not only against the Rio government but also against the monarchical principle itself. One of the most serious broke out in 1824 in Pernambuco, where the local notables were incensed that the monarch had named a new president for the province without consulting them. The rebels were militant republicans who wanted a Brazil free of any royalty. The battle against these and other republican rebels thus elevated the monarchy to the level of defender of Brazil's territorial integrity. The republicans "elected" their own president, whom the imperial authorities unsuccessfully attempted to deport. The rebels then issued a proclamation creating "the Confederation of the Equator." They gained adherents in Paraíba do Norte, Rio Grande do Norte, and southern Ceará. But the imperial forces had superiority at sea, and so conquered the Pernambucan capital of Recife and crushed the rebellion. Just as they would have in colonial times, the crown's representatives executed sixteen rebel leaders, including Frei Caneca, the publisher of the newspaper *Typis Pernambucano*, which had been the ideological voice of the Republicans in the area. The young nation survived this republican revolt, but more uprisings were to come in the course of the century.

The emperor's position was not improved by the outbreak of war in 1825 between his newborn empire and Buenos Aires over the attempt of Brazil's Cisplatine Province (roughly present-day Uruguay) to leave the Brazilian Empire and join Argentina. The Brazilian forces (including European mercenaries) were unprepared and unable to win, but English intervention ended the conflict and created the independent nation of Uruguay.

The cost of the war drained the imperial finances, undermined the value of the currency, and raised the cost of imports into Brazil. Since the latter were largely controlled by Portuguese merchants, the locals had yet another reason to feel lusophobic. In 1831, Rio witnessed a five-day "bottle-throwing" riot, in which the pro-Brazilian faction (the *cabras*, or "goats") attacked the houses of the pro-Portuguese (*pés de chumbo*, or "lead feet"). Dom Pedro I was caught in the middle of this rising tension. He may have been the symbol of independence in 1822, but now he was paying for the ambiguity inherent in a member of the Portuguese royal family leading the former colony to independence. He faced pressure from both Brazil and Portugal. In Brazil it was direct pressure from the higher military, who threatened to revolt if he remained in Brazil; in Portugal it was pressure from the monarchists, who wanted him, as the senior Bragança (Dom João VI had died in 1826), back on the Portuguese throne. In 1831, he returned to his homeland, leaving behind his five-year-old son, Pedro II, as the claimant to the Brazilian throne.

In addition to the problem of the succession of power, Brazil had to come to terms with the fact that Great Britain was now the guarantor of Brazil's survival as a new nation. Although U.S. recognition of Brazilian independence came first (1824), Britain was the leading European power of the day, and so its action (1825) was more crucial.

Britain had long been a key actor in the history of Portugal and therefore of Brazil. Portugal's political alliance with Britain went back to the fourteenth century. By the eighteenth century, Britain was Portugal's most important trading partner. And the Royal Navy had saved the Portuguese crown from capture and deposition by Napoleon's armies, thereby guaranteeing new importance for Brazil.

This British support did not come cheap, however. As noted earlier, in 1825 Brazil had agreed to pay the $7,000,000 debt Portugal had incurred with Britain to finance the fight against Brazilian independence. Second, there was another treaty in 1825 continuing to grant British goods preferential tariffs in Brazil at rates lower than charged to the Portuguese. Third, an 1826 treaty forced Brazil to commit itself to ending the African slave trade within a few years. The Brazilian legislation in 1831 reluctantly passed a law banning the trade, but failure to enforce it made the ban ineffectual. Finally, the Brazilians signed a treaty in 1827 giving British subjects the right to be tried by special British courts within Brazil.

All these measures underlined the fact that the British were now the dominant foreign actor in the Brazilian economy, both in trade and in direct investment. They were supreme in banking, shipping, communications, and insurance. Brazil had passed from the Portuguese crown to the British sphere of influence in what historians would later call "informal imperialism."

Uprisings under the Regency

When Pedro I reluctantly returned to Portugal in 1831, leaving his five-year-old son (Pedro II) to the mercies of a succession of regents, he also left an elite that was divided about how Brazil should be governed and, indeed, what kind of nation (or nations) Brazil should be.

In the middle were supporters of the Brazilian monarchy and Pedro II. They believed Brazil should continue as a single country, remaining as an empire but totally independent of Portugal. Called by Boris Fausto the "moderate liberals," they believed in the defense of individual liberty (for the elite, of course); were drawn primarily from the centrally located provinces of São Paulo, Rio de Janeiro, and Minas Gerais; and controlled the machinery of imperial government in Brazil. They were helped by the loyalty the hereditary monarchy stimulated among the largely illiterate, socially hierarchical, common population in Brazil. Even to many within the elite, the emperor was revered as the incarnation of absolute power. But the moderate liberals were not unambiguously helped by this reverence for the monarchy, because there were potentially two contenders for the Brazilian throne.

The other contender, of course, was Pedro I, now back on the throne of Portugal. And his existence created the first of two factions opposed to Pedro II and the moderate liberals. This group was called the "absolutists." They, too, believed Brazil should be an empire, but they wanted to bring back Pedro I and restore the united empire of Portugal and Brazil. They also favored a stronger monarchy than the moderate liberals and were more inclined to subordinate individual liberties to strengthen the crown. The absolutists were supported by the merchants, many of whom had been born in Portugal. Since Brazilian businessmen and planters (many of whom were quite patriotically Brazilian) were typically indebted to these merchants, feelings between the two groups ran high. The absolutists drew their support primarily from coastal cities, including Rio.

The other group opposed to Pedro II and the moderate liberals were the "exaltados." The exaltados wanted greater provincial autonomy than the moderate liberals. Some even favored a republic. They had regional support throughout Brazil, helped by the fact that most Brazilians, including many of the elite, identified with their *patria*—i.e., their regional homeland (*patria paulista* or *patria bahiana*, for example)—before they identified with Brazil. At the extreme, the exaltados believed there should be no united Brazil—that the provinces should become independent states, as had happened in Spanish America.

The first regency to rule in the name of Pedro II was actually a triumvirate, chosen to represent each of three regions where the moderate liberals were strong. This triumvirate lasted from 1831 to 1834 and created many of the legal institutions the Empire needed but still lacked when Pedro I headed back to Portugal. Two initiatives under the triumvirate are worthy of particular note. The first was the application of a Criminal Procedure in 1832 (the criminal code had been passed in 1830), which instituted habeas corpus, henceforth the Brazilian citizens' first line of defense against illegal arrest—effective for the elite, virtually a dead letter for the rest of the population. The second, which had almost immediate repercussions, was the Additional Act of 1834. This act, approved by parliament, amended the Constitution of 1824 by giving increased powers to the provinces. Under this act, each province was allowed to create a provincial assembly, which could control taxation and expenditure in that province as well as appoint local officials.

Supporters of the act, which was referred to by many as the regency's "experiment with decentralization," hoped that this deliberate weakening of Rio's imperial government, especially in financial affairs, would create greater unity within Brazil as a whole by recognizing the legitimacy of a Brazilian's first loyalty to his (few worried about political views of women in this era) *patria*.

The result was disastrous from the central government's viewpoint. Brazil erupted in a series of regional revolts. These revolts serve as a reminder that

Brazil was subject to the same forces of fragmentation that split Spanish America into several separate countries. Brazil survived as a single nation, however, with central authority successfully defeating every revolt.

The first revolt, the War of the Cabanos in Pernambuco (1832–35), began even before the Additional Act was passed in 1834. The instigators of this uprising were fighting to demand the return of Pedro I and the suppression of the regency. Attracting primarily lower sectors of the population, including Indians and slaves, the movement gained support from the absolutists in Rio, resulting in some street fighting in Rio itself. The revolt was weakened by the death of Pedro I in 1834 and was finally crushed in 1835, by which time the regency triumvirate had been replaced by a single regent, Father Diogo Antônio Feijó. He had been chosen by a narrowly based electoral body that represented the provinces and was authorized to choose a single regent. Father Diogo, in failing health, was himself forced out of the regency in 1837, to be replaced by a fierce defender of central authority, the future Marquês de Olinda.

The first major revolt after passage of the Additional Act was the War of Cabangem (1835–40). It erupted in Belém, the port city for the lower Amazon and the capital of the province of Pará. The initial fighting was between the monarchists (whatever their stripe) and the regionalists, fueled by the strong anti-Portuguese feeling stimulated by the presence of Portuguese-born merchants. It escalated into a social struggle between the elite more generally and a proletariat composed largely of Indians. Atrocities to prisoners were commonplace on both sides, with the Indians withdrawing into the interior and being hunted down by imperial troops. The death toll in Belém was staggering—30,000 in a province whose population before the conflict was estimated at about 150,000. The slaughter during the War of Cabangem stands as further contradiction to the claim of Brazilians and others that Brazil was blessed with a nonviolent past.

Two other major revolts erupted in the Northeast. Both spread from fighting among the elite to genuine social conflict, with Afro-Brazilians and poor whites capitalizing on the political unrest to attack authority more generally. These social uprisings led to particularly grisly reprisals against the underclasses who lost.

The first (the Sabinada) was a direct challenge to the Empire. It occurred in Bahia (1837–38) and began with a manifesto by the rebels declaring a "free and independent state." What the elite protagonists called "the nonwhite rabble" joined the battle, raising the specter of race war. The rebels attempted to blockade Bahia, but they were easily defeated by the central government, with a death toll of about 1,800.

The second revolt in the Northeast was the Balaiada (1838–41) in Maranhão, the second most northern province in Brazil. It was a region where bandits were common. But this fighting also grew into a social rebellion, with a rebel band including a column of 3,000 slaves capturing the major town of

Caxias. The imperial army finally recaptured the town, in a shrewd counter-insurgency campaign under the leadership of Brigadier Luiz Alves da Lima e Silva. His forces used unconventional movements, including infiltration of rebel lines, to demoralize the enemy. In reward for his exploits, Lima e Silva was made baron of Caxias, under which name he went on to quell a revolt that was much more dangerous to the Empire. (In 1869, he was elevated to duke of Caxias.) The leader of the slave column was hanged in 1842.

The revolt that first earned the baron of Caxias his place in history was the Guerra dos Farrapos revolt in Rio Grande do Sul, which began in 1836 and dragged on for a decade. The Riograndense rebels declared an independent state in 1838, the "Republic of Piratini," thereby gaining de facto control of the lucrative interregional commerce in leather and meat and posing by far the most difficult political problem for the Empire of any in this decade of revolts. The reason was the revolt's location on the border with Uruguay. At the time of the revolt, Uruguay had only recently been created (1828), largely through the good offices of the British, as a buffer state between Brazil and Argentina. The Empire could not afford to drive the Riograndense rebels into secession from the Empire, which would have created an independent state that might potentially ally with Uruguay and Argentina against Brazil. Nor could the Empire placate the rebels by conceding to them the kind of autonomy that would almost certainly tempt *patrias* in other parts of the country to set up their own "republics."

The man given the task of managing this delicate balancing act was the aforesaid baron of Caxias. He pursued a twofold strategy that succeeded brilliantly. First, he waged a relentless and winning military campaign to recapture Rio Grande do Sul. Then, to conciliate the losers, whose separatist emotions were still running high, he granted amnesty to all and, in the name of the Empire, assumed all the rebel republic's debt. His approach was to be copied by the central government in dealing with later regional revolts, even into the twentieth century.

Recentralization

The imperial government had had enough of its experiment in decentralization by 1840, a year that saw two major turning points in government. First, the parliament revoked the powers delegated to the provinces in the Additional Act of 1834. Second, the powers behind the throne decided to tap into the latent reverence among many Brazilians for the hereditary monarchy by proclaiming the majority of Pedro II. Given that the new monarch had just turned fourteen, this was quite a gamble. The hope was that the pomp and circumstance of his installation as sovereign would have a favorable symbolic effect strong enough to spill over into political support for consolidation of the nation. It was a vast country he inherited. Rio was three days from Santos (the principal Paulista port) by ship, another difficult day overland to the city of São Paulo, eight days to Salvador (Bahia), twelve to Recife, and thirty to Belém.

To say that a new fountain of political support for consolidation was not immediately obvious is an understatement. The year 1842 saw three more uprisings in São Paulo and Minas Gerais. These were easily suppressed. Once again the baron of Caxias was the victorious commander. The end of the decade saw a more serious revolt, the Praieira (1848–50) in Pernambuco.

By this time, there were two rather than three political factions among the elite. The death of Pedro I in 1834 had broken the will of those who backed a united empire with Portugal. The pro-Empire forces had become largely one imperial party, the Conservative party. The proregionalists had become primarily the Liberal party. In 1848 in Pernambuco, the Conservatives were in power and, as was typical in those days of patronage, had thrown out the Liberal appointees in the police and National Guard and installed their own supporters. The Liberals refused to accept this replacement of *their* appointees and took up arms. The ensuring conflict, as had happened elsewhere, was compounded by an outbreak of rioting among the populace against the Portuguese-born merchants in the port city of Recife, an outbreak that served to support the regionalist interests of the Liberals. The rebels, who had been influenced by the radical ideas that underlay the revolutions of 1848 in Europe, took up the cry of federalism, though stopping short of advocating a republic, and (in a mixture of xenophobia and anti-monarchism) demanded the expulsion of the Portuguese-born and an end to the "moderating power" of the sovereign. The imperial forces crushed the revolt in 1850. It was the last major regionalist challenge to the centralized monarchy. From this point, the nation-state was to hold the upper hand.

The Role of Pedro II

The term "moderating power," as noted in an earlier chapter, referred to the monarch's position as the balance wheel of government. It was at his invitation that governments were formed and dissolved. It was he who chose who should be Senator from among three province-chosen nominees. And it was through the crown that national patronage, the politicians' lifeblood, flowed. The success of Pedro II's role would depend on how he used his moderating power and how the elite perceived that use.

Pedro II brought a natural flair to his job. Even at age fourteen he was stable, balanced, and discreet. The young emperor had another asset. As his father had said on the eve of his departure in 1831, "My son has the advantage over me of being Brazilian, and the Brazilians like him. He'll reign without difficulty and the constitution will guarantee his prerogatives." As his reign progressed, he earned a reputation as being fair and objective, projecting the image of an honest and ethical sovereign who would not hesitate to discipline politicians who were caught straying from his strict standards. Here he resembled Queen Victoria, his British contemporary, whose long reign (1837–1901) largely paralleled his own. Pedro II became increasingly a point of political reference for the elite, who used his rectitude and firm hand to distance their own country from the "unstable" Spanish American republics. It was only after 1870 that, visibly aged and exhausted by the Paraguayan War, he became an easy target for politicians who wanted a scapegoat.

Pedro II strengthened his image of civilized urbanity and rectitude by making a habit of presiding over sessions of the Brazilian Historical and Cultural Institute, Brazil's leading learned body of the day. He was especially interested in Brazil's indigenous heritage and took the trouble to learn and speak Guaraní, the most widely spoken Indian language. He also subsidized Brazilian writers and intellectuals to research in European archives the treaties that supposedly defined Brazil's boundaries. Several of these beneficiaries of imperial largesse, such as the poet Antônio Gonçalves Dias, won fame as the leaders of the "Indianist" Romantic movement that dominated Brazilian letters at mid-century. Pedro II also maintained personal links with foreign savants, such as Louis Pasteur, the Comte de Gobineau, and Louis Agassiz.

Dom Pedro II, Brazil's second and last emperor, a popular and long-lived monarch who had the fortunate knack of governing in the English parliamentary manner.

In his public image, the emperor was in tune with his Victorian era. But he was his father's son in at least one respect: Pedro I had been a notorious philanderer, and Pedro II also had an active extramarital life, though his was vastly more discreet than that of his father, who made few concessions to public decorum. Ever mindful of the importance of keeping up appearances, Pedro II required his many mistresses to return his love letters. In a rare act of indiscretion, however, he himself kept them all—to be discovered a century later by an archivist who leaked them to the press. Perhaps that was how he intended things to go—that the world should discover his flesh-and-blood self at some safe interval after his death.

For three decades after Pedro II's succession in 1840, Brazilian politics were dominated by two parties, the Liberals and the Conservatives. This political environment was similar to that of Victorian Britain in the sense that it provided an institutionalized mechanism for alternating power peacefully among the dominant factions of the political elite. But the achievement becomes much more noteworthy when it is remembered that Brazilian parties operated in a country far less advanced, both economically and socially, than Britain. In the nineteenth-century Spanish American republics, for example, contests for power frequently involved civil war and dictatorial rule. And Brazil itself had until very recently been a nation rife with political disagreements at the regional level that often escalated into armed conflict.

Although the two Brazilian parties were accused, at the time and by later commentators, of being indistinguishable versions of a single elite, there were in fact real differences between them. They both supported a unified Brazil under the monarchy. But the Liberals, who had their primary strength in São Paulo, Minas Gerais, and Rio Grande do Sul, supported at least some decentralization. The Conservatives, strongest in Bahia, Pernambuco, and Rio de Janeiro, tended to be strong supporters of a centralized bureaucracy.

It is true that Brazilian electoral politics of the period was often a game in which the stakes were patronage and governmental support for local interests, and the tools were regular doses of bribery, intimidation, and fraud (not unlike British politics only a few decades earlier). But the monarchy was truly consolidated and its authority universally acknowledged, if only implicitly, throughout the country. The Conservative party was dominant between 1850 and 1863, successfully leading to what came to be known as the "conciliation"—a muting of party conflict and an agreement to avoid controversial issues. Politics became routinized. Meanwhile, coffee production was rising and boosting export earnings, allowing the crown to avoid further foreign indebtedness with London between 1840 and 1857.

The Rise of Coffee

The exhaustion of the gold and diamond mines by the second half of the eighteenth century made the Brazilian economy again dependent on agricultural

EXHIBIT 3-1

Principal Exports as a Percent of Brazil's Total Exports, 1650–1970

Years	Sugar	Coffee	Cotton	Other (including minerals & manufactured goods)
1650	95.0	–	–	5.0
1750	47.0	–	–	53.0
1800	31.0	–	6.0	63.0
1841–50	26.7	41.4	7.5	25.4
1891–1900	6.0	64.5	2.7	26.8
1921–30	1.4	69.6	2.4	26.6
1945–49	1.2	41.8	13.3	43.7
1970	4.9	35.8	6.0	53.3

Source: Thomas W. Merrick and Douglas H. Graham, *Population and Economic Development* (Baltimore, 1979), p. 12.

exports, with cotton and rice now complementing long-time exports of tobacco and sugar. By 1830, a new product had appeared: coffee, an export that would fuel Brazil's export economy for the next 140 years. (See exhibit 3-1.) Coffee was first successfully commercialized in the late eighteenth century in Brazil in the province of Rio de Janeiro, where the soil was highly adaptable to the coffee bush. In the 1830s and 1840s, that province became the center of coffee cultivation, with the city of Rio as the export center. Rio housed the banks, brokerage houses, and docks that connected Brazil to the world coffee market in western Europe and North America. Slaves were the main source of the considerable labor needed to plant the coffee trees, cultivate them, and harvest what would become the coffee beans. Some slaves were acquired from the slave trade, which, though technically illegal since 1826, continued until 1850. Others were purchased from the less profitable sugar plantations, especially in the Northeast.

The soils of Rio de Janeiro province were progressively depleted by the intensive coffee cultivation, as the hilly topography helped to accelerate soil erosion. But Brazil had no shortage of unutilized (or underutilized) land. Although production in Rio remained high, by midcentury the center of coffee cultivation was moving south and west of Rio, spreading into the provinces of São Paulo and Minas Gerais, where the soil proved as productive as Rio soil at its best.

The southward march of coffee and the rapid rise of Brazilian production generated an increased demand for labor. With the end of the slave trade in 1850, the southern provinces were forced to rely on the purchase of slaves from domestic sources, especially in the North and Northeast. This created a demographic shift southward, similar (though on a lesser scale) to the eighteenth-century shift toward Minas Gerais during the mining boom. (See exhibit 3-2.)

EXHIBIT 3-2
Percentage Distribution of Slave Population by Region in Brazil, 1823–1887

| Region | Percent | | | | |
	1823	1864	1872	1883	1887
North	4	2	2	2	1
Northeast	53	49	32	28	28
Southeast	38	44	59	63	67
South	2	4	6	6	2
West	3	1	1	1	1
Total (%)	100	100	100	100	100
Total number	1,163,746	1,715,000	1,510,806	1,240,806	723,419
Rate of Growth (between years)	0.9	−1.1	−2.1	−16.5	

Source: Thomas W. Merrick and Douglas H. Graham, *Population and Economic Development* (Baltimore, 1979), p. 66.

The northeastern masters who sold their slaves received payment, but this capital inflow did not stop northeastern politicians denouncing the "loss" of their labor force as it migrated to the more prosperous South.

The continued shortage of labor in São Paulo led a few planters to import European immigrants to work as sharecroppers on the coffee plantations. The most famous planter who tried this approach was Senator Nicolau Vergueiro, who recruited a group of German and Swiss immigrants in the 1840s. The Brazilian planters paid the passage for these immigrants and promised to provide a job, acceptable working conditions, and fair earnings in return for labor. The experiment failed, perhaps because of the inherent incompatibility of slave and free labor in a single plantation setting. In any case, many of these immigrants protested to their home governments that they were being treated like slaves—protested so vehemently, in fact, that Prussia responded by prohibiting immigrant recruitment by Brazil. The failure of this and other experiments with European immigrant colonists reinforced the conservative planters' view that there was no alternative to slave labor. The opposite conclusion—that the labor shortage could no longer be met by slaves and that abolition might be an indispensable prerequisite—took longer to sink in.

The system of landownership in colonial Brazil—a succession of royal land grants made personally by the monarch—had led to a pattern of ad hoc land claims that had more to do with actual physical possession (such as squatting) than legal recognition. By 1850, the growth of commercial export agriculture, especially coffee, had dramatically raised the stakes of landownership, and the prospect of increased immigration of free labor from Europe (with the slave trade cut off) raised the urgent question of how the new wage laborers could

Brazilian coffee sacks being unloaded. Brazil long reigned as the leading exporter of coffee to the world market. (Time & Life Pictures/Getty Images)

be made to stay on the plantations instead of settling on the still abundantly available unused land.

In 1850, a land law was passed in Brazil, decreeing that public land could now be obtained only by purchase from the government or by payment of taxes to regularize land agreements already made, making access to land more difficult for small holders. The law's application favored the large holders, especially those involved in export agriculture, and this was exactly its intent. In fact, the chief purpose of the law was to promote the large plantation system. The only way to have lessened the hold of large landowners would have been to impose a stiff tax on uncultivated land. Such a tax was proposed several times after 1850, but was consistently and successfully blocked by large landowner interests.

Twelve years later, the United States, in which small holder access to land had always been easier than in Brazil, took a very different tack. The U.S. government passed the Homestead Act of 1862, encouraging small land holdings by making land grants to small farmers who promised to cultivate the land. The contrary path taken by Brazil has had major implications for economic inequality in modern Brazil, because it institutionalized the concentration of legal land ownership in a country where land was the principal source of wealth.

The Emerging Problems with Slavery as an Institution

In 1830, Brazil was the largest slave economy in the world, with more slaves than free persons. But Brazil's slave population was not replacing itself, requiring Brazil to depend heavily on slave imports. There were three major reasons for this dependence on imports. First, because of its historic reliance on the slave trade, there were far more male than female slaves in Brazil, reducing the birth rate for that reason alone. Second, Brazilian slaves were kept in such grim living conditions that their health was jeopardized, further reducing the child-bearing capacity of the Brazilian female slave population. In the mid-nineteenth century, for example, the life expectancy of a Brazilian slave was about 66 percent that of a Brazilian white man (leaving aside free persons of color), in contrast to the United States in the slave period, where a slave would expect to live almost 90 percent as long as his master. Finally, despite their callousness about slave conditions on the plantations, Brazilian slave masters were much more likely to free the slaves they had than were their U.S. counterparts, perhaps because they were so used to being able to replace lost slaves through the frequent (monthly, according to most estimates) deliveries of new slaves from Africa.

British pressure to end the slave trade, therefore, threatened the very heart of the Brazilian economy. The British, like the other European settlers of the New World, had, of course, profited from African slavery for centuries through their slaveholding colonies in North America and the Caribbean. They had also profited from investments in the slave trade itself. And it was a rare British politician or cleric who found any convincing moral rationale against enslavement before the eighteenth century. By the late eighteenth century, however, British public opinion in general had moved toward abolition with the network of Methodist churches giving powerful support to the abolitionist campaign. As Enlightenment ideas produced new attitudes toward human relations, the reduction of humans to sub-human status for economic gain began to arouse passionate opposition in Britain as immoral and unchristian.

This moral shift became so powerful that in 1833 the British Parliament prohibited slavery in the British Atlantic colonies. Public opinion was also pressing the British government to suppress the flourishing slave trade from West Africa to the rest of the slaveholding New World. The main motivation was indeed moral and ideological, but an economic dimension also entered the political calculus, because leaving the British Caribbean colonies without a slave trade put them at a competitive disadvantage (in labor costs) vis-à-vis slave economies such as Cuba and Brazil. Ending the slave trade throughout the world would have the coincidental advantage of redressing this competitive imbalance.

So the British put growing pressure on Brazil, which was felt in several ways. In 1826 Britain had pressured Brazil to sign a treaty agreeing to end the slave trade within three years. Although there was no support for this measure among the Brazilian elite, they could hardly explicitly resist the British, to whom they were heavily indebted both politically and financially. Successive Brazilian governments dealt with the problem by simply neglecting to enforce the 1826 treaty, a negligence they applied also to an 1831 law that declared all slaves subsequently entering Brazil as automatically free. Slave ships continued to unload their human cargoes on the Brazilian coast, in open defiance of the legal ban. Britain's Royal Navy, the world's premier naval force, set out to intercept the slave ships and liberate the slave cargoes. Although they had some successes, a massive flow continued to arrive through the 1830s and 1840s. Despite outrage expressed in the English press and parliament, about 712,000 new slaves poured into Brazil during these two decades, averaging as many as 35,000 a year. (Since the trade was technically illegal after 1831, these figures are only estimates.)

Under pressure from the coffee growers and other landowners, who argued that Brazil's economy would collapse if denied a secure supply of slaves, the Brazilian government continued to ignore its diplomatic commitment to Britain until 1850, when the Brazilian parliament finally passed legislation (the Eusebio de Queiroz law) definitively outlawing the slave trade. The reasons were several. Most important was increased British naval pressure after the Brazilian government refused in 1845 to renew the treaty that had obligated it to suppress the trade. Royal Navy cruisers then cracked down on slave ships headed for Brazil, seizing almost four hundred between 1845 and 1850. This stepped-up intervention, which extended into Brazilian harbors, presented a major threat to Brazilian sovereignty. A second concern motivating the Brazilian elite was a loss of confidence in their ability to control the slaves after they reached Brazil. The successful slave rebellion in Haiti in the 1790s had struck fear into the hearts of slave owners throughout the Americas. This fear was reinforced in Brazil by the Malé slave revolt in Salvador, Bahia in 1835. From then on, the police and politicians, especially in Rio and Bahia, warned that the newly arriving African slaves had great explosive potential—warnings that were confirmed by a revolt of fugitive slaves in Rio de Janeiro province in 1838 and fugitive slave participation in the Balaiada revolt (1838–40) in Maranhão. Finally, Brazilian authorities were alarmed by the outbreaks of yellow fever and cholera in the 1840s. Medical researchers traced the source of these epidemic diseases to recently arrived African slaves, providing another powerful piece of self-interest for ending the trade.

In 1850, the Brazilian cabinet finally agreed to stop the slave traffic which, even by Brazilian law, had been illegal for almost two decades. The

Brazilian government was now truly committed to enforcing the law, and it was estimated that only 6,100 more slaves entered Brazil (clandestinely) from 1850 to 1855. The slave trade continued only to Cuba, where it was finally ended in the 1860s through combined pressure from the British and Spanish governments.

The end of the trade had grave implications for Brazil. As already discussed, continuous imports of slaves were essential to fill the labor needs of the plantations. Although the planters, whose ports were under pressure from the British navy, accepted the final abolition of the trade, they remained pessimistic about its effects on the future of Brazilian agriculture. As the Italian Jesuit Antonil had remarked two centuries earlier, the slaves were "the hands and feet" of Brazil. How could the country survive without its limbs?

The Question of Abolition

When Brazil established its independent empire in 1822, slavery was firmly entrenched. Slavery was central to the economy in every region of the country. The dynamic new coffee sector, for example, depended entirely on slave labor. At the same time, new shipments of slaves were pouring into the country. Slavery had no serious opposition. On the contrary, it was an essential part of Brazil's view of itself.

By 1850, the Brazilians' position on slavery made them increasingly isolated on the world scene. In 1863, U.S. President Lincoln's Emancipation Proclamation freed slaves within the Confederacy, and in 1865 the U.S. Congress freed the rest by constitutional amendment. That left Cuba and Brazil as the only major slave states in the Americas. Brazil's isolation was reinforced by increasing pressure from Europe, especially Britain and France. In 1870, for example, a committee of French intellectuals, led by Victor Hugo, wrote Emperor Pedro II, urging him to abolish slavery immediately. In his 1871 speech from the throne, the emperor acknowledged Hugo's letter and promised to work toward abolition. In fact, Pedro II had first become convinced of the need for abolition in 1865, when he visited the Brazilian front during the war against Paraguay (see discussion following). The emperor found that the Paraguayans' citing of Brazilian slavery made effective anti-Brazilian propaganda.

Neither the planters nor the political elite defended slavery with the racist arguments common to their counterparts in the United States. Rather, the position of the Brazilian supporters of slavery was pragmatic. They argued that slave labor was essential to Brazilian agriculture and therefore to the Brazilian economy. But the fate of the slaves was not, in fact, simply about labor supply, important though that issue was. The slavery issue also struck at the heart of the white elite's sense of identity. The issue for them was Brazil's future racial composition and how it would affect the distribution of power.

To understand this (normally) unstated preoccupation of the white elite requires an understanding of Brazil's nineteenth-century racial demography. (As can be seen from exhibit 3-3, the racial balance of the Brazilian population changed significantly in the nineteenth century.) In 1798, the Afro-Brazilians, slave and free, were twice as numerous as the white population. But of the almost 2 million Afro-Brazilians, one-fifth (four hundred thousand) were free. Two decades before independence, in other words, Brazil already had a significant free population of color. Thus, Brazilian society had already had experience in incorporating (with widely varying degrees of economic freedom) manumitted or free-born Afro-Brazilians.

Central to this process was the mulatto. We have seen how the colonial Brazilian economy had created space for mixed bloods, especially mulattos, to rise socially, at least to a limited degree. That trend continued in the early Empire. Before 1850, for example, the *Guarda Nacional*, a kind of militia, allowed its ordinary soldiers to elect their officers. Since the ranks comprised men of color, mulatto officers frequently won the elections. Mulattos nonetheless remained vulnerable in a hierarchical system where the top was always white. Revealing on this score is the case of Antônio Pereira Rebouças, a mulatto and father of the famous abolitionist André Rebouças. In 1824, Antônio, a distinguished lawyer and secretary to the government of the province of Sergipe, was formally accused by white landowners of planning a slave uprising and "a general massacre of all whites." Antônio was cleared in a public hearing, which was a credit to imperial justice. But it was a painful reminder of how any successful mulatto's color could be used against him.

In 1872 (date of the first national census), Afro-Brazilians still outnumbered whites, but by a smaller margin. From two-to-one in 1798 the ratio had dropped to three-to-two. The most dramatic change in the nonwhite

EXHIBIT 3-3

Brazilian Population Growth by Ethnic Origin, 1798–1872

Ethnic Origin	1798	1872	Average Annual Percent Growth, 1798–1872
European	1,010,000	3,787,289 (a)	1.80
African (and Mixed)	1,988,000	5,756,238 (b)	1.44(c)
Free	406,000	4,254,428	
Slave	1,582,000	1,510,810	
Indigenous	252,000	386,955	0.58
TOTAL	3,250,000	9,930,478	1.52

Notes: (a) Includes 383,000 foreign-born reported in 1872 population.
(b) Includes 1,351,600 estimated slave imports.
(c) Freed and slave are combined because it is impossible to separate the effects of natural growth, manumission, and importation in their growth.
Source: Thomas W. Merrick and Douglas H. Graham, *Population and Economic Development* (Baltimore, 1979), p. 29.

population was the growth of the free Afro-Brazilians, who now outnumbered the whites (4.2 million to 3.8 million). The slave population had remained about the same as in 1798.

What had been true in 1798 was even more true in 1872: Brazil's free society was heavily multiracial. Debate over abolition could not, therefore, be a debate over how free Brazil might react if it faced, for the first time, a future influx of ex-slaves. For better or for worse, the assimilation process had begun on a large scale long ago.

Nonetheless, the overwhelmingly white Brazilian elite often spoke as if their country had no such racial history. They talked as if they could start *de novo*. Most who addressed the subject believed the country's only hope was to become racially whiter (*branquear*), thus resembling the powerful nations of the North Atlantic. But how would the masses of illiterate, unskilled free Afro-Brazilians, not to speak of the ex-slaves, fit into this picture? Thus the abolition debate involved more than the legal institution of slavery. As the aftermath of Brazil's war with Paraguay made increasingly clear, it involved a reappraisal of Brazilians' view of themselves.

The Paraguayan War

In March 1865, Paraguayan forces trooped across Argentine territory (after being denied permission) to Uruguay, with the intention of countering recent Brazilian intervention there. Brazil claimed it had acted to protect its many citizens living in Uruguay by sending military forces to depose the Uruguayan government and replace it with a pro-Brazilian one. Paraguay's subsequent invasion of the neighboring Brazilian province of Mato Grosso was meant to undo the Brazilian intervention, but it ended up triggering a war that pitted Paraguay against the combined forces of Brazil, Argentina, and Uruguay (which had hastily formed a "Triple Alliance") in a conflict that was to last five years. The key to understanding this war and Brazil's involvement in it is the geography of the region.

After the Amazon, the La Plata river system is the largest in South America. It furnishes essential transportation to four countries: Brazil, Argentina, Paraguay, and Uruguay. (See exhibit 3-4.) For the last three of these it is the most important waterborne outlet to the Atlantic Ocean and therefore to seaborne contact with Europe and North America. For Brazil at that time, the Paraná River—one of the tributaries of the La Plata, which is technically an estuary—served the important strategic function of connecting Brazil's coast and its far western interior. Since land travel to the Brazilian interior was extremely time-consuming and insecure, the best route from the east coast was to sail down the Atlantic coast to the mouth of the La Plata, up the La Plata to the Paraná River, and up the Paraná River to the Paranaíba River. Any interruption to traffic on the Paraná would disrupt this vital military and economic link between the two regions of Brazil.

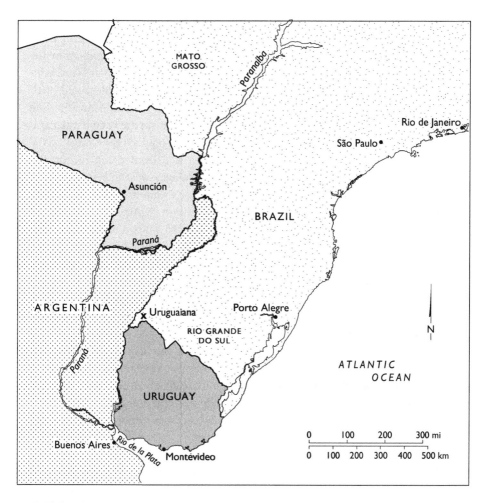

EXHIBIT 3-4
La Plata River basin.

Brazil's involvement in the La Plata region went back to the colonial era. We have seen how Brazil was drawn into war in this area in the 1820s. The result of that clash was an agreement, brokered by the English, to create the nation of Uruguay. By the same agreement, Brazil was guaranteed navigation rights to the La Plata and its tributaries. In subsequent decades, Brazil's economic interests in the region grew, especially in Uruguay, where they were directed by Brazil's premier banker and industrialist, Baron Mauá.

The stability of the La Plata region had depended on the cooperation of Brazil and Argentina, the two principal regional powers. Paraguay was a most unexpected threat to this stability. A small, poor, Guarani-speaking country, it had only recently emerged, under a series of military dictators, as an ambitious new nation. In 1865 it was under the control of the latest of these dictators, Francisco Solano López, whose political and personal motivations have long been debated by historians. This colorful dictator's exotic image was enhanced by his Irish-born mistress, whom he had brought back from a trip to Paris and who bore him five sons. A histrionic and flamboyant madame, she attempted, with understandable difficulty, to impose Parisian tastes on bucolic Asunción. She was cordially hated by the ladies of the European colony in the Paraguayan capital and was later to be blamed as the inspiration for López's more savage acts.

International tension in the La Plata area had been rising during the 1860s because of rival efforts by the Brazilians, Paraguayans, and Argentines to manipulate politics in Uruguay, where two factions were struggling for power. One Uruguayan faction, alleging hostile intervention by Argentina and Brazil in 1864, sought help from Paraguay. There followed a chain-reaction of challenge, defiance, and miscalculation, which eventually pitted Paraguay against both Argentina and Brazil. Solano López was so confident of his nation's military prowess that he was little inclined to be intimidated by his larger neighbors. Believing that Paraguay's independence was endangered by Argentine and Brazilian dominance in Uruguay, and nurturing a tragic overconfidence in his nation's strength, he decided to intervene. His first step was to seize a Brazilian steamer on the Paraná River, which was carrying the new Brazilian president-designate of the province of Mato Grosso. The crew and passengers were interned and the ship's flag was made into a rug to bedeck López's office in the presidential palace. Paraguay had brought about the Brazilian nightmare: The fluvial lifeline to its interior had been cut. No less important, its flag had been defiled.

López next launched a bold strike into Mato Grosso, where his troops enjoyed a series of rapid victories over the ill-prepared, ill-equipped, and poorly commanded Brazilians. These reverses sobered the Brazilian officers, who had predicted a quick victory for their troops. In particular, the Paraguayans carried off a valuable cache of captured military stocks, leaving the Brazilian defenders undersupplied and mortified. A second offensive in Rio Grande do Sul ended very differently. A six-thousand-man Paraguayan force fell into a trap at Uruguiana and surrendered without a fight. Pedro II had the pleasure of witnessing this victory.

From this point on (October 1865) combat shifted onto Paraguayan soil. But there were many Brazilian losses yet in store. The logistical challenges alone were staggering. The expedition sent from Rio in 1865, for example, consumed nearly four months in traveling 280 miles. A third of the troops were lost on the way to smallpox, malaria, and desertions. The column finally met the Paraguayans in combat in 1867, suffering a disastrous defeat near Laguna. That Brazilian agony was immortalized by the young writer Alfredo D'Escragnolle Taunay, a member of the expedition, in his 1871 work *The Retreat from Laguna* (first written in French and then translated into Portuguese by the author's son).

The Argentines' contribution proved to be small, leaving the Brazilians to furnish the majority of forces, both army and navy, to fight on. The Brazilian army was led after late 1866 by the same baron of Caxias who had quelled domestic rebellions earlier in the country. The first few months of the war prompted a wave of volunteers as a burst of patriotism took hold of young Brazilian men. In truth, Brazil did not have a proper national army when the war began. It numbered little more than 18,000 troops, many not available to move south. But once the initial pro-war enthusiasm faded after 1865, the imperial government could not attract enough "volunteers." In 1866 it turned to slaves, who were offered their freedom in return for joining up. This measure aroused the indignation of one Liberal politician, who declared, "To call slaves to defend, alongside free men, the integrity of the Empire and to avenge insults from a small republic is for us to confess before the civilized world...that we are incapable, without help from our slaves, of defending ourselves as a nation." Ironically, the author of those words, Viscount Jequitinhonha, was a mulatto who favored gradual abolition. One reason the army was short of soldiers for the Paraguayan campaign was that local commanders in Brazil feared that depleting their ranks might make them unable to deal with slave revolts at home. Paraguayan propaganda cast racist aspersions on the invading Brazilians, dubbing Pedro II "El Macacón" ("the Big Ape").

The Paraguayan army's reputation for being large (said to number 80,000) and well equipped was somewhat overdrawn, but the Paraguayan soldiers proved to be skilled guerrilla fighters, fighting with a ferocity and self-sacrifice the Brazilians could seldom match, and managing to hold off the invaders for two more years. The harsh combat conditions gradually hardened the Brazilian forces, who were finally able to virtually eliminate the Paraguayan army in a series of battles in 1868. Given a population base of perhaps 400,000 in 1864, the 60,000 Paraguayan soldiers who had been killed, captured, or maimed represented an exorbitant loss. By any rational calculation, the war was over. But López assembled another army (of boys, women, and old men), which held out for two more years by fleeing into the hills and forests and launching scattered guerrilla attacks.

The politicians back home in Brazil, who were absorbed in increasingly partisan bickering, began asking why their forces should go on fighting a war that should have been over. There were ugly charges of corruption in procuring supplies. The Liberal party press was especially shrill in its criticisms of the conduct of the war. The Brazilian commanders, in turn, accused the politicians on the home front of back-stabbing the war effort just when they were within reach of victory. And, indeed, the original agreement among Brazil, Uruguay, and Argentina (the Triple Alliance) had committed the combatants to achieving unconditional surrender of the enemy. Pedro II backed up the army by insisting on a fight to the finish. For the emperor, who seemed to have lost his usual pragmatism and good sense, the war had become a personal duel with the Paraguayan dictator. It had also become, in his view, a crucial test of his country's ability to prove itself a "modern" disciplined nation. When the U.S. government was making strenuous efforts to mediate the conflict in 1867, for example, Pedro II told a confidant, "Above all we go on and finish the war with honor. It is a question of honor and I will not compromise." In late 1868, he wrote of "López and his influence," arguing that "it is necessary to destroy completely this influence, whether direct or indirect, by capturing or forcefully expelling López from Paraguayan territory." But the emperor could no longer count on the Liberal cabinet, led by Zacarias de Góis e Vasconcelos, to continue his crusade. He had to turn to the Conservatives to finish the job.

Caxias resigned as commander-in-chief in 1868. Dom Pedro named his own son-in-law as the new commander, the Conde D'Eu, who had the dubious honor of presiding over the mopping-up operation. He also took the opportunity to abolish slavery in Paraguay, a gesture that earned him the enmity of many Brazilian slave owners, who feared the extension of abolition to Brazil.

The end came when Solano López, whose paranoid suspicions had led him to execute many of his own relatives, was hunted down and killed by Brazilian troops in March 1870. The nation of Paraguay had been reduced to rubble, its dead were estimated at 200,000 (no one knew exactly), and its male population had shrunk by as much as three-quarters. The Brazilian military occupation of Paraguay continued for another six years.

Ostensibly, Brazil had achieved its objectives. First, it had defeated Paraguay and eliminated its leader. Second, it had gained some marginal territorial concessions from the Paraguayans. Third, it had asserted itself as a major military power in South America's most volatile geopolitical region. As if to symbolize this triumph, the Brazilian troops carried off the entire Paraguayan archives to be stored in Rio. The Paraguayans had not only lost the war; they had lost the written record of their own history.

Along other dimensions, however, Brazil had not done so well. Emperor Pedro II had optimistically described the war when it began as a "nice electrical shock" to the nation. But looking back from the 1890s, Joaquim Nabuco, the noted legislator-historian-diplomat, found his society had been gripped by a malaise painfully exposed by the army's inept response to Paraguay's invasion of Rio Grande do Sul and Mato Grosso in 1864. There had been a decline in dedication to "public service," Nabuco said, which he attributed to an indolence produced by climate, race, and social habit. "For Brazilians, the old Portuguese discipline was too heavy, too exhausting, like the old clothes and old manners, for a society that just wanted to relax and go to sleep."

To the many observers who shared Nabuco's perception, the five-year war had led Brazil to a variety of uncomfortable confrontations with its own reality. First, the Brazilian army had received very bad press in the United States and Europe for its allegedly brutal tactics against Paraguayan civilians. This reinforced the Brazilian elite's preoccupation with their country's image abroad as uncivilized. Second, Brazil's attitude to slavery was irretrievably changed. The slaves who had been recruited to fill out the ranks of the Brazilian troops in return for their freedom after the war had acquitted themselves well in battle (although they had been ridiculed in the Paraguayan press as "monkeys"). And their performance had given Brazilian officers a new appreciation for the capacity of Afro-Brazilians. This became very important when the Brazilian military was later called upon to pursue runaway slaves. No less important was the realization that Brazil had been able to win the war only by enlisting thousands of slaves. Where was the "whitened" nation the elite yearned to inhabit?

Third, the war had deeply affected the military as an institution. The commanders' successful battle with the politicians over the conduct of the war set a precedent for increasing officer involvement in imperial politics. Officers were now suspicious that the civilians might sacrifice Brazil's military interest for their own purposes. The Paraguayan War therefore set the stage for growing military-civilian tensions during the 1880s.

Fourth, the war had a decisive effect on political party alignments. The forced recruitment of soldiers had especially aroused the opposition. In the war's early years, the Liberal government had been increasingly at odds with the emperor and the Conservative-controlled Senate over government finances, patronage questions, and the management of the war. In 1868, the baron of Caxias had resigned from his command in Paraguay, ostensibly for health reasons, and had been rewarded by the emperor with the title of duke. In fact, the new duke of Caxias was in good health. He had resigned in order to use his prestige with the emperor to help his Conservative colleagues in Rio force out the Liberal cabinet. In the ensuring crisis, the incumbent cabinet resigned and the Liberal party split. Although the Liberals retained a majority in the Chamber of Deputies, the emperor invited the Conservatives to form a government, which they did. The emperor's action alienated the Liberals because it was the first time the emperor had ever authorized a party to form a government when it had a majority of votes against it in the Chamber of Deputies. In the process, Pedro II lost the aura of a wise and benign monarch without partisanship and was charged with the abuse of his "moderating power." The war had also taken its toll on him personally. His hair had turned almost white and he now appeared much older than his relatively young age of forty-five. In reaction to the emperor's action, the Liberal party issued a manifesto calling for such measures as decentralization, limited Senate terms, an autonomous judiciary, religious freedom, and gradual abolition. Dissenters in the left branch of the Liberal party issued an even stronger manifesto, followed in 1871 by their decision to split off and form a new Republican party, which called for an end to the Empire.

All in all, the war had a profound psychological effect on the Brazilians' view of themselves. Brazil had entered the conflict with little respect for the Paraguayan troops. Years of heavy combat casualties cured the Brazilians of that arrogance. It had taken largely Afro-Brazilian troops to achieve victory. It had also taken burdensome new loans from England to finance the war. The Paraguayan War more than eradicated the government's efforts to stabilize the federal budget following the military expenditures necessitated by the revolts of the 1830s and 1840s. Victory over such a small, poor, and desolate country hardly qualified Brazil for the annals of glorious warfare, despite the triumphalist rhetoric of some patriots in Rio. On the contrary, it raised fundamental questions about whether their own ill-integrated society was ready to join the race to modernity.

4

The Making of "Modern" Brazil

A New Generation and the Military Question

The elite generation reaching maturity around 1870, three generations removed from their forebears who broke with Portugal, were too young to identify automatically with their emperor or their empire. In addition, they were much more uneasy than their fathers about being part of a slavocracy. In addition to the simple passage of time, two doctrines had reached Brazil that helped weaken the hold of earlier commitments and beliefs.

The first was positivism, a doctrine holding that every rationally justifiable assertion can be scientifically verified or is capable of logical or mathematical proof. Auguste Comte, the acknowledged leader of French positivism, had developed a dogma that was particularly admired by the younger army officers of the Rio Military Academy. Comte maintained that the course of history, like the nature of social reality, was subject to scientific law. He thus rejected both theology and metaphysics, arguing instead for a "religion of humanity." Although Comte was a prophet of secularization and one of the spiritual fathers of the modern technocrat, he also advocated strict limits to the role of the state, especially when it came to higher education and religion.

Brazilian positivists, in fact, spanned a wide range of beliefs. On one side of the pure followers of Comte's doctrine were religious positivists so doctrinaire that they founded their own Brazilian Positivist Church in 1881 and demanded doctrinal fidelity from all members. They eventually "excommunicated" the mother Positivist Church in Paris. On the other side were more pragmatic thinkers who agreed with Comte's rejection of Catholicism but did not accept his dogma about historical stages and the circumscribed role of the state. The middle-of-the-road positivists in Brazil were known as "heterodox" positivists. A good example in this group was the São Paulo physician and public health pioneer Luiz Pereira Barreto, who published in 1874 the first Brazilian treatise written from a systematic positivist position. Positivism's appeal was strong in late nineteenth-century Brazil because it was the only doctrine offering a strong and coherent structure to pose against a dissolving Catholic ethos. Positivism maintained a strong if diffuse influence in twentieth-century Brazil, not for its detailed doctrines but for its intellectual style—above all, the appeal for a scientific approach to understanding society and history. It was similar to the appeal that later made Marxist thought important in Brazil.

The second doctrine influencing the new generation was republicanism. The idea was not new in Brazilian history, having inspired regional revolts in the 1830s and 1840s, but it had faded with the consolidation of the Empire. Now republicanism revived as younger Brazilians questioned whether monarchy, with its accompanying socioeconomic ethos, was the best system for their country. The rapid industrialization of the United States reinforced this doubt in a Brazil that remained overwhelmingly agrarian. Furthermore, Dom Pedro II, once the unifying symbol of the Empire, was now physically and psychologically weaker. His colossal mistake in judgment when he insisted on calling for a Conservative government in 1868, despite the Liberal majority in the Chamber of Deputies, has already been discussed. It was the last straw for the more militant Liberals. Their manifesto, when they left the traditional Liberal party to found the Republican party in 1871, declared that "National sovereignty can only exist, can only be recognized and practiced in a nation whose parliament has the supreme direction and pronounces the final word in public business." The signers left no doubt about their orientation: "We are from America and we want to be Americans."

The younger generation's discontent soon took an extreme form in the army. Pedro II had weathered the political crisis surrounding the Paraguayan War partly because his senior army commanders stood together. By 1880, however, these officers were retired or dead, replaced by a younger generation which noted, among other things, that the overall imperial budget had increased by 70 percent during the period between 1871 and 1880, while the military budget had grown by only 8 percent. They wanted more manpower and new equipment, and they were suspicious that the husband of Princess Isabel, heir to the throne, might have his own reasons to sabotage their budget demands. The implausibility of those suspicions showed how deep the ill will against the prince had gone.

The army commanders also faced a wide class gap between themselves and their troops. The officers, mostly sons of professionals, came from the military academy. The enlisted men were conscripts, usually recruited under duress, illiterate, and serving against their will. The gap was long-standing, but the generation reaching maturity in the last quarter of the nineteenth century was newly sensitive to the danger that troops from the lower social orders might be unable (or unwilling) to maintain social control within the country.

All this was exacerbated by bad feeling between the military elite and the politicians. Open military criticism of cabinet ministers, which had begun during the Paraguayan War, had erupted in increasingly ugly confrontations between 1884 and 1889. Trouble had been brewing since the 1850s, with a faction of officers attacking the Empire for its excessive identification with the planters and lawyers and its failure to take the necessary steps—railway construction, promotion of industry, abolition of slavery, and encouragement of immigration—to modernize Brazil. As the ranks of the critics swelled, the growing controversy triggered a constitutional problem. Since military officers were legally subordinate to civilian ministers, when they spoke out against the government (and the topic was often abolition), the civilian minister of the army would discipline the offender, typically by placing him under house arrest. The resulting feeling of martyrdom among the officers combined with increasing rigidity and fear among their civilian superiors to become known in the 1880s as the "military question."

This was the environment in which the Brazilians finally abolished slavery.

Abolition and Its Aftermath: The Brazilian Way

Isolated arguments favoring abolition in Brazil can be found as far back as the era of independence. The preeminent leader of the period, José Bonifácio, was a strong abolitionist, although he believed abolition had to be gradual. In an 1823 draft speech, his attack on slavery was unmistakable: "By what sort of justice does a man steal another man's freedom, and worse yet, the freedom of this man's children, and of his children's children?" Emperor Dom Pedro I published an essay in that same year attacking slavery as "the cancer that is gnawing away at Brazil." The political implications of such a statement from the emperor were so grave that he was forced to use a pseudonym ("the Philanthropist"). Only in the late 1860s and early 1870s, however, did the abolitionist movement begin to gather widespread support, using the same arguments heard earlier in the United States and Britain. The Brazilian counterpart to Harriet Beecher Stowe's *Uncle Tom's Cabin* was the Bahia Romanticist poet Castro Alves's *Navio Negreiro* (*Slave Ship*). Both of these had a strongly Christian and humanist flavor and included the claim that "man is free neither when a slave nor when a master," in the words of Joaquim Nabuco. Nabuco, the scion of a Pernambucan elite family, was to become the best-known abolitionist with his publication of *Abolitionism* in 1884. But this white aristocrat was not alone in the leadership. He was joined by effective and eloquent Afro-Brazilian activists (all mulattos) such as José do Patrocínio, André Rebouças, and Luiz de Gama, who played key roles in mobilizing public opinion in the 1880s.

José de Patrocínio was a mulatto journalist and orator whose paper, *A Cidade de Rio*, was a leading abolitionist voice in the 1880s. André Rebouças was one of the most prominent mulattos of imperial Brazil. Trained as an engineer, he earned a fortune supervising the construction of the docks in Rio and numerous other Atlantic port cities. Of all the abolitionists, as noted, he was the only one to see the need for land reform. Luiz de Gama was a talented lawyer and a fiery orator. The presence of these three in the abolitionist leadership was another sign of the mobility of free coloreds in Brazil.

Foreign pressure also continued to play a part throughout the Brazilian struggle for abolition. Visitors to Brazil from the United States, Britain, and France in the 1870s and 1880s expressed their shock at finding slavery still alive. On the one hand, foreign advice angered Brazilian conservatives such as the Romanticist writer-politician José de Alencar, who played on Brazilian resentment at being subjected to "proclamations of European philanthropy" that prompted "obeisances to foreign opinion." On the other hand, criticism from abroad helped the elite realize that slavery was an obstacle to the country's emergence as a modern nation. In the words of the Anti-Slavery Society (written by Nabuco), "Brazil does not want to be a nation morally isolated, a leper, expelled from the world community. The esteem and respect of foreign nations are as valuable to us as they are to other people."

By the 1880s, although slaveholders in low-productivity areas such as the province of Rio de Janeiro continued to argue that they could not survive without slave labor, the writing was on the wall and everyone knew it. The plain fact was that they could not survive the labor shortage that was inevitable even if abolition was not passed. As already described, the end of the slave trade in 1850 combined with the low birthrate among the Brazilian slave population to guarantee that the slave population would eventually completely die out. Although total slave extinction was not predicted to occur until well into the twentieth century, Brazil's labor shortage was already acute.

Efforts to bring Europeans to Brazil to work in the plantations had largely failed, in good part because it seemed to be impossible to preserve tolerable working conditions for free labor in a slaveholding environment. As already mentioned, many of the earlier immigrants had complained so vociferously about their inhumane treatment that several German states had outlawed all Brazilian recruitment of immigrants in their territory. It was becoming clear to those who gave it any thought that, since slavery and immigrant labor could not work side by side, slavery would have to go.

This conclusion became even more logical as some planters, especially in São Paulo, began to ask whether free labor might be as effective as and perhaps cheaper than slave labor. Equally important, landowners were discovering, especially in São Paulo, that maintaining control of their labor force did not necessarily depend on its legal status. Neither the economic survival nor the political dominance of the planters was dependent on slavery. In the short run, of course, these planters had no intention of giving up their slaves without compensation. Such a measure, they argued, would destroy Brazilian agriculture, and Brazil's economy along with it. This was a major sticking point for the government, yet how could the government raise the funds to pay for the 1,510,806 human beings (by the 1872 census) still in slavery? One answer, which appealed to the establishment politicians, was to abolish slavery in stages.

In 1871, parliament passed the "Law of the Free Womb," freeing all children henceforth born of slave mothers. But the slaveowners were given a huge concession. The child now born "free" was required to render service to the mother's master until age twenty-one. An alternative provision for the government to buy the freedom of the newborn child was seldom exercised. Although the law was an important precedent, the more militant abolitionists were not satisfied with this long-term solution. They wanted total and immediate abolition.

The militants did not have their way. The anti-abolitionist forces blocked further legislation for more than a decade. Finally, in 1885, the parliament passed the Sexagenarian Law, which freed all slaves over sixty years of age, and established standards for gradual freeing of all slaves, with indemnities for owners. Cynics noted that few slaves ever lived to be sixty. Statistics from 1872 show that the life expectancy of the Brazilian male slave was only eighteen years. Furthermore, how were the newly freed to survive? There was no organized effort, even among abolitionists, to provide the emancipated with land, education, or housing.

As the political ferment increased, the slaves became important actors in their own drama. By their resistance, often requiring great courage, they gave the lie to the racist stereotype (entertained by whites then and later) of the Afro-Brazilian as inherently passive and unable to defend himself. By 1887, slaves were staging mass escapes from plantations, especially in São Paulo. The escapees formed fugitive communities (called *quilombos* in the colonial era) near Santos and on the Rio beaches. Furthermore, the army officers who had previously followed orders to hunt down runaways began rebelling against such orders.

The struggle ended on May 13, 1888, when the parliament approved total and immediate abolition without compensation (the "Golden Law"). The opposition vote was concentrated among the deputies from the province of Rio de Janeiro (seven of the eight negative votes). Since Pedro II was in Europe, the Golden Law was signed by Princess Isabel, who thereby won the title of the slaves' benefactress. A carnival of celebration erupted in Rio as Brazil joined the company of "civilized" nations.

Unlike abolition in the United States, which was achieved at the cost of a bloody civil war, abolition in Brazil was a gradual, drawn-out affair. How Brazil achieved abolition revealed much about the country's emerging political culture. First, the political elite succeeded in containing the growing social conflict within a strictly legal framework. Second, the landowners deflected any challenge to the structure of landholding—a crucial question for the future of Brazilian agriculture. Third, the elite had demonstrated its skill at compromising without endangering its own position. In the 1850s, this skill had been called "conciliation," and it would continue to be a key tactic used by the elite in their subsequent dominance in Brazil. Abolition, for example, helped divert attention from Brazil's "social question"—the euphemistic term used in the era to describe government policies on social welfare as well as to control the lower classes. By a simple legal gesture, the elite had "solved" the problem of an obsolete system of forced labor. This fit with the Brazilian elite's tendency to see socioeconomic questions in exclusively legal terms, rather than in structural or social class terms.

Abolition now opened the way for the redefinition of Brazil's system of social stratification. Previously, slaves made up the bottom of the social pyramid. Now that category was removed, yet color would remain a key mark in establishing social status even though everyone of color was now juridically

Joaquim Maria Machado de Assis, Brazil's greatest novelist, a mulatto whom contemporaries insisted on calling "white" because of his widely recognized eminence.

free. In practice, this would not necessarily alter the complex system of race relations, in which the lack of a clear-cut color line made room for limited mobility of mixed bloods. In that system, the top of the pyramid was occupied almost entirely by whites. But there continued to be no absolute color line (like the rest of Latin America and unlike the post-1890s United States), which had made it possible for small numbers of Afro-Brazilians, primarily mulattos, to rise socially, occasionally to the top of the pyramid. Obvious examples were André Rebouças, the engineer and prominent abolitionist, and Machado de Assis, Brazil's greatest novelist and founder and long-time president of the Brazilian Academy of Letters.

The coming of abolition also stimulated a dramatic surge of immigration into Brazil that must have surpassed the hopes of its most fervent supporters (see exhibit 4-1), no doubt helped by the Sociedade Promotora da Imigração (Society for Promoting Immigration), organized in 1886 by the planters in the richest coffee state, São Paulo. The number of immigrants entering Brazil jumped from less than 33,000 in 1886 to 132,000 just two years later. They went primarily to São Paulo and the South. The largest number entered through the immigrant hostel in Santos (the port for São Paulo) and were then assigned to the coffee fields.

During the wave of immigration to Brazil that followed abolition, the largest number came from Italy, with the second largest from Portugal, followed by Spain (see exhibit 4-2). These immigrants assimilated easily into Brazilian society and culture. Their language, if not Portuguese, was closely related to Portuguese, as were their cultures. They were typically highly versatile, often trying out their work skills in different industries, from agricultural labor to textiles to metallurgy. They were also mobile across national boundaries, moving among Argentina, Brazil, and the United States. They were often capitalistic in their mentality, seeking to maximize the acquisition of new skills and the accumulation of savings.

EXHIBIT 4-1

Immigrants to Brazil, 1872–1910

Years	Number of Immigrants
1872–1879	22,042
1880–1883	26,393
1890	106,819
1895	164,831
1900	37,807
1905	68,488
1910	86,751

Source: Armin K. Ludwig, *Brazil: A Handbook of Historical Statistics* (Boston, 1985), p. 103.

EXHIBIT 4-2
Immigrants to Brazil, by Nationality, 1872–1909 (percent)

	1872–79	1880–89	1890–99	1900–09
Italian	25.80	61.80	57.60	35.60
Portuguese	31.2	23.3	18.3	31.4
Spanish	1.9	6.7	13.7	18.2
Germans	8.1	4.2	1.4	2.2
Other	33.0	4.0	8.9	12.4
TOTAL	100	100	100	100

Source: Thomas W. Merrick and Douglas H. Graham, *Population and Economic Development* (Baltimore, 1979), p. 91.

These immigrants helped create the notion of a Brazilian "melting pot," where ethnic differences would be dissolved in the creation of a single nationality. Missing from this optimistic picture, which the elite liked to promote, was the huge population living in Brazil before the immigrants arrived. Italian immigrants might find assimilation easy, but what about the illiterate, unskilled Brazilians, overwhelmingly of color? For the modern observer an obvious question arises: Why did the planters of the Center-South fail to recruit from the large body of free labor elsewhere in Brazil?

The answer is several-fold. First, the planters, like the elite in general, had little faith in nonwhites, who were most of the existing Brazilian labor force. The imperial elite considered the Afro-Brazilians, for example, physically inferior and incapable of serious work habits. In spite of the grudging admiration felt by the army for the Afro-Brazilian exploits in the Paraguayan War—and the military fear that they were capable of aggressive fighting back if they were hunted down as runaway slaves—a leading military publication made clear in 1882 what it did *not* want as a recruitment source: "the lazy Negro race, whose education and heritage leaves it without energy, and can only be motivated by prodding." Second, they thought European immigrants would bring the qualities the Northeasterners lacked, including needed skills. Third, some planters thought the immigrants would be easier to control than freedmen. Finally, once in Brazil the European immigrants would presumably help improve the ethnic stock. This point is important to a discussion later in the chapter about the elite's preoccupation with Brazil's image abroad.

In preparation for that discussion, the next section recounts the story of the end of the Brazilian Empire, which fell in 1889, fast on the heels of abolition.

The End of the Empire

As the 1880s wore on, Pedro II's health continued to deteriorate. He traveled repeatedly to European spas, seeking a cure for his diabetes, without success.

Back in Rio, he was losing the close touch he had always maintained with his ministers. By 1887, he had also lost the popular appeal that had once helped bring the country together. The Rio press was openly speculating that he had lost his mind. He even became the butt of popular ridicule, with cartoonists depicting him as "Pedro Banana." The prospect of the succession of his daughter was also very unpopular. Princess Isabel and her consort had failed to win elite support for reasons that did no credit to their detractors. For Isabel, gender was the problem. The elite was by definition male and utterly unaccustomed to seeing a woman in authority. The Brazilians had never had a female monarch and the small insular world of politically powerful men was openly hostile. For her husband, the Conde d'Eu, nationality (he was a French-born nobleman) was the problem. Despite being culturally Francophile, the Brazilian elite was nationalistic when it came to the royal family.

Dom Pedro II had once been a symbol of national unity, presiding skillfully over Latin America's most stable political system. But the new generation of elite Brazilians now had doubts about the monarchy as an institution. The monarchy's most radical critics, the Republicans, were open in saying that the institution was not just an anachronism to be repackaged, but a genuine obstacle to national progress. Brazil, in their view, had outgrown the need for a moderating power.

By late 1889, multiple currents of discontent were swirling, but none seemed truly revolutionary. The Republicans, for example (only two members in the Chamber of Deputies from 1884 to 1889), were no serious threat either to the monarchy or to the two established political parties. Those two parties seemed more concerned with nominations of government officials than with the form of government itself, and were, in any case, even less in touch with popular sentiment than in earlier years because the franchise had become steadily more restrictive during the Empire. For the 1821 elections (for the Constituent Assembly), there had been virtually universal male suffrage. The Constitution of 1824 introduced a property requirement, which was increased in 1846. In 1881, a new electoral law drastically tightened the property requirement and excluded illiterates (thought to be a prime source of fraud), while making the vote optional. The effect on voter turnout was dramatic. Electoral participation dropped from 13 percent of the total populace (excluding slaves) in 1872 to 0.8 percent in 1886. The 1872 percentage was never regained until the election of 1945.

Although the Republicans had converted relatively few of the civilian political elite, they had made serious inroads among the discontented military, especially the positivists among them. On November 15, 1889, a group of junior officers, determined to intervene despite a lack of broad civilian support, convinced Marshall Deodoro da Fonseca, their commander, to rise from his sickbed and lead a coup against the emperor. Deodoro was also motivated by fear that the emperor might invite one of the marshall's political enemies to form a new government.

Like most major political transitions in Brazil, the fall of the Empire was virtually bloodless. The emperor simply accepted the military ultimatum. He and his family grabbed a few belongings and made their way, under military escort, to the Rio docks. There they boarded an ocean steamer to exile in Portugal. Brazil's imperial experiment, unique for its length and viability in the New World, was over.

The Brazilian Empire had been overthrown by a military coup, not a social revolution, and the Republic began as a military government. A military junta assumed power while much of the imperial elite withdrew from politics, some even choosing exile. The military lost no time in collecting their payoff from the coup. Military salaries were immediately increased 50 percent, a new law was passed regulating the retirement or immediate promotion of almost all higher officers (the army officer corps was notoriously top-heavy), and the army was authorized to expand from 13,000 to 25,000 troops.

The Republicans, previously a minority, took charge of shaping the new institutions. From 1890 to 1891 a newly elected constituent assembly wrote Brazil's second Constitution. The key author was Rui Barbosa, a Bahian deputy and noted legal scholar, who was to be finance minister in the new government. The 1891 Constitution's most important feature was radical decentralization. Brazil was now to become a federation, a goal long urged by provincial rebels. Each state (formerly province) would now directly elect its own governor and legislature, and would have extensive powers, such as the authority to contract foreign loans, to levy interstate tariffs, and to maintain militia. The Constitution of 1891 thus gave carte blanche for the economically most dynamic states—such as São Paulo—to direct their own development. The new Constitution also replaced the monarchy with a directly elected president, who was to be Brazil's symbolic and functional head of government. Clearly, power would now rest with the Republican oligarchies of the leading states. The property requirement for voting was abolished but illiterates (and women) were still excluded.

The Republicans also created new symbols to celebrate Brazil's entrance into the world without monarchs. The new flag bore the slogan "Order and Progress" (a positivist phrase) and Republican-commissioned paintings and graphics featured a half-clad female figure modeled on the comparable "Marianne" heroine of the French Revolution. The Roman Catholic Church was disestablished. At the same time, the Republicans set out to extinguish all evidence of the Empire. As the new finance minister, Rui Barbosa ordered the burning of the slave trade records so as to destroy all trace of what Rui considered a shameful chapter in Brazilian history. (This step also had the great advantage of making impossible any attempt to compensate the slaveholders.) The highly prestigious Colegio Pedro II was renamed the Ginásio Nacional (until 1911, when it regained its old name) and the heraldry of the royal family was banned. No more aristocratic titles could be created.

But Brazil had to do more than adopt a new flag, disestablish the Church, and eliminate titles if it wanted to join the outside world as an equal economic partner. Brazil had to change the image it presented to the world in order to compete with its neighbors in the dynamic North Atlantic world. Among the other South American states, Argentina, in particular, was already showing spectacular success in attracting both immigrants and investment.

Selling Brazil

With the Paraguayan War over and slavery abolished, Brazil had eliminated two obstacles in the way of achieving respectability in the wider world. Now it set to work to improve its image still further. One tack was to produce glossy volumes showing how modern Brazil was in its transportation, education, and communication systems. Gross exaggerations, of course, but they and exhibits with a similar purpose were shown off proudly by Brazilians at international events such as the Paris Exposition of 1889 and the Chicago Columbian Exposition of 1893.

More fundamental efforts were made in Europeanizing the physical appearance of its cities—in particular its capital city, Rio—and in "whitening" its population.

As Brazil entered the twentieth century, its cities retained many of the sights, sounds, and smells of their colonial past. In Rio de Janeiro, it was an ambiance that repelled many foreign visitors. Rio had a reputation for disease, especially yellow fever. Italian shipping lines even advertised their voyages to Argentina as making "no stops in Brazil." Save for minor changes made in the mid-1870s by Rio Branco's government, the layout of Rio's streets had changed little since the eighteenth century. They were narrow, crowded, unhygienic, and difficult to navigate. Sanitation was primitive and the water supply suspect. In short, Rio was a poor advertisement for a country hoping to join the North Atlantic march to modernity.

The Brazilian elite looked longingly at Paris, which Baron Hausmann had transformed with his grand boulevards. They knew there was a desperate need to bring Brazilian municipal services up to standard. It would not be easy, however, because wealthy interests, especially the many Portuguese building owners, had much to lose from the demolition involved in any major rebuilding of Rio.

The 1902 election of President Rodrigues Alves, a Paulista, set the scene for a major campaign to attack this problem. The Rio mayor, Francisco Pereira Passos—also a Paulista—presided over a massive rebuilding of downtown Rio, including the construction of two wide boulevards branching out from the docks. To create the needed right-of-way, 590 buildings had to be demolished. Many of these (known as *cortiços*, or tenements) had housed working-class families who were now forced to find new housing, often much further from their work. Whether intending to or not, the political elite was turning downtown

Rio into a "rabble free" zone that would impress the foreigner and keep the "dangerous classes" at a distance.

There was now room to construct stately new public buildings, such as the Biblioteca Nacional and the Teatro Municipal (modeled on the Paris Opera). In their "European" style, they resembled new public structures recently erected in Buenos Aires and Mexico City. The Rio elite described this ambitious rebuilding program as "Rio civilizing itself." Yet the rebuilding touched only the traditional downtown, doing nothing for those in the *favelas* (shanty towns) already covering the Rio hills.

The renovation of downtown Rio was accompanied by a major public health campaign, supervised by the noted medical administrator Oswaldo Cruz. The campaign's principal goal was eradication of the *Aedes aegypti* mosquito, the carrier of yellow fever. (President Rodrigues Alves had lost a child to the disease.) This required eliminating or treating all standing water where mosquitoes could breed. The campaign aroused impassioned opposition as the health officials (dubbed *mata mosquitos*, or "mosquito killers") went from door to door. A simultaneous campaign to require vaccination against smallpox provoked even stronger opposition, which managed to delay the campaign's start for five years. The positivists were the most militant opponents, especially of compulsory vaccination, which contradicted their concept of personal freedom. They were joined by community organizers, who were reacting to the frequent government invasions of their neighborhoods. Finally, the health campaign was seen by many Afro-Brazilians as aimed at liquidating their African culture (traditional cures, etc.). In 1909, Oswaldo Cruz declared Rio to be free from yellow fever and all other major epidemics. Subsequent statistics show this did not apply to the poorer sections of the city.

The public health crusaders hoped to extend their work into the interior, where disease and malnutrition were more serious than in the major cities. Most of the resources, however, went to the coastal cities. These contained the loudest political voices and were the best venue to impress foreigners.

"Whitening" Brazil

In the effort to improve Brazil's image abroad, the elite were particularly concerned about race. Although the percentage of the population classified as white in the Brazilian Census had increased between 1872 and 1890, the increase was modest and large proportions of Brazilians were still classified as black or mulatto in 1890. (See exhibit 4-3.) It was in the area of race that Brazilians felt especially disadvantaged vis-à-vis largely white Argentina, their prime South American rival.

In contemplating their position, the post-1870 Brazilian elite soon fell under the influence of European and North American doctrines of scientific racism, which pointed to biological and historical "evidence" to justify their claims of white superiority. These claims, in turn, underlay a new phase of

EXHIBIT 4-3

Racial Composition of Brazil's Population, 1872 and 1890*

Race	1872 Number (millions)	1872 %	1890 Number (millions)	1890 %
White	3.78	38.1	6.31	44.0
Mulatto	4.19	42.2	5.93	41.4
Black	1.96	19.7	2.09	14.6
Total	9.93	100	14.33	100

*Excludes the indigenous population.
Source: Brazilian Censuses, 1872 and 1890.

European and United States territorial expansionism, as imperialism and racism went hand in hand. In the aftermath of its civil war, the United States had even adopted a legal system ("Jim Crow") to keep the races physically separate in public places.

But Brazil could hardly hope to copy the United States in race relations, because its nonwhite population far exceeded that of the United States as a proportion of the total population. How then could Brazil become whiter? We have seen earlier in the chapter that the elite preferred the hiring of immigrants from Europe to the hiring of nonwhite workers within Brazil. In fact, Brazil strongly promoted *European* immigration, even while at the same time it rejected Chinese coolies as an alternative labor source for fear of "mongolization." Only after Europeans stopped coming to Brazil, around the beginning of the twentieth century, did the Brazilian government reluctantly turn to Japanese immigrants, for whom they actually created a new racial category: "whites of Asia."

The elite also developed a novel theory that miscegenation, combined with high ("natural") Afro-Brazilian mortality would, in time, "whiten" the population. In other words, white Brazilians were betting on race mixture, a process that horrified white North Americans, to gradually turn themselves into the equivalent of the superior race. In the words of João Batista de Lacerda, a leading doctor and anthropologist, "in the course of another century the mixed bloods will have disappeared from Brazil. This will coincide with the extinction of the black race in our midst." Lacerda's confident words were spoken at the First Universal Race Congress in London in 1911.

As the Brazilian elite began accepting scientific racism, social reality took an ominous turn. The end of both slavery and the Empire had cast race relations into a new light in the eyes of the victorious Republicans. Rio now loomed as a "black city" with a raucous culture that did not fit the ideas of the Europeanizing elite. Although little is known about this as yet, it appears that Brazilian society became institutionally more race conscious after the birth of the

Republic, as mobility for nonwhite Brazilians apparently began to decline. The barriers were never legal, unlike in the United States. But unwritten color bars were observed, for example, in the Ministry of Foreign Affairs, the officer corps of the navy (the army was slightly less color-prejudiced), and the higher levels of the Catholic Church.

The Reality behind the Facade

In the early 1900s, the vast majority of Brazilians (almost 84 percent in 1900) lived in the two main coastal areas—the Southeast and the Northeast—as they had throughout Brazil's history. This historic pattern of settlement, once described as "crabs clinging to the coast," broke down only slowly, with the Southeast and the Northeast still accounting for over 70 percent of the population in 1991. (See exhibit 4-4.) Although there had long been important exceptions, such as the inland state of Minas Gerais, the vast majority of states bordered on the sea and most had as their capital city a coastal port. It was not that the elite lived exclusively in the coastal cities. Virtually all had family connections with landowners and visited their farms and ranches in the agriculturally developed zones. But traveling to the distant and less settled interior was far less frequent.

The most dramatic illustration of this geographical divide between coast and interior was the military siege of Canudos in the 1890s. This interior town, several hundred miles from the state capital of Bahia, housed a religious com-

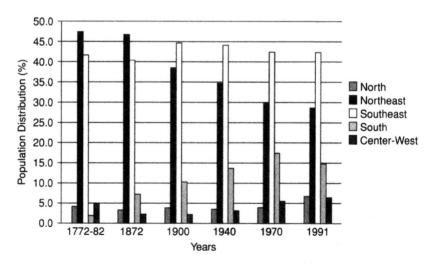

EXHIBIT 4-4

Distribution of Brazilian population by major regions, 1772–1991. From [1872–1970] Thomas W. Merrick and Douglas H. Graham, *Population and Economic Development* (Baltimore, 1979), p. 119, and [1991] Instituto Brasileiro de Geografia e Estatística, Diretoria de Pesquisas, Population Census.

munity headed by a lay clergyman, popularly known as "Antônio Conselheiro" ("Anthony the Counselor"). In 1895, the community ran afoul of local authorities in a dispute over a failed delivery of wood. The townsmen killed several police in the resulting clash, and the Bahian state authorities called for federal help. Rio responded by ordering the federal army to end the trouble.

Although we do not know the exact nature of the community's religious orientation, they were self-proclaimed monarchists and were clearly prepared to defend their homes. They had good reason, since the authorities had virtually declared war on Canudos. The conflict escalated in stages. First, the state government of Bahia tried to subdue the community. When that failed, Bahian authorities enlisted the federal government, which was then being pressured by fanatical Jacobins (the label for extreme Republicans) in Rio who wanted to extinguish all traces of monarchism. The news that the Canudos resisters were monarchists only increased Jacobin demands that the national army intervene.

The federal army's initial attacks failed, as the Canudenses fought with unexpected ferocity. The army commanders had underestimated their enemy (who used guerrilla tactics) and overestimated themselves. Frustrated and humiliated, they redoubled their efforts, having to mount three expeditions before they could declare victory. In the end, it took Krupp canons to demolish the defenses. When the dust cleared, not a single male defender of Canudos had survived. The women and children were herded together and shipped elsewhere. The human cost to the army was also heavy. Of the twelve thousand soldiers who fought in the siege, five thousand had been wounded or killed.

The three-year war of extermination at Canudos might have gone unnoticed by the rest of Brazil had it not been for Euclides da Cunha, the journalist-intellectual who immortalized it in his 1902 book *Rebellion in the Backlands* (*Os Sertões*). Euclides, a former army officer, was astounded by what he saw when he arrived from São Paulo to cover the unfolding story for *O Estado de S. Paulo*, the city's leading daily. He admired the defenders' military skills and their raw courage. At the same time, he was uneasy because, by the racist doctrines of the day, he had to regard the locals as half-breeds whose "unstable" nature boded ill for Brazil's future.

But Euclides's main message was about the gap between the politicians and bishops on the coast, who had an army to enforce their will, and the neglected masses of the interior. His book made a major impact on the small reading public, despite his dense prose. Any reader of *Os Sertões* could understand the desperation that had driven the Canudenses to revere their preacher and defend their homes. Antônio Conselheiro was, after all, a lay preacher filling the void created by the failure of the Church to staff its parishes in the interior. And many who never read it knew its story, especially since army officials loudly attacked the author for highlighting their incompetence.

The existence, let alone the fate, of Brazil's indigenous people was virtually ignored by coast-dwelling Brazilians well into the twentieth century. A pioneering Brazilian ethnographer wrote as late as 1913 that "even now...the census takers do not reach the savages of the wild interior, and quite recently Colonel Rondon (see below) discovered in the state of Mato Grosso a numerous tribe of which only the name, and that vaguely, had been known." The intermittent European-Indian coexistence of the early colonial days was long past. The Indians had been assimilated, annihilated, or pushed beyond the margins of Portuguese (and later, Brazilian) settlement. As a result, the Indian was as exotic a figure for most Brazilians as he was for the schoolchildren of Europe and North America. In the words of John Hemming, an English expert on the history of the Brazilian indigenous, "Indians were becoming curiosities rather than a serious threat."

That the Indian reappeared in Brazilian official thought was due to the efforts of dedicated public officials such as Cândido Rondon, an army officer and a positivist. Rondon first encountered Indian settlements in his role as an army officer on assignment to build telegraph lines through the interior. He decided to devote himself to the protection of the remaining "unassimilated" Indians. In 1910, he became the first director of the Service for the Protection of the Indians (SPI) and laid down strict guidelines for its operation. The SPI's mission was the difficult one of bringing basic services (health care, education) to the Indians without destroying their culture or social structure. This noble ambition was bound to collide with other Brazilians' determination to destroy any Indian who blocked their way to the land, minerals, or animals they wanted. It was an unequal contest, and the Indian population continued to decline. (Indian demographic growth after 1960 reversed this trend.)

The drama of opening up the vast interior brought to Brazil a wave of foreign explorers drawn by the stories of the country's natural and material riches. In 1913, former U.S. President Theodore Roosevelt arrived for an epic trip down the Dúvida (now Roosevelt) River, accompanied by Rondon. Roosevelt, ever the adept of challenging physical feats, plunged into his jungle adventure, ending up with a broken leg and a near fatal fever. On his return to the United States he sang the praises of Rondon and wrote a stirring account (*Through the Brazilian Wilderness*, 1914) of his journey. His enthusiastic description of Brazil's resources was a reaction typical of the many Americans and Europeans who were now discovering the country's economic potential.

Brazil now saw a succession of scientists who attempted to take an inventory of the inland expanse and its social problems. "Brazil is a vast hospital," was the gloomy diagnosis from one. Perhaps the most famous was Carlos Chagas, a brilliant medical researcher who helped eradicate malaria in several regions. He is best known for conquering in 1909 a deadly disease that bears his name (Chagas Disease) and had been blinding and even killing its victims in the interior. He identified the carrier (a beetle that lives in walls and ceilings of mud dwellings) and spent great effort educating public authorities about how to fight the carrier and the disease.

Pioneers such as Rondon and Chagas led a growing campaign to educate the public to understand that so many Brazilians were unproductive because of disease caused by unmet medical and sanitary needs. Their efforts would lead to major health campaigns in the 1910s and 1920s, campaigns that helped thoughtful Brazilians challenge the determinist racial and climatic theories that had so often dominated the elite's discussions of Brazil's place in the world.

Coffee Fluctuations, Emerging Industry, and Urban Labor

The explosion in coffee production that had caused the Brazilian economy to boom in the mid- to late nineteenth century turned into a liability in the early twentieth century, when the world coffee market ran a surplus, primarily because of Brazilian overproduction. Export earnings declined with drops in coffee prices abroad, which was exacerbated by an increase after 1898 in the exchange value of the Brazilian currency (due to an increase in foreign capital inflow). Since Brazil was by far the world's largest coffee producer (75 percent of world production in 1900–01), the temptation was natural for the Brazilians to use their market power to manipulate the price. (The Brazilian term for this was "valorization.") With that goal in mind, the governors of its three leading coffee-producing states—São Paulo, Rio de Janeiro, and Minas Gerais—signed a valorization agreement in 1906 known as the "Treaty of Taubaté," which aimed to limit production and exports in the hope of raising international coffee prices to pre-1900 levels by withholding Brazilian coffee (production had doubled in 1906) from the market. The large expense of storage was partially covered by foreign loans, which the federal government began to guarantee in 1907. This agreement did not raise prices but it could have been a factor in preventing them from declining more. (See exhibit 4-5 for fluctuations in the quantity and international value of coffee exports between 1870 and 1910.) It was also a sign that Brazilian politicians and planters were willing to use government power to interfere with the operations of the market, both world and domestic, more than their laissez-faire rhetoric would suggest. Other examples abound. In the years between 1889 and 1930, the federal government ended up acquiring—primarily as rescue operations—and operating such important enterprises as the Banco do Brasil, Lloyd Brasileiro (shipping), and a number of railways.

Most underdeveloped economies have either continued to depend largely on primary products for their export earnings or have failed in their efforts to industrialize. This was not the fate of Brazil.

EXHIBIT 4-5
Brazilian Coffee Exports

	Quantity (per thousand 60 kg. sacks)	International Value per Thousand Sacks (thousand lbs. gold)
1870–71	3.8	7.8
1880–81	3.7	11.6
1890	5.1	17.9
1895	6.7	22.4
1900	9.2	18.9
1905	10.8	21.4
1909	16.9	33.5
1910	9.7	26.7

Source: IBGE, *Estatísticas Históricas do Brasil*, 2nd ed. (Rio de Janeiro, 1990), p. 350.

The Roots of Industrialization

Brazil had been creating industry, on a small scale, since the early nineteenth century. Its tactic was to manufacture for domestic consumption those products for which costs were lower than the competing imports. By and large these were products whose value was low in proportion to their weight—making their price as imports particularly exorbitant relative to their true value. Soap, construction materials, and beverages were prime examples. Textiles were another area for early industrialization, since their needed capital equipment was relatively inexpensive to import. Most capital goods and technology-intensive products—such as railroad rails, locomotives, turbines, and field artillery—continued to be imported for many years to come, paid for by export earnings primarily from coffee and natural rubber. Foreign firms often supplied the necessary electric power for the industrializing sector. For example, Light and Power, a Canadian firm, supplied electricity in Rio and São Paulo.

Industrialization occurred largely without government support until about 1930, because most of the political elite believed that industrialization was against Brazil's long-run economic interests. Here they were repeating the doctrines of their creditors in Europe and North America, who were still schooled in the doctrines of Manchester Liberalism—i.e., a belief in free market economics, with minimal government intervention and a reliance on free trade. Brazilian tariffs, for example, were intended primarily to produce revenues, not to protect domestic industry (approximately 70 percent of federal revenues came from import duties between 1890 and 1910). Furthermore, there was no strong industrial bourgeoisie to press its claims with the politicians. Even when presidents such as Floriano Peixoto in the 1890s or Afonso Pena in the early 1900s engaged in pro-industry rhetoric, they were far from ready to take the comprehensive steps (monetary policy, allocation of foreign exchange) required to give their words substance.

In spite of doctrinal beliefs, however, industrialization proceeded, albeit modestly, largely as an unintended consequence of other government policies (especially on exchange rates), which, though usually designed to protect the primary goods export sector, helped the domestic industrialists as well. It is true that an ostensibly high tariff was instituted in 1895, followed by a more modest tariff in 1900, which remained in force until 1930. But tariffs were never intended to jeopardize Brazil's "agricultural vocation," as the coffee growers and their apologists liked to say.

An ambitious industrialization policy would have required much more than higher tariffs. It would have required ample credit, an efficient financial system, incentives for capital goods imports, and increased investment in human capital (especially education) and infrastructure. Such a comprehensive policy, which Germany and Japan were then pursuing, was never even a question for the overwhelming majority of the Brazilian elite. Nonetheless, by 1910, São Paulo, for example, was on the path that would make it by the 1960s the largest industrial park in the developing world. As the leader in modernization, São Paulo was also in the vanguard as measured by such modernization criteria as public education, sanitary facilities, and transportation. This gave Paulistas a sense of superiority with respect to the rest of Brazil. In fact, though, other parts of Brazil were making slow progress on the industrialization front, primarily the center-south states of Rio de Janeiro and Minas Gerais and a few regions outside that area, notably Bahia in the Northeast.

Industrialists, a high proportion of whom were of Italian or Lebanese descent, were often overshadowed politically by the export-import merchants who operated through powerful commercial associations. Not infrequently, however, merchant and industrialist overlapped, as in the case of Francisco Matarazzo (1854–1937), an Italian immigrant who was involved in both importing and manufacturing. After arriving in São Paulo in 1881, he first established a foodstuff-importing firm and then began to manufacture containers for distribution of his food imports within Brazil. There were links not only between industrialists and export-import merchants but also between those two groups and the bankers. And merchants and bankers were also linked to the coffee growers. The resulting web of contacts was extremely important in facilitating the transfer of a capital surplus from agriculture to the emerging industrial sector, just as the infant industry theory of development would have prescribed.

Brazilian factory owners, like their capitalist counterparts everywhere, faced the need to enforce worker discipline. Brazilian workers, many of whom came from the countryside, had to be taught to adapt to the process of mass production, which meant the tyranny of the clock. Employers often preferred immigrant workers, who were sometimes better trained in the rhythms of urban work. In fact, however, most of the industrial workplaces were relatively small. Metalworking, for example, was dominated by shops of less than ten employees. In these cases, the ambiance was not one of mass employment but something closer to the intimacy of small agricultural units. Large-scale factories were restricted to a few industries, especially textiles.

A further problem was illiteracy. Since most native-born Brazilians, especially of rural background, lacked basic schooling, they could not follow written instructions. This deficiency favored immigrants, who were more likely to be at least minimally literate.

The working conditions and pay in Brazilian factories left much to be desired by modern standards. The textile industry, for example, which employed mostly women, made its employees work long hours in poorly ventilated plants. It is worth remembering, however, that in this era working conditions in Europe and North America were also, by today's criteria, grossly substandard. Laws to protect workers were passed only around the First World War in Britain and even later in the United States. It is also far from clear that urban working conditions were worse than those facing agricultural workers. Brazilian factory workers in major cities such as São Paulo and Rio enjoyed one advantage over all other workers in Brazil. They had better access to government services and better prospects for their children's mobility (even if still pretty limited).

Most urban workers were not, however, employed in industry. Even in the major urban centers of São Paulo and Rio de Janeiro, most worked in the service sector or the informal sector. Service workers, who included shop clerks, trolley drivers, household domestics, and building custodians, often faced a work routine as unrelenting as that of the factory. Service workers in small family-owned businesses worked at the pleasure of their employer and had little recourse in case of arbitrary treatment by employers.

The informal sector included street peddlers, washerwomen, messenger boys, prostitutes, petty thieves, and vagrant handymen. Many came directly from the countryside and returned there when times got bad in the city. They escaped enumeration in the census unless they turned up on the police blotter, and lived outside the realm of formal regulations and structures. Workers in the informal sector aroused particular anxiety among the elite. Politicians and journalists frequently attacked them as "the dangerous classes," always ready to revolt. They were the target of regular police repression and received little mercy from the court system.

Worker Organization and Employers' Strategy

Brazil's first labor unions appeared in the 1880s, among the dock workers and the railway workers. Not coincidentally, they emerged at the same time as the arrival of immigrant workers who had union experience in Spain and Italy. These unions, relatively and not surprisingly weak, were led primarily by anarcho-syndicalists who hoped to end all formal organization of the workplace in the long run and believed a utopia would arrive when the workers had gained full control. In the meantime, the anarcho-syndicalists fought for better working conditions, higher pay, and worker organization as the key to radical democracy. Their chief rivals were the socialists, who thought only an eventual socialist government would solve the workers' problems, but fought, meanwhile, for short-term concessions. Local political differences influenced the fortunes of the two groups, with the anarcho-syndicalists dominating in São Paulo and the socialists dominating in Rio.

Any labor union organizers of this era faced serious obstacles. First, they were constantly repressed by the government and the police, who consistently supported the employers whatever the particular issue of the moment. More important was the enormous vulnerability of the workers themselves, who knew there were masses of other applicants for their jobs. Industrial workers who challenged their employers could be, and were, summarily fired and replaced by new hires. The mere threat of such action was often enough to maintain discipline. Given such a labor surplus, especially the potential in-migrants from the countryside, this was no idle threat. The work of union organizers was also made more difficult by the overwhelmingly rural background of Brazilian workers. The rural sector had a strong tradition of deference to elites. The concept of collective action, such as striking, was not easy to sell to these workers, especially if it meant lost wages. Finally, fear of retaliation was rife. Employers routinely blacklisted labor organizers and circulated their names to other employers. Furthermore, police tactics against strikers were extremely harsh. When, for example, São Paulo railway workers struck to protest a 10 percent wage cut in 1906, they were met with mass arrests and military intervention on the trains, making workers hesitant to follow their union leaders. Given these obstacles, it is hardly surprising that organized labor was a minor force at best in the Brazil of 1910, although it had the potential for growth and increased power in the future.

Brazilian urban employers followed the same management logic as their counterparts in the North Atlantic economies. They wanted to keep wages as low as possible, in which they were aided by the fact that virtually no benefits (health, pensions, etc.) were routinely provided. The concept that employees were also consumers, vital to the growth of the economy—as capitalists were beginning to understand in the United States and western Europe—had not yet penetrated South America. Consumption above the minimum remained the privilege of a small stratum. There were, as elsewhere, rare "enlightened" employers—Jorge Street, a São Paulo factory owner, was one of these, but his paternalistic policies (such as employer-furnished housing) were rarely duplicated. Employers typically harbored racist attitudes and doubted their workers could ever rise above menial tasks. Conspicuously missing was an appropriate recognition of the value of skilled labor, not only for industry but also for the multiple tasks of a modern economy. While the industrialized countries (and Argentina) were pouring money into public education at the turn of the century, Brazil continued to neglect this basic form of resource development. In 1900, only about one-quarter of the population was classified as literate.

In 1920, the proportion was essentially the same. The result was a shortage of skilled labor, which reinforced the lack of capital needed for the operation of a more advanced industrial society.

Evaporation of the Oligarchical Consensus

The Republican political system had operated smoothly since the emperor's bloodless overthrow in 1889 because of the cooperation of the principal state governors. The dominant political machines in each state were led by the Republican parties, which included some former Liberal and Conservative party members who chose to support the Republic. As long as there was agreement among these state machines, they could deliver the popular vote necessary to win a national presidential election for the official candidate.

But trouble began when the officially designated candidate for the 1910 presidential election, Governor João Pinheiro of Minas Gerais, died in 1908. The Republican party bosses of the leading states could not agree upon a new candidate, leading to the first seriously contested presidential election of the Republic. The official nomination went to a general, Marshall Hermes da Fonseca. He ran as a civilian (having retired from the army) but was soon accused of heading a military conspiracy to subvert civilian rule. He did not help his cause by his stubborn refusal to quit wearing his uniform. His prime accuser—and campaign opponent—was Senator Rui Barbosa, chief author of the 1891 Constitution and the country's leading orator and legal mind.

Rui was a throwback to the liberal political tradition of the Empire. As a prime representative of the legalistic culture that had long produced utopian interpretations of Brazilian reality, he saw Brazil as a liberal democracy where human rights and the rule of law should and could prevail. Rui's Brazil, of course, was not the Brazil of Canudos or of the São Paulo factories. His accusation that the official candidate was a military threat infuriated many army officers, who felt their professional honor had been impugned. By framing the choice as between military and civilian government, Rui had raised a red herring. There was in fact no danger of a military takeover at the federal level. The real danger of political instability was at the state level.

Irresponsible though it may have been, Rui's campaign tactic successfully cast him as a courageous lawyer defending constitutionalism against would-be tyrants. Although Rui lost the election, he reinforced the appeal of the kind of abstract legalism so evident among the abolitionists. In fact, Rui spoke eloquently also of the "social question," but that was lost amid his charges of militarism, which cast him as the ultimate *bacharel*, the erudite lawyer armed with endless legal formulae and a precarious hold on political reality.

A Message from Below

In 1910, the elite view of a harmonious Brazil was again shaken from another quarter: The navy enlisted men revolted. The navy was one of the most racially segregated institutions in early twentieth-century Brazil. The officer corps was entirely white and the enlisted ranks virtually all black or mulatto—segregation that resulted not from any legal provision (as in the United States) but from custom.

Whipping was commonly used to discipline enlisted men—a practice that continued even though it had been outlawed briefly by federal decree in 1889. The mutiny began as a protest against whipping but soon grew into a full-scale revolt. The black sailors overpowered their white officers and seized control of two dreadnoughts (the *Minas Gerais* and the *São Paulo*) anchored in the Rio harbor. Taking command, the sailors maneuvered the ships around the bay, threatening to shell the city if their demands were not met. Unfortunately for Foreign Minister Baron Rio Branco, the mutiny coincided with the presence of distinguished foreign visitors, including Lord Bryce, the noted English constitutional scholar. Bryce later wrote, "we were lunching at the Ministry of Foreign Affairs...when suddenly the heavy boom of the guns was heard, and continued at intervals all through the repast." Rio Branco's attempts to sell his visitors on Brazilian progress suffered an embarrassing setback.

The Rio elite, aghast at the menacing sight of the dreadnoughts and their guns, were both stunned and impressed by the mutiny. On the one hand, they were ashamed to have such a "barbaric" eruption occurring in their supposedly Europeanized city—a threat, moreover, that came from Afro-Brazilians, whom the elite wanted to eliminate through whitening. On the other hand, they were amazed at the navigational skills of the black sailors. How could supposed illiterates direct such complex vessels?

Naval officers negotiated a truce with the rebels, guaranteeing them fair treatment—a promise that was not kept. Instead, the rebels were herded off to an isolated island (appropriately named "Snake Island") to face torture and lengthy imprisonment. The navy had answered the black sailors' protest with repression, the response perfected so well over the centuries of slavery. Rui Barbosa attacked the unconstitutionality and immorality of the government's behavior in a blistering speech in the Senate in May 1911, thereby deepening the growing rift between civilian and military.

Economic Strains

As the nineteenth century turned into the twentieth, Brazil ran into problems with its primary export earners, coffee and natural rubber. Coffee earnings had become unreliable, as we have seen, when coffee developed a surplus on the world market. Brazil's response—to hold part of its production off the market— was only partly successful. Although the strategy made sense in theory, it had two defects. First, by maintaining high prices it attracted other coffee-producing countries, especially Central and South American, into the market. Second, the profits were diverted, much going to coffee brokers based outside Brazil, and some to the bankers and the federal government.

Brazilian problems with its rubber monopoly were of a different sort. Rubber was a product unique to the huge trees of the Amazon forest, and was now in heavy demand to make tires for the rapidly growing number of internal combustion engine vehicles in Europe and the United States. Between 1900 and 1910, Brazil was the world's only natural rubber exporter, but it lost its monopoly on this export when the British and Dutch planted their own rubber trees in the East Indies. Exhibit 4-6 shows the trend in Brazil's rubber exports over the period, highlighting the dramatic drop in value per quantity exported as Brazil lost its monopoly. A publicity-seeking English adventurer, Henry Wickham, later claimed to have smuggled out a shipment of Brazilian rubber tree seeds and delivered them to the hands of British growers. In any case, the Brazilians' hold on the world rubber market was broken.

These difficulties by no means neutralized Brazil's long-term growth. Indeed, Brazil's economic growth between 1850 and 1913 was relatively high by international standards, averaging 2.4 percent (constant prices) a year. (The average annual growth for western Europe and North America from 1870 to 1913 was 2.7 percent). The difficulty was that Brazil's population, thanks partly to immigration, was growing almost as rapidly, averaging 2.2 percent a year. Thus, Brazil's per capita growth—the crucial measure of the economy's capacity to raise the standard of living—was significantly lower than the overall growth rate of the economy. In fact, the gross domestic product per capita (measured in constant terms) in 1913 was actually no greater than it had been in 1870. (See exhibit 4-7.)

A rubber boat plying the Amazon River. Brazil's frantic and fantastic rubber boom was ended by a blight that destroyed virtually all Brazil's rubber trees.

EXHIBIT 4-6

Quantity and Value of Natural Rubber Exports, 1900–1920

Year	Quantity	% Change from Previous Year (quantity)	% Change from Previous Year (value)
1900	24,302	+16.9	+6.1
1905	35,393	+11.1	+28.5
1910	38,547	−1.2	+30.2
1915	35,165	+4.9	−0.3
1920	23,586	−29.1	−51.8

Source: IBGE, *Estatísticas Históricas do Brasil*, 2nd ed. (Rio de Janeiro, 1990), p. 347.

EXHIBIT 4-7

Population and Gross Domestic Product (GDP), 1850–1913

	1880 (base year) = 100				Annual Percentage Rate of Growth			
	1850	1870	1889	1913	1851–1870	1871–1889	1890–1913	1851–1913
Population	61	82	119	214	1.5	2.0	2.5	2.2
GDP (@ current prices)	24	78	119	442	6.1	2.1	5.9	4.7
Total GDP (@ constant prices)	49	85	108	220	2.8	1.3	3.0	2.4
GDP per capita (@ constant prices)	80	104	91	103	1.3	−0.7	0.5	0.4

Source: Raymond W. Goldsmith, *Brasil 1850–1984: Desenvolvimento Fincanceiro sob um Século de Inflação* (São Paulo, 1986), p. 134.

None of the possible options for increasing Brazil's economic growth seemed open to Brazilian policymakers around the turn of the century. The first option would have been to slow down population growth by reducing immigration or by encouraging smaller families, but this option was unthinkable in the Brazil of 1900. The elite fervently believed in increasing their country's population as fast as possible. Brazil's problem, they argued, was a *falta de braços* ("lack of arms"). Restricting population growth was precisely the opposite of what policymakers thought Brazil needed.

Another option would have been to accelerate growth, so as to overcome the drag of a rapidly growing population. Here Brazil faced a clear limit. Brazil's capacity to increase its exports, and therefore its domestic growth rate, was limited by its foreign markets. As was becoming clear by 1910, growth in those markets was not rapid enough to sustain the growth in exports Brazil needed to increase significantly its per capita growth rate. The gamble on export-led growth was not meeting expectations.

A third approach to higher growth would have been to concentrate on the domestic market by channeling investment into sectors that produced for domestic consumption, but such a strategy would have run into two difficulties immediately. First, Brazil lacked the technology and the capital goods needed for massive industrialization (as opposed to the moderate level achieved). In addition, the prevailing economic ideology of Manchester-style liberalism, widely endorsed by the Brazilian elite, strongly condemned attempted industrialization in "peripheral" countries such as Brazil. Further, there was powerful opposition to industrialization from the urban merchants, who had an obvious stake in maintaining Brazil's dependence on imported finished goods.

Even if Brazil had chosen to concentrate on its domestic markets, it would have needed to make massive investment. Since exports would almost certainly not have generated the surplus capital needed to finance that investment, the capital would have had to come from within Brazil. But that would have required extraordinarily high domestic savings rates. Such savings would have required sharply reduced consumption, something few democracies, then or since, have ever achieved.

All this is not to say that these options were inherently impossible in the decades after the Republic's creation in 1889. Rather, it is to say that the historic odds were heavily against adoption of policies that could have increased economic growth per capita fast enough to close the gap in living standards between Brazil and the North Atlantic industrial economies.

5

Building to a Dictatorship and World War II

The Shock of World War I

The Brazilian elite had believed in Europe as a cosmopolitan, politically stable, mature model for Latin America. They had imbibed its philosophies, embraced its literature, and celebrated its great men. Despite copying the U.S. constitutional structure, Brazil's soul was still European. Suddenly, the peace of a century was shattered. (The last continental conflict in Europe had been the Napoleonic Wars that ended in 1815.) The European powers slid into a horrifying war of attrition as millions of conscripted soldiers died or were mutilated in battles over seemingly meaningless meters of mud.

For the first three years of the war, Brazil remained neutral. Most Brazilians favored the Allied side, not surprising given the elite's strong identification with France. One Brazilian faction, a distinct minority, favored Germany. This movement, with strong links to the German colony in the South of Brazil, argued for continued Brazilian neutrality. In addition, although the army as a whole did not have a position, certain senior military officers favored Germany. Whether favoring or not favoring Germany, the military as a whole were happy to participate in, and even stimulate, discussion of Brazil's possible mobilization, believing that it could only help them in their battles for increased budgets.

Also fanning the flames of the debate over Brazil's intervention were two recently formed civic associations which argued that Brazil must make its own way in the world—contradicting the elite cosmopolitanism typical of the Republic. The first of these was the Liga da Defesa Nacional, with the prominent poet Olavo Bilac as patron. Founded in 1912, it had close links to the army and was dedicated to creating civilian support for the military, especially on such issues as compulsory military service and increased appropriations. The second was the Liga Nacionalista, which was founded in July 1917, centered in São Paulo, and focused less narrowly on the interests of the military.

Brazil, like the United States, was jolted out of its passivity by the German high command's 1917 decision to launch unrestricted submarine warfare in the Atlantic. The Brazilian Congress finally chose to join the Allies, making Brazil the only Latin American belligerent in the Great War.

As the European war dragged on and German submarines closed the Atlantic sealanes, Brazil, like the rest of Latin America, was cut off from its principal trading partners. Before the war, Brazil had had little incentive to pursue trade relations with other Latin American countries, since all produced primary products and all needed to import finished goods from the North Atlantic industrial economies. Now the war had deprived Brazil, along with its neighbors, of its regular supply of industrial goods. (See exhibit 5-1.) Furthermore, its exports were blocked by German submarines, reducing its ability to earn the foreign exchange needed to pay for imports.

Historians have long argued that the restriction of trade caused by World War I stimulated Brazilian industrialization. Recent research has shown, however, that the supply of imported capital goods, such as machine tools, was not and could not have been replaced by domestic production. Thus, the drop in sophisticated capital imports brought on by the war actually delayed further industrialization. Yet there was a positive aspect: The foreign exchange accumulated during the war later helped finance the surge of capital goods purchases after 1918.

EXHIBIT 5-1

Brazilian Imports of Industrial Equipment, 1890–1920

Years	Pounds Sterling*
1890	819,011
1895	985,722
1900	535,963
1905	891,185
1910	1,733,234
1914	1,157,885
1916	375,121
1918	424,971
1920	1,271,030

*At 1913 prices.
Source: IBGE, Estatísticas Históricas do Brasil, 2nd ed. (Rio de Janeiro, 1990), p. 385.

The Brazilian elite hoped their entry into the war would bring their country world status. Argentina, Brazil's big rival on the international stage, had remained neutral, partly out of a desire to avoid joining any alliance with England and the United States. Brazil's material commitment was admittedly minimal, limited to a hospital unit sent to France, along with a few officers who saw combat with the French army. Even so, Brazilian politicians and intellectuals thought that their action, contrasting so sharply with Argentina's, would increase their influence among the North Atlantic democracies.

Brazilian diplomats and politicians alike were convinced that the next step would be a seat on the Permanent Council of the newly founded League of Nations. (Gaining that seat was a "question of national dignity," in the words of Brazilian president Artur Bernardes.) The Brazilians launched a vigorous campaign but ultimately failed to win the seat, partly because of opposition (expressed through ugly infighting) from the other Latin American delegations. Frustrated in its campaign to win a permanent seat, Brazil withdrew from the League in 1926 in protest. It would take more than a tardy entry into a distant war to make Brazil a major power.

The Economy after the War

The First World War dramatized a change in the pattern of world trade that had begun before 1914. Most important was the relative decline in Britain's world economic position vis-à-vis Germany and the United States. Britain had to spend much of its overseas investment to finance the war effort. Furthermore, British technology, industrial skills, and productivity were all lagging behind those of the United States and Germany. The momentum sustaining Britain's rise to world economic predominance in the nineteenth century had irretrievably slowed. It was still Brazil's primary foreign investor, but it was losing ground, especially in industry. During the course of the 1920s, U.S. and German investment in Brazilian industry rose significantly, with the United States going from $50 million in 1914 to $557 million in 1930. This represented a more than eightfold increase in the U.S. share of total foreign investment in Brazil. Brazil's fortunes in the competition for foreign investment would from now on depend increasingly on the United States and Germany.

Although the Brazilian economy came out of the war years with high inflation, the economy proved remarkably resilient in the 1920s. Brazil was still heavily dependent on coffee exports, just as it had been before the First World War. Fortunately, world prices for Brazil's exports started to climb in 1923 and had more than doubled by 1925, a level maintained with only a slight decline until the crash of 1929. These high prices enabled Brazil to increase its imports by 150 percent between 1922 and 1929. In the same period, Brazilian industry was able to double its imports of capital goods (the essential element for further industrialization). What these data tell us is that Brazil was using much of its export earnings to finance the imports needed for industrialization. In other words, Brazil was diversifying its economy away from dependence on agriculture.

The rapid growth of industry in the 1920s created the opportunity for more effective organization of the urban labor unions. In fact, however, unions continued to be weak for reasons discussed earlier—the small scale of most workplaces, the surplus supply of workers, and, most notably, the unending repression of union activity by employers, police, and government.

One of the most significant developments within labor and the left was the founding of the Brazilian Communist Party (PCB) in 1922. The PCB subsequently succeeded in recruiting many of the former anarcho-syndicalists, who had dominated urban labor organization before the war. By 1930, the PCB had become the best-organized force on the left.

The economic bubble burst when the world capitalist economy collapsed in 1929. The price of coffee, which still earned 70 percent of Brazil's foreign exchange, declined 50 percent between September 1929 and January 1930. Brazil lost all its foreign exchange reserves in a few months as traders cashed in their Brazilian currency for gold, dollars, or sterling. The government's commitment to orthodox economics had led it to guarantee conversion of Brazilian currency at a fixed rate, virtually ensuring exhaustion of the country's foreign exchange reserves.

Brazil, along with the rest of Latin America, now faced bleak prospects. The collapse of capitalism at its center in Europe and the United States had left the peripheral economies, such as Brazil, with no formula for recovery. Brazilian policymakers, like their counterparts elsewhere in Latin America, entered a policy vacuum, as experts from London and New York advised them to apply new and stronger doses of economic orthodoxy—a major ingredient of which was to cut government spending and balance the budget.

More through inadvertence than design, the Brazilian government failed to follow the prescribed treatment. Federal expenditures continued to increase, and budget deficits were ubiquitous throughout the 1930s and World War II. One particularly large expenditure was buying excess coffee stocks that had resulted from the 1929 world crash (coffee plants take seven years to mature, making the matching of supply to future demand largely a gamble). The government's intent was to pacify the angry planters at home while boosting coffee prices abroad. The result, as a product of monetary expansion, was to stimulate overall demand in the Brazilian economy and thus spark an early recovery in Brazil—a recovery that was quicker and stronger than that in the United States. It also brought a new stimulus to Brazilian industrialization. It is tempting to credit the emerging Keynesian doctrines with this result, but John Maynard Keynes had yet to publish his *General Theory*, and he was unknown in Brazil. With foreign exchange scarce enough to make imports prohibitively expensive,

Brazilian industrialists were presented with a protected national market. Their domestic supply of capital goods was also larger than during the First World War, thus giving an alternative source for many of the industrial goods that had previously been imported.

Brazil's Uneven Development

The economic diversification following World War I had extremely uneven effects. Industrialization was concentrated in the South and Southeast, especially in the triangle formed by the states of Minas Gerais, Rio de Janeiro, and São Paulo. When the First World War began, Rio still had more industry than São Paulo, but in the 1920s São Paulo overtook it once and for all, increasing that state's share of Brazilian industry from 15.9 percent in 1907 to 45.4 percent in 1937.

Between 1900 and 1940, Brazil continued to see a significantly regional shift in its population, led by the decline in the Northeast's relative share (from 38.7 percent to 35 percent) and the increased share of the South (from 10.3 percent to 13.9 percent). Although the Southeast's share was virtually constant (going from 44.9 percent to 44.5 percent), that population's education and skills had improved disproportionally.

While the Southeast and South were making economic progress, the Northeast and the North (especially the Amazon Basin) suffered a decline. Sugar, which had been the economic basis of the Northeast, proved less and less competitive on the international market, and no other crop appeared to replace it in sufficient quantity. Although the Northeast's share of the population decreased (from 38.7 percent in 1900 to 35 percent in 1940), its absolute population remained large and highly fertile. This meant a widening gap between the resource base and the population in that area.

The Amazon Basin was another area on the margin of development. It had earlier enjoyed a boom based on natural rubber, but that bubble burst in 1912 when competing sources came onto the world market. The region then returned to a low-productivity gathering economy, carried out by a widely dispersed (half person per square mile before 1960) and malnourished population. The area attracted little attention from national politicians or the elite, although it was a never-ending source of fascination to North Americans and Europeans, both scientists and laymen.

In spite of diversification and major economic growth in the urban regions of the South and Southeast, Brazil remained predominantly rural. As late as the 1940 census, for example, less than a third (31.2 percent) of Brazil was urban. Transportation was difficult and slow, with less than 1,800 miles of paved highway in the entire country. Rapid communication had to be by telegraph or radio, which since the 1920s had become the principal form of mass communication. The print press existed only for the wealthier literate Brazilians in the larger cities.

New Currents in the 1920s

The 1920s saw increasing discontent with the liberalism that had been the underlying influence of the Brazilian Republic since its creation in 1889. The military were active participants in this restive discussion, but the cultural community and the intellectuals also took part.

The First World War gave the Brazilian army a welcome opportunity to lobby for its long-standing needs. The army had had no foreign combat experience since the Paraguayan War forty years earlier. The army commanders knew their equipment was obsolete. They also were extremely aware that their training methods were inadequate. Even though their fighting skills had only been tested at home, those tests had had pretty disastrous results. Their record during the revolt at Canudos has already been described in chapter 3. The war of the Contestado in Santa Catarina (1912–16) was another case in which committed civil resisters, headed by a charismatic leader protesting the building of a railroad across their land, held the federal army at bay far longer than it had expected and inflicted considerable loss of life through selective guerrilla-type raids. Protest as they might, however, Brazil's entry into the European war did not help the military significantly in their struggle to modernize equipment or training, leaving them at the end of the war feeling inadequate and ill done by. In the words of one military historian, "the cavalry had no horses, the artillery had no artillery pieces and the infantry had no rifles."

The end of the war also stimulated new questions, particularly among the junior officers, about Brazil's failure to catch up with the economic growth rates of Argentina and the United States. Unlike the military's intellectual discontents in the late Empire, when they were influenced by the then-new doctrines of republicanism and positivism, there was no clear ideological rationale for the military discontent of the early 1920s. It most commonly took the form of attacking liberalism as an ill-considered aping of a foreign formula. In this, the younger military were mirroring the views of dissenters among the civilian society more generally, as discussed further below.

Particularly active in raising these unsettling questions were the junior officers who had been sent for training with the German army. They had returned from Germany in 1912, founded a journal, *A Defesa Nacional*, and organized a lobbying group to promote new ideas within the army officer corps. They became known as the "Young Turks," because they admired Mustafa Kemal (later Atatürk), who had transformed the Ottoman Empire by relying on the military.

As in the presidency of Marshal Hermes da Fonseca (1910–14), these young military malcontents started intervening in state party politics. The Republican parties in several states had splintered into warring factions, whose contenders frequently tried to enlist the local military on their side. But when the military did intervene, they were seen as destroying the supposed political neutrality of the army and giving credence to the image of militarism painted by Rui Barbosa in his unsuccessful presidential campaign of 1910.

The young officers' anger eventually burst forth in a typically Latin American form: barracks revolts. The young officers (whose ideas are discussed later) participating in these revolts were called collectively the *tenentes* (literally meaning "lieutenants"). The first revolt occurred in 1922 at the army fort at the tip of Copacabana Beach in Rio de Janeiro. Eighteen of the Copacabana rebels fled the bombarded fort and marched down the beach. It was to have been part of a series of coordinated revolts, but the would-be rebels in the other locales lost their courage. The revolt was quickly contained, with all the rebels either killed, captured, or forced into hiding. Another important but also unsuccessful rebellion erupted in São Paulo in 1924. The military revolt destined to become the most famous of this series was the last. Launched in 1924 in Rio Grande do Sul, it was led by Captain Luiz Carlos Prestes. Failing to achieve his objective of seizing a local military base, Prestes led a band of rebel soldiers, joined by a contingent of surviving *tenentes* from the São Paulo revolt, on a 24,000-kilometer, three-year march through the interior of southern and western Brazil. The "Prestes Column," as it became known, managed to elude state and federal forces for that entire time and thereby demonstrate the weakness (often the nonexistence) of government authority in large parts of the country. Prestes's rebels became national heroes, and Prestes himself achieved legendary status in public opinion as the "Cavalier of Hope." But exhaustion and dwindling supplies finally overtook them in 1927, when they dissolved the column and crossed into exile in Bolivia.

These revolts, particularly the success of the Prestes Column, left a significant mark on Brazilian politics. First, they demonstrated a profound lack of discipline in the army, with the higher commands never certain of being obeyed. Second, the rebels' ability to survive showed the ineffectiveness of the federal army and its lack of coordination with state and local authorities. Third, the revolts showed that some of the younger generation were ready to take up arms against the national politicians in power. Fourth, the successful resistance of the Prestes Column dramatized the weakness of the civilian political elite. As had happened with their military counterparts during the late Empire, neither the presidents nor the governors were able to impose authority over rebellious officers. As for the ideas of the rebels (the movement was called *tenentismo*), they were expressed in varying and seldom precise forms. During the late Empire, the junior military had been influenced by the new doctrines of republicanism and positivism. In the 1920s, the junior military showed a similar but less focused intellectual influence. They were infected by the growing wave of disillusionment with the Republic. But there was no clear ideological rationale for this discontent. Behind it all lay the general realization that Brazil had fallen behind in the struggle for modernity. They wanted a strong central government that would unify Brazil and put an end to "professional politicians becoming rich at public expense." The junior military also wanted progressive social legislation such as a minimum wage and child labor legislation.

Modernism, Brazilian Style

Until World War I, Brazil had been living its own version of the "Belle Époque." Its French-oriented literary and artistic world largely copied European styles, with little room for artistic originality. When the war ended, Brazil faced new and more varied European influences, as the traditional artistic canons of the Old World came under attack from radical innovators such as the futurists and the surrealists. Adventurous Brazilian writers and artists from Pernambuco, Minas Gerais, Rio de Janeiro, Rio Grande do Sul and, of course, São Paulo, headed for Europe soon after 1918 and absorbed these new ideas, which soon began to surface in Brazilian poetry, sculpture, and painting.

The benchmark year dating Brazil's entry into what came to be called "modernism" (not to be confused with the very different Spanish-American modernism) was 1922. In February of that year, a "Modern Art Week" festival was held in the city of São Paulo. It was no accident that the new movement would first appear in the Brazilian city whose material progress best entitled it to claim the title "modern." Modern Art Week was a series of expositions, plays, concerts, and poetry readings. It was financed largely by Paulo Prado, scion of a wealthy São Paulo family (their wealth had come from cattle and coffee) and led by Mário de Andrade, a multitalented mulatto (worth noting, since mulattos were not common in high artistic circles) artist, playwright, and musician, also from São Paulo.

This artistic revolt was fed also by a new postwar attitude toward the Afro-Brazilian. The early Republic had been dominated by the dogma of "whitening"— an elite belief that accepted the "scientific" superiority of the white (as preached in the learned quarters of the United States and west Europe) but went on to assume that Brazil would, over the next century at most, virtually "bleach out" the nonwhite element. Along with this went a view that the African per se (as in Afro-Brazilian art and religion) was primitive and barbaric.

Frontal challenges to this racist attitude were few and far between before 1918. Among the outspoken opponents of scientific racism in that era were the jurist-politician Alberto Torres and the educator-writer Manuel Bomfim. Their most distinguished predecessor was the literary critic Sílvio Romero, who extolled the African and Indian contribution to Brazilian culture in his 1883 history of Brazilian literature. Nonetheless, Romero, although an inspiration to later champions of Afro-Brazilian culture, could never bring himself to completely disown scientific racism.

Romero, Torres, and Bomfim all served as antiracist mentors for the new generation of Brazilian thinkers that emerged after World War I. Its most influential spokesman was Gilberto Freyre, the Pernambucan writer-sociologist who began publishing in the early 1920s his pioneering analysis of Brazilian social history discussed briefly in chapter 2. Freyre used Brazil's long history of large-scale racial mixing as clear evidence of racial harmony and what he saw as the resulting lack of racial prejudice in Brazil, especially in contrast to the United States. Freyre's writing (of which the high point was *The Masters and the Slaves*, first published in 1933), combined with that of like-minded writers, artists, and scientists, resulted in a radical reorientation of elite thought about race in Brazil. The nonwhite element—especially the African element—was now seen as a positive factor in Brazilian social formation. Racist conceptions, among at least a significant part of the elite, were increasingly replaced with emphasis on the roles of health and education in countering the apparent backwardness of nonwhites. The result of this intellectual *bouleversement* was to reinforce the transformation of Brazilian culture associated with the modernist movement. This artistic and literary transformation added another force undermining the Old Republic. The cultural upheaval helped deepen the generation gap and raise questions about the value system that had surrounded the Republic's creation. Fascism had already appeared in Italy and was showing strength in Spain and Portugal. Was Brazilian electoral democracy just another fragile ornament borrowed from a European civilization that was now discarding it?

Rise of Anti-Liberal Thought

Post–World War I attacks on liberalism were not unique to Brazil. European thinkers such as Oswald Spengler were producing grand theories to explain the decline of Western civilization. Sigmund Freud's theories, spreading rapidly among the intellectuals, also threatened traditional religion and morals. Conflict over values shook the United States, as epitomized by the prohibition experiment. What was unique to Brazil was a focus primarily on the alleged defects of the political system rather than on philosophical issues.

One such defect was the repeated breakdown of the political system itself into widespread fraud and voter manipulation on both state and federal levels. A second was disappointment at the failure of the economy to grow more rapidly, attributed by many to the faults of the political system. By 1920, Brazil's inability to match United States and Argentine development was evident to all. The ambitious republican promises of the late 1880s had not been fulfilled. Although having industrialized to a certain degree, Brazil remained dependent for export earnings primarily on a single product: coffee. The country had failed to win a seat on the Permanent Council of the League of Nations in 1926. Disease and illiteracy were rife. And the elite was beginning to take real notice of the huge gap between urban and rural Brazil.

When Brazilian critics looked to Europe, they found liberal electoral democracy challenged by bolshevism in Russia, by fascism in Italy and Germany, and by anarchism and corporatism in Spain and Portugal. All called into question the assumptions on which Brazil's Republic had been founded, suggesting that capitalism had to be eliminated or deeply transformed to enable industrial society to survive in the twentieth century.

The early 1920s brought to center stage a chorus of intellectual critics in Brazil. Most considered themselves disciples of the jurist-politician Alberto Torres, an anti-racist thinker before his time. He condemned racist doctrines as instruments used by foreign countries in their attempt to dominate Brazil's economy. A "historic" republican in the late Empire, Torres had been minister of justice (1896–97), and governor of the state of Rio de Janeiro (1898–1900), and later served on the Brazilian Supreme Court (1901–09). In 1909, however, he had become disillusioned with the entire constitutional system and resigned from the bench in order to publicize his criticisms. Writing mainly in the form of newspaper articles (his books consist primarily of collections of these), Torres's principal message was that Brazilians must study their own problems and devise their own solutions—that mindlessly applying foreign formulae was doomed to failure.

He was a highly idiosyncratic thinker in many respects. He vigorously condemned urbanization, for example, branding cities as pernicious and detrimental to Brazilian development, which he thought had to remain agrarian. His disciples, which included army officers writing in *A Defesa Nacional*, concentrated on the arguments that fitted their purposes—in particular, his critique of the republican political structure and the need to find Brazilian solutions for Brazilian problems (which became a virtual mantra for this generation).

Most prominent among the Torres disciples was Oliveira Vianna, a lawyer from the state of Rio de Janeiro, who expounded his views in a two-volume history of southern Brazil and numerous other writings. He charged that the Republic had been founded on idealistic formulae totally inappropriate for Brazil. And he argued that Brazil had lacked any tradition of grassroots democracy (such as in the colonial United States and early modern England), which he thought essential for a liberal democracy. For Vianna, therefore, the systemic breakdown now evident on the state and federal levels was inevitable. Representative democracy in Brazil was a sham. Real power lay in the hands of the bosses or "colonels." Vianna also extolled the "aryan" as Brazil's most creative actor. But here again, judging from the reviews, his readers neglected his racist arguments in favor of his political conclusions.

Vianna was joined in his political critique by lesser known but equally vociferous critics such as Gilberto Amado, Carneiro Leão, Pontes de Mirada, and Vicente Licínio Cardoso. They all argued that the evolution of the Republic had gone fundamentally wrong.

By the end of the 1920s, the republican system had more critics than defenders among intellectuals. The legitimacy of electoral democracy as practiced was in doubt, although its critics, including the *tenentes*, were notably vague about preferred alternatives. They drifted into talk of "national solutions for national problems," better representation of the entire populace, and the need for greater discipline. But there was little debate over the specific institutions needed to bring about such change.

The Disintegration of the Old Politics

As the twentieth century wore on one innovation of the Republic had increasingly dramatic implications for politics as usual: The decentralization stimulated by the new Constitution had resulted in greatly fragmented federal authority, just as capitalism was facing increasingly severe tests of its viability. (See exhibit 5-2.)

Ever since the Constitution of 1891, states could levy tariffs on goods crossing their borders and also could contract loans abroad. They also had authority over such key areas as coffee exports and railway construction. These powers had facilitated industrial development in regions such as São Paulo but had left poorer regions—such as the Northeast—to languish economically. Brazil's vast regions were drifting further from one another economically, a trend that was particularly alarming to many army officers, who feared that Brazil was coming apart.

This fear was exacerbated by another development. The continuing weakness of the national army had stimulated the major states to build up their own military forces. São Paulo hired a French military mission from 1906 to 1924 to train its state military, the Força Publica (which even included a cavalry brigade and the beginnings of an air force in the late 1920s). Rio Grande do Sul's state military had combat experience in the La Plata region. Added together, the troops of the state militias totaled more than the federal army. In São Paulo state between 1894 and 1930, the Força Publica routinely outnumbered federal troops stationed there by ten to one. Although many of these state militias acted more like police than soldiers, they were forces to be reckoned

EXHIBIT 5-2

Distribution of Government Revenues by Levels of Government

	Total Government Percentage of GDP	Percentage Participation by Branch of Government		
		Federal	Provincial or State	Municipal
1856	9.9	81.5*	15.5	3.0
1885–6	10.2	76.3	18.5	5.2
1907	16.4	65.8	25.4	8.8
1929	12.5	54.2	35.4	10.4
1945	13.2	55.7	36.1	8.2

*Average of fiscal years 1855–86 and 1856–57.
Source: Raymond W. Goldsmith, *Brasil 1850–1984: Desenvolvimento Fincarceiro sob um Século de Inflação* (São Paulo, 1986), p. 71.

with, calling the ultimate test of any central government (i.e., its monopoly of force) into question.

Most important, elections had lost their perceived legitimacy as a means of allocating political power in republican Brazil. However manipulated they may have been (such as in the exclusion of monarchist candidates in the 1890s), they had generally been tolerated by the elite (with the possible exception of 1910) in earlier decades. By the 1920s, this was no longer true. First, exercise of the franchise was increasingly clouded by allegations of fraud as state elections turned ever more frequently into electoral farces. It was impossible to settle such conflicts impartially because the incumbent state governments controlled vote-counting (elections and electoral law were strictly a state matter) and certified the winners. Claims of vote fraud usually centered on the countryside, where landowner-hired agents could readily manipulate semiliterate voters.

The presidential elections of 1918 and 1922 furnished ample ammunition for the system's critics. In 1918, the state party leaders could not agree on a new face to nominate for president and turned to Rodrigues Alves, the Paulista politician who had been president from 1902 to 1906 and who had presided over Rio's rebuilding, but who was by now old and politically very weak. Alves was duly elected but died before inauguration day. A substitute, Epitácio Pessôa, a distinguished jurist from Pernambuco, was found, elected, and inaugurated. But he lacked consensus support in the major states and was soon the target of internecine political battles that continued throughout his presidency.

The succeeding president, Artur Bernardes (1922–26), an autocratic ex-governor of Minas Gerais, proved even more divisive. He was a stern often vindictive figure who showed little inclination to conciliate. His election campaign began on an ugly note when pro-military sources leaked alleged Bernardes letters (later proved to be forgeries) mocking the army. And barracks revolts (such as at Fort Copacabana in 1922) early in his presidency forced him to rule by state of siege (complete with Amazonian internment camps), a poor omen for the system's future. By 1926, when the Paulista Washington Luís was elected president, the divisions among the state political machines went very deep. The politicians had done as much as the military, the artists, and the intellectuals to undermine the political system they had all inherited.

The Revolution of 1930

Preparations for the presidential campaign of 1929 occurred amid even more than usual suspicion and manipulation. The nominee of the majority of state machines was Júlio Prestes, the governor of São Paulo, the same state as that of the incumbent president, Washington Luís. This was significant because state rivalries were running strong, pitting São Paulo against the major states of Minas Gerais and Rio Grande do Sul and the minor state of Paraíba. The opposition to the official ticket formed a liberal alliance that nominated for President Getúlio Vargas, a former federal finance minister and currently governor of Rio Grande do Sul. His running mate was João Pessôa, a politician from Paraíba. During the campaign, the opposition, distrustful of the eventual vote count, had considered organizing a coup if Júlio Prestes was declared the winner, which he was. Many in the opposition cried fraud at the result, but Vargas decided they lacked the power to contest the election successfully. He changed his mind when João Pessôa, his running mate, was assassinated. Even though Pessôa's death was due to a romantic involvement enmeshed in local politics, it was the shock needed to mobilize the opposition to take up arms.

Vargas and his co-conspirators now set about organizing an attack on the incumbent federal government. As a first step, the governors of Rio Grande do Sul, Minas Gerais, and the rebel states of the Northeast used their state military to secure their states. They then convinced the part of the federal army stationed in Rio Grande do Sul to join them and were able to add a series of rebel columns from other regions. The collection of armed conspirators converged on Rio from the north, south, and west.

In Rio, President Washington Luís was determined to remain in office long enough to hand power to his fellow Paulista. But the military commanders in Rio decided that continued support for the incumbent president would prolong what looked like an impending civil war. When they suggested to Washington Luís that he resign, he refused. Cardinal Dom Sebastião Leme, the archbishop of Brazil, agreed with the Rio military and convinced the president that his time was up. Washington Luís went into exile.

At this point, the rebel columns had not yet reached Rio. The army and navy commanders of the Rio garrison declared themselves a ruling junta and began issuing their own decrees, even though the territory they in fact controlled was restricted to Rio. They even considered remaining in power. After a few days, however, Getúlio Vargas himself reached Rio with his comrades, who—in a gesture of gaucho machismo—hitched their horses to the obelisk at the foot of Avenida Rio Branco, a famous landmark in downtown Rio. The junta reconsidered and handed power to Vargas as provisional president.

Vargas's victory had been the work of a complex coalition, of which the political leaders of Minas Gerais and Rio Grande do Sul, resentful of São Paulo's dominance of national politics, were only one element. Second was the recently founded (1926) Partido Democrático of São Paulo, the sworn opponent of the state's ruling official Republican party. Third were the *tenentes*, who had rebelled against both military and civilian authority. Fourth were the coffee growers (many but not all of them in the Partido Democrático), who were angered by the federal government's failure to compensate them for the plunge in coffee prices. Such a heterogeneous coalition was obviously unstable, with potential strains that were bound to appear as soon as the provisional government started to make decisions.

Citizens of Rio welcoming rebel troops as news of the 1930 revolution's success reached the Brazilian capital. Revolutions were rife in South America at that time, and the overthrow of the Brazilian government was one of the most stirring. (© Bettmann/CORBIS)

The losers in 1930 were also numerous. First were the São Paulo Republican party bosses, who had supported Júlio Prestes. Second were the top army commanders, most of whom found themselves summarily retired. Third were the bankers, who had insisted Brazil cling to the gold standard and who now found their financial links abroad badly frayed by the abrupt change in government.

But most Brazilians hardly noticed the break in the legal succession in 1930. Their lives had been far more affected by the great crash, which had cost jobs and income. Real GDP per capita fell 4 percent in 1930 and another 5 percent in 1931. Nor had the revolution of 1930 brought any major change in property relations or working conditions, despite the creation of a federal Ministry of Labor, Industry and Commerce in 1930. Brazil was still a country where landowners, merchants, industrialists, and bankers controlled power. The source of most wealth was still rural, and there was still no talk of serious land reform.

Swing toward Centralization

The world financial crash of 1929 had created a powerful economic rationale for strengthening central government in Brazil. Vargas seized the moment, dissolved Congress, instituted an emergency regime (legitimized by decree on November 11, 1930), and assumed full policymaking authority via federal decree power. He was strongly supported by the newly ascendant army generals—led by the ambitious military politician General Góes Monteiro—as he named "interventors" to administer the states. The state governors (technically known as "presidents") had almost universally been deposed by the new provisional federal government. Only in Minas Gerais was the governor allowed to remain and act as the interventor.

This assertion of federal authority was bound to threaten the state political elites, and it did. The implications for tax collection and budget allocation were obvious. Equally important was the threat of federal intervention in state politics. Although São Paulo, whose internal political divisions had helped bring Vargas to power, had the most to lose, other state leaders, such as those of Minas Gerais and Rio Grande do Sul, also saw dangers ahead.

The confrontation between the Vargas government and São Paulo was not long in coming. The Paulista elite, among whose ranks were some who had favored Vargas, quickly recovered their solidarity. Paulista opponents had always suspected his intentions toward their state, and his former Paulista supporters soon concluded that he would never keep his promise to hold elections. The Paulista *amour propre* was especially offended when Vargas appointed a non-Paulista, João Alberto Lins de Barros, as interventor in that state. Since the interventor was the federal authority there to monitor the state government, this was an unmistakable sign that recentralization was under way. Despite his best efforts, João Alberto could not placate the Paulista politicians and press, which successfully turned him into a target of local ridicule and hostility.

As the Paulista political elite resolved to fight the new powers in Rio, they thought they had recruited the leadership of Minas Gerais and Rio Grande do Sul to join them. Unfortunately for them, their would-be allies chose to sit on the sidelines. In July 1932, the Paulistas launched their revolt, led primarily by army officers who had refused to join the Vargas-led conspiracy of 1930 and who, as a consequence, had been cashiered. The Paulista rebels were left to fight the federal army alone. The Paulistas mobilized their wealthy matriarchs to turn in their gold and silver jewelry to help finance the war. The city's metalworking shops produced homemade tanks, and a minor armament industry blossomed. But the Constitutionalist Revolution, as the Paulistas called their revolt, lasted only three months (July 9 to October 2, 1932). Vargas and his army commanders did not invade the city of São Paulo, where the revolt centered. Nor did they bomb it, as the government had done during the 1924 revolt in São Paulo. They merely surrounded it. Actual fighting was confined to the city outskirts. By October, the Paulistas surrendered, lowering their flag of secession. Vargas again reacted with restraint. He imposed relatively soft peace terms and even ordered the federal government to assume half the debt incurred by the rebels. The federal military were rewarded for their victory with a budget increase of 159 percent.

The unsuccessful revolt had discredited the Paulista political elite in the country at large. It seemed a reprise of the Paulista threat to secede in the late Empire, and confirmed fears in other regions that Brazil's most powerful state would always put its own interests ahead of the nation. It would be almost three decades before a Paulista occupied the presidency again. One consolation for the Paulistas was creation of the University of São Paulo in the mid-1930s. Intended to be the state's assertion of power on the intellectual level (and to compensate for its political loss in 1932), it was to become Latin America's premier university.

Vargas kept his promise (made before the São Paulo revolt) to hold national elections for a Constituent Assembly, which occurred in May 1933. These elections brought an important innovation. For the first time in Brazilian history, a Vargas-sponsored 1932 law instituted federal responsibility for guaranteeing an honest vote throughout the country. As noted, the voting had previously been supervised by *município* and state authorities, with much leeway for fraud and manipulation. Now a federal authority, known as Justiça Eleitoral (Electoral Justice), was in place to protect the secret vote.

The Constituent Assembly met in 1933–34 and produced a new constitution (the Constitution of 1934, Brazil's third), which was a mixture of political liberalism and socioeconomic reformism. There were now guarantees for an impartial judiciary, along with an assertion of new government responsibility for economic development and social welfare. Elections were held for president (Getúlio was elected to a four-year term by the Assembly, which had become the Chamber of Deputies) and for the state legislature. It looked as if Brazil was finally going to be allowed an experiment in modern democracy. Such, as we shall see, did not prove to be the case.

Ideological Polarization

The 1930s brought the ideological radicalization Brazil had lacked during its upheaval of the 1920s. Anchoring the left was the Brazilian Communist Party (Partido Comunista Brasileiro, or PCB). Founded in 1922, it was under the supervision of the Comintern in Moscow, though its subservience was concealed under an elaborate clandestine apparatus. Many of its members were ex-anarchists or anarcho-syndicalists, whose former organizations the PCB was gradually defeating within the power struggles of the left. The PCB was essentially limited to a few major cities (Recife, Rio, Pôrto Alegre, and São Paulo) and some mining areas in Minas Gerais. In the early 1930s, the party followed the Comintern line of all-out struggle against the forces of "fascism." This strategy led to the creation in 1935 of a leftist front called the "Aliança Nacional Libertadora" (ANL). Its titular head was Luiz Carlos Prestes, who had led a rebel column through the Brazilian backlands from 1924 to 1927, as already described. The Brazilian public considered him an ethically outstanding figure with no political commitments other than the good of Brazil. Unknown to the public, however, he had in fact joined the Communist Party and was now under direction from Moscow. The ANL included other parties, such as the Socialists, but control remained with the Communists.

In carrying out the Comintern strategy, the Brazilian Communists were faced with the same difficulty as their comrades in most Third World countries. Communist Party doctrine focused entirely on urban workers, the assumption being that working-class consciousness could best be cultivated among urban workers, while rural workers offered little or no revolutionary potential. Yet Brazil was still primarily an agrarian society. There was the further difficulty that even industrial workers in Brazil worked primarily in small establishments, where organizing was especially difficult. Furthermore, even the city workers came mostly from rural backgrounds and did not take easily to appeals for short-run sacrifice—e.g., the loss of wages while striking. The task of organizing such workers therefore ran into employee resistance as well as police repression. But whatever its difficulties with the workers, the Communist-dominated left had aroused the fears of the elite, both civilian and military. The politicians and the generals had long been suspicious of worker organization (the "dangerous classes," as they were known), and the Moscow-based Communist ideology gave the elite new reason to impose repressive laws.

There were also new groups on the right of the political spectrum. In the 1920s, for example, the Brazilian Roman Catholic Church underwent a revival as both laymen and clergy struggled to breathe new life into a weak institution. By the early 1930s, the revived Church was exerting new political force on the right. An even more important force was the Açâo Integralista Brasileira (AIB). Its members wore green uniforms, had a quasi-military hierarchy, and engaged in paramilitary parades and exercises. They also relished street confrontations with their enemies on the left. Although it bore an obvious superficial resemblance to European fascism, in fact the AIB lacked the racist (with the exception of a few spokesmen, such as Gustavo Barroso), expansionist, fully militaristic qualities typical of European—especially German—fascism. The Integralista vision was of a Christian Brazil based on a disciplined society, with little tolerance for revolutionary action on the left.

The Integralists attracted a wide following among the middle and upper classes, especially among naval officers and the clergy. They attracted some following even among urban workers in Rio Grande do Sul and were well represented in Ceará. Their most visible leader was Plínio Salgado, a Paulista writer who had been involved in the modernist movement in São Paulo. Gaining confidence from their swelling numbers, the Integralists sought national influence. Like the Communists, they were prepared to seek it through direct action rather than through the ballot box. Some foreign countries thought them to be a major political actor on the Brazilian scene—Benito Mussolini's government, for example, gave them direct financial help—and their possible link to European fascism began to alarm the British and American governments, which already saw Germany as a geopolitical threat in Latin America.

The Communists and the Integralists saw themselves as natural antagonists. They staged marches, counter-marches, and street fights paralleling what was happening in central Europe. This ideological radicalization helped contribute to the public's growing doubts about the effectiveness of electoral politics—a point that was dramatized in November 1935 when a faction of Communist officers and enlisted men attempted a coup within the Brazilian army. The PCB and Comintern were gambling on a military coup to overthrow the Brazilian government. This strategy would weaken the U.S. and British governments and strengthen the Soviet Union's international position. It involved little organizing of workers and little attention to the industrial heartland of São Paulo. It would be a proletarian revolution without a proletariat.

Detailed instructions for carrying out the revolt were given to Luiz Carlos Prestes in Moscow, where he had been since 1931. He reentered Brazil in mid-1935 with a precise timetable from the Comintern, whose non-Brazilian agents were laying the groundwork in Brazil. The revolt broke out in a series of uprisings in November 1935 at three military bases, in Natal, Recife, and Rio. The Comintern leaders were convinced that the Communist Party had sufficiently infiltrated the army to be able to seize power. But after brief fighting, with some casualties among officers and enlisted men, the pro-government army commanders crushed the revolts at all three bases. The Comintern and the PCB, who were apparently unaware that they were already under surveillance by the Brazilian police, had unwittingly played into Vargas's hands. They had given him the ideal evidence of the "Bolshevik threat."

The Vargas government had a propaganda field day after it crushed the revolt, circulating wildly exaggerated stories (later discredited by military records) about loyalist officers shot unarmed in their beds. Vargas immediately convinced Congress to declare a state of emergency, allowing police to suspend civil rights in their hunt for suspects. He now had the atmosphere he needed to intimidate opponents of whatever ideological stripe. It was a perfect backdrop for increased presidential power and the further centralization such an increase in power implied.

Getúlio Vargas as Dictator

For the next two years, Vargas convinced Congress to keep renewing the ninety-day state of siege. Throughout, his government enjoyed extraordinary police powers, stultifying political life and stimulating growing suspicions that Vargas was preparing his own coup. This fear was reinforced by the pro-authoritarian views of his two top generals, Pedro Góes Monteiro and Eurico Dutra, whose views assumed particular importance because, in the radicalized political climate, Vargas was becoming increasingly dependent on military support. Both generals admired German military skills and both doubted the capacities of the Anglo-Saxon democracies to resist German power. This was a view shared in many circles—even some in the United States—and with some justification. The U.S. army in 1938, for example, was no larger than that of Greece or

Bulgaria. As late as 1940, U.S. troops lacked rifles to use on maneuvers and had to be content with wooden cutouts.

Political attention in Brazil now focused on the upcoming presidential election of 1938. Vargas had been elected by the Constituent Assembly of 1933–34, which had provided for a direct election to follow in 1938. Vargas was constitutionally ineligible to run for another term immediately, although he could after a four-year interval. Vargas's opposition coalesced behind Armando Salles de Oliveira, a leading member of the Paulista elite who were now trying to gain through the vote what they had failed to gain by arms in 1932. The government-supported candidate was José Américo de Almeida, a writer and minor politician from the Northeast. The Paulistas believed their time had come as they solicited support among the anti-Vargas forces.

Vargas was indeed conspiring with his generals to stage a coup and thereby preempt the election. On November 10, 1937, congressmen arrived in Rio to find the Congress building surrounded by troops refusing them access. That night, Vargas announced over the radio to the Brazilian people that they had a new Constitution for what he termed the Estado Nôvo (New State). Brazil had become a full-fledged dictatorship. The new Constitution had provided for a plebiscite to approve the new document, but it was never held. As in 1932, the military was rewarded with an increased budget, up by 49 percent in 1937 over 1936.

The Paulista elite, who had feared just such a move, had lost again. Vargas's most prominent opponents were arrested or fled into exile. The public fell silent as censorship settled over the media and the police were given a free hand.

The Integralistas were initially pleased by the coup, believing they would benefit from this swing to the right. Their leaders expected fellow Integralista Plínio Salgado to be offered a cabinet post. But the Vargas government did the opposite, imposing new restrictions on Integralista activities. In response, a band of armed Integralists tried their own coup in March 1938, attacking the presidential palace where Vargas was sleeping. In the middle of the night, the armed Integralists, aided by disloyal palace guards, penetrated the grounds of the palace and began firing at the main building. What followed was more comedy than combat. Vargas and his then 23-year-old daughter, Alzira, appeared at the windows and returned fire. The Integralists hesitated and settled into a multihour siege. It took until dawn for government reinforcements to arrive, as Alzira kept making increasingly frantic phone calls to the military commanders. The surviving attackers (at least four were killed) were rounded up and ushered off to prison. Vargas now had the perfect excuse to repress the Integralists in addition to the Communists. Salgado sought exile in Portugal, and Brazil was left with no organized alternative to the new dictatorship.

If Vargas's coup simplified politics at home, it created problems abroad. The U.S. White House demanded an immediate explanation from Brazil's ambassador, Oswaldo Aranha. The U.S. government was preoccupied with the geopolitical implications of Brazilian events for any future war with Germany (Brazil's position on the Atlantic coast meant that it could play a vital role in controlling transatlantic air and sea traffic), and the U.S. military feared that the coup would move Brazil closer to Nazi Germany. They were well aware of Dutra's and Góes Monteiro's sentiments and had been struggling to woo them away from German influence. The presence of a large German-speaking colony in southern Brazil reinforced American worries about the future direction of the Vargas dictatorship. At the very least, the coup meant Brazil had deserted the ideological ranks of the democracies.

The Vargas Style

Getúlio Vargas was about as uncharismatic a dictator as the world is likely to see. He lacked the electric charm of his Argentine counterpart Juan Perón and never cultivated the melodramatic personal appearance of a Hitler or a Mussolini. Unprepossessing physically, his chief physical features were his paunch and a habitual ironic smile. But he used his unimpressive persona to huge advantage because he combined it with an uncanny ability to size up his fellow humans and induce his enemies to underestimate him. He was a superb listener and had the ability to convince most of his interlocutors, whatever their position, that he genuinely understood them, if not agreed with them. Although capable of appalling cruelty (he allowed the extradition of Luiz Carlos Prestes's German-born Jewish wife to Nazi Germany, where she died in a death camp), he preferred to turn enemies into collaborators. There is no evidence that he amassed inappropriate wealth while in office, although he did not hesitate to enjoy the full powers of the presidency.

Vargas was probably the opposite of a visionary, but he had firm ideas about where Brazil should be headed. Judging from his speeches and government initiatives in the years following 1937, he wanted, first and foremost, to build a strong central government—a goal enthusiastically shared by the higher military. This would require increased investment in education, economic development (to support industrialization at least in the military-related sectors), and increased integration of the lands to the west. Second, he wanted to project Brazilian power abroad, which would require a stronger position in international trade. Third, he wanted to improve social welfare for urban workers. Here he had a non-economic goal in mind: A satisfied set of government-controlled unions would furnish Vargas with a political base.

Vargas's strategy during the Estado Nôvo (1937–45) was to rely on the military for political stability and on his technocrats for administration. Here, Vargas was borrowing from both European fascism (discarding electoral democracy) and the American New Deal (relying on modernizing technocrats). Fundamentally, he and his intellectual apologists, such as Azevedo Amaral and Oliveira Vianna, justified the Vargas dictatorship on the grounds that Brazil could ill afford the "petty politics" of an open society, given the dangers from its enemies, internal and external.

This rationale led directly to the repressive apparatus that accompanied the Estado Nôvo. Most visible were the police, who in Rio were commanded by the notorious sadist Filinto Muller. His staff even had a secret working agreement with the German Gestapo. Torture of political suspects was frequent and there was no reliable recourse to the courts, given the government's constant invocation of the National Security Law. There were also detention camps at such distant sites as the island of Fernando de Noronha, off the northeastern coast. One survivor of a camp in Alagoas, Graciliano Ramos, wrote a searing memoir of his suffering in *Memórias do Cárcere* (published only in 1955), which became a classic of Brazilian literature and later a highly successful film. And there was omnipotent censorship, carried out by the Departamento da Imprensa e Propaganda (DIP).

Corporatist Inroads

In 1937, the southeast triangle formed by Minas Gerais, Rio de Janeiro, and São Paulo, along with a few urban centers elsewhere on the coast, was approaching a modern capitalist economy. As early as 1900, part of its urban work force (a very small fraction of the Brazilian total) had become organized in unions, as we have seen. In some industries, such as the railways and the docks, they had won benefits, including pensions and holidays—something unheard of elsewhere in Brazil. Most workers, however, even in the cities, were neither unionized nor covered for benefits.

Brazil's industrial unions had begun to show strength in the 1920s and particularly the 1930s, when political turmoil had brought the question of workers' social welfare to the forefront. In the contemporary industrialized world, the least interventionist model was the United States. England, in contrast, had instituted government-sponsored social insurance before the First World War. Germany had acted even earlier, under Bismarck in the 1880s. Spain, Portugal, and Italy were now experimenting with the new form of social organization known as *corporatism*. Vargas and his technocrats chose the corporatist route.

The intent of corporatism was to facilitate the adoption of modern capitalism while avoiding the extremes of laissez-faire permissiveness on the one hand and total state direction on the other. The idea was to establish separate corporate entities (syndicates), each representing specific economic sectors. Each sector had its own syndicates. Both employers and employees were members of the syndicate for that sector. The coordination of relations between these corporate entities was the national government's responsibility, eliminating conflict between competing syndicates and leaving the last word (on wages, benefits, and working conditions) to the central government.

Vargas's primary corporatist target was labor. Since fear of labor and the left had in part prompted the repressive policies followed after 1935, Vargas was concerned to protect himself against the potential threat of labor unrest while also seeming to turn the other check. Much inspiration for the new legislation (especially the labor law of 1943) came from the Carta di Lavoro of the Italian fascist state.

Over the course of the 1930s, government technocrats, led by the lawyer and political philosopher Oliveira Vianna, used their arbitrary powers to shape a network of officially established labor unions (organized by trade) at the local level. Each *município*-based union was barred from direct relations with other *município*-based unions within the state, even of the same trade. State federations and national confederations were permitted, but these were also barred from having direct links with local-level organizations. The Ministry of Labor collected and channeled all union dues (equal to one day's pay a year automatically deducted from the worker's paycheck), and exercised veto power over all union elections. Strikes were illegal between 1937 and 1946, and no direct bargaining existed between unions and employers. All workplace-level grievances had to be directed to government-appointed labor courts within the Labor Justice System (Justiça do Trabalho), which until 1946 were subordinated to the minister of labor. With respect to employers, Vargas was able to build on the existing trade associations, which were already organized by industry.

Each syndicate was in turn a member of a new statewide federation, such as the Federation of Industries of the State of São Paulo (FIESP). In 1943, the state federations were brought together in a National Confederation of Industry. This corporatist structure gave the federal government a convenient channel not only for regulating industry but also for co-opting industrialists in the process. The corporatist structures for labor and industry effectively took both sectors out of the active political process.

Vargas and his technocrats made no effort to extend this system to the rural sector, although legislation provided for future coverage. The rural sector got less attention because it represented less danger of worker mobilization—not only because rural workers were harder to organize but also because repression by management (the landowners and their hired gunmen) was easier in the countryside. Political power in the Brazilian rural sector—whether by the ballot or otherwise—was effectively controlled by landowners, who did not look kindly on any type of worker organizations. In this respect, Brazil was much easier to handle within a corporatist system than Mexico, where rebel movements regularly stimulated rural worker uprisings.

A New Search for National Identity

The advent of the Estado Nôvo was a decisive victory against the liberalism of the Old Republic, with many anti-liberal critics now joining the dictatorship. A leading example was Francisco Campos, a Mineiro intellectual who had directed educational reform in his state. He wrote the authoritarian Constitution of 1937 and went on to serve as Vargas's justice minister. Azevedo Amaral, another leading anti-liberal, edited an official magazine, *A Nôva Política*, which published authors supportive of the Estado Nôvo. Finally, as noted, Oliveira Vianna, one of the most famous enemies of liberalism, helped draft and administer the corporatist labor laws.

The Vargas dictatorship had a keen sense of the political importance of popular culture as a way of cementing government support by making Brazil look good in the international context. One example was soccer, where Brazil excelled in international competition, as it does today.

Soccer had been introduced into Brazil and much of South America in the late nineteenth century by British businessmen and sailors. The game (called *futebol*) quickly caught on, with private clubs and factories sponsoring white, upper-class amateur teams. By the 1920s, a democratization had begun, with Afro-Brazilians beginning to appear on teams. By the 1938 World Cup, even Brazil's national team was no longer all white. Meanwhile, the Vargas government in 1941 created a National Sport Council, which formed an organizing umbrella for the extensive national network of private soccer clubs. Vargas's lieutenants channeled government money to fund the national team. Subsequent success was impressive. Brazil is the only country in the world to have qualified for every World Cup since 1930. There are few accomplishments that mean as much to Brazilian national identity as Brazil's supremacy in soccer, and Vargas was one of the first politicians to appreciate the political payoff from supporting it.

A second example of promoting popular culture was the Rio Carnival. As in the case of soccer, there had been a spontaneous growth of private groups dedicated to a popular pastime. In this case it was samba, a unique Brazilian music and dance form born among the shacks of poor Afro-Brazilians in the late nineteenth century. By the 1920s, the "schools" of samba singers and dancers had become the centerpiece of the annual pre-Lenten Carnival.

Vargas's was the first federal government to promote the samba schools and the Rio parades (previous support had come from the municipal government), which became an internationally recognized symbol of Brazilian culture. This policy, which was clearest after the coup of 1937, not only had an economic rationale (to attract tourism) but also sought to play a role in strengthening the nation's new sense of its own identity as at least partly Afro-Brazilian through such powerful instruments as music and dance. Finally, the government launched an extensive program of restoration of historic (especially religious) architecture, sculpture, and painting. Restoration of the Imperial Palace in Petrópolis was a good example. Another was inviting the famous French architect Le Corbusier (aided by a Brazilian team of architects) to design the much-celebrated Ministry of Education and Culture building in Rio in 1936 (construction finished in 1943). All these programs were designed to help soften the dictatorship's image of repression and censorship and present it as the promoter of national culture and, therefore, national unity. It was no accident, of course, that DIP, the agency in charge of all censorship, also handled public relations for the government, including the sponsorship of cultural events (as well as political rallies). Each samba school, for example, had to clear with DIP its plans for its annual Carnival appearance.

A darker side to the Vargas-sponsored preoccupation with national identity was the attempt to "protect" the country from those defined as "un-Brazilian," such as those of Japanese or Jewish descent. They were subject to discrimination, both official and unofficial, although it never approached the comprehensive and systematic level of Nazi Germany. Such measures were largely restricted to closing newspapers, schools, and organizations deemed "foreign."

Juggling the International Options

By 1934, the pattern of European geopolitical confrontation had already become clear. Nazi Germany had its eyes not only on its European neighbors, but also on increased influence in the Western Hemisphere. It had identified Brazil as a prime trading partner and proceeded to exercise leverage over this bilateral relationship. The mechanism was a special German currency used to pay for Brazilian exports, which could be redeemed only by buying German exports, making it a form of tied trade. From 1933 to 1938, German-Brazilian trade rose sharply—primarily Brazilian cotton in return for German industrial goods—with Britain the principal loser.

The Germans were interested in more than trade, however. They also wanted to draw Brazil into the German politico-military sphere. They systematically cultivated Brazilian army officers known to be admirers of German military prowess. They also offered Brazil arms and technical training. Just as in the pre–World War I period, the U.S. government worried about this German strategy. The State Department denounced German trade policy as discriminatory, and the U.S. military tried to counter the German offer of arms and training. In this effort they failed. Vargas had tried to get U.S. military equipment first, but the U.S. Congress, a very isolationist body during the 1930s, outlawed foreign arms sales by the United States.

Throughout the period, Vargas's police and intelligence forces often relied on British agents for information about other foreign penetration of the country. The army's rapid response to the 1935 Communist revolt probably owed much to British intelligence in identifying the Comintern agents. The British joined the Americans in watching nervously as Nazi and Italian agents operated both openly and clandestinely in Brazil. For example, Germany's official airline, Condor, was a known conduit for German intelligence (as was Pan American for the United States).

Brazilian public opinion was the target in a battle over which side to support in the coming European war. Elite sentiment still heavily favored the Allies for cultural reasons, and until their suppression in 1935, the Communists had also been effective in promoting anti-Nazi opinion. But some Brazilians, as in 1914, favored Germany, regardless of the historical ties of culture.

Vargas had shown an inclination to look to the United States for military links. As noted, he had tried to buy arms from the United States before turning to Germany. In 1937, he had also offered President Roosevelt the use of Brazilian coastal bases. This offer had been refused, presumably because Roosevelt could not afford to alienate the isolationist Congress by looking as if he were preparing for war. And a Brazilian bid to buy surplus U.S. destroyers also fell through when U.S. authorities caved in to Argentine protests against the planned sale. When World War II finally broke out in 1939, Roosevelt and the United States chose to remain neutral. So did Vargas and his generals, while continuing to cultivate relations with the Axis powers. At the same time, however, Vargas kept his options open by his 1941 approval of a Pan American Airways project (under U.S. army contract) to modernize airports in the North and Northeast.

On December 7, 1941, the Japanese bombed Pearl Harbor. Immediately after this, Hitler declared war on the United States, removing Roosevelt's problem with the isolationists. Brazil did not declare war until mid-1942. By then, even the fence-sitters could see that the military odds had tipped in favor of the Allies. The 1941 invasion of Russia had caught the Wehrmacht in a ferocious Russian winter, and the German U-boats were taking heavy losses in the Battle of the Atlantic. Brazil could not wait much longer if it hoped to extract any attractive compensation for entering the war.

Brazil had at least two assets the Allies needed. One was raw materials, including natural rubber, quartz (essential for radio communications), and other minerals. The other was its coastline, which offered air and sea bases at strategic points on the Atlantic Ocean. Vargas won an attractive deal. Brazil agreed to supply the raw materials and furnish the bases in return for U.S. military equipment, technical assistance, and financing for a Brazilian steel mill (located at Volta Redonda). This alliance made Brazil the United States' most conspicuous Latin American partner in the war. Furthermore, it set the precedent for American government support of basic industrialization in a Third World country.

Brazil's entry into the war had an important implication for politics at home. The decision to join the democracies was a blow to the authoritarians who had argued that democracy had no place in Brazil and had assumed Vargas agreed with them. Vargas and his generals, by calling that assumption into question, were setting the stage for a debate that would eventually end Vargas's dictatorship.

World War II and the Rise of U.S. Influence

As Brazil entered the war, a wave of American officials, both military and civilian, came to Brazil. Brazilian officers now cooperated closely with the U.S. Navy and Army Air Corps in waging anti-submarine warfare, a process that included supplying the Brazilians with American planes and ships, as well as land weapons. In turn, that meant the need for U.S. military maintenance personnel in

Brazil itself. By 1943, the Brazilians and Americans had built a network of modern military air and sea bases along the coast of northeast Brazil.

Along with the U.S. military offensive in Brazil came a cultural offensive. President Roosevelt appointed the multimillionaire Nelson Rockefeller to direct a new office to promote improved cultural relations with Latin America, with Brazil a prime target. Rockefeller's office recruited talent such as Orson Welles and Walt Disney to make films aimed at strengthening pro-U.S. opinion. Especially memorable was the cartoon ("Saludos Amigos") that sent Donald Duck to Latin America to meet his Spanish- and Portuguese-speaking cronies. The Brazilian was a parrot ("Zé Carioca") who delighted Brazilian audiences. Rockefeller's offensive also included visits by American writers and artists, who reinforced the U.S. cultural impact in Brazil.

Behind these activities lay longer-run U.S. objectives. One was increased U.S. economic penetration of Brazil. Although American investment in Brazil already exceeded British investment there, U.S. investors were anxious to make further inroads. In the area of mass culture, U.S. penetration had been steadily increasing since the First World War. Between 1928 and 1937, for example, 85 percent of the films shown in Brazil came from Hollywood. In advertising, U.S. firms were becoming dominant by the 1930s and the entire field was "Americanized." Wartime collaboration offered an excellent basis for the later U.S. economic offensive. U.S. aircraft came to dominate not only military but also civilian use. American industrial specifications and commercial measurements became more frequently used in Brazil. American brand names were becoming better known. And English was now the third most frequently spoken foreign language (after French and Italian).

Vargas's desire to identify Brazil with the Allied cause led him to offer three Brazilian army divisions to fight the Germans in the Mediterranean theater. Brazilian officers were enthusiastic about the idea. Vargas had two major purposes in insisting on a Brazilian military role. One was to dramatize Brazil's role as the only Latin American country to commit land forces under its own flag in the war (a Mexican air force unit fought in the Pacific and many Mexicans volunteered for service in the U.S. Army). The second was to touch Brazilian pride and give the public a patriotic reason to rally behind the government.

To emphasize that this was a national effort, Vargas wanted the troops recruited countrywide. He insisted that every state be represented, whatever the quality of the local recruits. The resulting force was highly heterogeneous, lacking common training and completely devoid of combat experience. The U.S. military command had also worried about the physical condition of these troops—doubts that proved justified when the Brazilians were able to furnish only one healthy division. Preparations in Brazil misfired even for the healthy troops. The commanders expected to be fighting in North Africa, so the troops were provided with summer uniforms. The Brazilian expeditionary force (Força Expeditionária Brasileira, or FEB) was assigned to operate with the U.S. Fifth

Army, however, which was driving against stubborn German defences in mountainous terrain north of Rome, just as a harsh winter was setting in. The Brazilians were thrown into battle without winter clothing to scale a precipice on which the Germans had commanding gun positions. Caught in murderous fire, they suffered heavy casualties and withdrew in disorder.

Though hardly surprising, given their troops' lack of combat experience and insufficient clothing, failure in their first combat engagement was extremely upsetting to the Brazilian commanders, who turned to the Americans for help and advice. The Brazilian troops went through rapid retraining and soon reentered battle, where they performed significantly better, helping to capture Monte Cassino, the historic monastery that marked a principal German position. The Brazilian combat record in Italy subsequently became a subject of bitter controversy. The official accounts stressed the very real Brazilian heroism after retraining, but the critics (including some Brazilian officers) stressed the early combat failure, which they unfairly blamed on incompetent commanders.

Brazil's combat involvement left a significant legacy. First, it furnished a basis for the country's claim to a major postwar role—a sentiment that resembled Brazil's similar hope upon emerging from World War I. This time, however, Brazil's military participation had been much greater and hopes were high that the political rewards would be commensurate. Second, sending the expeditionary force greatly increased the Brazilian army's prestige. As the only Latin Americans to fight in Europe, Brazilians could hold their head up among the Allies. Third, joint combat in Italy strengthened the ties between the U.S. and Brazilian militaries, even though Brazil remained very much the junior partner.

Brazil's economy had emerged from the Depression sooner than that of either the United States or England, a recovery that was sustained by the Second World War. (See exhibit 5-3.) As production rose, Brazil benefited from receiving war-related American technology and equipment. Brazil also received such items as railway rolling stock and trucks. Meanwhile, the disrupted shipping lanes had cut Brazilian consumers off from imports, forcing them to turn to Brazilian producers. A domestic paper industry was one of the beneficial results.

The war also greatly accelerated governmental centralization. The need to ration essentials, such as petroleum, put new power in the hands of the Vargas government. Allocation of most resources had to go through a national mobilization board, thereby bringing São Paulo industry under increased direction by the federal government.

A final economic effect of the war was a surge in inflationary demand as the general mobilization led to an overheated economy. This pent-up demand could not be met without imports (which were under wartime restrictions). In Rio, the cost of living between 1939 and 1945 almost doubled, and in

EXHIBIT 5-3

Gross Domestic Product 1925–1945 (indexed to 1929 = 100)

Year	Current Prices	Constant Prices (i.e., real growth)
1925	87.9	76.2
1928	102.3	98.9
1929	100.0	100.0
1930	83.6	97.9
1931	74.3	94.7
1933	88.8	107.6
1935	105.0	120.9
1937	136.4	141.7
1939	154.3	151.8
1941	188.8	157.7
1943	266.5	166.5
1945	411.1	184.8

Source: Raymond W. Goldsmith, *Brazil 1850–1984: Desinvolvimento Fincarceiro sob um Século de Inflação* (São Paulo, 1986), p. 147.

São Paulo it almost tripled, creating a significant problem for postwar economic policy.

Collapse of the Dictatorship at Home

When Vargas assumed dictatorial powers in 1937 and canceled the presidential election scheduled for 1938, he promised to hold presidential elections in 1943. It was his acknowledgment of Brazil's tradition of electoral democracy, even as he was snuffing it out. As the date neared, few expected Vargas to keep his promise. In 1943, Vargas announced that the wartime emergency would not permit the uncertainty of a presidential election and postponed the resumption of electoral politics "until after the war."

The anti-Vargistas, who doubted he ever intended to surrender power, grew increasingly preoccupied as the war neared its end. Every politically conscious Brazilian could see the contradiction: Brazil was fighting dictatorships yet itself had a dictatorial regime. In early 1945, all eyes centered on Vargas. Would he allow a free election and thereby put at risk his fifteen-year rule? In late February, his government issued a lengthy "constitutional law" that called for the popular election of a new president. The only eligibility requirement was to be a native-born Brazilian at least thirty-five years old. Vargas qualified on both counts.

Already a domestic opposition had appeared with the 1943 Manifesto of Mineiro leaders. Vargas's exiled opponents also began returning and in mid-1945 helped organize, along with Brazil-based Vargas opponents, a new party, the União Democrática Nacional (UDN). The UDN was dominated by the liberal constitutionalists who had fought Vargas since 1931. Their strongest support came from the middle and upper civilian classes and army officers. Interestingly enough, the UDN initially included leaders of the (still illegal) Communist Party, now enjoying prestige by its association with the hero Luiz Carlos Prestes and with the victorious Soviet Red Army. (The Communists withdrew from the coalition in June 1945, although numerous Socialists stayed in.) The UDN, suspicious of Vargas's motives, demanded that he resign. They were supported by state politicians who were maneuvering for position in a post-Vargas era.

Vargas maintained an ambiguous stand up to the last minute. He scheduled an election for October but declined to define his own role. As campaign preparations began, Vargas and his aides encouraged the creation of two more new parties. The first was the Partido Social Democrático (PSD) led by the Vargas-appointed political bosses of the leading states. It was preeminently a party of the "ins." The second was the Partido Trabalhista Brasileiro (PTB), intended as the political arm of the newly organized urban workers. Suddenly, another group materialized to further alarm Vargas's opponents: A movement called the "Queremistas" emerged with the slogan "Queremos Getúlio" ("We Want Getúlio"). They appeared to have support from the presidential palace as well as from labor union and Communist Party leaders. Again Vargas remained enigmatic, refusing to endorse or denounce the Queremistas. Such a refusal was tantamount, in the view of his opponents, to proof of his worst intentions.

The army generals in the Rio area—led by General Góes Monteiro, who was influenced by the UDN—shared the worry of the opposition. So did the U.S. ambassador, Adolph Berle, who suggested publicly (by praising "the solemn promise of free elections") that Vargas resign. U.S. Secretary of State Edward Stetinius also visited Brazil to plead for redemocratization. The suspicions of all parties were confirmed: President Vargas tried to instigate a nationalist reaction to Berle's intervention, but it was too late. The army command served Vargas with an ultimatum: Unless he resigned immediately, the army would besiege the palace, cutting off all water, power, and other supplies. Vargas decided he had no choice but to accept and cooperate in a bloodless coup. He resigned and returned to his ranch in Rio Grande do Sul.

Once again the generals had presided over a fundamental change in the constitutional structure of Brazil. It was a script familiar from 1930, 1935, and 1937. They had been motivated in part by wishing to head off a Perón-type regime in Brazil. Only weeks earlier, Argentina's General Juan Perón had been freed from military-imposed house arrest and restored to power as the urban workers cheered. Perón's worker mobilization was a clear threat to the Argentine army and to the established social order. The Brazilian generals wanted to foreclose any such threat at home.

6

Returning to Democracy, for a While

The 1945 Election and the Dutra Period

When the military sent Vargas back to his ranch, they ensured that electoral democracy returned to Brazil. The presidential election was held as scheduled in December 1945, with six million votes cast. This was three times as many as voted in 1930—the last presidential election—making the Brazil of 1945 a far more national polity than the oligarchy that had collapsed in 1930. In the 1945 election, party labels had some meaning in the large cities. But in the countryside and small towns, political allegiances (with party labels) still went to one or another local political clan whose origins went back at least to the Old Republic, if not the Empire.

The presidential election of 1945 was primarily a contest between two military officers. It was won by General Eúrico Gaspar Dutra, who ran on the PSD (Partido Social Democrático) ticket—a party composed of state party bosses and some São Paulo businessmen. He had been war minister from 1936 to 1945, serving as a pillar of Vargas's authoritarian Estado Nôvo. Now he had the support of the many state bosses wanting to preserve their influence under the new democratic regime. His chief opponent was air force brigadier Eduardo Gomes, who ran on the UDN (União Democrática Nacional) ticket. Gomes, a survivor of the Fort Copacabana revolt of 1922, a hero in the defense against the 1935 Communist revolt in Rio, a prominent opponent of the coup of 1937, and the top officer in the Brazilian air force (established in 1942), was generally recognized to be an upright, highly moral soldier. His reputation appealed to the relatively small middle- and upper-class electorate but failed to reach other voters in sufficient numbers to win.

EXHIBIT 6-1

Popular Vote for President, 1945

Candidate	Vote
Eúrico Dutra (PSD)	3,251,507
Eduardo Gomes (UDN)	2,039,341
Yeddo Fiúza (PCB)	569,818

Source: Walter Costa Porto, *O Voto no Brasil* (Brasília, 1989), p. 262.

The major surprise of the 1945 election was the support enjoyed by the Communist Party candidate for president, Yeddo Fiúza, who received almost 10 percent of the vote (exhibit 6-1). The Communists' success is in good part explained by strong worker discontent over the rapid inflation created by World War II. Continuing industrialization, though patchy, had enlarged the working class and the Communist Party had worked hard to recruit within it. The voters chose a new Congress, which, in turn, wrote a new Constitution. Debates over how the new Constitution (Brazil's fifth) should be shaped were dominated by demands to restore power to the states and municipalities. Orator after orator identified strong central government with dictatorship, in a concerted effort by the elite to legitimize devolution of power. The Constitution of 1946 reflected this objective. It retained the position of president as head of the national government but restored the power of the purse to Congress. This had the result of returning considerable power to the state political machines, although less than they had enjoyed under the Old Republic.

Although the electoral base in 1945 was a great deal larger than it had been in 1930, socioeconomically Brazil was, in the parlance of the day, still a "backward" country. Its industry was limited to a few large cities. Chronic disease was widespread and regular medical care nonexistent for most of the population. Overall life expectancy was forty-six years, with life expectancy in the Northeast under forty years. The economy continued to depend on coffee exports.

Even so, Brazil appeared to enjoy an enviable economic situation in 1945, in good part because it had accumulated significant foreign exchange reserves from war-imposed import restrictions. But in 1946–47, a flood of imported consumer goods, along with the buying up of foreign-owned public utilities, soaked up these reserves. Large-scale worker strikes in São Paulo in 1947 aggravated the situation, alarming both the Dutra government and the São Paulo economic establishment. In the face of the deteriorating economic situation, which led to a severe foreign exchange shortage in 1948, the Dutra government relied on the traditional emphasis on export promotion—greater promotion of coffee sales combined with import controls. There was no serious talk about promoting industrialization.

Reacting to the deteriorating political situation, the Dutra government remembered, and repeated, Vargas's warnings of the 1930s. They depicted the strikers as tools of Moscow, which (not coincidentally) helped justify the almost universal rejection by employers of wage demands by their workers. The growing confrontation between government and business on the one hand and the workers on the other looked like a rerun of the polarization that had led to Vargas's crackdown on the Communists and most of the left in 1935. Sure enough, the Dutra government resorted to political repression in 1947, the domestic imperatives for which were greatly reinforced by pressure from the United States.

By the late 1940s, the U.S. national security establishment was committed to fighting the Soviet threat everywhere. This included an offensive by the State Department and the Pentagon to convince Latin American governments to break diplomatic relations with the Soviet Union and to repress local Communist Parties. In 1947, the Dutra government broke off relations with the Soviet Union and pushed the Supreme Electoral Court to outlaw the Communist Party. The labor union leadership and the federal bureaucracy were systematically purged of Communists and militant leftists. In January 1948, the Congress expelled its fourteen Communist deputies and one senator. The shadow of the Estado Nôvo extended over a newly democratic Brazil.

The chief beneficiary of the PCB's suppression was the PTB (Partido Trabalhista Brasileiro, or the Brazilian Labor Party), which now had more room to recruit among workers. The PTB was the third major party (along with the UDN and the PDS) founded in 1945. Its patron was Vargas, who hoped to create a Brazilian version of the European Social Democratic parties. The Communist Party, per se, never regained the electoral influence it had during the 1945–47 period, although the PTB leaders developed informal pacts with the Communists, many of whom subsequently operated under PTB electoral cover. Communism as an ideology remained a powerful force among intellectuals and labor unions, however, for the next twenty-five years.

Vargas Returns

As Brazil's participation in the Second World War continued, Vargas had worked on finding a new rationale for trying to keep power. Beginning in 1943, he and his technocrats had begun to stake out a new political position, the keynote of which was an appeal to the urban working class. Its immediate application was an expansion of the labor union system, where the federal government predominated in managing relations between employers and workers. Vargas left the details to his labor minister, Marcondes Filho, who supervised the codification of the labor laws in 1943 and worked to strengthen government ties with the few leading unions. That meant using patronage to build a political following among the union leaders. A similar strategy was being followed in

Argentina, albeit with a heavier hand, by Colonel Juan Perón, who from 1943 to 1945 was the labor minister in an Argentine military government.

The creation of the PTB in 1945 was an extension of this strategy of cultivating union leadership. Vargas saw this party as the electoral arm of his populist strategy. In the last two years of his dictatorship, he was constructing a direct appeal to urban workers. This effort was cut short in October 1945, when fear of his intentions led to his ouster, but Vargas continued to elaborate his populist strategy in the years of the Dutra presidency. He had been elected in December 1945 as a senator from both Rio Grande do Sul and São Paulo, as well as deputy from seven states. Although he took up his Senate seat only briefly, withdrawing as soon as he had secured a public position from which to spread his message, he made many speeches after 1946 criticizing the government for failing the working class.

From Oligarch to Populist

Vargas worked hard to maintain his links to the traditional power sectors. Many state political bosses now in power had benefited from his earlier rule, and the São Paulo industrialists owed Vargas much for the business directed their way by his war effort. Finally, as a *fazendeiro* in Rio Grande do Sul, Vargas had the sympathy of fellow landholders, who were grateful he had never threatened the existing system of land tenure. For them, his newly minted populism was purely for urban consumption and was thus a strategy with which they could happily live.

While Vargas worked to transform his image from dictator to democratic politician, his longtime opponents did everything possible to sabotage that effort. The leading São Paulo newspaper (*O Estado de S. Paulo*), for example, never referred to Vargas by name, but only as the "ex-dictator." They had a ready audience. Vargas, never notably popular in São Paulo, still had the image of the Machiavellian figure who had betrayed democracy in 1937. He was also hated by some state political bosses, who had lost their access to federal power during his dictatorship. Nevertheless, Vargas was relatively successful in shedding the dictator image. By nature a genial personality, he played on the well-known Brazilian inclination to let bygones be bygones in politics.

Political divisions after Dutra's election played into Vargas's hands. The liberal constitutionalists, best represented by the UDN, expected to be the prime beneficiaries of Vargas's overthrow in 1945. They were bitterly disappointed when they lost the 1945 presidential election to General Dutra, the candidate supported by Vargas. They did win respectable representation in Congress, however (29 percent in the Chamber of Deputies, as against 53 percent for the PSD), where they could continue preaching the doctrines of traditional liberalism and prepare for the 1950 presidential election.

As for the left, it had regrouped after the Dutra government outlawed the Communist Party and purged the unions in 1947. The PTB was left as the principal national party with appeal to the urban worker, although that appeal sometimes failed, as in São Paulo, where the PTB remained weak. Thus the government's anti-Communist move of 1947 played into the hands of the populist electoral strategy Vargas had been elaborating since 1945.

By 1949, the international lines of conflict in the Cold War were drawn, with the U.S. government pressuring Brazil, along with the rest of Latin America, to join the United States in confronting the Soviet-led bloc. The intelligence agencies of both the United States and the Soviet Union (and later Fidelista Cuba) gave both financial and training assistance to their favored Brazilian organizations, often in clandestine circumstances. The Communist Party received funds and logistical support from Moscow. A wide range of Brazilian politicians and organizations got money and organizational help from Washington (via the CIA and other agencies). The Brazilian military, for one, readily absorbed U.S. doctrines through such institutions as its Higher War College (Escola Superior de Guerra), created in 1949 with U.S. help and blessing. With the outbreak of the Korean War, the U.S. government pressed Brazil strongly to send combat troops to fight alongside the United States. (The Vargas government successfully resisted.)

The political center was poorly defined in the Dutra years. It was most often identified with the PSD, which represented a wide social spectrum, including landowners, industrialists, and parts of the small middle class. The PSD was the least overtly ideological of the major parties and, therefore, in the best position to bargain.

With the political lines so fluid in 1949, predictions about future trends were especially dangerous. Public opinion research had hardly begun in Brazil (the first poll by IBOPE, the pioneer firm, was in 1945), and voting patterns were too recent to furnish a basis for prognostication. It was in the context of this fluid situation that voters saw Vargas emerging from his "exile" in a new and democratic incarnation.

Vargas's carefully laid groundwork to run for the presidency in 1950 included more than establishing himself as a populist. He also paid attention to the pragmatic task of getting the support of powerful political groups. First, he got assurances that the military would not veto his candidacy or his taking office should he win. This assurance was facilitated by General Góes Monteiro, Vargas's onetime collaborator during the Estado Nôvo and a still influential figure among the generals. Second, Vargas enlisted the support of three key political forces that could form a winning coalition. One was Adhemar de Barros, governor of São Paulo and an early proponent of the populist style in politics (meaning an appeal to urban voters based on public works, social welfare benefits, and an efficient voting machine). Adhemar wanted to run for president but was willing to back Vargas now in return for Vargas's later support of his own bid. Another was the PSD, which had its own candidate, but for which Vargas was able to split the support by wooing its regional chieftains, especially in Minais Gerais. The PTB, which was a growing force in selected states, rounded out the list.

The vote showed the extent of Vargas's skill. In a multiple field of candidates he received 48.7 percent, nearly an absolute majority. His chief opponent once again was Eduardo Gomes of the UDN, who received only 29.7 percent, while Christiano Machado of the PSD received 21.5 percent. Gomes, the loser in the 1945 presidential election, seemed to have learned little about Brazil's move toward change. During the campaign he actually went so far as to advocate repeal of the minimum wage law. By contrast, Vargas attacked the Dutra government for having neglected industrialization. In Rio, where the left was comparatively strong, he sounded a particularly populist note: "If I am elected on October 3rd, as I take office the people will climb the steps of Catete [the presidential palace] with me. And they will remain with me in power."

Vargas's Legislative Program Runs into Trouble

Once back in power, Vargas broke definitively with the liberal economic policies partially reinstated by the Dutra government. Implicit was his assumption that Brazil would need to promote industrialization if it were to overcome the balance-of-payments bottleneck that had become only too obvious during the Dutra years. An able team of young technocrats soon began to develop

Getúlio Vargas, back in power in 1951 as a democratically elected president, presenting the prize for best costume at the Rio Carnival. Vargas's interest in and promotion of popular culture was already evident in his 1937–45 dictatorship. (Popperfoto/Getty Images)

a plan for national economic development. The first step was creation of the National Bank for Economic Development in 1952. Here Vargas and his technocrats were drawing on the work of the Joint U.S.-Brazil Commission on Economic Development (1951–53), which, composed of technical experts from both countries, had produced an analysis of Brazil's primary economic needs. Since energy supplies were perennially inadequate to support industrialization (government concern on this count went back to 1938), the government proposed to create state enterprises in oil and electricity. Such measures violated the liberal prejudice against state intervention in the economy and provoked heavy criticism from UDN politicians and orthodox economists. The president defended his measures by invoking patriotism, nationalism, and realism in the face of the changing world economy—placing a heavy bet that his nationalist appeal would overcome the elite consensus favoring economic liberalism.

Vargas's proposal for a state enterprise in petroleum became the most controversial measure of his new presidency. The government's original proposal called for a mixed public-private corporation, called Petrobrás, with a de facto state monopoly over the central operations. That proposal was sent to Congress in 1951, unleashing a two-year national debate. On the right, supported by U.S. opposition to the proposal, spokesmen attacked it as dangerously interventionist. On the left, the Communist Party (acting partly through surrogates) demanded a full state monopoly. They exploited the public's distrust of international oil companies and charged that government supporters were on foreign payrolls. The U.S. government's opposition to Petrobrás only reinforced the fury of the left. Vargas was caught in the middle.

The danger in this confrontation was compounded by the involvement of the army officer corps. Its nationalist wing passionately supported Vargas's proposal for strategic purposes. They wanted Brazil to develop its own oil supply so it could be self-sufficient in time of war. But the other military faction, the anticommunists, attacked the proposal as collectivist state intervention that would move Brazil toward the Communist camp. The disagreement within the military was ominous for Vargas, who knew that to remain in power he had to retain the undivided support of the top officers.

The fight over Petrobrás did not turn out as Vargas had hoped. The UDN, intending to outflank and embarrass Vargas, switched position and announced in favor of a total state monopoly. By such a reversal they hoped to steal the nationalist flag from Vargas. Congress passed this more extreme version, ruling out the private participation provided for in the government proposal. This outcome saddled Vargas with a more statist law than he had wanted. It also meant that he had lost control over the legislative process.

As the Vargas government devised its new economic strategy, it also faced serious trade problems. World coffee prices had declined sharply, thereby shrinking Brazil's foreign exchange earnings. The result was a growing balance-of-payments deficit (see exhibit 6-2), which the International Monetary Fund

EXHIBIT 6-2

Brazil's Balance of Payments, 1950–1954—Inflow Minus Outflow (US$ millions)

	Commercial Balance(a)	Net Services	Transfers	Net Capital	Errors & Omissions	Surplus (+) or Deficit (−)
1950	425	−283	−2	−65	−23	52
1951	68	−469	−2	−11	123	−291
1952	−266	−336	−2	35	−26	−615
1953	424	−355	−14	59	−98	16
1954	148	−338	−5	−18	10	−203

(a) Exports minus imports.
Source: IBGE, *Estatísticas Históricas do Brasil*, 2nd ed. (Rio de Janeiro, 1990), pp. 581–85.

(IMF) blamed on Brazil's allegedly inflationary domestic policies. In 1953, under pressure from the IMF and the U.S. government, Brazil launched a stabilization program to correct the balance-of-payments deficit. Vargas turned to his longtime political ally Oswaldo Aranha, who was named minister of finance, to carry out the program. Stabilization was a bitter pill for Vargas to swallow for two reasons. First, it would preclude any economic growth for the rest of his term. Second, it was bound to arouse popular opposition since it involved restricting credit and holding down wages.

Suicide

As 1954 began, events were closing in on Vargas. Economic crisis had made his government more vulnerable politically. His enemies, especially in the UDN and military, smelled weakness. The bitter debate over Petrobrás had inflamed ideological opinion in Brazil and aroused military suspicions about Vargas's intentions. A campaign to drive Vargas from office began. It was led by Carlos Lacerda, a venomous journalist and leading orator as a UDN politician, who now devoted his formidable talents to vilifying the president. Lacerda controlled a newspaper (*A Tribuna da Imprensa*) that carried his message on a daily basis. Lacerda's more moderate UDN colleagues (who could not bring themselves to adopt his language) were exhilarated by his attacks and began to see him as a powerful weapon against a president whose return to power they had never accepted.

Vargas's supporters, especially among the PTB, were on the defensive because Vargas had been reelected in 1950 by a loose coalition ranging across the political spectrum. His former supporters among the wealthy now saw him as dispensable, and his support on the left was too weak to neutralize the current scale of attacks. This political impasse reflected the inherent limitation of the populist political strategy Vargas had increasingly adopted since 1953. Populism, in the form of wage hikes, nationalist economic initiatives, and patronage for the faithful, had not created a political base that could withstand an onslaught of civilian conservatives and a military looking for reasons to mount a coup. The same lesson would be learned by Argentine President Juan Perón in 1955 and by Brazilian President João Goulart in 1964.

Vargas, who had wavered between orthodox and nationalist measures, now swung decisively toward nationalism. The first indicator was wage policy. Vargas's labor minister was a young PTB politician from Vargas's local region in Rio Grande do Sul, João Goulart (the man who would be Brazil's president from 1961 until his own ouster by the military in 1964). Goulart was a Vargas protégé. On the minimum wage, which had not changed since 1951, Goulart recommended a 100 percent increase, infuriating the right, especially the military. This action was in part a response to the massive industrial strikes (such as the "Strike of the 300,000") which had shaken São Paulo in 1953. Put in the proper perspective, Goulart's recommendation was not patently absurd. Such an increase would have represented a real raise (i.e., more than compensated for inflation) over the 1951 level but would have left the minimum wage still far short of many prevailing industrial wage rates. Furthermore, the minimum wage varied widely by region, with São Paulo levels considerably higher than those in the Northeast. Yet Goulart had become a political liability and saw he had to resign.

Vargas accepted Goulart's resignation, leading observers to expect the president to settle on a lower increase. On May 1st, however, he announced as a fait accompli exactly what Goulart had recommended: an increase of 100 percent. This act alarmed employers and confirmed military suspicions that Vargas was plotting a thoroughgoing radical populist strategy. Many employers refused to honor the wage decree, even though it had been legitimated by the Federal Supreme Court. The result was a wave of strikes and strike threats across the country. Once again the UDN charged that the president had no commitment to maintaining "order."

The second indicator of Vargas's political swing was a possible organization of rural labor unions. The Estado Nôvo labor laws had never been extended to the countryside, thereby maintaining Vargas's strategy of avoiding any threat to landowners. In February, however, Goulart had proposed, along with the minimum wage increase, regulations to recognize rural labor unions, thereby threatening to expand the Vargas populist strategy to the rural sector.

For Vargas, this strategy came too late. The final chapter of his presidency began in June 1954 with a UDN attempt to remove Vargas by constitutional means. It was decisively defeated when the Chamber of Deputies rejected an impeachment motion by 136 to 35. The UDN would have to resort to other means. The weapon at hand was Carlos Lacerda, who was also a candidate in the October congressional elections, in which his principal opponent was Getúlio's son Lutero. (Lacerda won.) By early August of 1954, Lacerda's campaign attacking Vargas had seized the imagination of the Brazilian public. Among the more sensational (and utterly unsubstantiated) charges was the claim that Vargas had secretly negotiated an alliance with Argentina's Juan Perón, presumably to fortify a "syndicalist republic" in each country. It was the kind of face-off even the politically uninitiated could understand. Furthermore, Vargas had conspicuously failed to create an effective public relations capacity to counter his critics. Those around Vargas were alarmed by the effects of the attacks on the president, who became withdrawn and depressed. The faithful tried to fight back.

One of Vargas's most faithful followers was Gregório Fortunato, the president's Afro-Brazilian bodyguard and chauffeur. As he listened to the voices of alarm in the palace about Vargas's plight, he decided to act—contacting a professional gunman and instructing him to eliminate Lacerda.

The would-be assassin stalked Lacerda in front of his apartment near Copacabana Beach and fired at him from across the street. The bullets killed an air force major, Rubens Vaz, who was acting as Lacerda's bodyguard, but only wounded Lacerda in the foot. (His detractors thought it should have been in the mouth.) The gunman had done the ultimate disservice to Vargas and his chauffeur. Lacerda continued his attacks, now even more dramatic from his hospital bed, and the air force officer corps created a board of inquiry to investigate their fellow officer's assassination. It was not difficult to trace the killer to the presidential palace. Vargas's opponents were now able to accuse the president of harboring an accomplice to murder.

Vargas probably did not know of Fortunato's plot to kill Lacerda, but he certainly knew his palace was out of control. He was shaken by the revelation that Samuel Wainer, his journalist friend and key supporter (as editor of the pro-government daily *Última Hora*), had gotten sweetheart loans from the Bank of Brazil. This confirmation of corruption around the president led Vargas to remark "I feel I am standing in a sea of mud."

Vargas's days as president were clearly numbered. If he did not resign, a military coup was inevitable. Yet if he did resign, he would abandon his long-cherished image of himself as a leader single-mindedly devoted to the welfare of the poor. He began to describe himself as a martyr opposed by powerful and selfish forces, both domestic and foreign.

Vargas's advisers and his cabinet were divided over how he should react. Some wanted him to resist, if necessary with arms. Others called the situation hopeless and warned that the president's safety was in doubt if he did not promptly resign. On August 24th, Vargas held a lengthy cabinet meeting in the Catete presidential palace to discuss his next move. He said nothing about what he intended to do, but his closest advisers were troubled by his mood. They had more reason to be troubled than they realized. What they did not know was that Vargas had talked of suicide in his diary—the existence of which was not revealed until many years later—as early as 1930.

The president left the meeting, retired to his Catete palace bedroom, reached for a revolver, and fired once into his heart. The sound reverberated through the palace. His longtime ally, Oswaldo Aranha, rushed into the bedroom and burst into tears.

The political climate was transformed. Before the suicide, an atmosphere of hostility had been aimed at the president; now, a wave of outrage was aimed at his tormentors. The streets filled with pro-Vargas demonstrators who attacked the offices of the conservative newspaper *O Globo*. Lacerda went from hero to hunted man. He soon left Brazil for an extended exile.

By his suicide, Vargas had turned the tables on his enemies in the UDN and the military. He had neutralized what they had planned to be a smashing political victory. They wanted not only his removal but also the reversal of his policies and the displacement of his political network. Their agenda was now impossible, given the state of public opinion. Vargas may have been dead, but his influence was very much alive.

A brief socioeconomic profile of Brazil around this period is a useful context for interpreting the political history of the ten years following Vargas's suicide.

Population Growth, Regional Disequilibria, and Migration

The Brazil of the late 1940s and 1950s was in the midst of a population explosion. The long-standing public health campaigns against epidemic disease had begun to pay off. Brazil's fertility rate (at over six children per mother) was among the highest in the world. This, combined with plunging mortality rates (cut by two-thirds between 1940 and 1960), produced population growth rates that put a great burden on Brazil's economy. Schools, hospitals, and clinics were all inadequate.

The post–World War II years also saw continuing economic divergence among Brazil's regions. São Paulo's share of national industry had risen from 36 percent in 1940 to 47 percent in 1950, to 54 percent in 1960. The largest losers from this concentration of new industry were the Northeast, which fell from 12 percent to 8 percent, and Rio de Janeiro, which went from 27 percent to 17 percent. The concentration in São Paulo was hardly surprising, since it resulted from the same economies of scale that have produced similar patterns in every industrializing country.

The fact that São Paulo was producing about half of Brazil's GDP and more than half of its federal revenues led politicians from the poorer areas to attack São Paulo as exploiting the rest of Brazil—attacks that had ample precedent in Brazilian political tradition. Politicians from the Northeast, in particular, argued that their region had become a virtual colony of São Paulo, attacking São Paulo's industrial products as overpriced and leading to unfair "terms of trade" between the regions. This argument was given its most sophisticated form by a brilliant economist from the Northeast, Celso Furtado, as in his seminal book *The Economic Growth of Brazil* (first Brazilian edition in 1959).

In essence, the northeasterners were appealing to the conscience of the ˷ in the South, a case that was strengthened by a devastating drought that struck the Northeast in 1958.

Other lagging regions got far less attention than the Northeast. The most obvious was the Amazon Basin, where Brazilian settlement was still extremely thin. Another was the far west, the Campo Cerrado, where fertile land was cheap but often inaccessible. The truth was that the Brazilians were still largely following the pattern of their Portuguese ancestors—in the quote cited earlier in the book "clinging to the coast like crabs."

As already discussed, employers in the Old Republic, especially in the center-south, had concentrated on looking for new workers among immigrants from other countries. When large-scale in-migration from abroad declined after World War I, however, employers looked more seriously for workers from other parts of Brazil. This flow, unlike the earlier flow from Europe, was not organized or subsidized by the employers; rather, it was a spontaneous process of individual Brazilians and their families responding to economic signals across the country.

Although there are no official statistics on internal migration, estimates from census data and population growth rates indicate the trends. In the years from 1940 to 1950, the largest movement was out of Minas Gerais and into Rio, São Paulo, and Paraná. In subsequent years, there was also significant migration from the Northeast to São Paulo.

Such migration had several effects. First, it deprived the sending states of many enterprising and talented citizens. Second, it fed a pool of surplus labor that helped to keep wages down and thus reduce potential union militancy in the industrial cities. Third, it reinforced the national character of Brazil's culture. In-migrants from other parts of Brazil brought with them their music, folklore, cuisine, and style of life. This influx and its resulting human contact helped to bridge regional differences (although it also produced a backlash, as in the Paulistas' frequent scorn for northeasterners). Many street corners and *praças* (squares) in São Paulo and Rio, for example, became known for their Sunday night congregations of migrants from distant states. Finally, as the migration of Brazilians within the country increasingly replaced the recruitment of foreigners, Brazilian society would henceforth be made up primarily of native-born Brazilians. For better or worse, the era of hoping for redemption from Europe was now over.

It was during the immediate post–World War II period that Brazil began to see the emergence of the vast cities that would characterize urban life from then on. Brazil's urbanization differed, however, from that of Argentina, Chile, Mexico, or Venezuela. Those countries all had a single dominant metropolis, the capital. In Brazil, the official capital of Rio de Janeiro had to share dominance with São Paulo. Brazil was, therefore, saved from focusing the vast majority of its attention on a single city.

Brazil's rapid urban growth, as elsewhere in Latin America, has been criticized for having attracted huge populations that concentrated in the informal sector because the cities lacked the formal sector jobs to support their
populations. The urbanization process was indeed chaotic. In-migrants, finding no housing, swelled the shantytowns, sprawling developments (called *favelas*) that typically appeared on the city edges and often became more populous
than the formal city. Although the outside world saw a relatively favorable picture (for example, in the film *Black Orpheus*, which romanticized *favela* life in
Rio de Janeiro), the growing *favelas* frightened the urban elite within Brazil.
They were, in the eyes of the well-to-do, the "dangerous classes," despite the fact
that the thousands of domestic servants serving peacefully in the homes of the
upper classes came from these very ranks.

Yet it should be remembered that such urban growth had its logic. The
rural masses chose to move to the city because they perceived their economic
opportunities to be better there and knew they could move back to the countryside if city conditions became bad enough. Their underemployment in
the urban economy simply reflected the labor force stratification implicit in
the countryside from which they came. These "marginal" inhabitants strove
to improve their life by upgrading their shacks or by moving to better housing. This mobility within the marginal population was integral to economic

Favelas in the Catumbi district of Rio de Janeiro. These
slum communities of self-constructed shacks are made
from stolen building materials, nestled in a labyrinth of
illegal electrical connections. They were originally spawned
during Rio's massive urban rebuilding as it "civilized itself"
during the early 1900s. (© Paul Almasy/CORBIS)

growth. The marginal urban dwellers were nonetheless viewed with wariness by the middle and upper classes.

Despite the rapid growth of cities, more than half of all Brazilians in the 1950s still lived in the countryside. Most rural dwellers had little knowledge of their government. Medical care and schools were usually nonexistent. People communicated by word of mouth. The one regular link to the outside world was a radio. Between 1945 and 1960, for example, the number of radio stations in Brazil increased from less than one hundred to more than eight hundred. Travel to the nearest town was done on foot or horseback. Access to buses, trucks, or automobiles was difficult and expensive.

But rural Brazil was far from homogeneous. Alongside a large subsistence sector consisting of farmers cultivating their own small plots or working as share-croppers (with their numerous children working in the field) was large-scale agriculture. Coffee plantations in São Paulo and Paraná, sugar plantations in Pernambuco and Alagoas, and wheat farms in Rio Grande do Sul were worked by wage laborers. And there were some higher productivity elements.

One was the network of dynamic Japanese truck-farming colonies in São Paulo, Paraná, and Pará. Organizing large cooperatives, they pooled their skills to become the largest food supplier to the city of São Paulo. Another exception was the network of settlements by German (along with Ukrainian and Polish) descendants in Santa Catarina and Rio Grande do Sul. These farmers mastered medium-scale commercial farming and also provided the public services (especially education) that most of rural Brazil lacked.

Rural Brazil also produced its own cultures. There was a distinctive music and folklore (including humor) for each region. The Northeast become famous for its tales of banditry, the best-known heroes of which were Lampião and his companion Maria Bonita. Their exploits became celebrated in poetry, song, and film. In southern Brazil, the familiar figure was the *caipira*, or backwoodsman, who was the subject of endless folklore, such as observed in the children's festivals on St. John's day every June. This cultural construction from the countryside became an integral part of Brazilian national culture.

Quantitative indicators of Brazil's highly stratified society during this period are sparse. Income distribution data were not yet gathered in Brazil, and wealth data were also nonexistent. Aggregate data for such items as infant mortality and life expectancy are available, but there is no breakdown by income. The qualitative picture is clear, however.

The widest social differences were found in the countryside, where a landowner's or merchant's income was many times that of a subsistence farmer, and those at the bottom had virtually no hope of mobility.

Urban areas were also strictly stratified, although the divergence between top and bottom was slightly less. In the city, at least the chances for mobility through public education, though small, were higher. At the bottom were the urban workers in the informal market. They had no fixed employment and survived through ad hoc jobs, often as street sellers. One up from the bottom of the scale came the manual workers, such as bus drivers, janitors, factory workers, and mechanics. They fell below the middle classes, not only in pay but also in education. The small middle class consisted of the professions and the government bureaucracy. These were nonmanual workers with at least a secondary education, and attuned to urban values. Above them were the high-income earners and major wealth holders. They held the lucrative positions in commerce, law, industry, and finance, usually coming from families with extensive links to rural landholding.

This social hierarchy retained much of the flavor of Brazil's colonial era. Those at the top were treated with great deference by those below. The parallel with the power of the slave-master relationship comes to mind. The way to survive was to find a powerful *patrão* (patron) to act as one's protector. Collective action was not a rational option within this world. Rather, the premium was on promoting one's individual fortunes and those of one's family. The devices used reflected the social system. Brazilians relied on such institutions as the extended family (even a distant relative might prove a valuable contact), the network of friends (the *panelinha*), and co-godfatherhood or godmotherhood (*compadresco*).

The political implications of this social ethos were far-reaching. It favored strong leaders, personalistic politics, and minimal collective action. As a cultural atmosphere, it was unfriendly to both the merit system of hiring and promotion and to the creation of loyalties to parties or movements.

A New President, Juscelino Kubitschek, Elected

The public's reaction to Vargas's suicide robbed his opponents of their long-awaited triumph. They could not carry out their plans to disrupt the government. A presidential election was scheduled for 1955, but until then, the federal government was run by caretaker regimes (headed by Presidents Café Filho and Nereu Ramos). They lacked authority to make significant changes, however, even though inflation continued to increase and the balance-of-payments deficit failed to improve. Little foreign capital came into the country, exacerbating the effects of Brazil's low domestic savings rate. This boded ill for future growth. In 1955, however, new hope for economic development arrived in the form of Juscelino Kubitschek, who opted for growth with a vengeance as soon as he became president.

Kubitschek was a typical product of the Vargas political system. He had left his initial profession of physician to rise through the PSD party in Minas Gerais, having been mayor of the capital city of Belo Horizonte and governor of the state. His family name was Oliveira, but for political purposes he chose to use the Czechoslovakian name of an ancestor because he thought it would make him stand out among the field of Brazilian politicians. He was an ebullient politician, well used to the wheeling and dealing demanded in Brazil's wide-open politics. He won the presidency by successfully splitting his opposition, the UDN candidate General Juarez Távora, the PSD candidate Christiano Machado, and the São Paulo populist Adhemar de Barros, who ran under the banner of the Partido Social Progressista (PSP). Kubitschek thus assumed the presidency with only 36 percent of the vote, which contrasted with Vargas's 49 percent in 1950 and Dutra's 55 percent in 1945. Aside from being a minority president, he was also vulnerable vis-à-vis the military because of his Vargas connections and because his vice presidential running mate was João Goulart, arch enemy of the UDN and the conservative military. His presidency began on an ominous note. A group of air force officers stationed in Amazônia attempted a revolt against the new government in January 1956. The revolt was quashed, but it showed the new president would have little margin for error in dealing with the anti-Vargas military.

Political Strategy

Kubitschek's thin political base required him to maneuver carefully to maintain congressional support. The left painted him as the lackey of imperialism, selling Brazil out for short-term political gain. The right accused him of trying to curry favor with militant labor, giving as proof the large 1958 boost in the minimum wage (set at its highest real level since 1945). His own party, the PSD, avoided overt ideology but had uneven power across the country. Kubitschek's method of solidifying support was to make major concessions to both ends of the political spectrum.

An example of his efforts to placate the political left was his reaction to pressure from northeastern politicians, who complained that the South region was gaining unduly from industrialization, leaving the populous low-income Northeast even further behind. To quiet this complaint, Kubitschek accepted a proposal for a new federal authority, SUDENE (Superintendência para o Desenvolvimento do Nordeste)—based on a document ("Operation Northeast") by Celso Furtado—to promote northeastern economic development. A key device was a tax-forgiveness scheme to attract new industry or induce established industry to move from more developed regions. Significantly, land reform was ignored. The U.S. government, alarmed over the growth of peasant leagues in the area, also pledged to help in the transfer of technology and capital. An example of placating the right was how Kubitschek dealt with the military. Since he knew he was ultra-vulnerable on this front, he decided to spend heavily on new military equipment. The navy wanted an aircraft carrier, and so the government purchased an outmoded carrier from Britain and had it refitted in Holland.

He was successful enough in protecting his government from attacks by both left and right to complete his term and pass the presidency to a duly elected civilian successor. His economic strategy played an important role in that success. Whether his economic program was worth its cost (especially the building of Brasília) is a question that has been debated ever since.

The Economic Development Program

The first step Kubitschek and his technocrats took was to draw up a *Programa de Metas* ("Program of Goals"), a set of targets for increased production by sector. The objective was to bring together the state and the private sector in a high-growth strategy whose aim was to accelerate industrialization and construction of the infrastructure necessary to sustain it.

In ideological terms, the Kubitschek economic strategy was centrist. It included heavy public investment but also many incentives for private investment. In the public sphere, the National Bank for Economic Development was to channel funds to major infrastructure projects. In the private sphere, for example, a government commission solicited bids for the creation of a national automobile industry under favorable foreign exchange terms. Kubitschek and his advisers hoped to finesse the bitter ideological divisions that had helped wreck the Vargas government by providing benefits for everyone.

Kubitschek's economic strategy was very successful in reaching its primary objective of rapid economic development and industrialization. Virtually all the goals in the Programa de Metas were met. By 1961, when Kubitschek left office, Brazil had an integrated motor vehicle industry (created virtually from scratch) and was on the way to creating the many subsidiary industries vital to vehicle production. There were also impressive gains in electricity generation and road building.

In addition to the direct economic advances, there were more indirect political benefits from Kubitschek's economic strategy. His enthusiastic political style and personality reinforced the traditional Brazilian sense of optimism. Kubitschek stressed solutions rather than problems. He radiated confidence in the country and its capacity to join the industrial world. Even Brazil's national soccer team cooperated by winning its first world championship in Sweden in July 1958. The team's star was Pelé, who rapidly became known as the world's greatest player. The post-victory Brazilian mood was captured by Nelson Rodrigues, the playwright and sports writer, who observed that the myth of "Brazilian sadness" was on the run because "With this world title...sadness is a bad joke."

The ultimate example of Kubitschek's style was the building of Brasília. The idea of a new capital that would open up the interior had long been discussed, but few thought it would ever be built. The Constitution of 1891 had stipulated its construction, and a site had been selected as early as 1893. It was located in the state of Goiás, 630 miles from Rio de Janeiro and 700 miles from São Paulo. The spot was 3,800 feet above sea level and situated in a semiarid highland plain (*not* jungle, as foreign journalists often fantasize). During his presidential campaign, Kubitschek promised to build this new capital, and he meant it.

Once in office, he pushed the project hard, calling in the distinguished Brazilian architect Oscar Niemeyer and Lúcio Costa, a well-known Brazilian city planner. Both were profoundly influenced by French architects, especially Le Corbusier. With its futuristic architecture and ambitious urban planning, Brasília was to be a lesson to both Brazil and the world, a symbol of a new determination to settle the interior and leave behind the Portuguese habit of sticking close to the coast. The city was built in record time (even though there was no railway or hard-surfaced road connection and all the construction materials had to be brought in by air), much to the dismay of Rio de Janeiro, which lost its role as national capital when Brasília was inaugurated in 1960.

Brasília quickly captured the world's imagination. The inauguration brought a record number of journalists and photographers from all over the world. All the principal buildings were designed by Oscar Niemeyer, who was given a veto over any subsequent major construction. Lúcio Costa's prize-winning planned layout of the city was designed to make it look from the air like a sweptwing airplane, thereby symbolizing progress with the residential and business areas along the "wings" of the plane. Along the body of the plane were the government offices (each ministry was given a structure of precisely equal size) and cultural, banking, and hotel areas. In the "cockpit" of the plane was the Plaza of Three Powers, with imposing modern buildings for the executive, legislative, and judicial branches. Brasília proved, predictably, to be a one-industry (i.e., government) town, much like Washington and Canberra, other "new" capital cities built from scratch.

But there was also a negative side to Kubitschek's growth strategy, which stemmed from the way it was financed. Brazil's domestic savings remained chronically low, thereby keeping investment low. And the hoped-for inflow of foreign capital to supplement domestic investment was not sufficient to raise Brazilian investment to the level needed for sustained high growth over the long run. Yet Kubitschek would not scale back his ambitious economic plans, despite growing inflation and mounting balance-of-payments deficits.

Many economists criticized Brazil for what they called "inflation financing"—the financing of public sector deficits simply by printing money—because it inevitably redistributed income and wealth toward high-growth (including high-speculation) sectors. Such a shift could not continue indefinitely, because of the natural limits to such transfers and because eventually the losers in the process would be enraged enough to call a halt. The motto of the Kubitschek era was "fifty years' progress in five." His critics called it "fifty years' inflation in five." Kubitschek's inflation financing, as is often the case, stimulated intervention from outside Brazil.

Dealing with the World Economy

Kubitschek's determination to pursue his economic program ensured a continuing balance-of-payments crisis. Brazil's export earnings, which still came primarily from a few primary products, remained stagnant, even as its imports, including capital goods and inputs essential for industry, had grown. Brazil could sustain a deficit in the trade account only if it got foreign financing to make up the difference, either through foreign investment or through loans and grants.

Pursuit of rapid growth without adequate financing rekindled inflation in Brazil. Rather than slow down the program by reducing the government deficit, Kubitschek's team tolerated rising prices. Inflation and the payments deficit came together in 1958, as they had in the early 1950s, forcing Brazil to negotiate a stabilization agreement with the International Monetary Fund (IMF). Only with such an agreement could Kubitschek draw on IMF funds and cover Brazil's payments deficit. Like most stabilization programs, this one required tighter credit controls and wage restraints, as well as budget cuts.

The proposed IMF-approved stabilization program provoked furious opposition in Brazil. The left now had an ideal issue for attacking Kubitschek. They accused him of sacrificing Brazilian interests to the IMF and the U.S. government. Now approaching his last year in office, the president faced an uncomfortable decision. If he pursued stabilization in the face of opposition from the left, the economy would slow down, his Programa de Metas would be hurt, and his role as the dynamic promoter of Brazil's rush to modernity would be compromised.

Kubitschek took a gamble. He decided to break with the IMF and continue his economic program, at whatever cost. His decision proved widely popular. Congratulatory telegrams poured into the presidential palace. Editorial writers hailed him as the champion of a new nationalism. The left was disconcerted because he had stolen their thunder. The right hesitated, since they did not want to defy the patriotic outcry. Kubitschek's gamble paid off politically but disrupted relations with the world economy. Brazil had the thrill of defying orthodox financial experts, particularly in the United States, but there would be a heavy price to pay in reduced access to future foreign financing.

Any evaluation of Kubitschek's economic record must weigh the benefits against the costs—a calculus that depends on essentially normative judgments about the value of the different components.

On the positive side, Brazil gained invaluable technology, although often only through investment by foreign multinationals. Brazil also saw the growth of a national market, concentrated primarily in the center-south where the prospect of gaining a foothold attracted foreign firms, even if only through modest investment. Finally, Brazilian industrialists and managers began to believe that they could perform at world standards. This was an important psychological change related to the elite's long-standing doubt that Brazil could ever compete with the advanced nations.

But critics pointed to what they considered important costs in welfare effects. These included increased income inequality, since industrial workers earned more than those in the agrarian or service sectors. Of course, even industrial workers' incomes paled in comparison to that of the upper 2 to 3 percent comprising large landowners, major merchants, bankers, brokers, industrialists, and real estate moguls. Furthermore, the inevitable concentration of industry in the center-south meant exacerbating the income inequalities between that region and the rest of Brazil, especially the Northeast. Both of these effects—rising inequality among persons and among regions—were cited by those who doubted the appropriateness of orthodox-style industrialization in a country such as Brazil, with a large labor surplus and great regional inequalities. The almost inevitable link for developing countries (at least in Latin America) between rapid economic growth and growing income inequality has been dogging Brazil's economic policy debate ever since.

The Brief Presidency of Jânio Quadros

The campaign for Kubitschek's successor produced two political figures, each bizarre in his own way. Jânio Quadros was a loner who had built a political career on his charisma in the state of São Paulo. He began as a schoolteacher, later selling his history of Portuguese grammar door to door, but his true vocation was convincing middle-class voters he could clean up politics. He was a wild-looking figure—tall and thin, with a shock of hair falling over his brow, and one bad eye (the result of a childhood accident). He was especially adept at keeping the spotlight on himself by giving out tidbits of a story while spinning out the denouement. His campaign for the presidency in 1960 showcased this talent. His campaign symbol was a broom—to sweep out the corrupt incumbents. Quadros attracted such wide and enthusiastic support that he came across to the public as some kind of messiah. He was the choice of the UDN, which nominated him in the hope they finally had a winner. But Quadros set little store by party loyalty. In the midst of the campaign he renounced the UDN nomination to dramatize his independence.

Marshall Henrique Lott, Quadros's main opponent, was a former army minister. It was Lott who had played the key role in preempting the military coup aimed at stopping Kubitschek's inauguration. Now in 1960 Lott was naive enough to be convinced by the left (including the Communist Party) that he was the hero who could save the country. In fact, Lott was an inept campaigner and no match for Quadros.

Quadros won with 48 percent of the vote, much closer to an outright majority than Kubitschek's had been. His *modus vivendi* could hardly have contrasted more sharply with Kubitschek's. Instead of wheeling and dealing, Brazil would now enjoy transparently honest government, if Quadros could keep his promises.

Brazil's most important short-term problem in January 1961 was the economic crisis. Kubitschek had left the Treasury bare and had avoided the politically painful task of attacking inflation. Quadros assembled a cabinet that included numerous UDN figures and set about producing a new stabilization plan. As almost always with such anti-inflation plans, implementation had dire political implications for the government. By June, details of the plan were beginning to leak out. The IMF and the U.S. government were pleased by the Quadros regime's willingness to bite the bullet in economic policy. The left, along with some businessmen, was dubious.

Once he was installed in the presidency, Quadros's charisma proved to be a fading asset. With each passing day, his impressive electoral victory seemed to matter less, as he faced a bureaucracy and a Congress immune to campaign oratory. His bizarre personal behavior did not help. He would spend an inordinately long time obsessively positioning himself exactly in the middle of the rear seat of his limousine, for example. And he would issue without warning highly specific presidential orders (nicknamed *bilhetes* or "tickets"), as, for example, one outlawing perfume bombs at Carnival time (the alleged cause of his childhood eye injury). Political commentators began asking how he planned to govern. In fact, Quadros was making little effort to negotiate his program with the Congress. Instead, he spent his time striking sensationalist poses, such as the awarding of Brazil's highest medal for foreigners (the Cruzeiro do Sul) to the visiting Che Guevara in August 1961. It was becoming increasingly clear that Brazil might have elected a false messiah.

Quadros was never a politician given to the arts of negotiation, and his way of tackling the obstacles his stabilization program was facing in the Congress was, without warning, to resign. He evidently assumed it would be rejected and would force Congress to give him emergency powers—as had been given to General de Gaulle in the recent French crisis precipitated by Algerian independence. Unfortunately for Quadros, the Congress accepted his resignation. The former president immediately left the capital, heading by plane for the military air base of Cumbica in São Paulo. He sailed for Europe shortly thereafter, proclaiming, "I was compelled to resign, but like Getúlio, I shall return one

EXHIBIT 6-3

Major Party Representation in Chamber of Deputies, 1945–1962

	1945		1950		1954		1958		1962	
	Seats	%	Seats	%	Seats	%	Seats	%	Seats	%
PSD	151	52.8	112	36.8	114	35.0	115	35.3	118	28.9
UDN	77	26.9	81	26.6	74	22.7	70	21.5	91	22.2
PTB	22	7.7	51	16.8	56	17.2	66	20.2	116	28.4
TOTAL %		87.4		80.2		74.9		77.0		79.5

Source: Correspondence from Scott Mainwaring.

day, God willing, to show everyone who were the scum in this country." Brazil was left leaderless less than a year after the election of 1960. Brasília went into shock as the political scene degenerated once again into turmoil. The UDN had now lost what they had expected to be their entree to power. The one man with a hope of exorcising the ghost of Getúlio Vargas was gone. Even worse, Vargas's political heir, João Goulart of the PTB, was now in line to be president. He had been elected vice president because the electoral law allowed split voting and Goulart, as Lott's running mate, had outpolled Quadros's running mate, the UDN leader Milton Campos. In fact, since 1945, the PTB had grown steadily in power in the Chamber of Deputies, largely at the expense of the PSD. (See exhibit 6-3.)

The Succession of João Goulart

The prospect of Goulart's succession to the presidency alarmed the UDN and the military, who considered him a dangerous populist all too ready to accommodate the Communists and thereby help them to power. Goulart's location at the moment of his access to power could not have been a more dramatic confirmation that their fears were well-founded: He was on his way home from an official mission to the People's Republic of China.

Almost immediately after Quadros's resignation, the three military ministers issued a manifesto denouncing Goulart as a subversive and pledging to prevent his succession to the presidency. This salvo began an intense public debate. Those opposing Goulart were the well-known enemies of Vargas, especially from the UDN, which had just lost its access to power. Goulart's supporters dubbed themselves the "legalists," arguing that he had been democratically elected vice president and was thereby now the constitutional president. The loudest legalist voice was Leonel Brizola, the governor of Rio Grande do Sul, who happened also to be Goulart's brother-in-law (Brizola had married Goulart's sister). Brizola was a fiery PTB leader who aspired to the mantle of Getúlio Vargas. Fortunately for the legalists, the commander of the Third Army (stationed in Rio Grande do Sul) was on Goulart's side. Brizola decided to defy the military ministers. He invited Goulart to return to Brazil via Rio Grande do Sul, and he won a promise by the Third Army commander to repel any federal forces entering from the North.

Goulart arrived in Rio Grande do Sul and began preparing for the journey to Brasília. The centrist politicians in the Congress were so frightened by the prospect of civil war that they began negotiating with the military ministers to avoid a confrontation. In the midst of a bitter national debate, they struck a compromise. Goulart would assume the presidency, but with greatly reduced powers. The president would now preside over a parliamentary system (by constitutional amendment). Executive power would thus rest with a prime minister and a cabinet rather than the president. Goulart accepted this compromise, but only under protest. He vowed to campaign for the restoration of full powers (in a plebiscite scheduled for January 1963).

What was at stake in this struggle? The answer was the shape of Brazil's future. The country's accelerating population growth rate was increasing the ranks of job seekers. To create those jobs, Brazil badly needed to diversify its economic base. The debate over economic strategy in Brazil was polarized by the Marxists and statists on the left and the neo-liberals on the right. Vargas had tried to combine elements from the two. In the end, his balancing act had failed. Kubitschek had given new life to the trade-off between left and right. But with the succession of Goulart, Brazil now faced a repeat of the confrontation of 1954—a populist president, this time with an unstable political base and limited parliamentary powers, versus the military.

Populists versus the Military

Goulart lasted less than three years in the presidency. Throughout his presidential years he struggled to gain control over an increasingly divided political scene—a task that was vastly complicated by the heating up of the Cold War. Fidel Castro, triumphant in Cuba in 1959, was determined to export his revolution, and Brazil was one of the natural targets. President John F. Kennedy, elected in 1960, was equally determined to stop the Cuban offensive. The result was a clash of surrogates (Cuban, Soviet, U.S.) who tried, often successfully, to infiltrate, bribe, or otherwise influence Brazilian political parties, state governments, military officers, universities, professional associations, churches, and any other institution judged worthy of importance.

The Brazilian left had grown steadily since Vargas's return in 1951, but it had also become much more heterogeneous. One component was the Brazilian Communist Party, with its long experience of both open and clandestine politics. But the Communist Party was still scarred from repression during the Estado Nôvo and burdened by the memory of its abortive revolt in 1935. Furthermore, the Communists now had to contend with the cautious attitude of the Soviet Union (as compared with Fidel Castro) in promoting revolution in Latin America.

In addition, the party was outflanked on several fronts. On the left was the breakaway Chinese-oriented Communist Party of Brazil (Partido Comunista do Brasil), founded in 1962. This small but vocal group drew inspiration not only from the People's Republic of China but also from Cuba, where Fidel Castro had shown how to make a revolution by accelerating the dialectics of history.

Also important on the left were the many and varied "radical nationalists." Most passionate were the left-wing groups affiliated with the Roman Catholic Church. They had attracted many university students and aimed at creating political consciousness among the marginal masses, both urban and rural. The language of the radical nationalists was Marxist and many of their members had close links past or present to the orthodox Communist Party, although they were seldom under control of the latter and frequently followed a strategy that was all their own.

On the right were the traditional wealth-holders of Brazil. Their principal voice was the UDN and they relied on their links to the police and the military. They included landowners and many industrialists. Their trump card was the capacity of the military to intervene against their enemies.

The right attacked the legacy of Vargas despite the fact that many of their number had benefited greatly from Vargas's economic policies. In theory, they favored orthodox economic liberalism. In practice, they welcomed subsidies or protective tariffs when available, as in the coffee-support program. The right also relied upon the U.S. government as its ultimate support. They knew that pointing to the "Communist threat" would resonate in Washington, and some readily accepted secret U.S. funds for their electoral campaigns and propaganda battles.

Between left and right, the political center was shrinking. These were the politicians who were reformist but not revolutionary, who wanted to maintain the political game, and who often resorted to legalisms to solve social conflict. The centrist par excellence was San Tiago Dantas, a prominent lawyer and intellectual. He tried to relegitimize at least part of the left as consistent with democracy by dividing it into "positive" and "negative" wings. The positive wing, he argued, was ready to participate in democratic political solutions. The negative wing, in contrast, was committed to obstructing and delegitimizing the democratic process—gambling on replacing the existing system with a revolutionary regime. Dantas got his chance to rally the center when he became Goulart's finance minister in 1963.

The Economic Crisis Escalates

Along with reduced powers, Goulart inherited a worsening economic crisis. Inflation had risen from 25.4 percent in 1960 to 34.7 percent in 1961, and it was now producing serious distortions in economic decision making. It was also one of two signs to Brazil's foreign creditors that the government was losing control. The other indicator was the deficit in the balance of payments, which could only be covered by running down Brazil's foreign exchange reserves or by increasing the foreign debt. The promises of foreign help Quadros had negotiated were now suspended. Stabilization, that bugaboo of recent Brazilian presidents, was unavoidable.

San Tiago Dantas's arrival at the Finance Ministry offered a glimmer of hope. He was joined in early 1963 by Celso Furtado, the father of SUDENE, and they set to work drafting a three-year plan for Brazil.

Dantas journeyed to Washington in March 1963 and negotiated new agreements for U.S. and IMF support in return for a coherent anti-inflation program at home. When Dantas returned to Brazil he found himself the target of venomous attack from the left. He was accused of "selling out" in Washington, and memories of Kubitschek's break with the IMF began to flood the heads of the Brazilian public. This time, however, Brazil had no margin of foreign exchange reserves to carry out the Kubitschek strategy. To make matters worse, Dantas was diagnosed with lung cancer and had to resign.

Early 1963 had brought one source of relief to the government: In a national plebiscite, Brazilians voted to revoke the 1961 constitutional amendment that had imposed parliamentarism. Goulart now had full presidential powers. But the price of the change was high, ever deepening suspicions on the right, especially among the army officer corps. Would Goulart now attempt to lead Brazil toward the "syndical republic" which the right had long claimed he favored? Meanwhile, the radical left was even more anxious to demonstrate that the "popular forces" could assume power in Brazil—if not peacefully, then otherwise.

As 1963 continued, Brazil sank further into economic disrepute abroad. Foreign investment virtually ceased. Foreign suppliers were demanding immediate payment for anything they shipped, jeopardizing the adequacy of Brazil's supply of petroleum (more than half of which was imported at that time). The U.S. government had already written off Goulart as unreliable at best and revolutionary at worst, and was limiting its assistance to states with anti-Goulart governors, a policy the State Department described as favoring "islands of sanity." This favoritism reinforced the left's charges that the United States was intervening on behalf of reactionary forces in Brazilian politics. By early 1964, Brazilian financial markets were abuzz with rumors of an impending coup. Some days the alleged attackers were from the left, other days from the right. By March 1964, the annual inflation rate was over 100 percent.

The Goulart government had run out of conventional answers. The left was arguing that the time for conventional answers was over, and in March Goulart made a clear turn to the left. He had already called for measures that threatened elite control, such as enfranchising illiterates and permitting unionization of enlisted men in the military. He now launched a series of national rallies where he was to announce key presidential decrees (a way to bypass the federal Congress, where such measures could not pass). The first rally was scheduled for March 13 in Rio de Janeiro. The decrees to be announced included land expropriation and the nationalization of all private oil refineries.

That rally was followed by frantic organizing on the right to protest Goulart's allegedly anti-Christian, anti-family stance. These marches were organized by right-wing civic groups with links to other rightist groups in South America (some undoubtedly supported secretly by the U.S. government). Brazil was now set for a showdown between left and right.

As so often in Brazilian history (1889, 1930, 1937, 1945), the civilian political confrontation was cut short by a military coup d'état. It was organized by many of the same officers who had forced Vargas's ouster in 1954 and opposed

Goulart's succession in 1961. The intent was to end Goulart's presidency and with it, they hoped, the Vargas era. The coup organizers had energetically cultivated support among officers, successfully neutralizing Goulart supporters in their midst. The pro-coup forces also knew they could count on U.S. support, although the American officials were careful to keep any commitments secret.

On March 31–April 1, 1964, military units seized key government offices in Brasília and Rio. The military had expected to meet serious armed resistance—the left had boasted that the popular sectors would never allow the military to take power again, and the coup makers had taken the boast seriously. Goulart's justice minister, Abelardo Jurema, called for government supporters to fill the streets, but his pleas fell on deaf ears. The resistance did not materialize. The military and police quickly arrested key figures in the populist apparatus. Trade union leaders were the first target, but the purge soon expanded to include politicians and bureaucrats deemed subversive or untrustworthy. Violence was relatively limited, being most severe in the Northeast, where at least a dozen peasant league organizers and leftist leaders were tortured or killed.

Within days, the new government had consolidated power. At heart, it was an alliance between the military and the technocrats. The purged Congress promptly elected to the presidency General Castelo Branco, the army chief of staff, who had led the military conspiracy. The technocrats were led by Roberto Campos, a diplomat and economist and a leading critic of the Goulart government in its waning days. Campos brought with him a team of economists and engineers, many of whom had contributed to the creation of an anti-government think tank, IPES (Instituto da Pesquisas e Estudos Sociais), in Rio and São Paulo. They assumed power with clear and conventional ideas about how to contain inflation and restore Brazil to economic growth. The inflation rate for 1964 as a whole was already down from the over 100 percent annual rate prevailing when Goulart left office on April 1. (See exhibit 6-4.)

EXHIBIT 6-4

Annual Rate of Inflation, Selected Years, 1950–1964

Years	Inflation Rate (%)
1950	9.2
1955	11.8
1960	25.4
1961	34.7
1962	50.1
1963	78.4
1964	89.9

Source: Werner Baer, *The Brazilian Economy*, 6th ed. (Westport, 2008), p. 410.

Politicians from the UDN were the greatest political gainers. Frustrated by years of unsuccessfully fighting Vargas and his heirs, they had gained access to power via military intervention.

The anti-Goulart conspirators had assumed they would get immediate U.S. support. Carlos Lacerda, destroyer of three Brazilian presidents, went so far as to lecture Americans on their need to be grateful to the Brazilian revolutionaries for having saved such an important country from communism—and, in fact, U.S. President Lyndon Johnson recognized the new government within hours after the coup. The State Department, however, remained uneasy about the repression that followed Goulart's ouster and about the depth of the new government's commitment to economic and social reform, which had been a principal goal of the Alliance for Progress. Full credibility abroad would depend not only on the design of the new stabilization plan but also on the government's capacity to stick to it.

The speed and bloodlessness of the coup left Goulart supporters in total disarray. They began to realize how overconfident they had been, which led to much recrimination about responsibility for key errors. One question remained unanswered. How much freedom would the opposition be given to organize? And how would a military government treat its opposition?

This was hardly a question to detain João Goulart. He fled Brasília for his native Rio Grande do Sul. From there he left the country for Uruguay, where he settled into exile and became a highly successful cattle rancher. His former ministers were scattered among distant foreign capitals. The military had cast the populists from power.

7
Rule of the Military

The Generals Search for a Political Base

When the military took over the government in 1964, power within the officer ranks lay with the army, much larger than the other two armed forces and ultimately responsible for maintaining public order. The army officer corps, however, was less united than it appeared. The moderates ("soft-liners" in Brazilian parlance) believed their country was in peril because Brazilians had been misled by populist politicians and their left-wing allies. But they also believed the Brazilian public would come to its senses and that democracy could work once the "irresponsible" populists and the Communists were removed from the scene.

The "hard-liners" within the military had a more apocalyptic view. They distrusted *all* politicians, including the UDN. They thought only authoritarian measures could protect Brazil against the threats from the left. The hard-line leaders were led by officers with the most militantly anti-Vargas records, such as (among the older generation) Marshall Odílio Denys and General Jurandir Mamede. These hard-liners allowed the moderate military to take the lead in forming the new government in 1964, but behind the scenes they remained committed to tougher measures.

The military who seized power faced one extremely awkward political fact: They had no firm legal basis for their intervention. This would not have bothered many Latin American militaries, but the Brazilian officers had a strong legalist streak, and they wanted legitimacy. The civilian supporters of the coup had lacked the congressional votes to impeach Goulart, just as they and their predecessors had lacked the votes to impeach Getúlio Vargas in 1954. The constitutional path now would have to bend for the new military rulers to be granted emergency powers by the Congress. But the conservative congressional leaders balked.

On April 9, 1964, the three military ministers took matters into their own hands. They arbitrarily issued an "Institutional Act" (it became the first of many with that title), which had been drawn up by Francisco Campos—the same person, ironically, who had authored Vargas's authoritarian Constitution of 1937. The new act gave the Brazilian executive extraordinary powers, including increased authority to amend the Constitution, exclusive power to propose expenditure bills to Congress, and the power to suppress the political rights of any citizen for ten years. President Goulart had often complained that he lacked the authority to carry out his presidential duties. The military agreed with the diagnosis and imposed their own solution.

The military moderates then turned to the UDN, long-time enemies of the populists, as the political party to help them legitimize their takeover of power. Castelo Branco, coordinator of the coup and leader of the moderate military wing, was personally close to the UDN leaders and considered them the proper civilian inheritors of power. The UDN were happy to oblige. They had never won the presidency with one of their own (Jânio Quadros had accepted their nomination in 1959 but declared his political independence during the succeeding campaign) and were eager to take power at last. The military-UDN alliance elected Castelo Branco to the presidency—not an unexpected victory given that the electorate consisted of a Congress which had already been purged of leftist elements.

There were seeds of instability in the alliance, however. First, in joining with the military the UDN was going against its own ideological principles— dedication to legalism, defense of the Constitution, and keeping government small. Second, it was not clear that the UDN had sufficient appeal to win direct elections, even after the purge of the populists. If their electoral power turned out to be weak, the hard-liners in the military could not be counted on to let democracy of any sort continue, and in the event that they did allow some representative government, they would almost certainly look elsewhere for electoral support.

The policymaking arm of the Castelo Branco/UDN government was a group of economic experts dubbed the "technocrats." Their leader was Roberto Campos, an extremely articulate neo-orthodox economist who had helped define a new and more conservative development strategy in his extensive writings. Campos was appointed minister of planning. He was joined by Octávio Bulhões, a distinguished conservative economist who became finance minister. Joining them was a cadre of younger economists and engineers, such as Glycon de Paiva, a longtime critic of the government's petroleum monopoly. These technocrats now had the opportunity to reshape policy under the mantle of military power. One of the Castelo Branco government's first measures was a decree prohibiting Congress from increasing budget requests from the executive, a practice that had often undermined previous stabilization efforts.

These technocrats launched the same type of orthodox stabilization measures previous governments had tried to implement. They argued that they were governing in the name of honesty, common sense, and rationality—in other words, acting neutrally in the public interest. However, their measures did not turn out to be neutral in their impacts on different layers of society, as we shall see.

The new government also claimed a new international role. Brazil's military coup was the first in Latin America since the wave of democratization in the 1950s. It was thus an ominous sign for the U.S.-sponsored Alliance for Progress, which had aimed to strengthen democratic rule in Latin America by promoting economic growth and social reform. The military takeover of democracy in Brazil, Latin America's largest nation, suggested that U.S. strategy might have to be rethought.

In fact, promoting democracy had never been the sole aim of the United States. Another principal preoccupation for Washington was geopolitical: "Stop Castroism." Soviet influence must not be allowed to expand in the hemisphere was the logic. The Brazilian coup-makers's claim on U.S. support rested on this mission.

In the short run, the coup-makers succeeded in gaining U.S. support. The Lyndon Johnson administration recognized the new regime in Brazil less than forty-eight hours after the president of the Congress had declared the federal presidency vacant. The Brazilian congressional action was in fact illegal, since Goulart had neither been impeached and convicted, nor fled the country without congressional permission (the only two ways a living president could constitutionally lose office). President Johnson ignored this technicality in the hope that early recognition would help to strengthen the military moderates to resist a possible turn toward authoritarianism.

When neighboring Argentina, always closely linked politically to Brazil, suffered its own military coup in 1966, the Argentine generals used similar anti-Communist rhetoric to justify their intervention. Officers in both countries saw themselves on a common mission to save Western democracy from the "menace" on the left.

Growing Opposition, Growing Repression: 1964–1967

Two major issues emerged to coalesce an emerging opposition to the new regime: repression and economic policy.

The military government was quite open in its decision to purge the left wing from the political system. It was not so open about the fact that it also forced the retirement of several thousand civil servants, including a number of distinguished figures who had never been political partisans. Many were simply victims of personal vendettas by rivals promoting their careers by getting the ear of the military security officers. Negative reactions to these purges, plus antagonism to the loss of the democratic principles of liberal constitutionalism, were widespread. It should be noted that the press remained relatively free in this early period. Censorship of the media came later.

The new economic stabilization program was bitterly attacked by the left (and many in the center), which predicted that the anti-inflation program of Campos and Bulhões would create massive unemployment and facilitate sweeping takeovers by foreign firms, especially North American. Once again, the left portrayed Brazil as slipping under the heel of the United States and the IMF. The more extreme critics charged that the entire coup had been a U.S. production, with Brazilian officers merely carrying out Uncle Sam's instructions.

The August 1965 elections were the first formal test of the opposition's strength. State governorships were up for grabs, including those in the two key states of Guanabara (greater Rio de Janeiro city, which was then a state) and Minas Gerais. Pro-government candidates won in every state except Guanabara and Minas Gerais, where the winners were traditional PSD politicians of the Vargas stripe. Although both winners had reputations as wheeler-dealers, neither was a full-fledged populist.

Even so, the hard-line military were infuriated by the outcome, interpreting it as proof that Castelo Branco's dependence on the UDN would not work. Ominous threats swept through the officers' barracks in Rio de Janeiro. General Costa e Silva, the army minister and a sympathizer of the hard line, brokered an agreement with the president. As a result, using a freshly issued Institutional Act (No. 2), Castelo Branco and his advisers decided to replace the old party structure with two new parties. One party, ARENA (Aliança Renovadora Nacional) would represent the government, and the other, the MDB (Movimento Democrático Brasileiro), would represent the opposition. Castelo Branco chose this two-party structure out of his admiration for the Anglo-Saxon political experience and for what he saw as Brazil's positive experience during its nineteenth-century (largely two-party) parliamentary monarchy. The trick from the president's standpoint was to ensure a continuing majority for the pro-government party.

Triumph of the Hard Line

The issuing of the new Institutional Act and the reorganization of the party system did not quiet the opposition, but Castelo's critics increasingly focused on the effects of stabilization, which were felt through 1965 and 1966. The resulting fall in real wage rates and the public spending cuts provoked ever growing protest from opposition politicians and economists, who predicted that Brazil would never regain its growth path.

Castelo Branco had promised he would not extend his presidential mandate, which was the presidential term to which Quadros had been elected in 1960 and which Goulart had assumed in 1961. But as early as July 1964 Castelo had succumbed to intense pressure from his economic policymakers, who thought the presidential election scheduled for November 1965 would not allow time for their policies to show results. So he agreed to extend his term by fourteen months, to March 15, 1967. On that date, Castelo Branco passed the presidency to General Costa e Silva, the incumbent army minister and the second military president to be elected indirectly by the Congress.

The tense relations between the hard-line and moderate military were not helped by passage of two more Institutional Acts (Nos. 3 and 4). In April of 1968, a series of wildcat strikes erupted in Minas Gerais. Worker resentment against the steady fall in real wages had become so intense that the "safe" labor union leaders, appointed by the military in 1964, could not control their members. The hard line let this disruption go. But several months later, the government faced a new challenge to law and order. Students in Rio de Janeiro, always at the forefront of protest, staged noisy protest marches. This time the riot police turned out in force and the clash led to at least one death. These two incidents showed the hard line that the moderate military, although ostensibly repressive, were allowing continued public opposition. The hard-liners were determined to control both workers and students.

As 1968 continued, the political atmosphere became steadily overheated. The spark that started the final fire came from a speech by Márcio Moreira Alves, a young Rio congressman who challenged the honor of the military by suggesting that Brazilian women should protest military rule by withholding their favors from men in uniform. The hard line was livid at this ridicule and demanded Alves's immediate arrest. He eluded the authorities and slipped into exile in Chile and later France.

The hard-line officers decided the time had come for tougher measures. The president issued in December yet another Institutional Act (No. 5), which, unlike the preceding Institutional Acts, had no expiration date. Brazil was now a genuine dictatorship. Congress was closed (although not abolished) and all crimes against "national security" were subjected to military justice. Censorship was introduced, aimed especially at television and radio. Several prominent print media, such as the daily *O Estado de S. Paulo* and the weekly *Veja*, became subject to prior censorship (meaning their copy had to be cleared by an army censor).

Wire tapping, mail opening, and denunciations by informers became commonplace. University lectures were monitored and a wave of purges hit the leading faculties, especially in São Paulo, where a future Brazilian president, Fernando Henrique Cardoso, was forcibly retired from his professorship. Numerous other faculty were hit, losing their political rights for ten years. Security forces zeroed in especially on opposition clergy and students, among whom the doctrines of liberation theology were still influential.

The Arrival of the Guerrillas

The military takeover in 1964 had not stimulated any immediate significant armed resistance, but the government's record of growing repression gradually provoked armed opposition, which surfaced in 1969. One guerrilla group tried to apply Fidel Castro's strategy of rural guerrilla warfare to the cities. Their chief theoretician was Carlos Marighela, a former member of the Brazilian Communist Party and a founder of the breakaway Action for National Liberation (ANL) in 1968. In his *Minimanual of the Urban Guerrilla* he argued that a tightly organized cadre could bring down a dictatorship through urban combat.

More than a dozen guerrilla groups emerged in Brazil at about the same time, bearing a variety of labels, such as VAR (Vanguarda Armada Revolucionária—Palmares), ALN (Ação Libertadora Nacional), and COLINA (Comandos de Libertação Nacional). The combatants probably totaled fewer than five hundred, usually in their late teens or early twenties, although many others provided logistical support. These included committed Marxists and radical nationalists (many were Catholics attracted to liberation theology), mostly products of pre-1964 leftist politics but some joining after 1964.

The guerrillas first gained notoriety by robbing banks—forays that, at least initially, were highly successful. The poorly guarded banks were sitting ducks for the young robbers, who left the scene carrying their spoils, shouting revolutionary slogans and scattering anti-military flyers as they ran. The money was badly needed to finance their operations. The accompanying actions were needed to prove that the citadels of capitalism were not impregnable.

The guerrillas also resorted to a strategy of kidnapping prominent foreign diplomats. This had two purposes. One was to demonstrate again the weakness of the government. The second was to use the diplomatic hostages to bargain for the release of guerrillas captured earlier by the security forces.

The kidnapping began with the U.S. ambassador, Burke Elbrick, who was snatched from his black Cadillac limousine while riding home for lunch. The kidnappers offered to release Elbrick in exchange for fifteen guerrilla prisoners. After a fierce debate among the military, the government agreed to trade the prisoners for the ambassador's freedom. The precedent was thereby set for subsequent kidnappings and negotiations.

The guerrillas then turned to other diplomatic targets, including the Swiss ambassador, the German ambassador, and the Japanese consul general, in that order. In each case, the captors increased the number of prisoners demanded in exchange for the hostage, thereby gaining more and more publicity at the expense of the generals. In each case, the guerrillas won release of the prisoners.

The publicity did not help them win their case with the country, however. The guerrillas hoped to dramatize the exploitative role of foreign capital with the order of their kidnapping—in descending order of the country's investment in Brazil. But this symbolism was too subtle for the average Brazilian. It was also typical of the Brazilian guerrillas' tendency to overestimate the capacity of symbolic actions (especially in the face of censorship) to rouse a discontented population.

Although the kidnappings did not provoke an outpouring of public support for the guerrilla movement, they did provoke the security forces into ever more draconian security measures. They resorted to every method of surveillance and torture in their hunt for information. The truth is that even a mediocre military and police force could bring great pressure to bear on a small number of armed opponents. The danger of infiltration became so great that the guerrillas could not recruit new members, and their original number steadily dwindled as the arrests mounted. Within one year of their emergence, the trap was closing on the few guerrillas still at large. Marighela's strategy had been disproved. The cities were not hospitable to the guerrillas. Instead they had become, in Fidel Castro's own phrase, "the graveyard of the revolutionary."

The one major attempt to mount a rural front also failed after a promising start. In the Araguáia region of the Amazon Basin, a group of carefully trained guerrillas infiltrated a peasant area and gained the sympathy of the locals. The army sent in a force of poorly trained regular troops to clean out the area, which were easily routed by the guerrillas. The army then withdrew to train an elite corps of ten thousand counterinsurgency troops. Not surprisingly, they killed or captured all of the sixty-nine guerrillas in the area. But it took two years and repeated assaults, much like Canudos eighty years earlier. There was yet another historical parallel: The guerrilla commander was an Afro-Brazilian, Osvaldo Orlando da Costa, admired by his peers for his bravery. The victorious soldiers displayed his dead body to the locals, much as the Portuguese had done with the head of Tiradentes in 1792.

The armed opposition was totally liquidated by 1974. But that did not stop the military hard line from exploiting the claim of a continued guerrilla threat to keep the military moderates off balance and thereby justify its continued repression.

Brazilian Culture and the Generals

The nationalist energy generated in Brazil since Vargas's 1954 suicide accelerated during the presidency of Juscelino Kubitschek, a viscerally optimistic politician determined to establish Brazil's national self-confidence by every means possible. The supreme symbol of Kubitschek's drive for a new national identity was, as noted, the building of Brasília, which was typically Brazilian in its contradictions. On the one hand, Brasília was to be uniquely Brazilian, built far inland (thereby centering attention on the long-neglected interior of the country) and designed to give international attention to Brazil's leading architect and city planner, Oscar Niemeyer and Lúcio Costa, respectively. The result was a futuristic new city that proclaimed Brazil's entry into the modern world.

The new capital had its passionate supporters. Many young families praised its excellent climate, first-rate schools, excellent recreational facilities, and relative lack of crime. It was, they argued, an ideal place to raise children. Even those Brazilians who criticized the "artificiality" of so much perfect symmetry in the midst of a desolate plateau had to admit that their country had caught world attention. Famous European intellectuals such as André Malraux, for example, were calling Brasília "the capital of hope."

On the other hand, the inspiration for Brasília's basic conception was strictly French, which stimulated outspoken criticism. Gilberto Freyre, the most influential commentator on national culture and history, dismissed Brasília as "un-Brazilian." Some residents agreed, condemning the impracticality of glass-sided office buildings under an intense sun. Then there was the city traffic, unconstrained by a single traffic light in the maze of cloverleaf intersections. Intended to be a modernistic model of fluid flow, it soon set a national record for road accidents, leading to the tardy installation of orthodox traffic lights.

Whoever was in favor of or against it, the building of the new capital city and the new surge of industrialization were tangible evidence that Brazil was leaving behind the image of a sleepy tropical enclave. Other indicators of change also entered the cultural scene. Best known was "bossa nova," the subtle musical mixture of samba and jazz. It was born in the late 1950s, along with Brasília, and soon attracted worldwide attention.

Antônio Carlos Jobim, Brazil's greatest popular composer, whose new rhythms put his country on the world stage. Rio de Janeiro's airport was named for him after his death. (Associated Press)

Bossa nova musicians such as Antônio Carlos Jobim, Sérgio Mendes, and João Gilberto collaborated with American jazz musicians such as Stan Getz. Was Brazilian culture now penetrating the First World? Antônio Carlos Jobim and Vinícius De Moraes, the great lyricist of bossa nova, were even invited to write a symphony for the dedication of Brasília. The title of their work, "The Symphony of Dawn," paid tribute to Kubitschek's symbolism for the new capital. Although not performed at the dedication, the commissioning showed the link between this cultural movement and the ideological atmosphere of the era.

Bossa nova reached a climax in a highly successful Carnegie Hall concert by more than twenty Brazilian musicians in 1962. Their enthusiastic reception in New York (promotion by the Brazilian Foreign Ministry had helped) had great repercussions in Brazil—greater, some said, than their country's dazzling victory in the 1962 World Soccer Cup. Once again, Brazil was being recognized on the world stage.

Yet bossa nova had already faded by the time polarization led to the coup in 1964. Perhaps it was too subtle, too gentle for the turbulent climate shaking Brazil. Or perhaps it was too much a product of the cultural elite and its inevitably small middle-class audience. Bossa nova's fame, once brilliant in Carnegie Hall, soon proved ephemeral in Brazil.

There were other cultural fireworks in the early 1960s. One of the most notable was *cinema novo*, or "new cinema." It was closely linked to radical nationalism. The radical nationalists, as we saw earlier, believed that Brazil's relative backwardness was the result of foreign (especially U.S.) exploitation, which could only be countered by a strong state, a worker/peasant-oriented economy, and strict controls on all foreign economic and political participation. Its theoretical inspiration was Marxist, although its influence extended much beyond the Communist parties.

The radical nationalists rejected Kubitschek's entire economic policy as a sellout to international capital. *Vidas Secas* ("Barren Lives," 1963), for example, was a powerful portrait of a destitute northeastern peasant family reduced to desperation by a suffocating drought. The social injustice of their plight would be obvious to the Brazilian viewer who knew the facts about the grotesque distribution of power and wealth in the Northeast, then the largest pocket of misery in Latin America. *Deus e Diabo na Terra do Sol* ("God and the Devil in the Land of the Sun," but released as "Black God, White Devil," 1964) followed. In this case the peasant living in the parched Northeast is cheated out of his allotment of cattle and takes his revenge by killing the landowner. Although the film is hardly a call to revolution and spends most of its time in a complex depiction of messianism, the filmmaker leaves little doubt as to the source of injustice. It was a film likely to alarm the army generals who had the mission of maintaining "order" in the Northeast.

The implicit challenge to authority from the artistic left gained even greater tension in Ruy Guerra's *Os Fuzis* ("The Guns," 1964), where a truck loaded with food breaks down in a drought-stricken town whose starving inhabitants are held at bay by rifle-bearing soldiers. Once again the picture is of stark injustice, with even more radical implications since it is army troops who nervously hold off the hungry townspeople. The generals could not fail to get the message: their own fighting men could be alienated by subversive propaganda films.

The first phase of cinema novo was reaching its climax just as the Goulart presidency was careening toward destruction. Like the radical nationalists pushing Goulart to the left, "the cinema novo directors," in the words of a leading film critic, "searched out the dark corners of Brazilian life—its *favelas* and its *sertão*—the places where Brazil's social contradictions appeared most dramatically."

The coup of 1964 did not silence the left. On the contrary, the initial wave of repression (arrest of labor leaders, purge of the civil service, disqualification of politicians) did not immediately result in institutionalized censorship. From 1964 to 1968, the opposition retained space to maneuver. The most famous example was Glauber Rocha's *Terra em Transe* ("Land in Anguish," 1967). The film's events occur in the imaginary state of El Dorado, where a populist provincial governor, Felipe Vieira, chooses not to fight off a coup headed by a rightist politician with the revealing name of "Porfirio Diaz" (the Mexican authoritarian president). The analogy with Goulart and 1964 is obvious. Most of the film is taken up with a flashback depicting Vieira's political rise, complete with carnivalesque crowd scenes and frenetic behavior by the candidate. Rocha called it the "tragic carnival" of Brazilian politics, where "purity rots in tropical gardens." The film's effect is heightened by novel cinematographic techniques producing fragments that resist narrative synthesis.

Double entendre also flourished during the early years of the military regime. The master of this game was Francisco Buarque de Hollanda ("Chico Buarque"). Son of a noted intellectual, he had the knack of writing and singing songs that appealed to both sophisticated audiences and the ordinary Brazilian. Such compositions as "A Banda" (1966) and "Roda Viva" (1967) quickly established his fame.

After 1968, however, the cultural scene was subjected to strict censorship, including confiscation of suspect materials. Police informers were everywhere, throughout artistic circles and educational institutions. The penalty for falling afoul of the authorities was arrest, torture, and possibly worse. Many artists now fled into exile, leaving primarily the hacks and the conformists to fill the cultural vacuum.

Chico Buarque, for example, spent 1968 through 1970 in exile in Italy. Upon returning to Brazil, his first song, "Apesar de Você" ("In Spite of You"), was immediately banned because of its thinly veiled attack on military rule. Although rejecting the label of protest singer (he did not want to be typecast as an outsider), Chico continued composing and singing despite the censors' constant intervention. His success could be traced to his genius for combining traditional samba and bossa nova with his own playful originality.

His survival on the cultural scene after 1970 (he remained highly popular until redemocratization in 1985 and after) was a tribute not only to his ingenuity but also to the ineptitude of the censors, who never felt able to ban him outright. It was another sign that Brazil's military regime, although repressive, never reached the depth experienced in the counterpart dictatorships of Argentina and Chile.

The late 1960s produced another musical phenomenon involved in attempting to assert Brazilian identity in an unfree society. The movement was called "Tropicalism" and it owed its origins to a Bahian contingent led by Caetano Veloso and Gilberto Gil. They avoided overtly political messages but nonetheless ran into trouble with the censors. They chose to resurrect themes from the iconoclastic tradition of modernist writers such as Oswaldo de Andrade, whose 1920s avant-garde verse celebrated cannibalism as the only truly Brazilian characteristic. Veloso and Gil experimented with outrageously "tropical" costumes and ostentatiously honored Carmen Miranda, the ambassadress to Hollywood with the tutti-frutti hairstyle and the kitsch version of samba. Despite their ostensibly nonpolitical style, the Tropicalistas found the post-1968 atmosphere suffocating and went into exile in London in 1969. Their departure followed an episode of house arrest by the federal police in Bahia in late 1968. The military authorities could abide the (censored) subtleties of Chico Buarque, but they found Carmen Miranda and cannibalism too much to tolerate.

We now need to consider more explicitly the social context of cultural production after 1964. The foregoing discussion of cultural trends includes film, which was restricted in its impact. Brazilian filmmakers were at a great disadvantage vis-à-vis their competitors in Hollywood. The Brazilians were grossly underfinanced and lacking in technical resources. Above all, they were handicapped by poor distribution. Movie houses knew that Hollywood films, surrounded with their massive advertising and international glamour, would draw patrons. The kind of cinema novo films discussed above were often too difficult, too disturbing, and too heavy for the typical Brazilian. Popular music, on the other hand, especially after 1964, was more capable of reaching a mass audience via radio and television. For that reason it drew more attention from the censors.

The cultural medium that achieved the greatest impact during the military regime was television. In 1960, the year Jânio Quadros won the presidency, Brazil had fewer than 600,000 TV sets. By 1986, the year after the return of elected government, the total was 26.5 million, more than a fortyfold increase, aided by government-induced favorable installment terms. The number of stations had increased at an even faster rate. In 1964 there were only 14; by 1985, when the last general left the presidency, there were 150. In addition, a government-built network helped create a nationwide system. This meant that the federal government, through its licensing, could and did shape the ownership of the medium from which most Brazilians got their news and entertainment.

The most famous beneficiary of government favoritism was the Globo organization, the media and publishing conglomerate, which entered the TV field in 1965. Initially, Globo had technical and financial help for its fledgling TV enterprise from Time-Life, but the corporation soon dropped this link and emerged on its own as Brazil's most aggressive and professional TV network. Its expansion was openly favored by the military governments, which granted it the most attractive locations and facilitated import of the most up-to-date equipment. In return, TV Globo followed a strictly pro-government programming policy. This was a powerful asset for the generals, since TV Globo's evening news had 80 percent of the audience and its overall ratings far outweighed all the other networks combined.

By 1985, TV Globo had become the fourth largest network in the world, with a viewership of 80 million. Its skillfully produced evening *telenenovelas* (soap operas) developed a fanatical following. These *telenovelas* were exported to more than fifty countries, demonstrating that TV Globo's producers, writers, and actors had fashioned a product of universal appeal. For those who worried about Brazil's identity, it was another sign of success, however one might value it, on the world scene.

The private station owners got a further bonus from the heavy advertising by state corporations and banks. Advertising revenues poured in from every source, and rose from $350 million in 1970 to $1.5 billion in 1979. The sophistication of TV advertising grew along with the revenue. Brazilian ad agencies began winning international awards. The Americanization of Brazilian media, in the sense of ownership structure and production technique if not of U.S. programs, proceeded apace. If much of the programming was insipid and narcoticizing, could the same not be said of TV to the north?

As for the print media and fiction, military repression had the expected effects. Newspapers and magazines proved easy to control since no paper had a circulation of more than a few hundred thousand (such as O *Jornal do Brasil* and O *Estado de S. Paulo*) and Brazil was not known for being a newspaper-reading country. Direct pressure on the editors and owners was enough to create self-censorship, which made "prior censorship" regularly necessary on fewer than ten publications. The government had many other weapons, including manipulation of state-sponsored advertising (estimated at 30 percent of total revenue) and court actions against individual journalists, editors, and owners.

The more adventurous journalists responded to government pressure by creating an "alternative press," primarily weeklies such as *Opinião* and *Movimento*, which were outspokenly oppositionist and suffered frequent and large-scale censorship. These publications did, however, keep alive a critical spirit and were an important alternative to exile for opposition journalists. Interestingly enough, the alternative press died in the freer climate of the transition back to electoral government, thus ending one of the most creative chapters in the history of Brazilian journalism.

When it came to fiction during the military era, the story was similar to that of cinema. The audience was necessarily small, given the high incidence of functional illiteracy and the relatively high cost of books and poor sales distribution. Nonetheless, novelists produced works that gave their version of the experience of dictatorship, such as Antônio Callado's *Bar Don Juan* (1971), which depicted the short-lived guerrilla movement, and Loyola Brandão's *Zero* (1974), which laid out a disconnected series of tableaus located in a mythical country called "América Latindia." Both books were banned, although the censors relented on *Bar Don Juan*, and *Zero* was eventually printed in Brazil in 1985 after earlier publication in Italy. Finally, Ivan Angelo's *A Festa* (1976) was a look back at the height of the repression in 1970. The novel is set in Belo Horizonte, where a supposed influx of peasants fleeing from drought in the Northeast creates upheaval, while the local intellectuals lose themselves in sex and drugs. The parallels with Glauber Rocha's *Terra em Transe* are clear: It is another case of dissecting the illusion that had nourished the left before 1964, as well as showing their inability to deal with the repression that followed.

Culture in the military years was a reflection of Brazilian artists' confrontation with the realities of power in Brazil. More than a few myths had been destroyed. A large portion of the country's artists and intellectuals had endorsed the populist and often radically nationalist vision of the early 1960s. They realized, as the general-presidents succeeded one another, that those visions were dead for at least another generation.

The military governments did attempt one direct use of the mass media, the promotion of patriotic propaganda on the lines of "O Brasil Grande" ("Vast Brazil"). The theme was the traditional one of Brazil's destiny to become a great power on the world stage. This ambition could be traced back to turn-of-the-century literary figures such as Afonso Celso and Olavo Bilac. These enthusiasts had painted a great future for Brazil as a powerful modern nation, despite its real status as a minor power on the margins of international politics. Now the military thought the time had come to fulfill Brazil's destiny.

Proof of their commitment was to be found in the government's megaconstruction projects: the Itaipú dam (then the world's largest) on the Paraguayan border, the Transamazon Highway (crossing the world's largest rainforest), and the giant atomic energy project (utilizing a German technology never used before). All these multi-billion-dollar government-financed projects were supposed to help launch Brazil into the First World. They were given lavish coverage in the media, accompanied by patriotic music and liberal use of the national colors.

This brand of propaganda may have been effective in the 1968–74 period, when the Brazilian economy was growing by 10 percent a year, but the prolonged economic stagnation triggered by the 1979 oil crisis and Brazil's inadequate reaction to it made the public more skeptical. By the end of the last military presidency in 1985, censorship had finished and the generals had lost control of the media.

The Effects of Repression

Brazilians started journeying into exile as early as 1964, although the outflow accelerated in 1968–69. Those who fled included leftist politicians, intellectuals, academics, and artists, all convinced that they had no choice but to reconstruct their lives outside Brazil.

Many went to Chile, a democratic refuge where political pluralism was still a reality (until the military coup of 1973 brought the Pinochet dictatorship, which ensnared numerous Brazilian exiles). Chile was also attractive as a traditional ally of Brazil and as the center that had articulated a Latin American strategy of development. Other fleeing Brazilians joined intellectual and artistic circles in Mexico. Europe, especially France, also got its share of Brazilian refugees. France had long been the ideal refuge for Brazilians, and Paris soon had a large Brazilian exile colony. A small number went to Cuba and eastern Europe, to live under socialist regimes. Only a few exiles came to the United States, because its conservative climate (as symbolized by outspoken U.S. support for the 1964 coup) made it less attractive.

Exile came as a shock to these Brazilians, who, despite leaving, were passionate Brazilian patriots. Most felt painfully out of place abroad, where they began reexamining and writing about Brazilian history and the role of the left. Some simply repeated the Marxist or populist analyses they had been producing since the 1950s, for whom Brazil's authoritarian turn merely confirmed what they had long seen coming. The more thoughtful expatriates, however, began to question the assumptions behind the populist strategy of the early 1960s.

They now saw that the left had seriously miscalculated the balance of power. Established authority had not been about to crumble in the face of a populist offensive. On the contrary, the right and the military staged their own coup with ease. These exiles also began to rethink their rationale for opposing the military government. The public backlash against the military government was also weaker than they had predicted. One revolutionary, Herbert de Souza ("Betinho"), reflected on his pro-Maoist days, "We had arrived at the most extreme political madness. We were incapable of perceiving and gauging reality."

Forced residence abroad had another important effect on the exiles. It plunged some of Brazil's best and brightest into sustained contact with other societies, other cultures, and other political systems. Brazilians living in welfare states—such as Sweden, France, or Germany, in particular—found a capitalism quite different from that of Brazil. They also got to know societies where there was still room for political debate.

Meanwhile, the horrors of repression continued in Brazil. The victims of government torture continued to pile up through 1974. The repression was ostensibly aimed at the revolutionary opposition but in fact affected the entire society. To understand how, we must take a brief look at the role of repression in Brazilian history.

Although the elite had always preferred to view their country as fundamentally nonviolent, that is a very inaccurate reading of Brazilian history. Slavery, for example, had been based on physical brutality that included mutilation, merciless beatings, and execution, and had continued in Brazil until 1888, longer than anywhere else in the Americas. Forced labor of Amazonian Indians continued even longer. In the Brazil of the early 1960s, physical mistreatment of ordinary citizens by the police was still commonplace. In part, this was a legacy of the violence that had surrounded slavery. But it was also inherent in maintaining the highly hierarchical society that the Brazilian Republic inherited. From the beginning of the Republic in 1889, governments had repeatedly resorted to declaring a state of siege, thus allowing the suspension of judicial guarantees. During the popular protests against compulsory vaccination in Rio in 1904, for example, the crowds were bombarded by artillery. Over three hundred of the detainees were then deported, without any judicial proceeding, to a distant camp in the Amazon. Similar internment tactics were employed in the wake of the 1910 naval revolt.

Police mistreatment of the elite, on the other hand, was rare, not least because the police were members of the non-elite classes and were in awe of their social superiors. Examples of differential behavior were easy to find. Any arrestee who held a higher university degree, for example, was by law (created by the 1941 Penal Code) entitled to better jail quarters than common detainees. Any elite member who ran afoul of the authorities could count on quick help from his or her web of elite contacts. A prime indicator of the unequal application of justice was the gross leniency shown toward white-collar criminals such as stock market swindlers. Rarely did they suffer any meaningful punishment, while common suspects could usually expect the worst.

This system of differential justice was well understood by all Brazilians. It reinforced a hierarchical social structure that was tight but not impermeable. When Brazil grew economically, its elite expanded. Yet this mobility did not alter the hierarchy itself.

The elite had long been able to remain in ignorance of the true workings of the criminal justice system, but that changed with the highly authoritarian turn in 1968. The reason was that the revolutionary movement was led primarily by disaffected youth from the elite, not by workers. The militant radical nationalists, bitter over the coup, were prime recruiting material for the armed opposition. Many of them came from leftist Catholic youth organizations and university political groups (overwhelmingly elite in origin). The security forces interrogated all guerrilla suspects by methods that were normal for common criminals but not practiced on the elite. One was the "parrot's perch," where the victim was suspended naked on a horizontal pole and subjected to beatings and electric shocks. Another was to submerge the victim in filthy water and shoot just over his or her head whenever the body surfaced. For particularly difficult cases—i.e., where confessions or incriminating evidence were not forthcoming—electricity was applied to the genitals, eardrums, and other body apertures. Elite and non-elite alike were fair game. As word of this brutal treatment leaked out, the elite victims' families were truly aghast. Even the sons of generals faced the horror of torture.

This indiscriminate repression made many in the elite reconsider their support for the military government. Did the security threat really justify the government's barbarity? Slowly, elite institutions began to react. Best situated was the Catholic Church, whose bishops were outraged by the mistreatment of their clergy. Even conservative bishops who had enthusiastically endorsed the coup now denounced torture. A second elite institution that reacted, albeit more slowly, was the Bar Association. The few criminal lawyers who defended political prisoners and knew first-hand of the torture now tried to rouse their colleagues to action. The lawyers, the cream of the elite, began to discover a new meaning to the rule of law. Yet neither the Church nor the Bar had leverage against the military. The best they could do was spread a discreet word among the elite or leak information to friends abroad.

Even within the military there were signs of unease. Most officers had bought the official line (admitted internally but never publicly) that torture was used immediately after arrest to get "hot" intelligence that would "save lives." But the torturers sometimes continued their work for weeks or even months after the victim's arrest, when there was not even any tactical purpose to such brutality. The military command flatly denied any excesses, while informally officers made it clear that "war is war." In the short run, there was no recourse against the torturers. But there was a larger question. If military rule should end, would the Brazilian elite recognize that torture was in fact the latest expression of a repressive system sustaining the social hierarchy that had benefited them for so long?

Military Rule and Questions about Brazilian Political Tradition

The harsh reality of dictatorship raised another question for Brazilians. Was Brazil's political tradition inherently democratic or authoritarian? The coup of 1964 had ended the democratic era that had resumed in 1945. But 1945 had in turn ended the authoritarian era of 1937–45. What was "normal" for Brazil?

This question is complicated by the need to recognize that torture and repression are not the whole story of the military rule that began in 1964. For the vast majority of Brazilians, the victory of the hard line four years later probably made little if any difference in their lives. Some civilian politicians had been banned from public life, but there was no shortage of replacements, albeit of a less independent turn of mind. The higher military had not themselves assumed most of the administration of Brazil. Aside from critical areas such as security and communications, civilians remained in charge of the government machinery. In states such as Minas Gerais, for example, the politicians who allied with the military won much federal investment for their state.

Certain civilian allies (would-be right-wing theoreticians) of the military sought to help solidify the new regime by formulating a new compulsory educational curriculum known as "Moral and Civic Education." It consisted of an omnibus course (combining geography, geopolitics, conventionally oriented Brazilian history, and a dose of conservative civics) that was required at every level of education, public and private, from kindergarten to the doctoral level. The chief beneficiaries were the textbook writers, who rushed in to win a share of the lucrative new market. Nonetheless, the thinking elite worried about Brazil's image in the world. They had long believed military dictatorships in Latin America occurred only in Spanish America. They saw Brazil as an island of legality in the sea of Spanish American *caudillos* (traditional strongmen). They were right to be worried. Brazil's sharp turn toward authoritarianism in 1968 aroused immediate criticism abroad. The U.S. government, which had grown increasingly worried over the hard-line influence, expressed concern (the public language was mild; behind-the-scenes statements were stronger). Liberals and human rights observers in the United States and west Europe denounced the generals' new move as a signal that Brazil had betrayed its commitment to democracy and the rule of law.

However, although foreigners were denouncing the political tactics of the authoritarian regime, they continued to support Brazil's economic policy, which was yielding great dividends in economic growth.

The Economic "Miracle" Wrought by the Authoritarians

By the end of the Castelo Branco government in 1967, the stabilization program that began soon after the 1964 coup had achieved its principal economic goal: Inflation had been reduced from 90 percent in 1964 to 27 percent in 1967. Much of the foreign debt had been renegotiated and a foundation laid for renewed growth.

That growth appeared in 1968 and opened the way for a six-year boom, during which economic growth averaged the very high rate of 10.9 percent. The economic architect of this boom, as noted, was Delfim Neto, a young São Paulo economics professor recently appointed minister of finance in the new Costa e Silva government. Delfim eased credit in 1967, and the Brazilian economy responded with healthy growth, centered primarily in the industrial sector.

Financial help from the United States was important in establishing the environment for growth. The United States, as a single actor, could commit loan funds more rapidly than the international agencies. The sums were not large in relation to the size of Brazil's economy and its foreign debt, but the impact of U.S. aid was a powerful symbol, made more so by the praise U.S. businessmen, along with the U.S. government, heaped on Brazil for its economic turnaround.

A key policy change was in the financial area. Brazil had no central bank in 1964, and its financial system had verged on the chaotic. Octávio Bulhões and Roberto Campos began a reorganization when the military took over, which continued under Delfim Neto. Two policy instruments were crucial. The first was indexation (automatic adjustment for inflation), which had begun in 1964 for government bonds and became general in the early 1970s. Indexation helped maintain stable capital markets and prod the public to think in real rather than nominal economic terms. The second instrument was the "crawling peg," a system of small but frequent devaluations designed to maintain a realistic exchange rate (i.e., one that adjusted for the difference between the inflation rates of Brazil and the rest of the world). These continuous small adjustments avoided the need for any major devaluations, which had always proved disruptive. Both devices were defended as short-term measures to help in the transition to low or zero inflation. In 1974, that goal still seemed reachable.

The industrial boom stimulated by the easing of credit soon improved industrial wage levels. This also had the effect of increasing the earnings gap between industrial and nonindustrial workers, however. Furthermore, it stimulated rural to urban migration, dramatizing the income differential between the industrialized center-south and the poorer regions, especially the Northeast.

Economists had long argued that Brazil could neither stop inflation nor regain growth until it overcame the bottleneck in agriculture. The solution urged by the pre-1964 "structuralists" was land reform—i.e., redistribution of land ownership. Castelo Branco had promised meaningful land reform but was not able to follow through on his commitment. The agricultural bottleneck was broken however—at least in terms of production—not by land redistribution but by large-scale diversification away from coffee. Brazil became a major producer (and exporter) of orange concentrate (one Brazilian grower reportedly owned more trees than the whole state of Florida). Another virtually new crop was soybeans. Brazil quickly became the second-largest exporter of soybeans (after the United States) and a major supplier to Japan. There was also a steady increase in the production of domestic food crops.

The federal government's generous rural credit policy was one factor behind the increased agricultural production. The government's granting of export subsidies was another. Both policies benefited primarily the large commercial farms and were accompanied by the opening of new lands (Brazil had one of the world's largest reserves of unused arable land). The expansion spread into the *cerrado*, a vast western territory previously lacking transportation facilities. It also moved into western Bahia and the western Amazon Basin, with settlers arriving from states to the south, such as Minas Gerais and Paraná. In 1975, for example, the cerrado produced virtually no soybeans. By 1985 it was producing almost six million metric tons, a third of Brazil's soybean harvest. There was comparable success with rice.

The main beneficiaries of this agricultural boom were the large landowners, who were best situated to take advantage of the easier credit, export subsidies, and other government favors. Federal policy also favored export agriculture, rather than production of domestic foodstuffs. Nonetheless, the latter increased sufficiently to prevent food prices from endangering the boom. All of this had a cost: increased income differentials among regions and classes.

The Benefits and Costs of Foreign Loans

The economic boom was also successful in the external sector. The balance-of payments deficit that was such a major destabilizing factor in 1964 had been reversed by 1968, as Brazil expanded its exports significantly. But the good fortune did not continue indefinitely. The balance of payments went into deficit again starting in the mid-1970s and deteriorated thereafter. (See exhibit 7-1).

In 1973, OPEC, the price-fixing cartel of oil-producing and oil-exporting countries, imposed its first steep price increase. The effect on Brazil was immediate. Since it depended on imports for more than half its oil consumption, Brazil's import bill ballooned. Faced with a threat to the economic boom, Delfim Neto and his advisers decided to "grow their way out of the oil shock." To pay the bill they sharply increased their borrowing abroad, which they could do primarily on the accounts of Brazil's state corporations.

When a second OPEC oil shock followed in 1979, they took two additional steps to reduce oil imports. One was a massive program to produce alcohol fuel from sugarcane for use in passenger cars. Existing gasoline-fueled cars could run on a mixture of 20 percent alcohol and 80 percent gasoline. New car production was quickly shifted to models that burned almost all alcohol. The second step was to accelerate a 1976 program for obtaining German technology to build nuclear reactors. Here again, the goal was to find an alternative energy source for petroleum.

EXHIBIT 7-1

Brazil's Balance of Payments, Selected Categories, 1965–1985

Year	Exports Minus Imports	Net Services	Net Capital	Overall Surplus (+) or Deficit (−)
1965	655	−362	−6	331
1970	232	−815	1,015	545
1975	−3,540	−3,162	6,189	−950
1980	−2,255	−10,152	9,678	−3,472
1985	12,486	−12,878	−2,554	−3,200

Source: IBGE, *Estatísticas Históricas do Brasil*, 2nd ed. (Rio de Janeiro, 1990), pp. 583–85.

EXHIBIT 7-2

Annual Rate of Inflation, 1970–1985

Years	Inflation Rate (%)
1970	16.4
1975	33.9
1980	110.0
1985	235.1

Source: Werner Baer, *The Brazilian Economy*, 6th ed. (Westport, 2008), p. 410.

These steps did not ease the need for borrowing abroad, however, because Brazil had now adopted a strategy of "debt-led growth," aided by the availability of "petrodollars" from the oil-exporting economies. The strategy was understandable in short-run terms. World interest rates continued to be lower than the rate of inflation in New York and London, and Brazil could, for the moment, borrow at negative real rates of interest.

What had seemed sound borrowing strategy in the early to mid-1970s turned slowly but surely into a longer-term disaster. In 1979, OPEC again jacked up the price of oil. By 1980, inflation in Brazil had risen to over 100 percent a year (see exhibit 7-2), and oil was accounting for 43 percent of Brazilian imports. In 1981, a massive credit squeeze, led by the U.S. Federal Reserve Bank, hit the industrial world. Since the interest rates on Brazil's foreign loans were tied to world rates, the interest due on Brazil's loans—the largest in the developing world—shot up. Brazil, like the rest of Latin America, could not make its payments. Latin America went into default on its commercial bank loans, and Brazil's economic boom came to a halt.

The Winners and Losers

What role did labor play in this story? One feature of most developing economies is a relative surplus of labor—the result of the declining demand for labor in agriculture and the high population growth rates in such societies. Surplus low-cost labor can be a benefit or a liability, depending on one's perspective. Such a surplus can be an asset in that it produces a relative wage advantage in producing for export. It can be a liability in that it can depress wages and make union organizing more difficult.

Brazil exhibited both these effects. Its industries recruited cheap labor among rural in-migrants; at the same time, the ready availability of those workers acted as a drag on the wages and working conditions of unskilled and semiskilled labor. Low wages also kept down the level of consumer demand, especially for clothing and less expensive durable goods. Meanwhile, wages for the relatively few high-skilled workers increased rapidly, creating large wage differentials and relatively little labor-market mobility. Benefits from the economic boom were therefore distributed very unequally. At least half the labor force fell outside the formal labor market altogether, making them (in addition to earning very low cash wages) ineligible for the corporatist system of health care, vacations, and pensions created by Getúlio Vargas.

The lot of individual workers varied greatly by where they lived. Those in the industrializing center-south had a chance at the better jobs. Those in the countryside were the poorest. They were most numerous in the Northeast, but large pockets of rural poverty existed also in the South and West. The labor unions could do little in the way of working-class mobilization. The existence of a large surplus labor force inhibits union militancy even in an open society. Under the military regime, unions were subject to control and manipulation by the Ministry of Labor. How successful they could be in organizing if and when democracy returned was a question no one could answer.

Who got the income and wealth generated by the rapid growth of the 1970s? Any perceptive visitor to Brazil could have given an answer. Every large city had its construction boom, especially of high-rise apartments. The better-off "non-manual workers" (in the demographer's term) were acquiring luxurious quarters—at least compared with those inhabited by 90 percent of Brazilians.

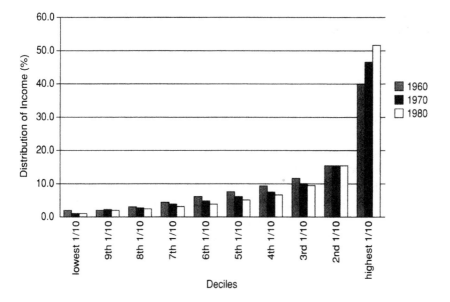

EXHIBIT 7-3

Distribution of income for the economically active population, by deciles, 1960–1980. From IBGE, *Estatísticas Históricas do Brasil*, 2nd ed. (Rio de Janeiro, 1990), p. 77.

How could this contrast be exposed in the language of economists? The official data on income distribution showed increased inequality (see exhibit 7-3). They were much cited by critics at home and abroad. But the data also showed that every income group had improved its absolute income level during the 1970s. The shares of the economic pie had grown more unequal but the absolute size of each slice had become larger. The publication of these data provoked great controversy. Critics of the government at home and abroad emphasized the growing inequality; government supporters emphasized the increasing absolute shares.

Other indicators, except of course civil liberties, showed steady improvement. During the 1960 to 1987–88 period, infant (under five) mortality dropped from 160 to 85 per 1,000. Over the same period, overall life expectancy increased from fifty-five to sixty years. Literacy rates rose, as did the number of homes with indoor plumbing (crucial for improving public health). Finally, access to radio continued to increase and television became a reality for many, transforming the leisure time of millions.

Perceptions of these facts were as important politically as the facts themselves. Brazil was becoming a test case for capitalism in the developing world of the 1970s. Its boosters called it an "economic miracle." Those on the left and left-center cited the data on income inequality as proof that the authoritarian regime was bent on rewarding the rich. (See exhibit 7-3.) They also pointed to continuing urban-rural inequalities. The government defenders, led by Delfim Neto, acknowledged the inequalities but dismissed them as inevitable in a vigorously growing capitalist economy. "The pie must grow before it can be divided up," they liked to note. They pointed to the large inequalities produced by U.S. and west European nineteenth-century growth—inequalities that had even grown in the early twentieth century before subsequently moderating. They argued that when Brazil was farther down the capitalist road it would exhibit more equal income distribution.

The left was in a difficult position with one aspect of this largely ideological debate. They had declared in 1964 (and before) that any stabilization program would plunge Brazil into a long recession. They were proved wrong. With inflation under control, Brazil had succeeded in resuming growth, however distorted the distribution of its benefits. Some critics acknowledged this point. Celso Furtado, for example, writing from exile in Paris, published a series of theoretical treatises explaining how, despite dire predictions, the economy had managed to resume growth. He even acknowledged that this growth strategy could continue to operate, however distasteful its social effects.

The debates over economic justice versus growth had their counterparts abroad. The World Bank now saw Brazil as a case of economic growth at the cost of social justice. The question to which no one knew the answer was whether this spectacular growth record could be achieved only by an authoritarian regime, and only at the cost of rising income inequality. Would the technocrats always need military protection to carry out their unpopular decisions? And would growth always require rewarding the rich so their savings could finance needed investment? Brazil was on the way to finding out.

The Road to Redemocratization

The initiative for political change, surprisingly enough, came from within the military itself. The leader was General Ernesto Geisel, who assumed the presidency in 1974 after his indirect election by the Congress. Geisel had the reputation of being a stern, humorless officer, known for going by the book. But he remained a Castelista (read: *moderate*), a trait that had grown stronger when he headed the military household during Castelo Branco's presidency. His political adviser was General Golbery Couto e Silva, a closet democrat whom he made head of his civil household. The subsequent internal history of the regime was the battle between the hard- and soft-line factions over a possible transition to civilian rule.

Golbery, a consummate behind-the-scenes maneuverer, started playing a complicated game with the civilian opposition. As of 1974, the Catholic Church was the most important other player. Its human rights advocates had long demanded an accounting for the several hundred missing Brazilians. Golbery met with the Catholic Church and other opposition leaders and promised to return with information from Geisel. At the same time, he was sending signals to labor union leaders in São Paulo. Golbery was widely distrusted, but his influence with Geisel could not be doubted.

The Geisel government accompanied this political maneuvering with an easing of censorship and police surveillance in 1974–75, a move that emboldened opposition groups. The Bar Association, in particular, became more aggressive. A few progressive business leaders from São Paulo called for a return to democracy. And São Paulo metalworkers began spontaneous meetings to protest wage policies.

For the rest of the Geisel presidency, which ended in 1979, authoritarianism was slowly eroded by the interaction of the soft-line military and the increasingly vocal civilian opposition. Neither could have succeeded without the other, but the process was long because of hard-line interference.

Battles within the Officer Corps

Not surprisingly, Golbery's overtures alarmed the hard-line military. They disdained him personally (calling him "the General from Dow" for his earlier highly paid consulting with Dow Chemical, an American firm). They also persuaded their colleagues in the repressive apparatus to begin a new security crackdown designed to discredit Golbery's contacts with the opposition.

The hard line's logic was as simple as it was absurd: They believed Brazil suffered from the malignant disease of "populism," "communism," or "corruption"—terms they used interchangeably. The more fanatical officers saw this malady as a challenge to Christian civilization, of which Brazil was presumably a bulwark. By this logic, pornography was as great a threat as Cuban agents. Unlike the Castelistas, who thought a few years of military rule would be enough of a convalescence to cure the disease, the hard-liners believed Brazil was suffering from an entrenched cancer that could be cured only by decades of harsh treatment. They also made sure to build their own network of cronies to guarantee themselves the best military postings and the best benefits. Although the Castelistas also distrusted most politicians, they came from the "legalist" Brazilian military tradition, believing that ultimately only popular elections gave legitimacy. After a decade of authoritarian medicine, the soft line now wanted a return to democracy under carefully controlled conditions.

This strategy, identified closely with General Golbery, implied several important rules of engagement. First, there could be no public admission of torture or other illicit activity. Second, no punishment could be permitted for those, military or civilian, who had served in the security apparatus. Third, all officers must follow the strict rules of retirement, which included a limit on "years in rank" (decreed earlier by Castelo Branco). In other words, the Brazilian army insisted upon rotation of its general presidents to ensure that no general was allowed to perpetuate himself in power. This principle, in particular, distinguished them from the Argentine generals, who failed to limit the term of their military presidents, making them perennial targets for overthrow. Finally, seniority by age was to be strictly observed.

The Castelistas had one important factor in their favor. The military government had never completely repressed the main civilian political institutions. The Congress remained open (although partially purged) and directly elected. It was also used to elect succeeding general-presidents. This approach contrasted with later military governments in Argentina and Chile, which simply abolished their legislatures.

Brazil's way out of authoritarianism was also influenced by the international context. The elite was highly aware of their country's image abroad, just as they had been since the nineteenth century. As a group, they identified strongly with the North Atlantic democracies. Brazil had been the only Latin American country to send troops to fight Hitler, and identification with the victorious allies was also central to the officer corps's identity. The use of torture and the abuse of human rights since 1964 had brought heavy criticism from churches (including the Vatican), politicians, and intellectuals in the United States and western Europe. The Brazilian elite's fear of social revolution (which was fading fast after a decade of repressive government) was being overtaken by their desire to return to the democratic world.

United States influence was crucial in this changing calculus, and after the authoritarian turn in 1968, U.S. approval of the 1964 coup began to be mixed with criticism. The economic boom of the 1970s gave the military some added legitimacy in the eyes of the outside world, but did not erase Brazil's repressive image. Thus, the Brazilian elite's desire for international respectability aided the soft-liners in their plans.

Manipulating the Electoral System

President Geisel had to worry about winning elections if he was to stay ahead of his hard-line enemies. In his first presidential year, he had decided to change a previous campaign rule that denied the opposition access to television. As a result, both parties were to be given free television time in the 1974 elections. The main opposition party, the MDB, won major victories in every state where voters were exposed to anti-government TV campaigns. As a result, the government lost its two-thirds majority in the Congress and therefore its ability to amend the Constitution at will.

What had been intended as a minor concession to critics turned out to be a major setback that put Geisel and Golbery in a dilemma. They wanted to change other electoral rules as well (to strengthen the government party's position) but could not now count on automatic congressional support. To deal with the situation, Geisel had to issue a series of arbitrary decrees ("The April Package of 1977"), which were in fact constitutional amendments. The Fifth Institutional Act had given the president this power, and he now used it to pack the Senate with nonelected presidential appointees and to unilaterally amend the constitution. The new senators were quickly dubbed "bionic," demonstrating both Brazilian wit and the influence of U.S. TV programs (the reference is to "the bionic man" on U.S. TV's *The Six Million Dollar Man*) in Brazil. Armed with these new weapons, Geisel and Golbery felt they could guarantee government party electoral victories and prevent the civilian opposition from gaining power. Golbery returned to negotiating with leading groups in civil society.

When Geisel left power in 1979, the path for the transition had been laid out. It was to be "slow, gradual, and certain," in Geisel's words. The fifth general-president was João Batista Figueiredo, hand-picked by Geisel. He apparently thought Figueiredo's genial personality would help give the military government a new face. Geisel, as noted, had been a stiff, rather stereotypically German figure (his father was an immigrant German schoolteacher). He never held a press conference in Brazil (there was one given abroad) or made any other gesture to woo the public. Yet Geisel played a crucial role in disarming the hard line and managing an extremely tricky transition back toward electoral democracy.

Figueiredo's easy manner made a favorable first impression, and he continued the process of relaxing authoritarian power while keeping the hard line at bay. In August 1979, the Congress passed (knowing the government would accept) an amnesty law which, as was typical in Brazilian history, applied to *all* political crimes, whether by the government or the opposition. The exiles, famous and not so famous, began streaming back home. Golbery remained as chief political advisor to the new president and continued his efforts to shore up the government party. He was aided by the bionic senators' presence, which gave him the two-thirds majority he needed to manipulate the electoral rules in the government's favor.

But the economic scene was daunting. Figueiredo inherited the intensifying debt crisis, which reached a breaking point in 1981–82. He brought back Delfim Neto as finance minister, but Delfim's skills at monetary manipulation could no longer match the world forces working against Brazil.

Figueiredo was, however, helped along on another dimension. A new generation of army officers had emerged who had graduated from the military academy since 1964. No longer necessarily anti-Vargas or even anti-Goulart activists, they were worried about their profession's image among fellow Brazilians. The lurid stories of torture now tarnished the entire military. Some military officers had even stopped wearing their uniforms in public for fear of ridicule. They saw the hard line as having dragged their profession in the dust. Nor were these officers as susceptible to the psychology of the "red scare" as their predecessors had been. The hard line was losing support where it counted most—within the army officer corps.

Meanwhile, in the civilian sphere a spirited campaign had begun to restore direct election of the president in 1985, with millions of supporters wearing T-shirts that read, "I want to vote for president!" It began, logically enough, with the PMDB, then picked up endorsement from top Catholic clergy, and soon became an enthusiastic movement featuring regional rallies that reached 500,000 in Rio and one million in São Paulo. The rallies featured pop singing stars such as Fafá da Belém and Elba Ramalho and even Brazil's leading soccer announcer, Osmar Santos. It was an outpouring of civic spirit unprecedented since the military seized power two decades earlier. Unfortunately, the effort fell short in the government-controlled Congress, where, despite enormous public pressure, proponents of the direct election of the president came up just twenty-two votes short of the required two-thirds majority. There was massive public disillusionment.

All attention was now centered on the jockeying for the presidential election, which would again be indirect, taking place in Congress. The generals faced a predictable challenge: The government party wanted to nominate a civilian candidate. The leading contender was Paulo Maluf, the indirectly elected governor of São Paulo in 1979, famous for his tough right-wing stand in Paulista politics. Maluf had inherited great wealth (from both his own family and that of his wife) and was one of Brazil's most aggressive political campaigners. Many observers on the center and left found him crude and unscrupulous, not least for his use of the police, when governor, to suppress strikes and civic demonstrations.

The opposition had united behind Tancredo Neves, the governor of Minas Gerais and a political veteran of high office in the governments of both Vargas

Newly elected President Tancredo Neves. Embodying the hopes shared by all Brazilians of a peaceful return to democracy following military rule, he died before he could take power. (© Bettmann/CORBIS)

and Goulart. His personality and politics contrasted sharply with those of Maluf. He was a quiet, discreet, diminutive charmer who preferred the politics of intimate negotiation to public bombast. And he was known as the ultimate centrist.

Maluf's drive for the official nomination had set on edge the teeth of numerous PDS leaders. They disliked his style and worried that he could not be trusted as president. No longer afraid of the military at the top, they began to defect from the PDS, forming a splinter party (the PFL or Partido da Frente Liberal) with just enough congressional votes to give Tancredo the election. Tancredo was meanwhile negotiating discreetly with the military to assure them that as president he would treat them well. Not least was his promise to increase the military budget, which had lagged badly in recent years. The military's financial situation was certainly desperate. By the early 1980s, units at the Villa Militar, for example, had no ammunition for target practice, and the frontier units in Rio Grande do Sul were denied the ultra-modern military vehicles Brazil was exporting.

The defectors' strategy succeeded. The dissenting PDS votes (now under the PFL label) combined with those of the PMDB to make Tancredo the first elected civilian president since Jânio Quadros. His election met with public rejoicing and, more interestingly, minimal concern by the military. He was, virtually everyone agreed, the ideal leader to restore Brazil to the ranks of electoral democracies.

8

Redemocratization—New Hope, Old Problems

An Unintended Succession

The excitement surrounding Tancredo's pending accession to the presidency was short-lived. Following his tried-and-true methods of maximizing support, Tancredo was keeping the many contenders for office hopeful but in the air about their chances. Negotiations for the new cabinet were particularly intense—with Tancredo making promises left and right and keeping those promises close to his chest—when persistent rumors began to surface about his health. As time passed, it became increasingly clear to those in the know that the president-elect was seriously ill. The public knew that he needed surgery, but the gravity of his true condition was kept a closely guarded secret.

All hell broke loose on the eve of his inauguration in Brasília on March 15, 1985. Tancredo was stricken with such acute stomach pains that he was rushed to the nearest military hospital. Vice president José Sarney was hastily installed as provisional president and Tancredo underwent intestinal surgery. The scene at the hospital was a nightmare. Sterile conditions were impossible because of the crowds of political cronies and hangers-on that filled the operating room. Then, Tancredo's intestine ruptured. If the cause of his condition was an infection, the rupture certainly spread it into his abdominal cavity.

The surgeons declared their work a success, and the president-elect was said to be on the mend, but that was not the truth, as the spokesmen must have known. He continued to have dreadful intestinal symptoms, frightening his physicians into sending him by air to Brazil's best hospital, not surprisingly in São Paulo. By the time Tancredo underwent his seventh surgery, on April 12, the gravity of his condition, if not its cause, was widely known, stimulating a lengthy public vigil as millions of Brazilians directed their prayers to his hospital room. Hundreds of religious offerings, both Christian and Afro-Brazilian, surrounded the hospital entrance. As one journalist noted, "It wasn't just Tancredo in intensive care, it was the whole country."

Tancredo died on April 21, 1985, amid recriminations from all sides about the management of his medical care and the news releases about his condition. Had the care been incompetent in Brasília? Was there a cover-up in São Paulo? Rumors still persist that Tancredo died of stomach cancer and that his closest advisers kept it secret for fear that the news might derail the new democracy just as it started. The truth remains a secret. But the reaction of Brazilians to his death was certainly genuine. In São Paulo, two million people lined the street to bid adieu as Tancredo's body began its journey back to São João Del Rei, his birthplace in Minas Gerais. Tancredo's funeral was the most massive outpouring of public grief since the funeral that followed Vargas's suicide three decades earlier.

Once again, Brazil was to be governed by a vice president, José Sarney, Tancredo's running mate, who was suddenly thrust into the spotlight of full presidential power.

Sarney and the New Democracy

José Sarney was a long-time member of the political elite (he was first elected federal deputy in 1958) and PDS national party president from the poverty-stricken northeastern state of Maranhão. He had been put on the ticket as a concession to the PDS congressmen who had defected to vote with the PMDB to ensure Tancredo's victory. Sarney was an old-style politician for whom politics meant little more than getting elected and dispensing patronage. He soon used the patronage attached to the presidency to woo the PMDB, Tancredo's party.

Sarney's presidency faced two gargantuan tasks: rebuilding democracy after a hiatus of almost two decades, and resolving yet another inflationary crisis. To strengthen his own hand, his first action was to push to extend his term from four to five years. Intensive horse trading and generous dispensing of new television licenses to congressmen who were swing votes achieved the extended mandate he sought.

A return to open politics demanded a new Constitution and free political parties. The drafting of the Constitution was a task for the Congress (constituted also as a Constituent Assembly) that was elected in November 1986. Thus, the Constitution-writing task fell to a set of congressmen elected in the normal cycle of congressional elections. It took over a year to draft the Constitution of 1988, which was the result of one of the most intense lobbying efforts in the history of the Brazilian Congress. Lobbyists representing leftist groups in the Church, the union movement, and the human rights community were especially active. Much of its content represented a victory for populist ideas against many of the principles advocated by the military government.

The new Constitution stipulated a long list of citizen rights and reaffirmed such corporatist tenets as absolute job tenure for federal civil servants (Federal University faculty, for example, got tenure after one year of service). It was also nationalist in establishing the inviolability of Petrobrás, the state oil monopoly. These measures were all attempts by the heirs of the populist tradition to prevent another 1964.

The populists failed in their attempt to include a strong agrarian reform provision, however. The provision owed its decisive defeat to conservative congressmen, who were unworried at seeing Vargas-style corporatist measures continue in the urban sector, but wanted no truck with expanding property rights in the countryside. A new organization of rural landowners, the União Democrática Rural, outflanked the agrarian reform advocates through intense and effective lobbying. The conservative message was clear: Guarantees of human rights were harmless, but threatening land rights was another matter.

One of the most important constitutional provisions was a new allocation of federal revenues. The military governments had concentrated more and more spending power in Brasília, a concentration that caused frustration and resentment among state governors and mayors. Although this trend had reversed by 1985, the Constituent Assembly, whose members largely identified with the states and *municípios*, sought to further correct the balance by increasing the share of the federal revenues for lower levels of government. Before 1988, 44.6 percent of revenues went to the federal government and 55.4 percent to the states and municipalities. Now the division became 36.5 percent and 63.5 percent, respectively. The revenue shift was made without reducing the federal government's constitutional responsibilities, however, thus virtually guaranteeing permanent federal deficits. Seen in a larger context, it was a continuation of Brazil's long alternation between centralization and decentralization, both politically and economically. Previous pendulum swings had happened in 1830, 1841, 1889, 1930, 1937, 1945, 1964, and 1969.

Most Brazilian politicians and editorial writers congratulated themselves on their country's new "magna carta," praising its up-to-date democratic content. The problems inherent in some of its more exaggerated provisions would take longer to be appreciated.

The political party system presented a more intractable problem because the existing parties were badly fragmented. General Golbery had begun manipulating the electoral laws in the early 1980s in a successful effort to divide the opposition and thus assure a continuous majority for the government party. This fragmentation had now assumed a momentum of its own, however, which threatened the stability of the democracy Golbery had worked to achieve. Ever since the PDS, the government party, had lost its majority in the Chamber of Deputies in 1982, the number of parties had grown and the rules for their operation had become more lax—especially with legislation passed in 1985. Castelo Branco's 1965 plan for a two-party system had collapsed once military control was relaxed and the military needed to manipulate the vote to remain in power. By 1985, eleven parties were represented in Congress, and by 1991 the total had reached nineteen. Such fragmentation, accompanied by weak party discipline, encouraged individual wheeling and dealing by congressmen and made consensus on policy action, especially with regard to the economy, virtually impossible.

The effects of this fragmentation complicated an already delicate moment in the evolution of post-1985 democracy. With the first direct presidential election since the 1964 coup scheduled for November 1989, two major factors combined to make voter preferences unpredictable and potentially highly unstable. First, Brazil now had a huge electorate dominated by relatively young voters who had never faced a genuine choice at the polls. The total vote for president in 1960 was 12.6 million. In 1989, it turned out to be 82 million. Uncertainty about their preferences was aggravated by the fact that the minimum voting age had dropped from eighteen years to sixteen (although voting was compulsory only for those eighteen or older). The second factor contributing to potential instability was the election schedule, with elections at some level—federal, state, or municipal—planned for every one of the next four years. During the military regime the hard- and soft-line officers had disagreed on how unstable a free electorate might be. The answer was now at hand.

The Cruzado Plan

The main economic problem facing Sarney as he took office was the continuing foreign debt crisis stimulated by the "debt-led" growth of the 1970s, which finally caught up with the Brazilian economy in 1983. In order to meet payments on its foreign debt, the government resorted to both increased domestic public debt and money creation. This meant that servicing the foreign debt had forced the Brazilian government to feed the flames of inflation. Brazilian inflation was over 200 percent a year, and the Sarney government had to do something about it.

In late 1985, a group of young and innovative government economists designed a new stabilization plan. It was a heterodox plan, similar to the Austral plan that was simultaneously being attempted in Argentina. The term "heterodox" was meant to indicate that it differed from the "orthodox" plans long urged by the IMF. The plan began in February 1986 with the introduction of a new currency, the cruzado, to replace the existing unit, the cruzeiro. Prices, the exchange rate, and wages (after an initial adjustment) were frozen, and indexation was virtually eliminated. After this initial phase, a 20 percent annual wage increase was instituted (in line with Finance Minister Dilson Funaro's populist inclinations), and the monetary policy was expansive.

Brazilian President José Sarney speaks with officials aboard his jet. A typical political product of northeastern Brazil, he used traditional political wiles to survive in the turbulent days of redemocratization after Tancredo's tragic and untimely death. (National Geographic/Getty Images)

For the next few months the plan appeared to be a success. Inflation fell to less than 2 percent a month, negligible by Brazilian standards of the time. But a consumer boom ensued, with labor shortages provoking further wage increases. By mid-1986, the economy was clearly overheating. The corrective measures urged by the technocratic team were politically unpalatable to both Finance Minister Funaro and President Sarney, however, neither of whom wanted to cut short the boom.

The euphoria lasted through the November congressional and gubernatorial elections, in which Sarney and the PMDB won a stunning victory. Its delegation in the Chamber of Deputies went from 201 to 261 (out of 487), and its number of senators rose from 23 to 45. The PMDB also swept the gubernatorial elections in the most populous states. It looked as if the democratic opposition had finally won a decisive vote of confidence against the authoritarians. In fact, it was the swan song of the PMDB, which was about to begin a long and inglorious decline as its party identity eroded.

In addition to rampant inflation, there was trouble on the balance-of-payments front. The officially frozen exchange rate was becoming increasingly overvalued, as imports were favored and exports discouraged. The unmistakable sign of panic came in February 1987 when Funaro suspended interest payments on the foreign debts owed to private banks. It was the unilateral moratorium that Brazilian finance ministers had long been avoiding. It was also the last populist gesture of Funaro, who was struggling with terminal cancer.

EXHIBIT 8-1

Annual Rate of Inflation, Selected Years, 1980–1989

Year	Inflation % Variation
1980	110.0
1985	235.1
1987	415.8
1988	1037.6
1989	1782.9

Source: Werner Baer, *The Brazilian Economy*, 6th ed. (Westport, 2008), p. 410.

By 1987, the Cruzado Plan had become just another failed stabilization program. Indexation was reinstated as a way to live with inflation, and the public once again turned cynical about all government plans. We will never know for certain, of course, but there is a pretty fair consensus among experts that, if politics had not beaten the technocrats—if Sarney had put on the economic brakes at the right time—the Cruzado Plan stood a good chance of beating inflation and setting Brazil on a steady growth path.

Such was not to be the case. The last two years of the Sarney presidency saw the economy go increasingly out of control. Inflation for 1988 reached 1038 percent. Brazilians had long lived with inflation rates that seem unimaginable to Americans, but never like this. (See exhibit 8-1.) A poll in mid-January 1989 in greater Rio and São Paulo registered a 70 percent "no confidence" rating for the president.

The Debt Crisis and the Economy

The effects of the 1982 debt crisis were to linger for many years, as Brazil was obligated to spend much of its scarce foreign exchange on servicing its foreign debt. The only solution for the debt to the foreign commercial banks was to roll it over, which meant paying more interest in the future. New loans were unavailable at any price, since the commercial banks had stopped making new commitments. All this was accompanied by an inevitable drop in both public and private investment in Brazil. Real investment as a share of GDP averaged 23 percent in the 1970s but dropped to 17 percent in the 1980s.

There was still another source for Brazil's economic problems, which had to do strictly with Brazil's past economic policy decisions, especially since the 1930s. With the loss of export earning capacity after the 1929 crash, Brazil concentrated on "inward looking" development. The years of high tariff protection (identified with "import-substituting industrialization") had encouraged inefficiency in Brazilian industry. A notable example was the computer industry, where the government had banned both imported products and foreign-owned domestic producers. The logic for this policy came initially from the Brazilian military, who opposed dependence on foreign suppliers for technology crucial to weapons systems. The policy was quickly embraced by the economic nationalists in the civilian sector. The result was a domestic computer industry known for high prices, low quality, and out-of-date technology. Meanwhile, smuggling of foreign-made equipment became a major industry.

This industrial protection had been accompanied by an inadequate effort to import up-to-date technology more generally. A prime example was the automobile industry. Although its wage rates were low, Brazilian car makers had total costs that rivaled or exceeded those of western Europe. Finally, the public sector continued to be highly inefficient. State enterprises such as Petrobrás and the ports were infamous for their overstaffing and inflated salaries. Poor management of the state-owned electric utilities and telephone companies, along with the badly maintained rail and road system, also added to the cost of doing business in Brazil (foreign investors called it *custo Brasil*, or "the Brazilian cost").

These factors more than explained why Brazil was in economic trouble. There was no shortage of suggested solutions as the economists in and out of government offered their formulae. In the end, however, all solutions depended for implementation upon political leadership, and leadership was in short supply in the Sarney years.

Lost Investment

The mid- to late 1980s saw Brazil lose two types of investment. The first was reduced investment in the physical capital that was key to growth in the economy. The second was lost human capital from a brain-drain out-migration of Brazilians looking for better lives abroad.

Domestic investment in Brazil's business and public infrastructure was a major loser in the economic slowdown of the 1980s in Brazil. An obvious culprit was low consumer demand in the economy. With low wages, workers had less money to spend. Given the government's inability to cure inflation and resume growth, few sensible businessmen wanted to risk expanding their productive capacity. On the contrary, in many sectors (especially where competition was weak) businesses maintained high prices in order to compensate for low volume.

The government's decision to reintroduce indexation in late 1986 also contributed. In the short run, indexation, first introduced in the mid-1960s, had proven highly effective in neutralizing many of the price distortions produced by inflation and forcing economic actors—individual and corporate—to think in real, not nominal terms. But indexation produced its own distortions because it was not applied uniformly across the economy. By the late 1980s, there were scores of different indexation tables (with different rates of adjustment) applied to contracts.

The one type of contract for which full indexation was guaranteed was government debt. In order to finance the federal deficit, the Central Bank had to sell bonds to the public. In order to make the bonds attractive, they had to include full indexation and a high rate of real interest. The Central Bank also needed to make the bonds attractive in order to induce wealthy Brazilians (and foreigners) to keep their money in Brazil rather than sending it abroad. The need to finance the deficit, along with the need to prevent capital flight, further encouraged the use of indexation. The government achieved its purpose, at least partially. It was able to market its bonds, although by the late 1980s it was no longer able to stem large-scale capital flight.

The price of the Central Bank's decision on indexation policy was high, because it greatly encouraged financial speculation. Investors could routinely earn double-digit real returns on their capital by simply investing in government bonds. This helped make the banking sector the most profitable in the economy. It also resulted in a substantial diversion of capital from productive investment to financial speculation. The consequences were serious for Brazilian industry, which was not getting the capital it badly needed for modernization. Brazil was turned into a tropical paradise for financial manipulators. Finally, indexation had the effect of "institutionalizing" inflation. Its critics noted that indexation rarely achieved a reduction in the inflation rate. At best it perpetuated the current rate.

Public investment also suffered. One reason was that current tax revenues were swallowed up by government deficits. A second reason was the irrational pricing policy of the state enterprises. The weak federal and state governments of the 1980s kept prices down on such utilities as petroleum, electricity, water, and telephones, in a desperate attempt to slow inflation and win popularity. Unfortunately, however, prices lagged behind costs, pushing the major state enterprises into deficit and eliminating the surplus needed for investment. Successive governments postponed public-sector investment in the hope that it could be made up later. The quality of the utility services inevitably declined, and the quantity failed to keep pace with demand growth.

This serious lag in private and public investment had dangerous consequences for future stable growth. Should growth resume, industry would soon find itself operating at the limits of its capacity. Furthermore, Brazil's relative productivity was increasing little in this climate of stagnation and low investment. In the ranks of emerging capitalist countries, especially when compared with the dynamic East Asian economies, Brazil had become a conspicuous underperformer.

The Brain Drain

The brain drain during the 1980s of some of the best and brightest from Brazil was perhaps the strongest symbol of how low Brazil's morale had sunk. At less than 1 percent of the population, the size of the outflow may have been modest, but the fact that Brazilians were choosing to leave at all was the startling point. Brazilians had long been famous for their fierce loyalty to Brazil. Foreigners marveled at the patriotism of their Brazilian friends. Even in difficult times, Brazilians had kept alive the belief that theirs was the country of the future.

There was no major exodus even when doubt began to set in during the military government, aside from the political exiles whose circumstances forced them out. The economic boom of the 1970s undoubtedly provided an economic incentive to stay, even for Brazilians who may have been repelled by the repression. When Brazil returned to civilian government in the mid-1980s, genuine loyalty and optimism revived. The Brazilian pattern continued to be staying close to the home state. Going abroad was always temporary.

The disorganization, corruption, and economic chaos of the Sarney government sapped this patriotism. Brazilians began voting with their feet. Their prime destinations were the United States (610,000) and Japan (170,000), with a smaller number heading for Portugal, whose membership in the European Community made it attractive. Given its ill-defended borders and generally ineffectual immigration controls, the United States—and especially such cities as Miami, New York, and Boston—was a favorite destination for growing Brazilian exile communities. These Brazilians were leaving not for political reasons but because they wanted a better life. The influx to Japan consisted of Brazilians of Japanese descent who found they could earn more in a menial job in Japan than in a skilled profession in Brazil. The Japanese government strengthened the appeal by granting Brazilians of Japanese descent special visas. Japanese social welfare agencies even had to open offices to counsel the Brazilian arrivals, who were of Japanese ancestry but became disoriented because they could not speak a word of Japanese and because the Japanese did not accept them as authentic Japanese.

This loss of Brazilians to foreign countries was particularly painful because it often involved the most energetic and talented of Brazilian citizens. Furthermore, they were taking their talents away from Brazil primarily to the two leading world economies—an ominous sign of what critics called the "reversal of development" in Brazil. The fact that it was occurring under the new democracy made it particularly dispiriting.

Widening Gaps between Rich and Poor

A major factor contributing to the drain of Brazilians in search of a better deal abroad was ever-widening economic and social disparities within an environment of declining public investment. Income, education, health, housing, transportation—all were facets of Brazil's "social debt."

As already discussed, the economic boom of the 1970s had increased income inequality in Brazil. (See exhibit 8-2.) Income for all income groups increased, but the rich got richer much faster than the poor got less poor. In the years of stagnation during the 1980s, real incomes actually fell for some groups, especially those at the lower end of the distribution. This was caused, at least in part, by what economists call the "inflation tax." Those at the bottom had to

EXHIBIT 8-2

Income Inequality in Brazil, 1960–1990*

	1960	1970	1980	1990
Lowest 20%	3.5	3.2	3.0	2.3
Next 60%	42.1	34.6	30.9	31.6
Top 20%	54.4	62.2	66.1	66.1
	100	100	100	100
Top 10%	39.7	47.8	51.0	49.7
Top 5%	27.7	34.9	33.8	35.8

*Percent of economically active population with nonzero incomes.
Source: Susan Kaufman Purcell and Riordan Roett, eds., *Brazil Under Cardoso* (Boulder, 1997), p. 73.

operate primarily in cash, the value of which deteriorated sharply (often by 50 percent or more) between pay periods. Wealthier individuals could use checking accounts, which were corrected (indexed) for inflation and often added a small real interest rate, thus enabling their pay to retain its value between pay periods. Furthermore, with liquid assets of even a few thousand dollars, they could invest in government bonds, which paid a very high real interest rate. Finally, as always in Brazil, the effect varied greatly by region. (See exhibit 8-3.)

Employment measures were unreliable in Brazil, making it hazardous to measure unemployment among the lowest sectors. There were, however, other symptoms. An important one was crime. Crime rates in the major cities rose in the 1980s, and any visitor from abroad could see the effects. The gracious entries to the apartment buildings of Rio de Janeiro were now surrounded with

EXHIBIT 8-3

Hungry Persons* in Brazil, 1990

Region	Total	Percentage of Region's Total Population
North	685,204	13.9
Northeast	17,288,528	40.9
South	4,082,314	18.1
Southeast	7,982,453	12.4
Center-West	1,640,597	16.1
Brazil	31,679,095	21.9

*"Hungry" is defined as those persons whose income is inadequate to buy sufficient food.
Source: Anna Maria T. M. Peliano, ed., *O Mapa da Fome* (IPEA: Documento de política No. 14: Brasília, 1993).

Alexandre Heng Fai Tsang, the grandson of a prominent Rio restaurant owner, being escorted to safety from Tijuca National Forest sixteen days after having been kidnapped. Organized crime rings regularly kidnapped the rich to extort huge ransoms, leading many Rio residents to turn their houses into veritable fortresses. (AP Photo/João Cerqueira)

elaborate metal gratings to stop vagrants from camping on the steps. Wealthy Brazilians withdrew to expensive new apartment complexes surrounded by electronically controlled fences and guarded by 24-hour patrols.

The epidemic of kidnappings in Rio de Janeiro was a prominent example. They were committed by gangs, often in collusion with the police. And, although millionaires were the obvious targets, even small businessmen fell victim. The response of the wealthy was to hire more bodyguards and ride in armored cars.

Shop owners, annoyed by the presence of hordes of street children committing petty theft, periodically hired off-duty policemen to scare them away and, sometimes, to kill them. In mid-1993, such persecution reached a chilling climax. During the early morning hours of July 23rd, a contingent of well-armed Polícia Militar attacked a group of fifty street children sleeping on the sidewalk in front of Rio's Candelária cathedral. Seven children and one young adult were killed. In São Paulo, the violent hunt for "marginals" was delegated to an elite paramilitary police unit. These heavily armed and smartly uniformed police roamed the São Paulo streets in late-model Jeep Cherokee wagons looking for suspicious street people. They did not hesitate to shoot to kill, and they helped give São Paulo the doubtful honor of having the world's highest homicide rate by a police force.

Brazilians and foreign observers often asked whether this upsurge of crime represented the beginnings of a social upheaval. But ordinary crime did not represent any threat to the established economic order. At most, it was a minor redistribution of income by noneconomic means—i.e., coercion. In no sense did it represent collective mobilization against the established order. Revolution was never likely to come to Brazil at the hands of small-time kidnappers or car thieves.

In fact, the rise in crime probably worked against any greater awareness of social inequality. Violent crime reinforced the Brazilian elite's image of the lower classes as threatening. The result was a shifting of focus from the *trabalhador* (the worker who had a job and was contributing to society) to the *marginal* (the hustler who lived by his street smarts). Focusing on the marginals ("mere criminals") made it easier to ignore the plight of the many millions of hard-working Brazilians at the bottom. It also helped to strengthen the elite's long-time image of the lower classes as "dangerous" rather than "deserving." This effect on the perceptions of the elite was ironical, since it was the poor who suffered most from crime. Police seldom entered the urban slums except as "SWAT teams." In Rio, the hillside shantytowns (*favelas*) became centers for narcotraffic, with its attendant violence. The resulting firefights often killed or wounded innocent residents. But the rich and middle-class victims of crime got all the publicity, both because they made better TV and newspaper copy and because they were victimized in the best sections of town, which became major (negative) news for the international press, affecting the potential tourist trade.

Education and Health Care

Brazil's record in education was one of the worst in the developing world, and the 1980s saw a deterioration even in that dismal record. In major cities where public schools had once educated middle-class children, school systems were in physical decay and educational decline. Teachers' salaries were abysmally low (commonly less than $200 a month and less than $100 a month in the Northeast—in today's prices), and working conditions often equally bad. Brazilian schoolchildren were repeating elementary grades at a higher rate than in any other country. The wealthier middle class reacted by sending their children to private schools, which increased educational segregation by social class and undermined the creation of a cohesive sense of citizenship to which public school systems are dedicated.

The strange thing was that, in this area of public services, the deterioration could not be traced to budget cuts. In 1989, for example, United Nations statistics showed that Brazil was spending almost 18 percent of total public expenditures on education, a respectable share by international standards. The same could be said of Brazil's educational expenditures as a percentage of GDP. The problem clearly was bureaucratic incompetence or fraud. Far too little of the money reached the schoolroom. The results were high dropout rates and an army of half-literate children, most of whom entered the labor market before reaching the normal age for finishing grade school. Public schools had become so overbureaucratized, corrupt, and archaic in their pedagogy that business firms were routinely spending large sums to make up for the training their employees should have received at school. At a time when the East Asian tigers were reducing illiteracy to zero, Brazil was still struggling to bring its illiteracy rate (defined generously) below 20 percent.

Health care—another measure of investment of human capital—was also in a dreadful way in the 1980s in Brazil. Inadequate financing combined with structural disorganization to produce public health care significantly worse than it had been in the 1970s. As in education, what public money there was in the system—much of it in the form of numerous publicly funded, privately run clinics with questionable financial practices—was not reaching the patients. The better-off Brazilians were fleeing the public health care system in the same way as they fled the public schools, joining private health insurance plans that gave them access to special clinics and thereby reinforcing a two-tier delivery system. The super-rich could always fly to Miami or New York for the ultimate supplement in health care.

Housing and Communications

In housing, roads, and the telephone system Brazil also saw a turn for the worse in the 1980s. In housing, the middle and upper classes increasingly fled from the burgeoning urban crime by building massive iron barriers around their apartment buildings and hiring private security guards to protect their entrances. On the outskirts of São Paulo and Rio de Janeiro, for example, new housing complexes (one was called "Alphaville" in São Paulo) were complete with internal recreation areas so the residents did not have to leave even to have fun.

The road and telephone systems were starved into decay because of shrinking funds available for public investment. Deficits at every government level had reduced road maintenance, leaving gaping holes in the main inner-city streets (a Rio newspaper of the 1980s showed a Volkswagen disappearing totally into a pothole) and hazardous conditions on the highways. The main artery connecting São Paulo and Curitiba became known as the "death run." This lack of road maintenance was particularly injurious to the economy because Brazil depended overwhelmingly on road transportation—a dependence that was aggravated by a government decision in the 1950s to concentrate on highways rather than the rail system, which was rarely updated or expanded from then on.

The capacity of the telephone network, into which the military government had poured funds in the 1970s, had also fallen far behind demand by the late 1980s. Residential telephone numbers were regularly advertised for direct sale from one consumer to another in leading newspapers at thousands of dollars each. Low investment combined with failure to raise telephone rates reduced the funds available for the telephone utility's needed expansion. This delayed investment in transportation and communication increased the "Brazil cost" and damaged the country's competitiveness on an international scale.

Public Health: A Success Story

In sharp contrast to the deteriorating public services, Brazil's human-development indicators (monitored by the United Nations) showed steady improvement through the 1980s. Between 1960 and 1990, for example, as we saw earlier, life expectancy rose from fifty-five years to sixty-six years. Over the same period, the mortality rate of children under five years fell from 159 to 83 per 1,000 live births. A key variable explaining these health trends was the access of Brazilians to safe water supplies. That rate rose from 62 percent of the population in 1975–80 to 87 percent in 1988–90.

These figures are best interpreted by putting them into international perspective, however, based on the data gathered by the World Bank and the United Nations. First, Brazil was participating in a favorable worldwide trend. The average absolute improvement in life expectancy for *all* developing countries over the period was seventeen years, compared with Brazil's eleven years. Brazil's reduction of the mortality rate of children under five years was 48 percent compared with 52 percent for all developing countries. In terms of increased access to safe water, Brazil also showed percentage improvements, although less than the average for all developing countries. These improving trends, which were achieved regardless of the type of government or economic system, reflected certain global factors at work. One was urbanization, which made health services and safe water supplies easier to deliver than in rural societies. A second was modern technology, especially in medicine, which made it possible to control epidemic disease and infection at relatively low cost. A third factor was the role of international institutions, which were directing major aid to health and education, furnishing technology, capital, and expertise. The World Bank, for example, played a crucial role in expanding the safe water system in the Brazilian Northeast.

Brazil's slow progress compared with the average for all developing countries is all the more significant in view of the fact that Brazil has exceptional resources. Its 1989 per capita income ($4,951) was more than double the 1989 per capita average ($2,296) for all developing countries. Brazil was not using the resources it had to foster human development as effectively as other parts of the developing world—not an unexpected conclusion given that its income distribution was one of the most unequal.

There was one demographic indicator that brought good news for Brazilian planners: The population growth rate, which had been among the world's highest in the 1950s, had been falling steadily. In the 1970s, it reached an annual rate of 2.5 percent. In the 1980s, it fell to 1.9 percent and in the 1990s to only 1.3 percent. A prime cause for the decline was again urbanization, which increased from 35 percent in the 1950s to 78 percent in the mid-1990s. Another was the widespread recourse, often in government-supported clinics, to sterilization (usually tubal ligation) as a means of birth control.

This drop in population growth rate meant that the strain on overstretched public services such as education and health would be eased as there would be fewer children requiring schools and hospitals. That, in turn, meant lower requirements for investment in infrastructure. Eventually there would be a negative side if the trend continued, however, because there would be fewer workers in the labor force to support the ever larger retired population.

Changes Affecting Women

Brazilian women have traditionally played a small role in Brazilian public life, even though they won the right to vote sooner than in France or in most Latin American countries. When Congress approved female suffrage in 1932, it followed decades of lobbying by a small but dedicated band of middle- and upper-class suffragettes. But this expansion of the voter rolls did little to change the overall position of women in Brazilian society. The dominant middle-class feminine stereotype continued to be a passive, submissive being whose existence was defined as a dutiful daughter and patient wife, and who faced a male-dominated society that blocked her professional advancement in all fields except a few "female" roles, such as teaching and nursing. The reality was, of course, even harsher for the vast majority of working-class women. They had to combine child rearing (often as single parents) and paid work at miserable wages in order to survive.

The coup of 1964 highlighted the fact that the status of women had changed little in the intervening thirty years. In the polarization leading to military seizure of power, women appeared primarily as the middle- and upper-class demonstrators in right-wing demonstrations such as the "March of Family with God for Liberty," the caricature of the traditional "housewifely" role. The military government, through its subsequent manipulation of politics and the media, made it clear that it intended to reinforce that role. The few feminist organizations experienced the general repression of the left.

Ironically, two consequences of military rule after 1964 helped provoke women to challenge their traditional role, with the Catholic Church proving an invaluable ally throughout subsequent struggle. The first stimulus was the harsh repression of 1968–75, which took the greatest toll among the young guerrillas of primarily middle- and upper-class background. This was exactly the social sector that had supported the coup most strongly. Now their sons and daughters were being tortured in the police and military dungeons. This brutality brought rising protests, especially from the mothers, whose maternal indignation created a natural solidarity. As censorship eased in the late 1970s, these mothers organized widely noticed protest rallies that were the harbinger of a new brand of political activism among elite women. It was also at this time that many of these white middle-class women were gaining entry into the male-dominated professions (their numbers rose from 18,000 in 1970 to an estimated 95,800 in 1980) thanks to the growth of the technocratic state and the rapid increase in female university graduates.

The second consequence of the military regime for the women's movement was economic. The economically active female population had increased from 18.5 percent in 1970 to 26.9 percent in 1980. The rapid growth of the economy after 1968, however, was achieved in part by compressing real wages. This "squeeze" aroused indignation among urban workers, especially the working-class wives whose household budgets were buying less and less at the supermarket. In the 1970s, these women organized a movement called "Against the Cost of Living," which directly challenged government economic policy. This movement helped break down the women's fear of authority, gave them a sense of confidence in acting together, and could be seen also in major cities, where working-class women were instrumental in organizing neighborhood associations (Sociedades de Amigos de Bairros or SABs) that demanded improved services such as fresh water, paved roads, and functioning schools.

Another government policy, probably inadvertently, stimulated a rural counterpart to this urban organizing effort. This was a set of financial incentives, especially low-cost credit, paid to the owners of large farms, which enabled them to go in for capital-intensive agriculture and to get rid of their tenant farmers and squatters. Many of these were women who then turned to wage labor, often on the all-female agricultural work crews of *bóias-frias* (the term referred to the cold lunches they carried). These women labored (often cutting sugarcane to be processed in the alcohol program) hard and long and were badly paid. The miserable working environment and the propinquity of the women to one another led them to organize powerful rural unions. In 1984, sixty thousand *bóias-frias* cane cutters demanded and got union recognition. They then bargained successfully for better pay and benefits such as school instruction and medical assistance for themselves and their families (many had to bring children with them to the job).

The feminists, who were primarily middle class, raised their own range of issues, many of which had been simmering for years. One of the most important was reproductive rights. The existing legal system had been designed by male lawgivers. Under its constraints, access to information about (and availability of) contraception was expensive, and abortion was illegal (except to safeguard the life of the mother—a waiver rarely granted). Rich women had access to both at private clinics, but other women found family planning very difficult. Feminists demanded free and accessible contraception, as well as free legalized abortion. They also wanted free community-based daycare.

The feminist campaign had mixed success. It must be pointed out that, when push came to shove, feminists turned out to be very ambivalent about public subsidization of family planning for the poor. For example, daycare facilities were created in several Brazilian cities, a large number of them in São Paulo. There were no changes in the abortion law, however, leaving women with lower incomes vulnerable to dangerous back-alley abortions. In 1981, when São Paulo Governor Paulo Maluf—a right-wing anathema to the feminists, most of whom were left or center-left—launched a privately funded (through Japanese and American sources!), state-administered family-planning program, feminist organizations opposed it. They said that such programs were "genocidal," intended to manipulate poor (and especially nonwhite) women for the benefit of the white elite. By the early 1990s, the federal government had followed in São Paulo's footsteps with a comprehensive family-planning program. Under the banner of protecting the health of the mother, government clinics carried out tubal ligations, often in connection with cesarean births. Feminists, among other critics, claimed that the female patients were deliberately misled, that the "sterilizations" were part of a conspiracy to reduce the "inferior" population. Program defenders replied that all surgical procedures were voluntary and that the women were merely taking advantage of an opportunity to act on a long-felt desire to limit family size or to use sterilization as a solution to serious health problems.

Violence against women was another issue for Brazilian feminists. Wife (or female companion) abuse was widely known to be a serious problem among all Brazilian social classes, but the police and courts traditionally refused to recognize such behavior as criminal. Charges were routinely dismissed, even in cases when abuse by the man turned literally to murder. Judges routinely excused husbands actually convicted of murdering their wives from penalty by accepting a plea "in defense of honor," the claim that the wife was (or intended to be) unfaithful. In 1980, in São Paulo alone, 772 women were reported to have been killed by their husbands or lovers, who escaped penalty. This abuse of justice had become so common in Minas Gerais that a group of middle-class women organized an educational campaign called "Quem Ama Não Mata" ("He Who Loves Doesn't Kill"). Their efforts included visits to judges to convince them of the injustice of accepting the "defense of honor" plea when sentencing convicted wife murderers.

The campaign to stop court acceptance of wife-battering assumed greater visibility in 1985, when feminist groups convinced the governor of São Paulo to create a division for the protection of women in the state police. Specially designated officers (normally women—their office was dubbed the "women's police station") were posted at police stations to handle abuse complaints from women. In dealing with the state authorities, feminist leaders were soon caught up in party politics where corruption and loss of militancy was a constant threat. Although social attitudes on such a basic question were slow to change, at least the feminist campaign had altered somewhat the public discourse.

The ultimate target for the feminist campaign was the dramatic under-representation of women in leadership of such major institutions as state and national government, professional associations, and labor unions. For example, the Constituent Assembly elected in 1986 (which wrote the Constitution of 1988) had only twenty-six women. Once sworn in, they protested their minority status to the assembly president, pointing out that "we represent only 4.9 percent of the Constituent Assembly, while we are 54 percent of the population and 53 percent of the electorate."

Yet some progress was made. For the 1994 municipal council elections, the federal government fixed a minimum female candidate quota of 20 percent. Such a measure would have been unthinkable in the even more sexist atmosphere of the 1964–85 authoritarian regime. Women were still conspicuous by their complete absence on the directorship level of such important professional associations as the Ordem dos Advogados do Brasil (the Bar Association), with 52 percent female membership; the Associação Brasileira de Imprensa (the Press Association), with 40 percent female membership; and the Conselho Nacional de Medicina (the National Medical Association), with 31.5 percent female membership. And although by the late 1990s significantly more women were completing secondary school, women on the whole were earning 40 percent less than men. On the other hand, women had made real inroads in certain professions, especially in the more developed center-south. In São Paulo, for example, 44 percent of the newly registered doctors and 63 percent of the practicing dentists were women by 1997.

Pressure by women workers did lead to significant institutionalization of their interests in the two largest labor union conglomerates: the Central Única dos Trabalhadores (the CUT, or Central Union of Workers) and the Força Sindical (Union Power). In 1986, the CUT created a commission on the question of the woman worker and in 1993 established quotas for women in executive positions. In 1992, the Força Sindical created the National Secretariat for Women, Adolescents, and Children. As one woman union leader active in pursuing these demands put it, "We were educated to be sensitive, affectionate, maternal, everything that means being servile, accepting domination and thinking it's all wonderful. Now we're breaking with this, and we don't want to be anymore wives, mothers, housewives because we are entering public life. We are now going to have 'equal relations and an equal participation in the public world.'"

Despite its failures, such as the failure to achieve legalized abortion, the Brazilian women's movement became the largest, most radical, most diverse, and most effective of women's movements in Latin America. How did it happen? Sonia Alvarez, an expert in the field, suggests four factors: (1) Church support for community organizations, especially among the poor, both urban and rural; (2) the Brazilian left's intensive organizing of opposition groups in which women were prominent; (3) the military government's deliberate opening of political space (a policy known as *abertura*); (4) the government's granting women more organizing latitude than other elements of civil society because they saw women as less threatening.

From a historical perspective, two points are significant. First, a dissenting sector of the white elite had emerged to challenge politics as usual in the white male-dominated world. Second, there had been genuine mobilization among working-class women, both urban and rural. At times the two movements converged and cooperated, but more frequently they were drawn apart by issues of class, race, and ideology. It was a familiar story among the grassroots organizations that flourished at the end of the military regime. Once electoral democracy was restored, the political parties, with their patronage and animus toward ideology, filled the public space. The receding of the women's movement from the spotlight (although it is still much alive, if at a reduced level) reflects a familiar Brazilian dilemma: how to incorporate genuine citizen participation in a political system created for top-down government by a narrow white political elite.

Race Relations

Modern Brazilian race relations have been subject to a misunderstanding similar to that of foreign interpretations of African religion. It began in the nineteenth century, when North American and European travelers absorbed and passed on a mythic history of Brazilian slavery as peaceful coexistence compared with the brutality of slavery in the United States—a view that was reinforced by the violent confrontation of North and South in the U.S. Civil War. Reconstruction subsequently gave way to a long interval of legally enforced racial segregation in the United States, with racial violence a recurrent theme.

This version of the U.S.-Brazilian contrast was given added credence by Gilberto Freyre, whose book *Casa Grande e Senzala*, published in Portuguese in 1933, was translated into English in 1946 as *The Master and the Slaves*. His image of Brazilian slavery as having been "benign" and "humane" and its legacy as racial harmony was adopted and given wide exposure by U.S. historians Frank Tannenbaum and Stanley Elkins in their comparative slavery debate.

Not until 1954 did the U.S. Supreme Court rule that "separate but equal" is not true equality. But the period since 1954 has brought enormous change in the United States. The full force of the law became engaged in attacking racism in public life. Interventionist policies, such as affirmative action, stimulated the rise of a new cadre of African-Americans. Early in the new century, the U.S. race-relations scene is unrecognizable to those old enough to have lived in the pre-1954 system. African-Americans are now represented in highest echelons of public life, including the U.S. presidency as of early 2009, even though discrimination may not have totally disappeared in private life.

This sea change in U.S. society has helped generate a new look at Brazilian society. As late as the 1990s most of the Brazilian elite denied that they lived with racial discrimination, even though Afro-Brazilians were 44 percent of the population and hardly represented in positions of authority. These were dominated (with rare exceptions) by whites—Congress, the Foreign Service, the church hierarchy, military and police officials, and the prestigious professions such as law and medicine. Of the thousands of undergraduate and graduate students at the University of São Paulo (Brazil's most distinguished) in the early 1990s, for example, fewer than a dozen were Afro-Brazilian. There were even fewer Afro-Brazilian faculty members there, and this in a state with a 20 percent Afro-Brazilian population. And it should be remembered that this discrimination occurred in the absence of any legal or institutional support.

The lack of formal barriers made it easier for the white elite to continue describing Brazil as prejudice-free, without the racial conflict that, for example, was constantly reported for the United States. This state of denial was also helped by lack of quantifiable evidence either way until the late 1970s. In 1976, however, the Brazilian Census Bureau, generously funded by the military government, carried out an ambitious national household survey, generating the first reliable national data allowing connections to be made between race, employment, education, income, and other socioeconomic characteristics of the population. Analysis of these data revealed a clear pattern of discrimination against persons of color, with the worst discrimination against blacks, but pervasive discrimination against mulattos also.

This newly evident reality came as unwelcome, if not actually shocking, news to Brazil's white elite and left them vulnerable to Afro-Brazilian demands for reform. In the 1990s, Afro-Brazilians began pressing for interventionist policies such as affirmative action. As of this writing it is unclear whether affirmative action plans will be adopted throughout the society, but such institutions as the federal government ministries and the university systems are already being mandated to institute some form of racial quotas.

Although Afro-Brazilians are slowly increasing their penetration of the upper levels of society, the weight of color prejudice still lies heavily on Brazilian society. The key to more mobility for Brazilians of color lies in increased access to the educational system, which still excludes Afro-Brazilians or misdirects them in their search for more or better options.

Visitors to modern-day Brazil, especially North Americans, often ask why Afro-Brazilians have done so little to protest their plight. Why have they (aside from a very small band of militants) not demanded intervention to counter discrimination? The question reveals a basic misunderstanding of the dynamics of Brazilian race relations, which have proved remarkably stable because all the actors—blacks and mulattos, as well as whites—have believed in key elements of what might be called the "Myth of Racial Democracy." The first element is the belief that race is only a secondary variable in determining life chances. More important variables, in the view of most Brazilians, are social class and education or the luck of the clientalistic culture. Second, Brazilians know the patrimonial system militates against any mobilization from the bottom up. Afro-Brazilians, who are mostly at the bottom of the socioeconomic scale, are therefore doubly affected (class and race) by that deferential mind-set. Third, anyone trying to organize Afro-Brazilians on racial lines faces a problem unique to Brazil: the almost complete lack of nonwhite solidarity. This can be explained in part by the absence, at least since the eighteenth century, of any formal segregation or other form of official discrimination. The kind of parallel nonwhite institutions, such as produced by United States segregation, are missing in Brazil. The pervasive Brazilian aspiration for "whitening" (and therefore the denigration of blackness) has further undermined efforts of solidarity. Mulattos, for example, proved notoriously difficult to recruit for any racially oriented political project because they tend to see themselves as completely separate from the black community. In this respect they have implicitly accepted the myth of the "mulatto escape hatch," even though census data of the 1970s showed that mulattos did only marginally better than blacks (and much worse than whites) in employment, education, and income.

All these factors combined to cripple Afro-Brazilian organizing efforts. That could be seen in the fate of the Afro-Brazilian mobilization of the late 1970s. Afro-Brazilians took advantage of the climate of relaxed government control then to organize the Movimento Negro Unificado (Black United Movement). They protested incidents of veiled discrimination and demanded punishment of the alleged white offenders. They got considerable publicity but had little political effect.

Other Afro-Brazilians chose a different path in those years. Rejecting political protest, they called instead for recognition of Brazil's *cultural* legacy from Africa. They celebrated African-style art, music, language, and the Afro-Brazilian religion expressed in such rituals as *candomblé*. In effect, these "culturalists" were emphasizing the separateness of Afro-Brazilians, not their possible status for integration into a white-dominated society. Their net effect, however, was to divert attention from the fledgling Afro-Brazilian protest movement.

At the same time, some leaders of elite culture began to show increased awareness of the problem of racial discrimination. President Fernando Henrique Cardoso, who earlier in his career had authored pioneering research works on the history of Brazilian race relations, made a historic statement in 1995 acknowledging the existence of Brazilian racism and authorizing the creation of an Advisory Council on Race Questions. Other action on the elite level was equally noteworthy. *Veja* magazine, the fourth-largest newsmagazine in the world, ran numerous articles on incidents of racial discrimination, and *A Folha de São Paulo*, a leading São Paulo daily, followed the same pattern. As late as the 1980s, these archetypal organs of elite culture had been virtually ignoring the subject. Finally, the Federal University of Rio de Janeiro in the

Brazilian men practicing *capoeira*, a traditional Afro-Brazilian dance in the form of a mock battle. (AFP/Getty Images)

late 1980s mounted a major affirmative action admission program (the racial dimension was downplayed in the public discussion, although it was a deliberate objective), which, by emphasizing economic need for applicants, sharply increased the Afro-Brazilian enrollment.

Contemporary Culture

We have seen in the preceding chapter how cultural life reacted to military government. The period after democratization in 1985 proved to be quite different. The intense mobilization of the late 1970s and early 1980s seemed to have drawn down the energies of Brazil's artistic minority. In 1988, the leading novelist Ignácio de Loyola Brandão proclaimed "There is a crisis of creativity affecting the older writers, who are producing nothing, and which is blocking the young."

Bookstores that had few new literary works on their shelves overflowed with books on self-help, ranging from how to succeed in business to how to tolerate your mate. *Veja* magazine expanded its weekly best-seller list from fiction/nonfiction to include the new category of self-help. Many titles had a mystical ring. The guru Paulo Coelho was especially popular. The Brazilian reader had turned inward, away from the confusion and tension of contemporary politics and the endless social problems.

Yet there was one constructive reaction from the authorial ranks. Writers—especially journalists—published a series of outstanding biographies of leading historic figures. There was Jorge Caldeira on Baron Mauá (1995), the legendary (if failed) nineteenth-century entrepreneur; Fernando Morais on Assis

Chateaubriand (1994), the twentieth-century newspaper and TV magnate; Ruy Castro on Nelson Rodrigues (1992), Brazil's preeminent playwright of the 1940s and 1950s; João Maximo and Carlos Didier on Noel Rosa (1990), the famous Rio samba composer of the 1930s; and João Ubaldo Ribeiro with his epic *Viva o Povo Brasileiro* (1984), a novel encompassing all Brazilian history.

These books, all bestsellers, reflected a common desire to recapture the past through some unique personality. It was as if these authors were engaged in a common enterprise to reach beyond the nightmare of military rule to find the roots of a more authentic Brazil. The novelists also joined in the effort, as could be seen in Moacyr Scliar's *Sonhos Tropicais* (1992), a fictional portrait of turn-of-the-century public health hero Oswaldo Cruz, and in Rubem Fonseca's *Agôsto* (1990), a novel based on the last days and suicide of Getúlio Vargas in 1954.

As for film, the Brazilian industry had been in decline in the 1980s and became virtually moribund when the government eliminated federal subsidies to film producers in the early 1990s. But there was a revival in the mid-1990s, led by historically oriented films such as *Bananas Is My Business*, a documentary on the career of Carmen Miranda, and *Que É Isso Companheiro?*, a filmic reconstruction of the kidnapping of the United States ambassador by Brazilian guerrillas in 1969. Like the biographies and historical novels, these films met a public desire to connect with important moments in the past, thereby perhaps putting the post-military era in perspective. But none of this equaled the creativity and originality of the cultural scene of the 1950s and 1960s.

The Political Spectrum in the New Democracy

With the return to democracy, all parts of the political spectrum—left, right, and center—turned out to have changed during the military regime. Some understanding of the political landscape is useful in explaining the post-Sarney political world in Brazil.

The traditional left had been shattered by the intense repression of 1968–74. The left's most important point of reference had traditionally been the Brazilian Communist Party (PCB). As we have seen, the Communist Party had adopted a cautious strategy in the radicalized climate leading to the coup of 1964, outflanked on the left by the radical nationalists. Nonetheless, the PCB remained a key target for the government security forces, which killed, hounded into the underground, or forced into exile virtually its entire leadership. By the late 1980s, there was almost nothing left of the traditional PCB, now also suffering from its identification with the crumbling Soviet regime. By the mid-1990s, the party had renamed itself (as the Partido Popular Socialista) and was struggling to assume the guise of a social democratic party.

The militant guerrilla groups of the 1960s had not fared much better. The PC do B (the Maoist breakaway from the PCB), once dominated by João

Amazonas, had suffered heavily from the repression, and its few survivors also sought a more moderate socialist image. The MR-8 (the Eighth of October Revolutionary Movement, named for the day of Che Guevara's execution in 1967) was a guerrilla group that as an armed force was exterminated by the government but survived as a left-wing party. The remaining force on the left were the Trotskyists, who retained their intellectual position (radical Marxist but anti-Stalinist) and operated mainly within the PT (explained below). They had always been powerful critics of the PCB and were now concentrated in a new group on the left, the Convergência Socialista. They were a constant force for militant (not armed) action and fierce opponents of the trend toward "moderate" social democracy. Virtually all the left now agreed on one thing: They could not hope to overthrow the state by force; the illusions of the 1960s were gone. The left would now walk the electoral road, wherever it led.

Remains of the populist left, strengthened by the huge PMDB victory in the 1986 elections, still existed by the late 1980s, wielding considerable influence in the constituent assembly of 1987–88. Yet their long-run electoral appeal was uncertain. Only two of the surviving first-rank pre-1964 populist leaders of the left were still active: Leonel Brizola, who reentered public life as the governor of Rio de Janeiro in 1982 and won the governorship again in 1990, and Miguel Arraes, who had been deposed as governor of Pernambuco in 1964 but won back that post in 1986 and again in 1994.

Brizola commanded a strong emotional following, especially in the city of Rio de Janeiro, with a discourse that was unchanged since the 1960s. He advocated a militant economic nationalism, liberal benefits for government employees, and a generous education policy (emphasizing a new all-day public school program). He was also the only major politician of this era to recognize racial discrimination and call for its end. Brizola had earlier tried to capture the old Vargas party label of PTB but was blocked by government maneuvering. He then founded his own party, the PDT (Partido Democrático Trabalhista), with major strength in Rio de Janeiro and Rio Grande do Sul. Most of the public saw him as an aging *caudilho* (traditional strongman) whose discourse no longer matched post-populist Brazil. Nonetheless, he could not be counted out as a campaigner. Still the most charismatic political orator on the Brazilian scene, he was unmatched in his mastery of television as a medium for campaigning.

The newest party on the left was the Partido dos Trabalhadores (PT). Born in the labor union activism of the late 1970s, it had become a genuine national party through dedicated grassroots organizing across the country. Its greatest strength did not lie among industrial workers, however, as its name and origin might suggest. Its largest numbers were drawn from government workers, teachers, and middle-class professionals. Catholic activists were highly important PT members and were dedicated to directly attacking Brazil's huge social problems in both the city and the countryside.

The PT grew steadily in the 1980s, despite predictions that such an ideological party would not prosper in Brazil. Its representation in the Chamber of Deputies went from eight in 1982 to forty-nine (almost 10 percent of the Chamber) in 1994. Much of its appeal was its promise to behave as an accountable movement that would not sacrifice its principles for the sake of individual political egos.

In fact, the PT was less unified than it advertised. Moderate PT leaders knew that a truly radical message would be rejected by most Brazilian voters. The moderates' solution was to advocate policies similar to those espoused by the social democrats of western Europe. At the other extreme within the PT were the militants (often dubbed "Shiites") who wanted more radical confrontation with the economic and political establishment. They favored "political" strikes—i.e., strikes for other than specific economic claims—and were given to anti-capitalist rhetoric. At their most exuberant, the PT militants recalled the radical left on the eve of the coup of 1964.

Notwithstanding its problems, the PT actually came close to capturing the presidency in 1989. Their candidate in the presidential election was Luiz Inácio Lula da Silva (known as "Lula" for short), the leader of the São Paulo auto workers' strikes of the late 1970s. The PT ran an effective presidential campaign in 1989, capitalizing on the free television time allocated to all parties to display the many pop stars who supported Lula and draw attention to the myriad social injustices they planned to correct. The ineffectual Sarney government, paralyzed by surging inflation, offered a perfect target for this message. Lula was also aided by the personality of his opponent, Fernando Collor de Melo, who aroused mistrust among middle-class voters.

Collor proved to have a powerful appeal to the poor and to industrial workers, however. In the end, during the run-off between the top two candidates, Lula lost to Collor in a close race (37.8 percent to 42.7 percent, the remainder being spoilt or blank ballots). Collor carried both the state of São Paulo and its capital city—the birthplace of Lula's "new unionism" had failed to mobilize for him. But Lula had gained a huge nationwide vote. Whether this indicated a real move to the left by the Brazilian electorate was unclear.

The left also included other important groups. One was the CUT (Central Única dos Trabalhadores), an unofficial confederation of labor unions, closely linked to the PT, that was given to militant rhetoric and a readiness to call strikes. And the Catholic Church still furnished some important leaders for the left. Many served in human rights organizations and land reform groups, especially the Movimento Sem Terra. Many also operated through the PT. Finally, there were the progressive think tanks, such as IBASE (Instituto Brasileiro de Análises Sociais e Econômicas), devoted to research and advocacy on such social questions as street children, the environment, education, and police violence. The dominant intellectual in these ranks was the sociologist and social activist Herbert de Souza (known by the affectionate diminutive of "Betinho"), who organized massive civic efforts such as the Campaign Against Hunger, which collected food for distribution to the poor. There was also a myriad of other nongovernmental organizations, many supported by foreign funds, researching and lobbying on social issues from a perspective that reinforced a leftist critique of Brazilian capitalism.

The electoral right in the late 1980s grew out of the PDS, the government party created and nurtured by the military regime after 1965 and first known as "ARENA." It had split when a dissident wing formed the PFL in order to vote for Tancredo Neves's presidential candidacy in 1985. But both the PDS and the PFL embodied the tradition of the political "ins"—i.e., the establishment politicians who had always lived off the status quo of the Brazilian capitalist system.

After 1985, the PFL emerged as the main rightist party. It was strongest in the Northeast, where the traditional political machines gave it a natural home. In addition, many of its leaders had been beneficiaries of the military's manipulation of electoral rules between 1965 and 1985. It had not, therefore, been tested in truly free elections.

The right also included splinter parties, such as the PPB (Partido Progressista Brasileiro), which was formed in 1995 to bring together smaller conservative parties. In addition, there were ad hoc political movements such as the UDR, organized by the landowners in 1987 as a movement to block land reform. Their urban counterparts were the small businessmen who often faced daily harassment by street children and vagrants, especially in Rio de Janeiro. To rid themselves of this nuisance, merchants joined together to hire off-duty police to remove (and sometimes kill) the children. Both the UDR and the merchants represented the dark side of the Brazilian establishment, ready to use violence to protect their property rights.

Finally, the right included many former anti-Communists who remained opposed to the few remaining populists or militant leftists. The ideology of these rightists was free market economics. They promoted the writings of such First World conservative economists as Friedrich Hayek and Milton Friedman. Prominent among their spokesmen was Henri Maksoud, a hotel baron and avid promoter of neo-liberal ideas.

The right, therefore, consisted of a large body of traditional politicians, a smaller cadre of zealots prepared to use violence, and a band of wealthy lawyers and businessmen who longed for a free market (although not always conscious of what it might cost them).

The center had a more uncertain fate as of the late 1980s than either the left or the right. Its predecessor was the MDB, renamed the "PMDB" after the government's party reorganization of 1979. This was the coalition that had opposed the military dictatorship, serving as an umbrella for a wide range of pro-democracy voters. Yet the PMDB had never been a coherent party. Its raison d'être had been the fight against authoritarianism. When civilian government returned in 1985, the PMDB had no clear vision for Brazil. What should be the social and economic policies in a restored democracy? How much maldistribution of wealth and income were PMDB leaders prepared to try and change? And could their policies be sold to the voter, especially given the uncertain nature of the hugely increased and much younger electorate?

Before a start could even be made to face these questions in 1985, the party was caught up in the political misadventure of the Sarney presidency. The initial success of Sarney's stabilization program, the Cruzado Plan, caused the PMDB to enjoy a smashing victory in the November 1986 congressional elections, as noted earlier. But inflation was again rampant by 1987 and the elections at the end of that year showed that the public was greatly disillusioned with the PMDB, which never recovered politically. Henceforth, its image was set by figures such as Orestes Quercia, a São Paulo governor whose alleged corruption was of record proportions.

The PMDB therefore entered the 1990s having squandered the moral advantage it had gained from fighting the dictatorship, even though it remained the largest party in Congress. Virtually without ideas, dominated by irresolute politicians, it offered a weak alternative to the establishment on the political right.

Its decline led directly to the creation of a new party on the center-left: the Partido Social Democrático Brasileiro (PSDB), whose main founders were disaffected PMDB politicians from São Paulo. The leaders included Mário Covas, a Paulista senator, and Fernando Henrique Cardoso, an ex-university professor and a senator from São Paulo. Joining them was Franco Montoro, a former Christian Democrat and subsequently a PMDB leader as well as a former senator and governor of São Paulo.

The new PSDB defined itself as a social democratic party in the western European tradition. Its founders looked to the example of Felipe González, the then-highly successful premier of Spain, who had led that country's transition to democracy. They also admired the Portuguese socialists, who had eventually achieved the same transition after the fall of the Portuguese dictatorship. Roughly speaking, they accepted Brazilian capitalism but wanted to moderate its excesses through government reform. As their party symbol, they chose the toucan, the colorful Brazilian parrot-like bird with the huge beak, a symbol that delighted the cartoonists.

The political center also included many public figures and institutions wanting simply to avoid either extreme. A centrist view was typically taken by clergy, intellectuals, and businessmen, who hoped Brazilian capitalism could evolve toward the more egalitarian societies of the North Atlantic world. But they and the voters they represented could be attracted by extremists if the issues were polarizing. Rising crime, uncontrolled inflation, decaying public services, cynical displays of wealth by corrupt politicians—attractive schemes that claimed to cure any of these ills could push centrists to either side. As always in Brazilian history, maintaining a center position was a delicate balancing act.

One long-term political actor, the military, was notably absent from the scene. We have seen how they had played a key role at every juncture in Brazilian history since the 1880s. By the mid-1980s, however, the officers were tired, demoralized, and longing to return to a more "professional" role. Many observers thought this transition would be difficult and perhaps even stormy. They were proved wrong. Although the military retained their claim to authority in a few areas (such as Amazon policy), they assumed an increasingly lower profile after 1985. Their declining influence was seen most dramatically in their share of the federal budget. With the exception of one year (1990) the military lost budget share every year between 1985 and 1993, suffering a decline of one-quarter of their share over those years. Brazil had entered a new era. If the civilian elite failed to make democracy work now, they could hardly blame it on the men in uniform.

The Collor Debacle

Into this uncertain political atmosphere stepped Fernando Collor de Melo. He was virtually unknown nationally in Brazil until early 1989, when he began a television blitz to win the presidential nomination. Between March and early June, his approval rating in the national polls shot up from 9 percent to 40 percent. He had increased his TV exposure by buying the free TV time (apportioned under the electoral law in proportion to votes won in the previous election) of several small political parties. Although technically legal, this tactic was typical of the many questionable practices of the Collor campaign.

Collor was young, athletic, handsome, and highly telegenic. He came from the poor northeastern state of Alagoas but had grown up largely in Rio de Janeiro and Brasília, where his politically powerful family maintained residences. His father's family belonged to a powerful clan, the Arnon de Melos, which had long dominated politics in Alagoas. The father had taken his northeastern political ways to the federal Senate, where, in an argument, he had shot dead a former substitute senator on the Senate floor. But the older Collor was also attuned to modern politics, as shown by his close relations with television network magnate Roberto Marinho (of TV Globo) and his proprietorship of the TV Globo station in Alagoas. Young Collor's mother was the daughter of a prominent Rio Grandense politician who had once served as labor minister under Getúlio Vargas.

Fernando Collor de Melo began his national political assault by assuming the mantle of a crusader against corruption. His targets were high civil servants (*marajás*, or "maharajas"), whom he accused of living luxuriously at the cost of the Brazilian taxpayer. This strategy proved popular with the national electorate, who believed him despite the fact that Collor himself came from the Northeast, a region of notorious political corruption. His other principal message was a pledge to apply neo-liberal economic policies in Brazil—i.e., to shrink government and to privatize Brazil's labyrinth of state enterprises. This, he assured his TV viewers, would bring Brazil abreast of such countries as Argentina, Chile, and Mexico, which were already jettisoning protectionism and selling off their largest public companies. Soon, he promised, Brazil would be entering the First World.

Most important, Collor struck the pose of a messiah who could solve Brazil's problems by the force of his personality. In this he resembled Jânio Quadros, who had won the 1960 presidential election by running as a political messiah. Such a strategy clearly fit the mood of the many Brazilians who were becoming disillusioned with the return to democracy and were thus susceptible to a politician promising miracles. At the same time, his neo-liberal message appealed to business leaders, who sought a candidate committed to reducing the role of government in the economy.

The Election

With the reinstitution of direct popular election of the president, new electoral regulations provided for a new procedure. The president was to be elected in a two-stage process. In the first round, entry would be relatively easy (there were twenty-two registered candidates in the 1989 first round). If no candidate won a majority in the first round, then a second round (a runoff) was held between the top two vote-getters from the first round.

Since Collor was running so far ahead in the polls, it was assumed he would be one of the top two in the first round. Speculation therefore centered on the second spot for the two-person runoff in the final round. When the votes came in, Lula had defeated Leonel Brizola in the first round by running second to Collor. Lula was a kind of anti-messiah, the factory worker from São Paulo with fractured grammar and an unmistakably proletarian appearance (he was missing one finger because of an accident with factory machinery). On TV, Lula lacked the slickness of Collor but projected a reformist zeal that touched many viewers worried about Brazil's yawning economic inequalities.

During the run off campaign, Collor tried to frighten voters by calling Lula a dangerous radical who would expropriate their property. The PT predicted (correctly, as it turned out) that Collor, if elected, would run an unscrupulous government that would be disastrous for Brazil. Collor's scare tactics proved to resonate better with the electorate, especially in São Paulo, the homeland of Lula's labor movement. They also frightened wealthy businessmen (industrialists, contractors, etc.) into contributing enormous sums to Collor's campaign.

Collor assumed the presidency in March 1990 amid highly favorable publicity. The media had overwhelmingly supported him, with the foreign press largely following their lead. The U.S. government was especially delighted with Collor, believing he would adopt the neo-liberal policies the United States was preaching to all developing countries.

The Policies

Collor began his government with an economic bombshell. His advisers had warned that Brazil was on the verge of runaway inflation, now approaching 100 percent a month. The only solution, they argued, was a shock treatment, beginning with the freezing of all Brazilian savings accounts. Accompanying steps were a price freeze and the abolition of indexation. The public's initial reaction was disbelief. Many savers were furious that they were suddenly denied access to the money they had put aside. Large business firms were paralyzed because the financial reserves they had used to meet current payrolls were frozen. Economists doubted the long-run viability of the policy since it depended on inherently temporary instruments such as price controls and a savings freeze. For a few months, however, the therapy seemed to work. Inflation dropped to zero, and the fiscal deficit was dramatically reduced.

This dramatic attack on inflation was accompanied by the dismissal of thousands of federal workers—many of whom had been appointed in Sarney's flurry of patronage—on the grounds of redundancy and the government's fiscal emergency. The civil service unions protested, and the dismissed workers sought court orders to restore their jobs, which had been guaranteed by the liberal job tenure provision of the 1988 Constitution. Eventually, many won back their jobs through court action.

Collor's government also announced a phased schedule of tariff reductions that would bring Brazil from having some of the higher tariffs in the world to being in the 10–20 percent range found in other Latin American countries. This policy understandably worried those São Paulo industrialists who were not internationally competitive and would be hurt by cheaper imports. It was particularly embarrassing to those businessmen who had praised neo-liberalism in principle but now realized how it could hit them in the wallet.

Finally, the Collor government moved toward privatization. Brazil had over two hundred state enterprises, most of them money-losing. Collor announced that the government would begin auctioning off state enterprises to private buyers, including foreigners. Opposition to this came from several sources. Most vocal were the economic nationalists, especially in the PT, who defended the state sector as a bulwark of national sovereignty against foreign interests. The business community followed close behind. For sectors such as capital goods, purchases by state enterprises were crucial to their businesses, which had formed close relationships with such enterprises, often including noncompetitive bidding.

Collor implemented these economic policies through a flood of presidential decrees (*medidas provisórias,* or "provisional measures") in 1990, showing little inclination to negotiate with the Congress. He stuck to this imperial style on the assumption that his majority vote in the runoff presidential election would legitimize his boldness. By late 1990, however, his approach had aroused strong opposition. Although presidential decrees were valid only if ratified by Congress within thirty days, Collor simply issued them again if Congress refused. His opponents contested the constitutionality of this tactic, and in February 1991 congressional opposition, led by the PMDB, threatened to limit the presidential decree power. He now had no alternative but to negotiate with the Congress. From his inauguration in March 1990 through January 1991, the president averaged fourteen decrees per month. For the rest of his term, January 1991 to September 1992, he averaged less than one.

Unfortunately for the president, however, his economic program, like so many before it, was falling apart. Numerous exceptions had been made to the savings freeze, and the price freeze was also collapsing. The finance minister, Zélia Cardoso de Mello, tried a second shock treatment in early 1991, but it was too late. The government's gamble on breaking inflationary expectations had lost.

The president was able, nonetheless, to show some accomplishments. He signed a historic non-nuclear pact with Argentina, which laid to rest the fears of an atomic arms race in southern South America. At the same time, he scotched an apparent attempt by the Brazilian military to carry out a clandestine atomic weapons program. Further, he showed sensitivity to the long-standing problem of the indigenous peoples in the Amazon, designating huge new areas as exclusive reserves for the Indians. Finally, his measures on privatization and tariff reduction were important first steps toward making Brazil an internationally competitive economy. Perhaps these successes could have been sustained through his term, but something else was eating into his public reputation: growing tales of corruption at the highest levels of government.

The End

By early 1992, Collor's arrogance and unwillingness to negotiate with congressional party leaders—combined with the suspicions of corruption—had left him without any means of mobilizing political support. As had happened frequently in the past, the lack of strong ties among the Congress, the political parties, and the president was making Brazil ungovernable. In January 1992, the president turned to the political center to organize a new cabinet, jettisoning his corruption-tainted minister of labor and social security, Antônio Magri, and his health minister, Alceni Guerra. The new ministers included several PSD figures with the image of technical skill and honesty. The cabinet was further strengthened in May when Marcílio Marques Moreira, a respected banker-diplomat, became finance minister. It was dubbed the "last-chance cabinet." The hope of centrists was that Collor would be able to finish his term, if for no other reason than to secure the foundations of the democracy.

Their hope was soon overtaken by a burgeoning scandal involving the treasurer for Collor's presidential campaign. Journalists in Brasília had long described many in the Collor government as abnormally greedy (as opposed to usual political practice) in demanding payoffs from anyone dealing with the federal government. Such rumors had abounded about previous governments, but proof was almost always lacking. In the case of the Collor government, proof became abundantly public. The villain of the piece was P. C. Farias, a political fixer from Alagoas who had amassed a fortune, several mansions, and a jet plane (called the "black bat") through brokering political favors for many. As the treasurer for the campaign, he had successfully pressured so many wealthy donors that funds were still abundant three years after the campaign. Some said Collor and Farias were planning to use the money to found a long-term political dynasty.

In mid-1992, Collor and his collaborators became targets for a Watergate-style investigation. The heaviest blow was a magazine interview in May 1992 in which Collor's own brother accused the president of drug use, extortion, and sexual improprieties. Eventually, the congressional investigators extracted bank records that proved exactly how the millions had circulated within the presidential circle. Collor fought back via television speeches. Like former U.S. President Richard Nixon, however, who had once faced a similar personal challenge (although of a graver constitutional nature), Collor dug himself into a deeper hole with each TV appearance. As the evidence mounted, the Congress, many of whose members were no strangers to corruption, began to consider impeachment. They were given further momentum by massive street demonstrations against Collor in the major cities.

The Collor circle tried to buy off the congressmen involved, but to little avail. In July, a national poll gave Collor a "no confidence" rating of 69 percent. A comfortable majority (59 percent) thought he should resign the presidency. The Chamber of Deputies voted overwhelmingly (441 to 38) to impeach the president on September 29, 1992, and the Senate met and prepared to convict him on December 29. Only hours before the Senate voted, Collor resigned, hoping to escape the final stage of legislative condemnation. But the Senate was not deterred, voting against Collor (seventy-six to five) and suspending his political rights for eight years.

For the first time, a Brazilian president had been forced out of office not by military coup or military ultimatum, but by orderly vote of the Congress. Collor had done one great favor for Brazil: He had prodded the political class into proving that they could live up to their constitutional responsibility.

Another Vice President in Command

Yet another vice president had to assume the Brazilian presidency. Once again, as in the case of Sarney, the new president was a minor politician never considered to be presidential material. Itamar Franco was from the state of Minas Gerais, where he had been a leading political figure in the city of Juiz da Fora. His only national visibility had come via two terms as a nondescript senator. His party identification was PMDB, but he was a decidedly nonideological figure.

Although few had any idea of the policies Franco might adopt, he was initially given the benefit of the doubt by the press and by most Brazilians, who were grateful to see Collor gone and normal succession procedures followed. His original cabinet was hardly distinguished in terms of national visibility or political clout, although it did cover the political spectrum.

The most pressing economic issue was inflation. Collor's stabilization policies had failed, and inflation was again accelerating, but the new president showed little understanding of the economic forces at work. He preferred to look for villains among producers who raised prices on specific goods, such as pharmaceuticals. He also seemed indifferent to the burgeoning fiscal deficit. Above all, he had no stomach for undertaking the tough policies that stabilization required. Brazil was apparently condemned to continued drift.

France also expressed strong doubts about the wisdom of privatization and consistently threw roadblocks in the path of Collor's neo-liberal policies. His rhetoric often sounded like the economic nationalists on the left. He was also suspicious of reducing tariffs and liked to talk, à la the developmentalists of the past, about the autonomy of the domestic market. Franco's image was not improved by his sometimes bizarre behavior—he frequently contradicted his own statements and was unwilling to engage in sustained discussion of major issues. Finally, he restricted his political consultations to a narrow circle of longtime cronies from his hometown of Juiz da Fora, confirming his image as a provincial politician with little capacity to lead the country.

Franco was rescued by a late appointment to his cabinet. After constantly reshuffling his ministers, in 1993 he appointed Fernando Henrique Cardoso as minister of foreign relations. The highly intelligent, multilingual Cardoso was well known internationally. After a brief sojourn in the Foreign Ministry, Cardoso was soon invited to assume the Finance Ministry, which had proved a Waterloo for so many incumbents over the last fifteen years. Fernando Henrique accepted the post and assembled a team of outstanding economists, including Pérsio Arida, Edmar Bacha, André Lara Resende, and Gustavo Franco, many of whom had helped draft the Cruzado Plan back in 1986.

Back to Stabilization: The Plano Real

When Fernando Henrique was appointed finance minister, Brazil stood out as the only Latin American country that had failed to control inflation, and it was now said to be world champion in signing unfulfilled agreements with the IMF. The problem was fundamentally not one of economic diagnosis, although the treatment of the disease did demand considerable economic sophistication. Rather, it was political leadership. President after president had backed away from stabilization: Vargas, Kubitschek, Quadros, Goulart, and Sarney. Only Castelo Branco, fortified by an authoritarian regime, had pursued stabilization long enough to reach a successful conclusion.

Itamar Franco had seemed as unlikely as his predecessors to tackle stabilization. The difference between the fate of his stabilization plan and previous efforts turned out to be his choice of Cardoso as finance minister.

Cardoso's team formulated a complex strategy. First, they ruled out any shock treatment, such as a price and wage freeze. Second, they drew up a balanced budget for 1994, which the Congress passed. Third, they created a two-stage transition to a new currency. The first stage, which began in March 1994, was to last for four months and involved the creation of a new unit of value, the URV (Unit of Real Value), into which all previous values were converted. Meanwhile, the cruzeiro continued as currency, thus creating a dual set of prices. The objective here was to force the public to stop thinking in the currency values that had historically eroded so rapidly. This was also the stage for slowing down the "inertial inflation" (the inflation that was self-sustaining, without any new inflationary pressure), which all observers agreed had made rising prices a self-reproducing phenomenon.

The second stage, which began on July 1, was the introduction of a new currency, the *real*. The choice of name was ambiguous (it could mean either "royal" or "real"). In order to dramatize the government's commitment to stability, metallic coins were introduced. Soon, Brazilians were using coin-operated dispensing machines, a phenomenon unknown in Brazil for a generation.

In order to strengthen this approach, the government adopted a mildly overvalued exchange rate and imposed high real interest rates. The first measure was in order to fight inflation (with cheap imports). The second was to prevent the kind of runaway consumer boom that had occurred under the Cruzado Plan. Also scheduled was the gradual elimination of indexation over the following year. Finally, workers were left to negotiate wage increases as defined in the URVs. Thanks in part to the strong economy and good harvest in the last half of 1994, inflation-adjusted wages did not decline—as had happened during virtually all previous stabilization efforts—but instead showed increases.

The Plano Real met much initial skepticism. With Brazil's track record on stabilization, the doubts were certainly legitimate, but both stages worked smoothly. The success of the second stage—the transition to the new currency— was particularly striking, given the enormity of the challenge. The success was both logistical (getting the new currency to thousands of banks across a huge country) and psychological (getting the public to accept yet another new form of currency for their transactions). The morale of Brazilians could not have provided a better context. Just as the *real* was introduced, Brazil was on its way to winning an unprecedented fourth championship in the World Soccer Cup. Incredibly, Brazil had earlier in 1994 beaten the U.S. team on the Fourth of July. Could there have been a better omen for the Cardoso team?

Inflation dropped immediately, going from 1094 percent in 1994 to 15 percent in 1995. The last quarter of 1994 and the first quarter of 1995 saw industrial production surge (14 percent for the latter period, when GDP grew

EXHIBIT 8-4
Annual Rate of Inflation, 1991–1995

Year	Inflation Rate (%)
1991	480.2
1992	1157.8
1993	2708.2
1994	1093.9
1995	14.8

Source: 1991–1992: Werner Baer, *The Brazilian Economy*, 6th ed. (Westport, 2008), p. 410.

10.4 percent), with inflation continuing to drop. By December it had reached a monthly average of only .96 percent. Obviously, there had been considerable excess capacity in mid-1994. By early 1995, the short-run success of the Plano Real was assured. (See exhibit 8-4.)

There were several reasons for the early success of the Plano Real. The plan was intelligently conceived and implemented. It was helped by the high level of foreign exchange reserves that the Cardoso team had inherited, which (topping $40 billion in July 1994) gave Brazil the largest reserves in its history and among the largest in the world. Such ample foreign exchange gave Brazil a cushion as it cut tariffs. In fact, it lost $10 billion in reserves over the first eight months of the plan when the premature tariff cuts led to an import boom, but it had a large enough cushion to weather this loss. The large agricultural harvest of 1994, which kept food prices down, was another massive piece of luck.

There was good luck on the political side as well. Most of the Brazilian public turned out to really want an end to volatile inflation. In addition, the most likely opponents of the plan—the economic nationalists on the left— were disorganized, demoralized, and reduced in number. Their heart was no longer in the kind of IMF-bashing so successful in the Kubitschek era and in the mid-1960s. The PT had discredited itself by having immediately rejected the Plano Real as a cynical electoral maneuver. Understandable as this response was, it became more and more self-defeating as the plan's continued success became obvious. Finally, the well-informed knew their country was seen as the economic pariah of Latin America. The traditionally successful discourse about Brazil being too big or too special to conform to conventional economic cures was now falling flat. Furthermore, the stable cost of basic goods (especially food), combined with wage increases, had undercut much of the worker discontent that might have been tapped by the government's opponents. Finally, the Cardoso team made liberal use of the *medida provisória*, the executive decree power that allowed the president to temporarily bypass the Congress. In 1994, for example, the presidency issued 397 such decrees (Collor's maximum was 163 in 1990), often to implement unpopular economic measures.

The Presidential Election of 1994

The election for Franco's successor was set for November 1994. The campaign ended up dominated by the apparent success of the Plano Real, although it had not started out that way. In the early months of 1994, Lula, once again the PT candidate, enjoyed a huge lead in the polls, enticing his supporters to believe they were going to avenge Lula's defeat in 1989. The PT had, after all, predicted that Collor was an adventurer who would do his country no good, and Collor's fall from power confirmed their prediction. Furthermore, in early 1994 there was no strong figure from the right or center willing to contest Lula's lead. Cardoso was widely rumored to be a candidate, but he did not confirm it until he resigned from the Finance Ministry in early 1994 (resignation was required under the "incompatibility law" for all candidates who were already holding office). Until July 1994, therefore, the PT considered Lula virtually a president-elect.

Cardoso did finally decide to enter the race in March 1994 and was immediately faced with some difficult choices. Because his party, the PSDB, lacked truly national strength, he knew he would have to seek an election alliance with one or more of the major parties. He first contacted the PT, exploring the possibility of a center-left coalition. Such a combination would have been formidable. For obvious reasons, however, the PT was unreceptive. They saw no reason to sacrifice their own candidate (relegating him to be Cardoso's running mate) when Lula was so far ahead. Cardoso then sounded out other parties on the center-left, such as Brizola's PDT, but Brizola was determined to maintain his own candidacy for the presidency, despite his declining standing in the polls.

Cardoso finally succeeded in attracting support from the PFL, a remnant of the official party from the dictatorship and an unlikely bedfellow for Cardoso, given his political philosophy. A link with the PFL would identify him with one of the most traditional (and one of the most reactionary) political images in Brazil, opening him up to fierce attacks from the left. On the other hand, the PFL was now controlled by Antônio Carlos Magalhães, the governor of Bahia and acknowledged political boss of the entire Northeast. In a close election, the PFL might be able to deliver the winning margin by drawing on their political machines in the Northeast. Finally, the PFL was known to favor the neo-liberal reforms in Cardoso's platform. The PFL's ability to deliver a large regional vote was probably the most important factor in Cardoso's decision.

The PT was jubilant, believing that his alliance with the PFL would alienate enough centrist voters to ensure Cardoso's defeat. But the election did not turn on the question of the PFL. It turned, instead, on the Plano Real.

Once the campaign began, Lula and his advisers decided to launch an all-out attack on the Plano Real, charging that instead of ending inflation it would worsen the economic plight of the poor. Their decision was based on their assumption that the plan would either fail or at least alienate many voters. This decision, made despite early warnings that the public was reacting favorably to the plan, was reached as part of a larger conflict within the PT. The more militant wing wanted an aggressive campaign, believing that was the only way to maintain Lula's early lead. The more moderate wing did not wish to present too radical a face to the Brazilian voter, fearing the militants' zeal might alienate the average Brazilian. The militant wing won out—a decision that did not seem as unreasonable in late July 1994 as it does in hindsight.

The Plano Real proved a rapid and continuing success, and Lula's poll numbers began to drop. Fernando Henrique Cardoso was elected president with an absolute majority (54 percent of the valid votes) on the first round. By the second round in November, which was restricted to runoffs for the posts for which no candidate had received an absolute majority, Fernando Henrique's party's triumph became even broader in that PSDB candidates won the governorships in the key states of São Paulo, Minas Gerais, and Rio de Janeiro. The congressional picture was more mixed. Despite Lula's defeat, the PT had once again increased its congressional delegation (from thirty-five to forty-nine), and the PMDB, despite its visible decay, remained the largest party in the Congress.

The political nature of the new Congress was actually quite uncertain. Extreme party fragmentation (eighteen parties represented in the Chamber of Deputies) suggested that getting any coherent program through Congress could be a Herculean task. Fernando Henrique had won the largest electoral majority of any president since 1945, but as Collor had demonstrated, electoral majorities can be perishable assets when it comes to governing.

The Cardoso Government's First Term

For its first three years, the Cardoso government's top priority remained stabilization. Presidential policymakers knew that conquering inflation, after so many failed attempts, would take time. Yet success came much faster than most expected. By 1996, inflation had dropped to 11 percent and by 1997 to only about 4 percent.

This remarkable record, equal only to President Castelo Branco's success from 1964 to 1967, required continuing battle, especially over the federal budget, where the structure favored continuous deficits. Other areas also needed constant attention. The balance of payments had run a surplus in the half-dozen years before 1994 because continued protection and low growth had depressed imports, while exports remained strong. Now that Brazil was beginning to reduce tariffs, the long-run outlook for the trade balance was more doubtful.

Another area of worry was the financial system. It had overexpanded during the 1980s, with much of its profits coming from the "inflationary float" the banks earned from financial transactions. The rapid fall in inflation after 1994 reduced this float and thus threatened bank profits, forcing several major bank failures (including some of the largest, such as the Banco Nacional and the Banco Econômico). This process required costly government bailouts.

Finally, there was the problem of inflationary expectations. Brazil had lived through one of the most pervasive inflationary experiences in the world, with the Brazilian public becoming sophisticated in defending itself financially. Policymakers knew that any significant recurrence of inflation would signal that stabilization had failed again. The Cardoso government thus had to fight against extreme public skepticism about its ability to hold the price line. Based on stabilization experience elsewhere in Latin America, the government realized it might well take the rest of Cardoso's term to squeeze inflation out of the economy.

The stabilization battle necessarily involved a campaign to reduce deficit spending, which had become a way of life at every level of government. The most obvious confrontation was in the federal Congress, where members were always interested in enjoying the fruits of federal patronage. The battle also went on at the state level, especially with the state banks, notorious for running up large debts (usually incurred to fund political campaigns or pet projects of incumbent officials) and then blackmailing the national government into bailing them out. The leading example was Banespa, the São Paulo state bank, which by 1994 had run up a debt of more than $25 billion. After years of wrangling, the São Paulo state government and the federal government reached a complex agreement in November 1996 whereby the latter helped refinance the debt of the bank (and the state of São Paulo) in return for the forced sale of state assets (including the railways and the electricity system) and the temporary takeover of the bank by federal authorities.

The Cardoso government also faced a vast federal, state, and local bureaucracy with a remarkable talent for reproducing itself. The largest single increase in government expenditure during the Sarney presidency, for example, had been for personnel, representing a fiscal time bomb for the future because the generous government pension system would have to fund them when they retired. As of March 1998, the government had succeeded in getting the preliminary two-thirds congressional vote to reform the notoriously generous federal pension system. The final vote in October 1998, however, was a rejection.

A further priority of the Cardoso government was privatization of state enterprises, which under Franco and Collor had been subject to numerous delays. But the process of auctioning off ownership of large public corporations proved more difficult than anticipated, with establishing appraisals of the corporations' value especially controversial. It was also difficult to find satisfactory buyers since few private interests had the large-scale capital needed. As a result, domestic pension funds were at first often the winning bidders, with substantial foreign buyers ready to bid only in such areas as telecommunications. One of the government's motives in pushing privatization was the prospect of gaining cash that could help reduce federal deficits, which had given stabilizing governments an important boost in Argentina and Mexico. But this was just beginning to occur in Brazil, where most of the buyers in the early 1990s had paid in nonnegotiable government bonds. Nonetheless, by mid-1998 the government could show considerable success, having privatized (by sale or lease) more than fifty firms in such areas as steel, fertilizer, and iron ore. In almost every case, efficiency immediately increased.

Finally, there was the question of measures to improve the social welfare of the ordinary Brazilian. The need for public investment in education, health, transportation, and communications was enormous. Unfortunately, however, the necessary federal funds were not available in the short run (although tougher tax collection helped raise revenues) and the urgent need to balance the budget meant that they could not be expected soon. Cardoso's government had to content itself with essentially token gestures such as putting computers in school classrooms, a measure that was much cheaper than raising teachers' salaries.

Agrarian reform was one area of social policy that would not wait. In recent years, landless workers had organized a protest movement (Movimento Sem Terra) that organized land invasions, especially in the South and in the Amazon Basin. Landowners fought back, usually with the support of local police. In April 1996, military police killed twenty-three workers in a bloody confrontation in the Amazonian state of Pará.

Nationwide indignation over this incident provoked the Cardoso government to promise a complete investigation, but the workers could expect little relief. Local landowners and their sympathetic military police had almost invariably proved beyond the reach of federal authorities, as shown in the reaction to a similar wave of killings in the Amazon during the previous August. Furthermore, the Cardoso administration had rejected a policy of simply handing out land, especially in small units, on the grounds it was counterproductive economically. Nonetheless, by mid-1998 INCRA, the land reform agency, had made record-breaking distributions of government-controlled land.

Human violence was not the only ill plaguing the Amazon. The relentless destruction of the rain forest had also disturbed thoughtful Brazilians and became a prime issue in the international ecological movement. Since 1960, fires and chainsaws had stripped an area of Amazon vegetation cover larger than all of France. After a drop in the rate of destruction in the early 1990s, there was an increase in 1995 and an even greater upsurge in 1996. Inadequate budgets for the environmental ministry, combined with indecisive leadership in Brasília were giving the loggers (many illegal) and the slash-and-burn settlers near free rein. Even with the best will in the world, Brasília, with its few hundred inspectors, could not have established effective control over an area larger than western Europe.

The government was also well aware of how little it could do on social welfare. One obvious reason was lack of funds, a plight produced by the urgent need to reduce the federal deficit. Modest steps were taken in education, such as raising public teachers' salaries (pitifully meager in the primary and secondary schools) and establishing an educational TV network for all schools. But knowledgeable observers argued that the biggest problem continued to be the waste, diversion, and mismanagement of whatever funds were appropriated. That had much to do with corruption and perverse incentives existing on the state and local level—ills that would take more than a few years to cure.

In one respect, the Cardoso government scored a victory for the poorest Brazilians: The rapid decline in inflation had suddenly raised the average buying power of consumers who dealt only in cash because the deterioration of their income between pay periods was now less. (The better-off, in contrast, had been able to keep their liquid funds in fully indexed checking accounts.) Furthermore, abundant harvests helped to keep food prices down. A 1996 government study showed that between July 1984 and January 1996, the percentage of poor in the six largest metropolitan regions had declined from 33 percent to 25 percent. By the end of 1997, it was estimated that the real value of the minimum wage had risen 27 percent since 1994. This reflected a deliberate government policy of using minimum wage policy to target the poorest.

The greatest squeeze was felt by the middle class, which in Brazil means roughly the fifth to the thirtieth percentile from the top of the income distribution. This class was especially hit by the price increase in "non-tradables"—i.e., the goods and services that were not in international trade and were therefore not subject to price competition from imported substitutes. Most prominent were rent, school tuition, restaurant meals, and all personal services.

Going for a Second Term

As of mid-1998, Brazil seemed in suspended animation economically. The Real Plan had proved a brilliant success as to its original purpose—drastically reducing inflation, inducing the public to think in real economic terms, and sanitizing a bloated financial system—yet it had not put the Brazilian economy back on the strong growth path that was essential if the country's enormous social needs were to be met. Nor was it clear, despite Brazil's record foreign exchange reserves, that Brazil had the competitive capacity to expand its role in world trade. All these questions were essentially on hold, as the Cardoso government appeared determined to stick to the stabilization-oriented economic strategy begun in 1994.

The year 1997 did not prove so easy, however. Trouble had been brewing in East Asia, the region of rapid economic growth since the 1960s. The crisis was financial: plunging stock markets and currency values. First hit was Thailand in July, but the virus soon spread to Malaysia, Indonesia, the Phillipines, and South Korea. In every case, investors dumped equities, at the same time demanding hard currency for whatever local currencies they held. The cause of the panic was belated recognition that many East Asian financial institutions lacked accountability, transparency, and professional management. Many had made bad loans, resulting in bank portfolios of dubious quality. Furthermore, some East Asian currencies were overvalued.

Most important in the short run, however, was the self-reinforcing nature of the panic. The faster currency traders demanded hard currency, the sooner the countries under siege ran out of foreign exchange. It was a vicious circle. It was also a repeat of the financial crisis that had hit Mexico three years before.

Brazil soon began to show signs of catching the Asian virus, which had been exacerbated by a financial crisis in Russia as well. A sell-off hit the São Paulo stock market, which fell 22 percent in the last two weeks of October. At the same time, speculation battered the *real*, causing the Central Bank to spend a substantial part of its foreign exchange reserves. Rumors flew about possible bank failures. The New York investment house of Morgan Stanley warned its clients that Brazil had become the number one global risk.

The fears turned out to be exaggerated. The São Paulo stock market stabilized (by the end of 1997 it was still up 34.8 percent for the year), and the *real* survived attack, with the Central Bank by December still holding more than $55 billion in foreign exchange reserves (the total reached over $70 billion by June 1998). But the government's successful counterattack required extreme measures. First was a huge jump in interest rates to 40 percent per annum in real terms. This was aimed at holding the "hot money" of investors who might be tempted to withdraw their dollars from Brazil. It was also designed to reduce demand for imports, which were contributing to a dangerously increasing deficit in the balance of payments—by October running at 4 percent of GDP, well ahead of the government target. The second action was a package of fifty-one reform measures, which included budget cuts and tax increases designed to produce a net saving of $18 billion.

However effective in staunching the immediate crisis, these measures also had negative effects. The ultra-high interest rates would be deflationary, possibly driving the economy into negative growth in 1998, an election year. This would inevitably set back the effort to improve living standards, which depended above all on rapid growth. Higher interest rates would also be costly to the government, because they would raise the cost of financing the large domestic public debt. Finally, continuing to maintain an overvalued exchange rate—a key element of government policy—would postpone facing up to a basic cause of the disequilibrium in the external sector. Brazil had reduced its short-term international vulnerabilities by making itself hostage to short-term capital movements and a large-scale domestic economic slowdown.

President Cardoso reacted vigorously to the crisis, pledging that Brazil would never give in to the speculators. Finance Minister Malan was even more optimistic. He argued for the chance to "emerge from the crisis better than before." As for the once-famous East Asian Tigers, he predicted that the "Latin American economy is beginning a new phase, while Asia is finishing a cycle." It was a curious way to introduce Brazilians to yet another bout of austerity. Brazil, three years after successful stabilization, was again having to postpone rapid growth and increased investment in human capital, the only viable paths to greater social justice. Cardoso's challenge was compounded by a renewed speculative attack on the Brazilian currency that began in August 1998. By early October Brazil's foreign exchange reserves had fallen from $73 billion to $47 billion.

Politically, the strategy had not changed since 1994. That strategy was an ad hoc approach, weaving together a shifting coalition of party and regional support. Given the fragmented party system, this style was probably inevitable, but it did involve one unforeseen consequence: a steady weakening of Cardoso's own party, the PSDB, as the president relied for support increasingly on the conservative PFL. Instead of investing in the strengthening of his party, which had been created with such fanfare in 1988, Cardoso invested in himself as Brazil's political solution.

He had long chafed under the one-term rule and as the end of his term was approaching decided to invest all his energies in achieving passage of a constitutional amendment legalizing a second presidential term. Cardoso was following the successful precedents of Presidents Menem of Argentina and Fujimori of Peru, both of whom had been widely criticized for their authoritarian tendencies. But Cardoso passes his decision off in his memoirs as "causing no constitutional harm," simply "bringing Brazil's presidential system in line with that of the United States and many other countries."

The political capital required to bring off this feat was enormous. To make himself eligible to run in 1998, he needed a two-thirds vote, twice, in each house of Congress. Between January and June 1997, the Congress—succumbing to a political blitz from the presidential palace—approved the amendment (80 percent of the Senate voted in favor on one of the votes). Cardoso later reaped something of a whirlwind from what turned out to be considerable resentment at his high-pressure tactics, even within his own coalition. As Cardoso remarks in his memoirs, "The election itself became nearly an afterthought," in part because the public faced a Hobson's choice of sorts. The election of Lula, on the one hand, would make a default on Brazil's international obligations a virtual certainty. Fernando Henrique and his people on the other hand, though facing a crisis of confidence, were promising all would be well if they were given the necessary time to effectuate a lasting solution. The public chose the latter, with opinion polls showing a clear majority in favor of Cardoso running for a second term. On October 3, 1998, he was elected for a second term with 53 percent of the vote to Lula's 32 percent.

Social Justice Delayed

The promise of a solution to the debt crisis was not to be. The IMF did grant Brazil a $40 billion aid package shortly after Cardoso's reelection. But it was contingent on large future spending cuts that had to be approved by Congress. Cardoso introduced a bill to save nearly $5 billion by raising the pension contributions of highly paid government workers. It was defeated, with some members of his own coalition helping vote it down. After that the denouement was only a matter of time, helped on by several state governors (led by Itamar Franco, who had become governor of Minas Gerais) choosing to default on their state debts to the federal treasury and blaming Cardoso's "cruel and unjust" economic policies for forcing their hand. On January 15, 1999, the *real* was forced to float. Between mid-January and the beginning of March, the *real* lost nearly two-thirds of its value. But, amazingly, hyperinflation did not reappear, and the currency value settled down. For the year as a whole, prices rose just under 9 percent.

As 1999 continued, the Cardoso administration turned to another troublesome problem: whether and how to continue the privatization of state enterprises, which President Collor had launched earlier. Passions on the subject ran high, especially on the left. Much of the public had come to see these enterprises as a symbol of national sovereignty. But, at least in the 1960s and 1970s these firms had been frequently inefficient, running chronic deficits that the federal treasury had to cover. Now some firms had improved. The fundamental questions were: Which of the remaining state enterprises should be sold off? Who should be eligible to bid? And how would the Brazilian economy be altered by a massive shift in economic ownership? The answer to the last question depended crucially on whether the buyers were foreign or domestic.

For most workers (except those employed in the state enterprises), these debates were academic. Rather, the average worker in the economy wanted to know why his pay had been frozen or was even shrinking. This trend was dramatized by the result of the minimum wage adjustment in 1999. The workers got a small increase, but, as with most such increases in Brazil, the additional money was quickly eaten up by inflation. The unpleasant fact was that most Brazilian workers (including millions in the informal sector) were locked into wages much lower than those paid in neighboring countries such as Argentina and Chile. The culprit was Brazil's low economic growth rate, which left no margin for income gains at the bottom.

Not surprisingly, President Cardoso was harshly criticized for his mediocre economic record, in particular for "arbitrarily" continuing the Plano Real, thereby saddling Brazil with an out-of-date set of economic targets. Cardoso was especially vulnerable to this criticism, since he had been the father of the Plano Real as well as its chief defender. The Catholic Church's Conference of Bishops was among the chief critics. It sponsored a series of nationwide demonstrations against the Cardoso economic policies. The conference even called for a national plebiscite on whether to continue making payments on the country's foreign debt. Another important critic was Ciro Gomes, a former northeastern governor who had attracted a center-left following. He also attempted a nationalist appeal. But the tight reins imposed by the IMF left little room for innovation. Like it or not, Brazil had little prospect for significant short-run action to change the situation. Surprisingly enough, however, by October 1999 the official GDP forecasts turned upward, and Brazil's gross domestic product for 1999 as a whole rose very slightly.

Cardoso had also had the bad luck to inherit one of the world's most financially disastrous federal pension systems. The fund was in the red due to many participants taking early retirement with high cash rewards (and the fact that retirees paid no contributions). In October 1998, the Cardoso government had attempted to revise the system but met rejection from the Congress. Later that month the government was able to get some participant contributions increased, but the system continued to threaten bankruptcy.

There was also trouble in the realm of the federal police. Cardoso had appointed a new director-general. Unfortunately for the president, his nominee turned out to be a suspect in torture sessions against political prisoners in the 1970s. He was quickly withdrawn in favor of Agildo Monteiro Filho, the first black man to head the federal police force.

On the noneconomic front, however, Cardoso used his second term to strike a major blow for social justice in the area of race. Cardoso had a long-standing and well-deserved reputation as a passionate critic of racial discrimination in Brazil. In 2001, he put his convictions into action. His government issued a decree applying to all federal ministries, ordering them to establish affirmative action quotas for personnel recruitment of Afro-Brazilians and women, among other minorities. He accompanied this legal action with a series of widely publicized speeches deploring the current situation and urging the country, both publicly and privately, to redress the balance caused by past inequities. The president also directed the Ministry of Foreign Affairs to implement a special program that would assist Afro-Brazilian candidates in preparing for the entrance exams to work in the diplomatic corps. President Cardoso declared, "We need a diplomatic corps...that reflects our society, which is multi-colored and will not present itself to the outside world as if it were a white society, because it isn't." In early 2002, the president also issued an executive decree creating the National Affirmative Action Program, which mandated government agencies as well as companies with government contracts, to adopt "percentage goals" for hiring blacks, women, and handicapped people. These policies have engendered a widespread debate in Brazilian society about their efficacy in rooting out long-term forms of discrimination.

Selling Off the State

The year 2000 dawned with favorable economic news. Most important, the *real* had become undervalued relative to the dollar. Brazil now had a powerful incentive to export because its selling prices to the rest of the world were down. Despite the good fortune, the federal government still faced a huge deficit, with the pension system continuing to be a major liability. At least federal tax revenues were cooperating by setting record levels. For the first time in Brazil's history, tax revenue exceeded 30 percent of GDP. This was all the more notable in view of the decades-long prediction that Brazil's weak tax collection system would never produce the needed revenues.

Cardoso had one more weapon he could use to attack the fiscal crisis: the *"medida provisória,"* the constitutional provision power noted earlier as empowering the president to legislate by fiat. Once issued, such a decree remained valid for thirty days if not overridden by the legislature. But *medidas* could be reissued every month and often were. The legislature paid little apparent attention. It was not a new issue. All presidents since 1985 had used this device, for a grand total of 6,110 times. Cardoso defended it as essential in dealing with issues of taxation and finance. In fact, its frequent use meant that executive-legislative relations were not operating normally. In 2001, Congress finally passed a constitutional amendment increasing control over the *medidas provisórias*.

On one front, the official neo-monetarist policy was clearly succeeding: Brazil's labor costs had plunged to among the world's lowest. One Brazilian economist calculated that Brazil's industrial labor costs were a startling 20–55 percent of those in South Korea, Taiwan, Singapore, and Hong Kong. This result had been an explicit neo-monetarist aim: to turn Brazil into an ultra-low-wage economy in the industrializing world.

Meanwhile urban crime continued to be a blight. In 2000, local bus number 174 was hijacked in one of Rio's better suburbs. Live TV picked up the hours-long seizure as the terrified passengers were held at gunpoint. The police botched a rescue attempt, accidentally shooting the last hostage held by the hijacker, who was carted off in a paddy wagon and executed by the police on the way to the prison. TV audiences were traumatized, and the public was scared off taking buses for months.

On another key financial front, the Congress finally passed the Law of Fiscal Responsibility, which limited city and state payroll spending to 60 percent of their respective tax revenues. This control over traditional overspending was now strengthened by penalties of up to four years in prison for officials who violated the new rules. It was a milestone in the struggle to cap municipal and state expenditures.

For the worker, unfortunately, this fiscal tough-mindedness produced little benefit. A February study by the Confederation of Industries showed 1999 real wages dropping below even their 1995 level. And this was after several years of modest nominal increases. The PT and their allies kept up their drumfire of criticism, charging that Cardoso's continued neo-orthodox policy was responsible for massive injustice. In May, Cardoso maneuvered the Congress into approving a new minimum wage law. The new level, however, was little better than the existing level.

The Cardoso regime maintained its commitment to privatization. Each sale of a government enterprise provoked charges that the price was scandalously low. For the average Brazilian, there was only one explanation: corruption. These charges continued for years. But the opposition lacked formal proof. Despite the attacks, privatization was pushed through to a successful close, except for the electrical power sector and Petrobrás, the government-controlled national oil company. By early December 2000, most major state enterprises had been sold off, as Brazil was caught up in the privatization wave sweeping Latin America. The negative aspect of the government success was that the billions received in sales were quickly swallowed up by the treasury, which used them to meet short-term balance-of-payment deficits. There was another result from this shuffling of assets as well. Due to its aggressive direct investment policy, Spain had now replaced the United States as the number one foreign investor in Brazil.

Meanwhile, the specter of scandal was spreading elsewhere in the public sector. Suspicion centered on the labor turmoil in São Paulo. The new building housing the headquarters of the regional labor authority was a showcase of corruption—a decade behind its construction schedule with almost a million dollars in missing funds.

Early in the new year, speculation began about the upcoming presidential election. In March 2000, a straw poll rated Lula number one and Ciro Gomes number two in the forthcoming presidential race. São Paulo's ex-mayor, Paulo Maluf, was the perennial candidate on the right. The PT appeared to be the strongest opposition party with Maluf, as always, a wild card. Pressure from the countryside was omnipresent. In May, the MST (Movimento Sem Terra—Movement of the Landless) invaded federal buildings in eight states, demanding faster land reform. One of MST's biggest mobilizations, it failed in its intended goal; in the end it alienated much of public opinion.

Brazil in the Shadow of an Argentine Default

In the chaotic and conflicting political climate of 2001, any presidential candidates could expect a wide-open fight. The latest candidate to declare was Jader Barbalho, a former senator whose fortune had come from questionable contracts with the federal government. Barbalho exemplified a dying breed: the regional political boss who commanded all patronage in his region. The few remaining bosses of his kind, mostly from the Amazon and the Northeast, were actively opposing Cardoso's reform plans. But time was not on their side.

The impending Argentine financial collapse continued to preoccupy Brazilian policymakers. Could Brazil's economy survive an Argentine financial debacle? Argentine Finance Minister Cavallo's bravado in defending his currency stabilization structure sounded hollow as his country hurtled toward default. By contrast, Brazil had some good news. It could point to an important success in the fight against AIDS. An aggressive treatment program had reduced AIDS deaths by 85 percent since 1995. Brazil had jumped to the forefront in the campaign against this scourge. The government has also led an international campaign to force pharmaceutical companies to license generic drugs that control HIV.

Meanwhile, Brazilian politics was being transformed by the PT's rapid growth. The prospect of Lula's possible arrival in power continued to agitate the political scene. Could a former metalworker really be expected to respectably fill the presidency? In an effort to quiet doubts, a leading PT spokesman, Aloizio Mercardante, said in June that the PT was committed to stability and a continuing reliance on foreign investment.

Shortly thereafter, Cardoso's Finance Minister Pedro Malan gave evidence of economic confidence by announcing that Brazil would not need to renew its current IMF loan. That was music to the ears of Brazilians who had tired of hearing that every economic policy move required consultation with Washington. But the Brazilian economy soon demonstrated again how little room for maneuver the policymakers enjoyed. Foreign investment was down, Argentina faced an imminent default, internal inflation was flaring up, and energy shortages were threatening to paralyze industry. Instead of reducing reliance on the IMF, to increase its safety margin the Cardoso government negotiated another $15 billion in IMF credit, acceptance of which was dependent upon cutting spending.

If days looked dark in Brazil, they were much darker in Argentina. The Argentine authorities faced a no-win situation. Every option seemed closed. Increasing the money supply, for example, was impossible because Argentine law required that pesos in circulation equal available dollar reserves. But the latter were exhausted. Nor was increased government spending a solution, because the government was under strict IMF budget controls. The ultimate way out, floating the peso, would rapidly bankrupt the many Argentines with large dollar-denominated accounts. The Cardoso government, for its part, was struggling at this time to open Brazil's relatively closed economy and establish a more consistent foreign investment policy—with Cardoso and Malan gambling that Brazil, under their direction, could weather the Argentine storm.

On one front Malan could report good news. The New Law of Fiscal Responsibility was taking hold, helping to produce primary budget surpluses on both state and federal levels. This was good news to the IMF, which required such surpluses in order to control Brazil's government spending. The financially weak pension system was another target of attempted reform. The current issue was whether to tax the Social Security income of retired federal employees, who had always been exempt. This issue, not surprisingly given who would lose if such a policy went into effect, was, and still is, highly contentious.

The previous year Brazil had witnessed the beginning of a multiyear fight over farmers' right to plant genetically modified soybean seeds, following a 1998 ban on the planting of such seeds. The supplier was the American chemical giant Monsanto. Radicals on the left challenged use of these seeds on environmental grounds. The stakes were high, since the seeds were much more fertile than existing seeds. Even without increased fertility, it cost 20 percent less to grow soybeans in central Brazil than in the United States, which was Brazil's main competition. Brazil was bound to be an even bigger exporter if the seeds were approved. (In 2004, President Lula was to sign a decree repealing the 1998 ban.)

The Cardoso government, despite ceaseless criticism from the PT, pressed on with its privatization program. Most of the transition to private ownership, including steel mills, iron ore mines, and aircraft manufacturing, had been successful. But the final step, which included primarily state telephone and electricity firms, provoked popular dissatisfaction with pricing, despite the fact that the total number of phone lines had nearly quadrupled since 1970 to about 50 million. The firms remained only partially privatized, including in particular the three principal power companies. In addition, the regulatory framework had been left vague, no doubt deliberately, leading to confusion over output, which, in turn, contributed to power shortages.

October saw a growing number of political quarrels. Lula was the front-runner, but other candidates were also generating interest. José Serra, the government health minister, an able and ambitious figure, began to stake out his own political position. His stronghold was São Paulo. His assets were his intelligence and his energy. His liability was his sharp tongue, which often alienated potential allies.

Tarso Jereissati, another presidential hopeful, had been a highly successful governor of Ceará. But he was relatively unknown in the South, where economic and political power was concentrated. Both he and Serra yearned to attack the style and record of Cardoso, but a practical alternative was difficult to formulate when the government propaganda was dominating the airwaves.

The opposition presidential candidates found themselves tempted to sound economically nationalist. Yet they were limited, knowing that Brazil's international debt position made it dangerous to risk alarming the bankers or the IMF.

Making it more difficult for the opposition, the Cardoso government had, despite obstacles, compiled a record of price stability and modestly increased purchasing power for the growing middle class. In his memoirs, Cardoso acknowledges that his main presidential goal was economic and political stability. The president's great liability was having failed to achieve economic growth and thereby make possible a meaningful reduction in poverty.

As 2001 ended, the prospects for the presidential succession remained murky. José Serra was losing ground, having been inept in maneuvering for the succession, and was winning only marginal support in the polls. Lula still led but was being crowded by the surprise candidacy of Rosanne Sarney, governor of Maranhão and daughter of a previous president of Brazil. Cardoso, unable to run again, was lacking in options to control the succession and was rumored to be considering throwing his support to Sarney.

9

Brazilian Democracy Takes a New Turn: Or Does It?

The real possibility of electing Lula president posed a challenge to Brazil that its elite had never faced before. No previous president—whether being democratically elected or coming from the military, whether radical or conventional—had come from the country's "masses." All were well educated, spoke with correct grammar, and were born into Brazil's ruling or middle classes. Lula, in sharp contrast, spoke grammatically fractured Portuguese and was clearly, and proudly, a member of the "have-nots." This alone made the election of 2002 a potential watershed. Added to this, Lula was the first serious potential president since the military coup of 1964 to espouse a socialist agenda. If he were elected, his administration could thus represent a very different approach to both the politics and economics of government. Lula in fact pursued a very conventional, internationally approved economic policy. How this combination worked out in Brazil's economic and social policy record makes interesting reading.

Lula Finally Becomes Legitimate

As politicians prepared for the presidential election, 2002 promised to be a busy year. It began with strong economic growth but also with a depressingly large deficit in the Social Security program. The South American scene also remained clouded by the growing monetary deficit in Argentina as the peso, still fixed against the dollar, became ever more severely overvalued. Brazil's misfortune was to be tainted with the investor suspicion that was justifiably aroused by Argentina, since outside observers tended to lump Brazil and Argentina together as to economic prospects.

The Economic Scene

Argentina finally had to devalue the peso, breaking the link with the dollar that Finance Minister Carvallo had guaranteed would last forever. That country's financial system collapsed like a house of cards, as Argentine debtors scrambled to meet their dollar debts. The collapse led to what bankers always feared in Latin America—a major default. Meanwhile, Brazilians were optimistic that their future exports to China and Russia would replace markets being lost in Argentina. The Brazilian policymakers, justifiably or not, thought they had avoided another default of their own.

This optimism was tempered in Brasília by policymakers' knowledge that international bankers had long memories and would not soon forget Brazil's 1,000 percent-a-year inflation of not too many years ago. Brazil's related problem, however, was its low economic growth rate. In the 1980s, the real annual rate had been a mere 1.8 percent, which many Brazilians attributed to the "unfair" world trading system. They intermittently sought relief by complaining to the W.T.O. over, for example, U.S. subsidies to its cotton producers. In 2002, Brazil's growth rate had increased very little from the previous year.

At the same time, Brazil was experiencing its usual spectacular bank profits. (Bank Boston, for example, in 2001 had its biggest profits in fifty-five years of activity in Brazil.) Such returns were hardly surprising given that the banks were charging virtually the highest interest rates in the world. But high interest rates, as always, contributed to hobbling Brazilian economic growth.

In foreign trade Brazil was struggling to penetrate the U.S. market. A case in point was Brazilian steel, which was so highly competitive in the United States that it provoked an internal U.S. demand for tariff barriers. In the air also was controversy over a contract an American firm had won for a huge electronic intelligence system in the Amazon Basin. Raytheon Corporation had won over the bid of a French competitor, and there were ugly charges that the Americans had cheated. Brazilian nationalists seized upon this as proof that any economic relations with the United States would mean exploitation. Cardoso notes in his memoirs: "I was always concerned that the terms of trade as dictated by Washington would be damaging to Brazil, particularly with regard to agriculture."

The 2002 Presidential Campaign

The build-up to the presidential campaign of 2002 was bitterly contested. Rosanne Sarney dropped out after a federal police raid found over R$1 million (Brazilian *real* currency) in cash of unexplained origin in her office. The investigators laid out the hundreds of neatly stacked bills for maximum television exposure. Sarney charged that the raid was the work of José Serra, a chief campaign rival, but public opinion considered this explanation lame and rejected her candidacy. Proof against Serra was indeed lacking, but it was undeniably true that he benefited from the new campaign space. The PFL was enraged and left the alliance with the PSDB, resigning all positions in the Cardoso government and not participating in the Serra election coalition. The PSDB ended up in an electoral alliance with the PMDB.

President Cardoso was also encountering personal embarrassment, which inevitably reflected on his party. MST militants decided on a publicity gesture consisting of invading a Minas Gerais farm owned by the president's family. The invaders easily occupied the lightly protected house and published photographs showing them relaxing over a sample of the president's liquor cabinet. But the incident turned out to be an opportunity to demonstrate Brazilian elitist political culture, rather than injuring Cardoso's personal standing. Cardoso successfully deflected opposition by not immediately expelling the invaders. And it all ended without violence. The president had the offenders arrested but did not press charges. The Minas Gerais state police failed to act under orders from Itamar Franco, who was still governor, so the farm was declared "under federal jurisdiction."

The leading presidential candidate was still Lula, which was provoking wild reactions abroad. Foreign observers alternated between shock at his Marxist speeches and relief when he shifted to more moderate language. Lula's authentic working-class background was a genuine political novelty. Born in poverty in rural northwestern Pernambuco, he grew up on the outskirts of São Paulo. He became a metal worker and eventually won a job in the automobile industry, which was considered the ideal factory employment at the time. He became active in the union, soon as president, and led a strike wave from 1978 to 1980 that challenged the military government's economic policies. As a result, he was arrested and removed from his union office and charged with violating the National Security Law, although the charges were eventually dropped. By early 2002, Lula's leadership had attracted a wide spectrum of followers. His advisers argued that Brazil's economic problems were the result of previous government incompetence. All observers agreed that the domestic debt had risen alarmingly under Cardoso. Servicing this debt was a heavy burden on the treasury. And it strengthened the fears of conservative economists who foresaw domestic bankruptcy just around the corner, even under Cardoso.

In July, a lesser-known presidential candidate appeared. He was Ciro Gomes, former governor of Ceará and Itamar Franco's last finance minister in 1994, who had also run unsuccessfully for president in 1998. A dynamic young speaker, Gomes had staked out a center-left position. Lula was still trying to shake off the image of someone utterly without experience in public administration. And his occasional grammatical lapses highlighted his working-class background. Were average Brazilian voters ready to elect a candidate who seemed so much like themselves? This was an important question, given that Brazilians had never elected anyone as president who was not from the educated elite. In any event, Lula came across well in a debate among presidential hopefuls and was, to the surprise of his detractors, declared the debate winner in a follow-up public opinion poll. A fourth candidate also joined the race. Evangelical leader Rio Governor Anthony Garotinho (PSB) stepped down from the governorship in April and was seen by some as a "populist" threat to Lula.

Lula's solid performance at home did not assuage his foreign skeptics. The PT advisers spent many an hour explaining to the foreign press how the Brazilian case differed from the Argentine. But it remained a distinction lost on many American bankers.

Cardoso was not idle as Lula fought for support. At the end of his eight-year presidency, the former president moved to consolidate his prestige and secure his legacy by calling for a summit meeting of all the presidential candidates, which was convoked by Central Bank President Arminio Fraga. The idea was that at the summit the candidates would commit themselves, if elected, to achieve a primary budget surplus in 2003, 2004, and 2005. Lula went even further. He promised also to support the recent agreement with the IMF. In fact, this agreement was an economic straitjacket that would guarantee the continuation of Cardoso's economic policy well past the end of his presidency. Under constant pressure to distinguish his position from that of Cardoso, Lula soon withdrew his support for the IMF agreement, highlighting his somewhat inconsistent economic stance as he sought votes.

October 6 brought the presidential election's first round. Brazil's rule was that if no candidate won a majority on the first round, the election would go to a runoff between the two leading candidates on October 27. Persisting foreign worries about Lula's economic views were reflected in a drop in foreign investment, as rumors of Brazil's impending default were heard again in New York and London.

In the first electoral round, Lula won 39.6 million votes out of 84 million, for a total of 46.4 percent versus 23.2 percent for Serra, 17.9 percent for Garotinho, and 12.0 percent for Ciro Gomes. Lack of an absolute majority initiated a second round. Lula's single opponent would be the person who placed second in the popular vote—José Serra, the Paulista economist who was Cardoso's minister of planning and later health and was maneuvering for center support. The campaign was hard fought, and Lula's advisers once again worried about how his fractured grammar would go over on TV. On October 28, Lula was declared the winner of the second-round election, receiving 52 million votes or 61.3 percent of the total, compared with Serra's 38.7 percent.

It was a dramatic moment in Brazilian political history. Lula had lost three earlier attempts to gain the presidency in 1989, 1994, and 1998. Now he stood as the first working-class Brazilian ever elevated to the Presidential Palace. Most reassuring for the PT leadership was the way in which the business community had come around to accepting the idea of a President Lula. It was as if the Brazilian bourgeoisie had decided the time had come to turn a new corner. Even the bond market reacted calmly when Lula was finally elected.

Lula's First Steps

Once elected, President Lula was cautious in forming his government. The key initial appointee was Antônio Palocci, a former physician and mayor of the city of Ribeirão Preto in the state of São Paulo, who became Lula's campaign manager in early 2002. He was named head of the transition team and later became the minister of finance. Palocci was known as an economic moderate and a tough figure in political maneuvering. He had already established himself as one of Lula's closest advisers. Another important early appointee, as chief of staff, was José Dirceu, also a centrist, who had been a leading hard-line guerrilla during the military dictatorship. By now, however, he had achieved the reputation of having guided the PT away from its radical positions after becoming PT national president in 1995. In 2002, Dirceu was elected federal deputy.

One of the major policy issues facing Lula was Brazil's policy toward the United States. The United States had been pushing hard for adoption of its proposed FTAA (Free Trade Agreement of the Americas) since December 1994. Brazil was a major skeptic, with Brazilians suspecting that the FTAA would be a device for the Americans to globalize their exports while making few trade concessions in return. This charge struck a chord among the PT left, which was always suspicious of U.S. motives.

Meanwhile, Brazil could be proud of how it had conducted the presidential election. By 2002, Brazil had become the fourth-largest democracy in the world. Its electorate reached more than 115 million, many of whom had never voted before. Despite predictions to the contrary, the electorate had been unmoved by the scare tactics of the right.

Perhaps surprisingly given its political history, Brazil since 1945 had had a relatively efficient electoral justice system that had kept fraud and voting disputes below the average of most Latin American republics. By 2002, voting had become 100 percent electronic throughout Brazil. The voting machine components were all made in Brazil, although the firm that devised the voting machine was later sold to a U.S. company. Once functioning smoothly, an achievement that had been several years in the making, there were almost no claims of partisan manipulation of the machines. It was a marvel, especially in comparison with the habitual accusations of fraud from both sides in so many North American electoral jurisdictions (of which the confusion in the state of Florida in the 2000 U.S. presidential election is a notable case in point).

The fear among the PT leadership was that Lula's election would only reinforce foreign doubts about the new government. There were some favorable signs, including a healthy foreign trade surplus, but all eyes were fixed on the international bankers. Would they ever give the PT government the benefit of the doubt? The PT girded for a war of nerves. The PT radicals were in for two shocks. First, President-elect Lula decided to continue the IMF program signed by Cardoso/Malan in August 2002 and actually increased the fiscal surplus target from 3.75 percent to 4.25 percent. Second, he appointed an international banker (Henrique Meirelles, who had just been elected PSDB deputy from Goias) to head the Central Bank.

Lula's left wing had additional concerns. They were preoccupied with fulfilling the PT's campaign promise to abolish hunger. Academic experts were agreed that hunger in Brazil was a matter of distribution, not production. There was enough food. It just was not getting to all the people. To change this meant getting buying power into the hands of the Brazilians who couldn't afford enough food on their own. One idea was a direct benefit program to enable the poor to buy food. Called "fome zero" (zero hunger) for a while, the plan was to build on a small program started under Cardoso to provide a single minimum wage benefit to poor families to enable their children to stay in school rather than having to earn money to help their families afford food. Another idea was a major increase in the minimum wage. Realism was brought to those deliberations by José Dirceu, who, on election eve, warned that the new government, if the PT won, would not be able to meet the new minimum wage being demanded by the unions, which would have increased the already huge social security deficit. Lula contented himself with the commitment to doubling the minimum wage by the end of his first term.

As the new government settled in, its foreign trade record strengthened. Foreign trade had doubled since 1990 and had now grown to just over $100 billion a year. This upward trend was crucial because a growing trade surplus was the only way Brazil could finance its foreign debt without putting unbearable pressure on the domestic economy. Another favorable trend from the standpoint of the government was the steady rise in overall tax revenues. These projections meant that the Lula government would have more room to maneuver than it had foreseen. On the other hand, some sectors of Brazilian domestic industry were overextended. The automobile industry was a prime example. It had expanded based on optimistic projections of the early 1990s. But lagging sales, which had persisted through the mid-1990s and into the new century, threatened the economy because auto production had long been viewed in Brazil as a prime source of employment. Continuing stagnation in that sector put increased pressure on other urban employers.

The new team contained some interesting faces in addition to Palocci and Dirceu. One was Marina Silva, a PT senator from the Amazon region and a politician closely linked to environmental movements, who became minister of the environment. Lula appointed the Afro-Brazilian singer and songwriter Gilberto Gil as minister of culture. Luiz Furlan, a well-known member of Brazil's private sector, took the post of minister of development, industry, and foreign commerce. It was hoped that he would be an effective link between the PT and the FIESP, the principal industrial lobby. The most controversial appointment was probably Meirelles, the former head of International Bank of Boston who was now Lula's president of the Brazilian Central Bank. This transition—from heading a prominent U.S. bank to Brazilian Labor Party politics—made Meirelles, rather naturally, suspect to the PT left wing. Geographically, Lula's cabinet appointments were distributed, per Brazil's usual balance, among the major states: São Paulo had five, Rio de Janeiro had three, and Bahia, Minas Gerais, and Rio Grande do Sul each had two. The cabinet was also notable for including two Afro-Brazilians and one with some Indian bloodline (Marina Silva, senator from the Amazon region). The PT did not win a majority in Congress and quickly had to build a governing alliance with other political parties to get any legislation approved.

The PT in Power

Lula's Inauguration Address on June 1, 2003, struck an eloquent chord in keeping with the PT's historic pledge to be the party of the people: "...the hour has come to transform Brazil into that nation we have always dreamed of: a sovereign and worthy nation that is aware of its own importance on the international scene and, at the same time, able to house, clothe, and treat with justice all its children."

This rhetoric confirmed the views of many in both Latin America and Washington that Lula's election was—for good or bad—Brazil's most important political event since the military takeover of 1964. The PT candidate had, for example, assumed a radical stance, explicitly attacking Brazil's alleged subservience to the IMF. He had, at least from time to time, promised a new policy that would break with Cardoso's monetarist orthodoxy. Furthermore, he had promised dramatic measures to help the poor. But could he—would he—keep any of those promises? After all, Cardoso and Finance Minister Malan had warned that servicing Brazil's colossal debt (internal and external) left no room for the PT's extravagant pledges to the voters. In effect, these critics argued that Brazil was decades away from being able to take the PT's proposed risks. Orthodox monetarism was not a policy choice, explained the Cardoso team, it was an unavoidable necessity. As Cardoso later said, "Brazil's constant financial troubles meant that the government was severely limited in terms of what it could spend....I would have loved to be able to spend billions of dollars on health care and education, but we just didn't have the money."

The stage seemed to be set for a new government to prove the contrary. But the scenery quickly shifted. The expectation (strongest on the PT left) that Lula would try to escape the lock step of neo-liberal policymaking was soon disappointed. His economic team, which was in any case mixed in its ideology, turned out to be also mixed in its policy recommendations. The initial comments of the new financial minister, physician-turned-politician Antônio Palocci, signaled caution.

One economic indicator, as we have seen, was a pleasant surprise: a trade surplus of $13 billion. Brazil had benefited from a worldwide rise in commodity prices. This could assuage, temporarily at least, worries about the balance of payments. A more troubling issue was electric energy, a sector in which privatization had bogged down. Significantly, as noted, almost all the large state enterprises had been sold off by Cardoso with the exception of three mega-hydroelectric firms and Petrobrás, the national oil monopoly. Lula decided to halt the privatization process, although he did not reverse the privatizations of the Cardoso government. The issue of whether or not the government should retain state-owned sectors of the infrastructure remained controversial.

The president's chief foreign economic problem was responding to the continuing U.S. campaign for its proposed FTAA. The idea was to create a continent-wide trade zone. Since this would inevitably be dominated by the United States, it was seen by Brazil as obviously intended to preempt Latin American initiatives such as Mercosur, which in any case had been weakened by Argentina's recent economic collapse.

Another problem the Lula government faced was the federal pension system. Riddled with outdated regulations that facilitated fraud and excessive payouts, it had an operating deficit that had now reached $20 billion a year. The Cardoso government had labored mightily for reform but was vetoed by the Brazilian Supreme Court (Supreme Tribunal Federal or STF). What the runaway system would cost the PT government if left unchecked was hardly calculable.

On yet another front, Brazil was seriously underfunding investment. That was dangerous, because it meant that Brazil was failing to lay the foundation for future growth. Might the answer be increased state investment? Economists generally say that investment should reach at least 25 percent of GDP to achieve higher growth rates. If so, the obvious instrument would be the National Bank for Economic and Social Development. But such an initiative would involve changing the existing budgeting priorities. It was out of the question for the moment, because the government had to avoid anything that might discourage foreign investment.

Interest rate policy also confronted the incoming government. The Central Bank, now under Lula appointee Henrique Meirelles, was following a hard interest rate policy, replicating essentially the course of his Cardoso-appointed predecessor. In January 2003, the Central Bank's actions kept Brazilian interest rates among the highest in the world. The new economic team believed such a policy was needed to control inflation. It was also needed to discourage Brazilian capitalists from converting their *real* assets into dollars.

At this point in Lula's first term, Palocci and Meirelles could feel satisfied with their short-term success. They had strengthened the *real* and convinced foreign bankers to increase their credit lines, even though the Central Bank continued to infuriate small-scale producers and consumers with its high interest rates.

Several other pieces of good news also helped Lula. Brazil's exports were flourishing. Brazil had emerged as the world's second-largest soybean exporter, even with the Brazilian legislative prohibition against foreign genetically modified seeds. In addition, race relations, a major PT concern, were seen as a Lula strongpoint. The president had nominated (a nomination that was later confirmed) a distinguished Afro-Brazilian for the Supreme Court. This was unprecedented and therefore a gesture of great symbolic importance. President Lula has now named six new STF judges, including a second woman (Cardoso had named the first, Ellen Gracie Northfleet, who became STF president in 2006 for a two-year term).

The oil sector brought further good news. In early 2003, Petrobrás announced that its oil and gas reserves, for the first time in its history, exceeded its long-sought goal of ten billion barrels, at which rate of increase, the firm added, Brazil would reach oil self-sufficiency in only four years. Such an achievement would be a great relief to Brazil's balance of payments, enabling the funds previously spent on oil imports to be used to help refinance Brazil's $260 billion debt (52 percent of the country's GDP!).

The various pieces of good news notwithstanding, the Lula government had to face the continuing social damage inflicted by Brazil's restrictive monetary policy, which Lula had inherited from his predecessor and continued into his own presidency. Rising unemployment helped depress real monthly wages, which in April 2003 had fallen 14.7 percent from a year earlier. In June, an ugly scene further dramatized the problem of unemployment. Some twenty thousand applicants appeared to apply for the 1,500 jobs as street sweepers and janitors offered by the São Paulo city government. It took tear gas and truncheon-wielding police to clear the scene.

Government finances for 2003 were also worrying. The federal budget was displaying its usual red ink despite the export boom. In order to reduce expenditures while retaining its stated commitment to food security, the Lula government looked for ways to cut the budget. R$14 billion were cut initially in 2003. The road-building program was one target. Defense spending was another. Both were cut. For example, the government postponed the purchase of twelve supersonic fighter-bombers for the air force.

Exports Take Center Stage as Lula Continues to Govern

In 2004, the second full calendar year of PT government, Lula's economic policy continued virtually indistinguishable from Cardoso's. But direct foreign investment, which the continuation of Cardoso's policies would supposedly attract, had fallen from an annual rate of $30 billion in the late 1990s to $9 billion in 2003. Spending on social needs (aside from the Social Security program) had actually fallen from $10 billion in 2002 to only $6.3 billion in 2003. PT militants had little to cheer about. Where was the social transformation for which they had campaigned so hard? And where were the supposedly compensating economic advantages of the pro-IMF stance?

This was one fight confronting Lula in 2004. He also had two new policy fights on his hands. The first was the rural violence generated by the MST. Lula appeared sympathetic to their continuing land invasions, yet he hesitated in adopting policy change. He had, for example, actually slowed down the federal land distribution program. The second fight was Brazil's resistance to U.S. pressure to cooperate in the American-proposed FTAA trade zone. Every collision with the United States raised the question of where Brazil was headed: More socialist or more capitalistic? More or less integrated into the world economy? Lula showed hesitation here as well, with these questions remaining unanswered within the PT-led government.

Lula's government was also dogged by Brazil's continuing reversion to its violent past despite its continuing modernization. In February, for example, three Labor Ministry inspectors were gunned down in Minas Gerais. They were investigating charges that local farmers were using slave labor—this more than a century and a quarter after the end of legal slavery in Brazil.

But early in May 2004, the PT government got a pleasant surprise from the foreign sector. The economic figures when released indicated that exports had leaped in the fourth quarter of 2003 to $26 billion—a 25 percent increase over the previous year. The increased demand for Brazil's exports had come from an international commodity boom combined with the growing sales of Brazilian manufactured products to China. But how far could this external demand take the Brazilian economy? Exports had traditionally been only 20 percent of GDP. How much higher could they go before hitting the ceiling of maximum Brazilian productive capacity?

The year 2004 also brought major innovations in the auto sector, which launched flex cars (able to burn both gasoline and alcohol or a mix of the two). These alternative fuel systems allowed drivers to adjust to the preferred fuel type. (Since 2007, Americans can also buy "E-95" flex fuel, with 85 percent ethanol.) Since the price of alcohol was only 70 percent that of gasoline, the potential for petroleum savings was great. But Brazil was not the hemisphere's only alcohol producer. The major potential competitor in the world ethanol market was the United States, although its capacity for ethanol production came from corn rather than the more productive sugar. But the U.S. economy showed no signs of reducing its dependence on oil, leaving Brazil with a clean field to develop its own sugar-based industry. (By early 2006, Brazil was the world leader, producing 40 percent of the sugar traded on world markets.) Furthermore, output was increasing by 20 percent a year. The comparative success of Brazilian ethanol is shown by the fact that petrol sold at the Brazilian pumps has been 25 percent ethanol, the highest percentage in the world, since the 1940s. Flex-fuel cars account for up to 30 percent of all new cars in Brazil. Presidents George W. Bush and Lula discussed new joint ethanol policies—a so-called OPEC for ethanol—in São Paulo on March 8–9, 2007.

Despite the favorable export trends and the increasing fuel savings, by mid-2004 the government was facing a severe shortage of investment capital. Unfortunately, foreign investment was still down. The PT was discovering that Lula's brand of conservative macroeconomic policy seemed incompatible with strong domestic growth.

The slowdown in the economy, as described earlier, had hurt Lula's popularity. His approval rating in the polls dropped in late June to 29.4 percent from 34.6 percent in May and 48.3 percent in August of the preceding year. The stakes were high. Lula's personal popularity was crucial for the PT government's legitimacy, since the cabinet was weakened by divisions within it.

Then, suddenly, the economic news took a turn for the better. The second-quarter growth rate estimate for 2004, when released in August, turned out to be 5.7 percent, the highest quarterly rate in years. In the autumn of 2004, Moody's and Standard and Poor's, the leading U.S. international credit-rating agencies, reacted to the good economic news by upgrading its Brazilian ratings from BB- to B+. Here was a signal, as Lula was heading into the last two years of his first term, that the PT government's economic moderation was at last gaining him a favorable nod from the bastion of capitalism.

With economic growth picking up, the PT's left wing thought it was time to raise again the issue of fighting Brazil's core poverty in earnest. The Lula government's initial plan was to base a national benefit program for the poor on two preliminary initiatives of the Cardoso government—Bolsa Alimentação, providing funds for nutrition for pregnant women and small children, and Bolsa Escola, aimed at keeping children in school. The new program, named "Bolsa Família," started off underfunded and burdened by poor administration and chaotic coordination with other government welfare programs. Disillusionment with the program was not lessoned when Brazil's most-watched Sunday evening TV program, *Fantástico*, ran an exposé alleging that local governments were steering federal anti-poverty funds into middle-class hands. The Lula government responded with a rapid expansion of the program. In 2003, the program had reached 3.6 million families. It was reaching 6.5 million families by the end of 2004 and 8.7 million families in 2005.

By the October 2004 midterm municipal elections, the downward trend in Lula's popularity had reversed. The PT was growing faster than any other political party, doubling the number of municipalities it had controlled in 2000. In addition to expanding its control of larger cities, the PT elected many more mayors in small towns. This reflected, at least in part, the continued movement of the party as a whole toward the center, since that was where the votes could be picked up. Those on the party's left seethed in frustration over their relative impotence.

The trade surplus was strengthening the rightward movement of the party by attaining apparent success in capitalist terms. In September 2004, for example, the surplus reached $24 billion, up 42 percent from the previous year's surplus as of the same date. But there was, as is often the case, a downside to this increase. The growing steam in the domestic economy raised worries about inflation. Overall wage growth was up to 11.09 percent for the year ending September 2004, raising the specter of demand inflation. Thus far, however, inflation was under control, with price growth lagging wage growth. The nonagricultural sector exports were also coming online, with the dynamic steel firm Gerdau leading the way.

Notwithstanding these favorable numbers, by the end of 2004 Lula's critics from both inside and outside the party had returned to the fray. He was again attacked from within for being too responsive to the harsh guidelines of the IMF and for failing to implement any policy that would fulfill authentic socialist goals.

Government Fortunes Further Reverse as the PT Tastes Scandal

At the two-year mark of the Lula regime (2002–2004), the macroeconomic results were reasonably satisfactory, in good part due to the success of the export sector. Economic growth had risen from 1.9 percent for 2002 to 5.2 percent for 2004, increasing Brazil's trade surplus from $13.1 billion to $33.3 billion.

So Brazil was finally reaping the benefits from the orthodox policies the Lula economic team had continued from the Cardoso regime. Furthermore, it had succeeded in remaining economically stable despite the monetary collapse in nearby Argentina and initial hostility of New York and London bankers.

In spite of 2004's economic good news, however, the Brazilian technocrats knew how far behind their country was in the world's growth race. Other major emerging countries were doing conspicuously better. Chile was at 9.5 percent annual growth, India at 6.5 percent, and Russia at 7.1 percent.

Meanwhile, now into his third year in office, Lula was getting heavy personal criticism. One issue was his penchant for foreign travel. As the president of a major developing country he could easily arrange invitations for state visits. And it was clear he was enjoying the foreign social occasions more than the task of hard political slogging back home. One sign of discontent with Lula came from the lower house of the federal legislature. The occasion was the election of its new president, necessitated by rules prohibiting the immediate reelection of the incumbent. In February 2005, a new president was elected. The position, which carried significant power and prestige, was won by Severino Cavalcanti, a member of the "allied" Progressive party that was part of the Lula coalition. Cavalcanti was soon accused of corruption, however, suffered a "seven-month miscarriage," and was forced to resign in September 2005. Communist Deputy Aldo Rebelo (PCdoB) was elected to complete the term (until February 2007). The press saw his election as a setback for Lula. But the press still considered Lula unbeatable should he run for reelection in 2006.

In mid-2005, however, Brazil was rocked by a series of revelations in Brasília that were far more damaging to the PT. The evidence was first detected in an investigation of corruption in the post office. Misappropriation of government funds abounded. Investigative reporters then turned up evidence that the PT congressional leadership had been systematically buying votes with cash of uncertain origin. The goal was to guarantee majorities on bills for which the government lacked enough votes to win honestly. At first the PT leaders vehemently denied the charges. Unfortunately for them, these were too well documented to be in doubt.

The major charges involved alleged payoffs by the government to congressional members looking to sell their votes on legislation that was crucial to the government. A key accuser was Deputy Roberto Jefferson, a talented orator and a leader in the Partido Trabalhista Brasileiro (PTB), who was probably settling old scores. In any case, his accusations received huge TV coverage.

Brazilian public life now became absorbed in the drama of the Brasília scandals. PT leaders defended themselves by pointing to similar corruption in the Cardoso government, a defense so weak that it gained no traction. Government prestige continued to slide.

August 2005 brought yet more revelations of substantial bribes. Duda Mendonça, the famed public relations impresario, whom Lula had insisted manage his 2002 presidential campaign, confirmed that he had been paid $3 million with "off the books" funds supplied by a mysterious middleman. Lula went on TV to claim he knew nothing of the revelations.

Was Lula another president en route to self-destruction like Vargas and Collor? The ethical superiority the PT had always claimed was gone. Lula was now enmeshed in the seamy side of Brazilian politics, which the PT had claimed it would never enter.

Meanwhile, public pressure on the PT, especially from the media, grew. Typical was the attack from a PT-supporting journalist: "How is it possible that a clique could assault our Brazilian state and provoke the greatest political crisis that our country has ever suffered?" Lula acted the innocent party in successive TV appearances. In one appearance in July, he rose in righteous indignation to challenge his critics:

> There isn't a woman or a man who has the courage to give me a lesson in ethics, morality, and honesty. My comrades, I have earned the right in this country to walk with my head high after much self-sacrifice. And it's not going to be the Brazilian elite which will make me bow my head. That is not going to happen.

The public didn't seem to be buying his self-righteous denials. Lula's support in the polls went from 35–36 percent in June–July to 29 percent in August 2005.

Roberto Jefferson continued his sideshow-style attacks, and the rot soon reached Lula's inner circle. But despite the weight of evidence against his party confidants, Lula continued to think he could outlast his accusers. The plot thickened in late 2005, as Brazil ran into an unexpected problem on the economic side: the strengthening of the *real*. Over the previous three years, the *real* had doubled its value in dollars, raising deep concern that the strengthening *real* would hurt exports. In the meantime, the government's economic hopes remained buoyant, since, for example, Brazil's increasing dollar reserves (from the *real*'s climb) made possible early payments on the foreign debt. (Brazil liquidated its IMF loan ahead of time in March 2005.)

By November 2005, Lula was facing increasingly unavoidable questions about his party's financing irregularities. Once again he brushed off his critics. But his poll numbers continued downward. Meanwhile, the countryside grew increasingly restless. In late 2005, some twelve thousand members of the Landless Workers Movement demonstrated in Brasília to protest the slow rate at which land was being distributed to the urban poor. After violent clashes with the police, the protesters agreed to meet with the president. The subsequent negotiations left an ambiguous accord, which pleased no one.

At the same time the government sustained another blow as the economy showed signs of weakening. Some diversion from the political scene was provided by a November visit to Brasília by President George W. Bush. But the climate was not exactly welcoming, since Brazilian public opinion was disenchanted with the Iraq War. The visit produced the kind of inconclusive communiqué that foreign offices cook up for such occasions.

As the year came to a close, the crisis deepened further. The president lost one of his most important political collaborators, José Dirceu. His demise was hardly a surprise. Dirceu, who had headed the PT presidential team, had already been accused of involvement in the scandal to buy votes. With Lula's support, Dirceu had been able to cling to his administrative power for several months thereafter. But in June 2005 he had been forced to resign that post because of the continuing publicity given the bribery case. He retained his congressional seat for a while longer. But now that, too, had gone. The Chamber of Deputies expelled him and banned him from electoral politics until 2016. Dirceu's magical journey from guerrilla hero to presidential kingmaker had ended. The Chamber also expelled Deputy Roberto Jefferson.

Meanwhile, Lula's popularity continued to take a beating. One poll showed that he would lose even to his long-time rival, José Serra, in a hypothetical presidential election.

The dark days for the PT government carried through the final months of 2005. It was as if politics had been transferred to another world. Leading PT political kingmakers such as Dirceu had been swept from the chessboard. The once-fanatical PT fans had long disappeared from the scene, and the party had lost its crusading zeal. In December 2003, the PT expelled one senator (Heloisa Helena) and three deputies who had voted against all Lula government proposals in Congress that year. In 2005, these people led the organization of the new PSoL (Party of Socialism and Liberty), which attracted many PT disaffected dissidents. The PT, in the midst of a political scandal reminiscent of what had led to Collor's impeachment, was lucky that the opposition was too weak to draw maximum partisan benefits. But the party's drive to "moralize" politics had certainly lost its steam.

The Last Year of Lula's First Term

The year 2006 was to be a crucial one for the PT government. It was assumed that Lula would run for a second presidential term. This would be the last year of a unique experiment in democratic rule by Brazil's first mass-based party. How would that government be judged by Latin America's largest electorate? That was the major question on everyone's mind in Brasília.

A new PT scandal did not help matters, when the press discovered that dozens of congressmen were accused of taking bribes to approve allocation of government funds to cover a fraudulent ambulance scheme. Lula rejected the charges by citing "betrayal" by unidentified aides.

Political observers had difficulty interpreting the likely political impact of this latest scandal. Then, just a week into the election campaign, yet another PT-linked scandal erupted. This was an attempt to implicate the opposition in a wiretapping scheme. As in previous incidents, Lula accused the opposition of undermining his campaign. Former President Cardoso ridiculed Lula's defense.

Calculating the odds on Lula's reelection was complicated. The conventional view for most of 2006 was that Lula was a sure bet for reelection. Evidence accumulated that the government welfare program had created a strong following, with the Bolsa Família now distributing (according to government data) $325 a month to 11 million of Brazil's 45 million families.

Lower-income families were further strengthened in 2006 by a large increase in the minimum wage (26 percent in real terms). The buying power of this largesse was preserved by the continuing low inflation rate. One leading analyst, Bolivar Lamounier, went so far as to claim "the poor electorates of the north-east have been turned capitalist."

Meanwhile, Brazil had been accumulating a huge positive trade balance ($30 billion annually in recent years). While this surplus enabled Brazil to pay off its long-standing international debts, it also pushed up the value of the *real*. That in turn reduced the competitiveness of Brazilian exports, causing major losses in such Brazilian industries as footwear and textiles.

Lula's political enemies had little luck in criticizing Lula's economic record, however, in part because Geraldo Alckmin, ex-governor of São Paulo and the candidate from Fernando Henrique Cardoso's party, came across as aloof and without electoral appeal in the less-developed states—little seeming threat to Lula's reelection. The only likely threat to Lula's smooth transition seemed to be the possible vote for the followers of Senator Heloisa Helena, the extreme left-winger who had earlier been expelled from the PT and helped organize the PSoL in 2005.

Heloisa, who was mounting an effective evangelical-type presidential campaign, had achieved a stubbornly loyal following of several hundred thousand voters—attracted by her accusations of Lula's "arrogance and political cowardice."

The Economy in 2006

The last year of Lula's presidential term turned out to be very favorable economically for the government. The Plano Real, a creature of Cardoso, along with conservative fiscal policy, continued to generate financial stability. That meant, above all, relative freedom from inflation, which only a few years before had reached rates so high as to render impossible any but the shortest-run capital market. Equally important, high inflation had precluded any saving, however modest, by the working class, along with the rest of the public. The cause was the "inflation tax" that reduced by inflation the real value of every financial transaction. When this de facto tax dropped sharply, all classes gained because their purchasing power improved.

As we have seen, Lula's economic policy had proved at least as conservative as his predecessor's. By 2006, the fruits of this policy were increasingly clear. The economy had responded well to the tight fiscal measures, which more than satisfied the requirements of the IMF loans Cardoso and Malan had been forced to negotiate in 1998 and 2002.

The Lula government enjoyed a particular streak of good luck at this juncture. In the early 2000s, the world economy had entered a primary products boom, of which Brazil took full advantage. Brazil had not enjoyed such a healthy trade surplus for decades.

Elsewhere the news was less favorable, however. The first negative was that slow growth had returned, reaching only 2.6 percent in 2005 and 2.9 percent, not much higher, in 2006. The danger of low total output, as usual, was that Brazil was not saving enough to finance badly needed investment. Brazil's capital needs were enormous in every sector—transportation, communication, education, national security, and housing.

The second economic shortcoming was in social welfare. Brazil's notoriously unequal distribution of income proved stubbornly unresponsive to any efforts to increase living standards at the bottom. This was due largely to the distributional effects of government spending, which heavily favored the middle- and upper-income groups. The one corrective for this maldistribution, the Bolsa Família program, consisted of low-interest loans and direct subsidies (cash, food, school fees) distributed to low-income families who kept their children in school. The funds are controlled by the mothers (who are given ATM debit-like plastic cards in their own names and exclusive access to the

PIN number needed for access, reflecting a popular prejudice that poor fathers cannot be trusted to handle the additional funds responsibly). These measures could be effective on the local level. But they would never add up to the fundamental changes needed to correct the growing social inequities that existed, though they certainly boosted PT popularity with certain classes. These inequities, among other things, had implications for race relations. Afro-Brazilians constitute 45 percent of the population but 64 percent of the poor.

In the short run, this policy of increasing the consumption of the poorer sectors fulfilled one of the PT's goals. It was instant gratification to the poorest. On the other hand, these transfer payments were a heavy drain on the national treasury, which left little money for investment in the badly deteriorating infrastructure. It was the familiar dilemma of consumption versus investment.

Some Lessons for Lula's Socialism

The Landless Movement

In the last year of Lula's first term, land reform was the most volatile issue to come to the fore, with the PT's efficient rural mobilization movement earning headlines worldwide. Brazil differed from most of Latin America in the historical context of land reform. Before the 1960s, for example, land reform had not been on Brazil's national political agenda, unlike in Chile or Mexico. National politics remained urban centered. In 1970, Brazil had become 65 percent urban. By 1980, the urban share had climbed to 70 percent. The political polarization around the João Goulart presidency in the early 1960s reached the rural sector, but not profoundly. It was only after the end of military rule that serious mobilization took hold, much aided by the radical wing of the Church. The later military governments (1970–85) had speeded up land distribution by passing out land titles to the homeless (a relatively cheap policy), but without the much more costly infrastructure investment (roads, schools, health posts, credit, technical assistance) the post-1985 civilian governments undertook to make the land usable.

The mid-1990s marked a take-off into intense rural conflict as reformist organizers focused on landowners and their protectors among the regular police force. The Cardoso government went on the defensive and made a score of land concessions in a calculated gamble that piecemeal concessions would rob the movement of its momentum.

What totally disrupted this scene of political give-and-take were two brutal massacres of landless protesters by official security forces in Corumbá in August 1995 and Eldorado de Carajás in April 1996 (the second year of Cardoso's presidency). These two events (heavily covered in the Brazilian and international media) catalyzed public opinion both inside Brazil and abroad. Within the country, the two incidents combined to mobilize domestic opinion and undermine conservative opposition to more aggressive land reform measures.

The Movimento Sem Terra (MST), the populist organization leading the regional landless movements, established a nationwide organization with important links to the left wing of the Church. The MST also got important support in organizing demonstrations from the PT and the central labor federation. The MST is linked to the Via Campesina organization in Latin America and has a new training school in Guararema, São Paulo, inaugurated in 2005 and funded to the tune of $1.3 million by Christian nongovernmental organizations (NGOs) in Europe.

At the end of his presidency, Fernando Henrique Cardoso had faced enormous pressure and tried to respond with further land concessions. The remainder of his term saw clashes focused on the landless. In late 1998, federal officials boasted that they had settled more than 282,000 families. In late 2002, the Agrarian Reform Institute claimed to have settled 600,000 families in eight years. Verified data are hard to come by. But there can be little doubt that in the end hundreds of thousands of landless Brazilian families realized their dream of having land of their own. In spite of these concessions, however, protests continued into the Lula presidency, which claimed to have resettled 381,419 families between 2003 and 2006.

Riots among the Criminal Population

Already in 2005, the Lula presidency began to be faced with a new phenomenon: prison breakouts organized from inside prison walls. The movement was fed by inmates who had long suffered inhuman conditions. The precipitating factor was the lax discipline in the miserably maintained cells, as the authorities lost control. The prisoners organized supporters to invade public institutions in the rural locations where many of the larger prisons were located. One of the first waves of attacks on security had occurred in Carandiru in 1992, where 111 died as the security forces mowed them down.

These ugly incidents mainly reflected the long-term decay of the penal system. The prisons were shockingly neglected, with horrendously deteriorated and dangerously overcrowded buildings. Prison discipline was notoriously lax, with free access, astonishingly, to cell phones due to corruption and bribes of prison guards. The result was a national network able to coordinate their plotting across prisons. Given sufficient numbers (including criminals on the outside as well as escapees), they could readily overwhelm local police forces. It was the dark underside of the social welfare crisis that the PT had talked about so much. The prison rioting and breakouts, as well as coordinated attacks on police stations, buses, and other public buildings in São Paulo in 2005 and 2006, were perpetrated by Brazil's best-organized criminal group—the PCC (Primeiro Comando da Capital)—which exerts control over 140,000 in the São Paulo prison system. These attacks humiliated the São Paulo government (PSDB) and presidential candidate Geraldo Alckmin in the run-up to the 2006 election.

Conflict with Bolivia over Natural Gas

In early 2006, Brazil found itself facing in Bolivia the kind of economic nationalism the Brazilian left had itself long preached. The issue was natural gas, of which Bolivia contained Latin America's largest reserves. Bolivia's newly elected President Evo Morales announced the abrogation of Brazil's gas contract, which it had earlier obtained on very favorable terms. Bolivia had long been one of the politically and economically weakest republics of Spanish America and had become a prime target for Brazilian penetration. By the late twentieth century, thousands of Brazilian farmers had moved across the border to settle on Bolivian territory. And Bolivia, as a weak neighbor, had seldom been an object of Brazilian respect. Bolivia's vulnerability was due to its relative underdevelopment, even as a Third World country. If there should be a confrontation between Brazil and Bolivia, the odds would be in Brazil's favor. On the other hand, this looked like Bolivia's chance to make up for lost time in asserting its own sovereignty.

In the 1990s, Brazil had negotiated a huge contract to import Bolivian gas, which supplied 50 percent of Brazil's gas consumption. For decades, Bolivia had been governed by politicians of European descent. But in early 2006 that political context changed dramatically when the Bolivian presidential election was won by a full-blooded Bolivian-Indian who had campaigned on a pledge to nationalize natural resources. This put Bolivia on a collision course with foreign investors and, coincidentally, with Brazil because of its huge natural gas contracts.

Once inaugurated, Evo Morales moved quickly, issuing a decree "nationalizing" the nation's hydrocarbon resources and ordering the Bolivian military to take control of all hydrocarbon installations. Morales also announced that any existing gas contract with Brazil was invalid because its terms had been "exploitive." Observers wondered whether the influence of Venezuela's Hugo Chavez was at work. Chavez had maneuvered himself into being the arch nationalist and Latin America's number one anti-American. Chavez's promises to Morales were never forthcoming ($2 billion to finance the hydrocarbon nationalization and some two thousand technicians to help train Bolivians to operate the Brazilian installations).

Brazil's reaction to the Bolivian challenge was twofold. First, President Lula was highly conciliatory. He did not resort to threatening invectives. His mild manner infuriated his Brazilian critics who expected—indeed, demanded—a more violent Brazilian response. But the latter was readily supplied by Petrobrás President José Sérgio Gabrielli, who insisted that any negotiation for new gas prices be settled within forty-five days. It was clear that any negotiated settlement would involve Venezuela, as well as Bolivia. The major question was how Lula's government would deal with the economic nationalists, who were the Bolivian counterpart to the PT's left wing. In early 2007, the impasses over the price structure of Bolivian gas were resolved, at least for the time being. Brazil agreed to double the price of gas piped to a private gas-turbine electricity-generating station in Cuiabá, Mato Grosso, and to prorate the main volume of gas piped to southern Brazil in accordance with its "quality"—higher caloric content, higher price.

The 2006 Presidential Campaign

The most important fact about Brazil's presidential campaigns is that the electorate votes purely on one man/one vote. Lack of an intervening body—such as the electoral college under Brazil's military government or the U.S. electoral college—favors a candidate with a personally identifiable following. Furthermore, the present provision for a two-candidate runoff ensures that the election will produce a victor with a clear majority (no plurality wins).

The second most important fact is that the campaigns are overwhelmingly covered by the media (particularly TV). There are political rallies attended in person by the candidates, but the political publics are completely absorbed by the TV coverage. And there is no lack of TV sets, even in the poorest sections of the country. Home ownership of TVs is estimated in the range of 100 million. Census data show that millions of homes have TVs but no running water. The government also allocates free TV time (in proportion to the party's vote in the last election, with some provision for new parties). This allocation guarantees all duly registered politicians at least some minimum of exposure in the same broadcasting bloc and is monitored by the federal electoral court to ensure that the media exposure rules are followed. The system facilitates the public presence of small and weaker parties, which would lack the resources necessary to purchase TV time if the system were not free.

By early 2006, Lula had regained much of his popularity. In fact, he had two bases of support. The first was the one he had focused on traditionally—the lowest classes. His hold on the lower-income segments, which had first been forged by his successful exploitation of his humble origins and his status as a factory worker, was strengthened by the Bolsa Família program, which was covering 11 million families (40 million potential voters) by the October 2006 elections. His recent increase in the minimum wage and continuing low inflation also helped. University of Brasília political science professor David Fleischer dubbed Lula equivalent to U.S. President Ronald Reagan in his Teflon quality—no accusations of scandal "stick" to him.

The second base of support was Lula's increasing ability to attract important segments of the middle class. There had always been an idealistic segment of the middle class that believed philosophically in social justice. But this group had been largely frightened off in previous elections by the specter of the international financial community and the threat of financial collapse. Lula's time in office had laid that specter to rest. In addition, Lula's expansion of government programs had increased the government jobs available to educated bureaucrats interested in public service.

Several personal factors also contributed to his popularity. One was Lula's manner. His occasional fractured grammar reminded the millions of lower-class Brazilians that their president was one of them. But Lula must also be credited with more political shrewdness than his detractors liked to acknowledge. Lula had not hesitated to demand the ouster of congressmen in his own party if they failed to support his policies. This was a show of general confidence bound to influence middle-class voters who had little stomach for the PT dissenters' typical tactics of tying up government with parliamentary procedures widely seen as self-interested.

By mid-2006, the opposition to Lula was getting nervous. In a late July poll, Lula enjoyed a comfortable lead at 44 percent, with Geraldo Alckmin, the main opponent, at 25 percent and the next candidate down at 11 percent. Alckmin, the former governor of São Paulo, was known as a very cerebral governor who excelled at public administration. In conformance with electoral law, he had to step down from his governorship to run. This deprived him of a powerful electoral machine. For much of September, the polls showed Lula hovering around the magic 50 percent mark.

But the first round of the presidential election disappointed the Lula supporters. Lula received only 48.65 of the valid vote. Alckmin's vote was 41.6 percent, distinctly higher than the 31–35 percent predicted by the public opinion polls in late September. This last-minute decline in Lula's vote was in large part due to the so-called Dossier Caper allegedly perpetrated by some "misguided" PT militants trying to buy documents to smear the PSDB candidate for governor in São Paulo—José Serra. In mid-September, federal police intercepted the cash transfer, and in late September photos of the bills (dollars and *reals*) stacked on a table were leaked to the press.

Some members of the extreme left seemed hopeful that they might mobilize a defeat for Lula, in return for his perceived betrayal of the economic mandate they thought they had given him in his first term. This threat was gaining increasing plausibility in the person of Heloisa, who received a respectable 6.9 percent in the first round—enough, if added to Alckmin's vote, to produce a statistical dead heat with Lula. Some bookmakers actually began to bet against a Lula victory in the second round.

In the end, such speculation proved groundless. Lula swept to an easy second-round victory with 60.8 percent of the valid votes cast. The first-round weakness appeared to have been the result of a momentary irritation with Lula on the part of the electorate. Accusations of new PT scandals uncomfortably close to Lula had seemed almost a daily occurrence during the later stages of the campaign. In addition, Lula (following the example of his predecessor, it must be noted) had deliberately sabotaged the last presidential candidates' debate by failing to show up. The no-show tactic had served Fernando Henrique Cardoso well, but it seemed to have backfired when Lula tried it. Lula did show up in the second-round one-on-one debates with Alckmin. And

President Luiz Inácio Lula da Silva in June 2006 during his reelection campaign, greeting fans at an occasion in Brasília celebrating an economic solidarity program. (AP Photo/Eraldo Peres)

obviously, when the chips were down, the electorate was not about to risk a Lula loss.

Lula's Second Term and the Outlook Ahead

As in his first term, Lula has given every evidence in his second term of being in control of his party and the government coalition. Despite continuing congressional scandals and the media criticism that accompanies them, his public opinion poll ratings remain high. He has proved himself a reformer from the inside, not the revolutionary his enemies had always branded him. Admittedly, the PT still has firebrands who preach the destruction of Brazilian capitalism. But such has not been Lula's position. As for his political style, he has felt secure enough to take highly publicized trips outside Brasília, both elsewhere in Brazil and abroad. By the end of his first term, Lula had been absent from the capital city for 337 days. A year into his second term, he took a seventh visit to Africa, with stops in South Africa, Congo, and Angola. Evidently, his physical presence has not been required to maintain governmental control or his popularity.

His reelection actually showed some widening in his locus of support. In 2002, his heaviest vote had come from better-off voters in the South and Southeast. In 2006, his success owed more to the poorer and less-developed North and Northeast. Not coincidentally, those were the regions that had benefited most from the Bolsa Família program, which in its most inclusive form provides $60–100 a month per family. Lula also benefited in 2006 from the recurrence of a curious pattern repeated from previous presidential elections in Brazil. In five of the preceding six of these, the most backward areas of the country voted for the incumbent government, whatever its political identity. This pattern served to increase Lula's majority in 2006.

Throughout 2007 and into 2008, Brazil's economy flourished, with GDP growth healthier than in many decades, even extending to industrial production, an area that had perennially lagged. Inflation, the curse of Brazil's economy through much of the post-1945 period, remained under control. Exports reached unprecedented heights and amassed record foreign exchange reserves. This boon financed significantly increased capital goods imports—badly needed to modernize the country's industrial plant. The economy was no longer hostage to the IMF, Brazil's foreign debt had been largely paid, and the Brazilian *real* reached exceptional strength for the currency of a developing country.

Foreign investment in Brazil was also very healthy, with the 2007 total nearing $35 billion, an all-time record. In the domestic world of Brazilian politics in the 1950s and 1960s, foreign investment had been highly controversial. Aggressive nationalists denied any positive role for foreign investors in Brazil, especially if they were American. But as Brazil increased control over its economy after the 1980s, attitudes changed. Policymakers discovered that foreign investment could be controlled by channeling it into what Brazil chose as its high-priority areas. Furthermore, accepting such investment no longer necessarily involved Uncle Sam, because Brazil's sources of foreign capital had diversified. Brazil's current major foreign investors include, for example, Spain, Germany, and Holland.

The world economic downturn of late 2008 and 2009 (as this book is going to press) has reduced Brazil's economic growth rate and slowed domestic production and exports. Growth is tipping to negative, but inflation is still under good control and Brazil's foreign exchange reserves are still healthy. The betting is that Brazil will emerge from the world downturn less damaged than many other countries.

Foreign policy developments have challenged Lula in his second term, but so far without bad results. The major challenge has come from Venezuelan President Hugo Chavez's drive to make his country a socialist power in the hemisphere and to increase its influence throughout Latin America and beyond. Apparent U.S. support for an abortive coup aimed at Chavez earlier in his presidency did not help his attitude toward the United States. In Central America, Chavez has shipped oil below cost to economically strapped Cuba. In South America, he has helped finance Argentina's long-unpaid foreign debt. Closer to home, he has eyed Bolivia and its first indigenous president, Evo Morales, an outspoken nationalist who has also benefited from Venezuela's low-cost oil, as a potential ally. The U.S. government, which has oil interests in Bolivia and opposes Chavez's squeezing of U.S.-owned companies, is obviously displeased.

Amid rising tensions, Brazil has been standing as an intermediary. As its close neighbor, Bolivia has long been within Brazil's acknowledged sphere of influence. In recent decades, thousands of Brazilian farmers and merchants have moved across the border into Bolivia, taking with them their language, currency, and families, and generating a hostile nationalist reaction in Bolivia. Morales's government decided to demand, with Venezuelan support, renegotiation of a large natural gas contract Brazil had signed with Bolivia. Lula made some concessions in order to resolve the issue and continues to take a calm tone with Morales, using the argument that "your [long-term] partner is Brazil, not Venezuela."

Lula's calm has also extended to his direct dealing with Venezuela, as he ignores Chavez's jibes that Brazil is just a stalking horse for America. Lula's forbearance sends the implicit message that, as the greater power, Brazil can ignore a lesser country's criticism.

Lula's Luck

Lula is a politician who has had the courage to combine social welfare measures on an unprecedented scale with orthodox monetary policy. He has also shown an awareness of the need for change. Early in his first term he made this promise: "We shall certainly change. We shall change with courage and care, humility and boldness, change with an awareness that change is a gradual and continuous process, not a single gesture with a violent backlash. It is change by dialogue and negotiation, without sudden menace or threats, so that the outcome will be consistent and permanent." He has, by and large, delivered on this promise. But in doing so he has benefited a great deal from profound changes that were well under way before he came to power.

One is a drop in Brazil's working-age population. Brazil used to have one of the fastest-growing populations in the world. Then, for complex reasons that probably include the many millions of U.S. dollars spent by NGOs on birth control programs, population growth began to decline and continued declining through the Cardoso and Lula presidencies. From 1980 to 2005, Brazil's annual net population increase fell from 2.7 percent to 1.9 percent. This trend eases the burden of financing essential social services, freeing more resources for general economic growth.

Another factor of great help to Brazil is the development of a cadre of highly trained elites, which began during the political turmoil of the military takeover more than forty years ago. It was a tense political scene back in 1964 when an American naval fleet was carrying guns and oil to reinforce the anti-Goulart military conspirators in Brazil. The supplies were not needed. Instead, Washington stepped up its already formidable flow of financial aid and diplomatic support. The U.S. government brain trust had years back decided that Brazil needed a dose of U.S. technology and know-how. The maestro of this process was the former Harvard professor-turned-ambassador to Brazil, Lincoln Gordon. AID, the U.S. foreign assistance arm, shifted into high gear (it had already been active in Brazil), drafting multiple plans to help transform along

American lines key institutions such as primary schools, police departments, and university faculties.

At least two areas of assistance had a positive long-term effect: economics and agronomy. Economics of the North American brand (via many exchanges with developed country universities) was effectively transferred to Brazil, which created a network of excellent university faculties there. These then produced economists up to the highest international standards. By the 1980s, they were already making their mark in U.S. and European universities, research institutions, and the IMF and World Bank. They also gave Brazil the expertise to guide its economy. At the same time, visiting faculty transformed the teaching and application of agricultural methods. These included the use of chemical treatments that neutralize acidic soil, which greatly boosted productivity. Applying techniques like these (which brought into production previously uncultivated lands) has helped make Brazil one of the world's leading food exporters. Some experts reckon that Brazil now has more potentially productive land than any other Latin American country. Such transfer of intellectual capital may be the one dimension in which the close alliance between the military governments and the United States has unambiguously paid off for Brazil.

Lula benefited also from economic reforms achieved by the Cardoso government that he succeeded. Crucial was the Real Plan of 1993–94, which tamed inflation while avoiding recession. This shrewdly conceived program was one of the most effective stabilization efforts of any major country in Latin America, and perhaps in the world, since 1945. A further Cardoso accomplishment was privatizing many of Brazil's state monopolies. Once privatized, they could no longer bleed the public treasury with chronic deficits. Additional benefits were the inflow of foreign capital to finance the independent firms that replaced the state monopolies and Brazil's steady trend toward freer trade. By 2000, Brazilian tariffs on goods coming into the country were minimal.

The Cardoso government also carried out a thoroughgoing reform of the private banking system, long one of the most profitable, if badly managed, in Latin America. These measures extinguished the most scandal-ridden institutions and created a private financial system able to withstand future external economic shocks. In a similar crackdown on government agencies, Cardoso decreed that they could henceforth use no more than 60 percent of their revenues to meet their payroll, including a most un-Brazilian proviso allowing workers to be terminated to meet the new standards. Yet another important inheritance from Cardoso was the Fiscal Responsibility Law of 1999, which limited permissible indebtedness at all levels of government.

External economic conditions also helped the Lula government—the buoyant world economy, especially the primary products boom. Brazil's export surge brought more foreign exchange to help modernize its economy, especially the industrial sector.

More Brazilian success came in the form of rapid expansion of ethanol production. Unlike the U.S. process, which relies on corn, Brazil uses sugarcane as its primary vegetable source, which produces several times as much energy per unit of land as does corn. In fact, Brazil had launched large-scale production of ethanol as early as the 1930s. Since then, large tracts of arable land have become cultivable, as noted, in the formerly barren Center-West. In the area of energy more generally, Brazil is also well endowed. Hydroelectric power abounds, and the country is self-sufficient in oil. An expert in offshore drilling, Brazil has recently announced the discovery of a huge new oil field deep in the ocean more than two hundred miles off Brazil's Atlantic coast.

What's Next?

Brazil has come a long way in its five centuries of change. What is needed now for the country to continue its progress? Several areas stand out as priority issues for Lula's successor.

The first is education. In late 2007, OECD, the Paris-based economic research center, released data on school examination results for fifteen-year-olds in over fifty nations. Subjects tested included mathematics, science, and reading. Brazil ranked fifty-third in math and fifty-fourth in science. In reading comprehension, it showed no improvement over a low score recorded earlier. Brazil is not only low in achievement scores for those who attend school. About 13 percent of Brazilians are totally illiterate, a rate exceeded in Latin America by only four Central American republics and Haiti. Much of this residual illiteracy is in the Northeast. Until the citizens in that part of the country are brought into the mainstream, the region will remain too much of a burden on the country as a whole for it to be able to ratchet up its productive capacity per capita to First World levels. Critics point to the corrupt and inept application of government education budgets, notwithstanding widely publicized reform efforts during the Cardoso presidency.

A second area crying out for reform is rampant corruption and violent crime. On the international index of corruption, for example, Brazil's standing in the world has been going steadily down: forty-fifth in 2002, fifty-ninth in 2004, seventieth in 2006, with a concomitant rise in street crime and penal facility violence. James Holston, an American anthropologist, has warned observers not to overinterpret the positive trends in Brazil: "Brazilian democracy has advanced significantly in the last two decades. Indeed, it has pioneered innovations that place it in the forefront of democratic development worldwide. Yet, precisely as democracy has taken root, new kinds of violence, injustice and corruption, and impunity have increased dramatically."

In addition, Brazil's dysfunctional legal system, which is rooted in the historical development of Brazilian law, adds substantially to the cost of doing business and is acknowledged to be a potentially treacherous problem for foreign investors. An obvious example is the cumbersome tax system—a tangle of federal, state, and municipal codes. A 2007 World Bank study found that it took a typical private company in Brazil 2,600 hours to pay its taxes—the longest time of any of the 177 countries surveyed. Other important areas in need of improvement include the law on public rights (for example, the right of eminent domain), legal records of ownership, judicial procedures that allow the same case to go around and around in the courts for almost indefinite periods, and the legal statutes themselves (including civil and commercial law). A drastic and urgent revision of the procedures of the penal code is also needed to reduce appeals and to streamline trials.

No review of Brazil's continuing challenges would be complete without mention of Brazil's highly unequal income distribution. Measured by the Gini index of inequality, Brazil typically registers a number in the upper 50s and lower 60s, compared with the mid- to upper 50s for most Latin American countries and the 30s to lower 40s for so-called developed countries. Worse, inequality in Brazil is known to have been increasing over time—worse in all but one of Brazil's twenty-three states and territorial units in the year 2000 than in 1990. A recent survey suggests that the downward trend may at last be reversing. According to a national survey by Datafolha, a São Paulo research agency, 20 million Brazilians moved up from the bottom two levels of a five-level income scale into the middle level between 2003 and 2007. Analysis showed that between 2003 and 2005 the upward movement resulted primarily from cash transfers (the Bolsa Família program and increased federal retirement pensions). In 2006 and 2007, the main causes of improvement were more fundamental—GDP growth, new job creation, and lower unemployment. The mobility in both periods was more apparent in the Northeast, North, and Central-West than in the South and Southeast. The improvement itself and its geographic distribution are hopeful signs indeed for Brazil's economic and social future.

SUGGESTIONS FOR
FURTHER READING

There is a vast bibliography on Brazilian history in Portuguese and English. What follows is a selection of some of the most significant works published in English over the last several decades.

Colony (1500–1822)

João Capistrano de Abreu, *Chapters of Brazil's Colonial History, 1500–1800* (Oxford University Press, 1997). Classical history of colonial Brazil.

Leslie Bethell, ed., *Colonial Brazil* (Cambridge, 1991). A collection of essays about colonial Brazil from the sixteenth to the nineteenth centuries.

Thomas M. Cohen, *The Fire of Tongues: Antônio Vieira and the Missionary Church in Brazil and Portugal* (Stanford University Press, 1998). Biographical study of the Jesuits' missionary work among Portuguese and indigenous peoples.

Gilberto Freyre, *The Masters and the Slaves: A Study in the Development of Brazilian Civilization* (University of California Press, 1986). Classic influential work on patriarchal society, slavery, and its legacy.

Richard Graham, ed., *Brazil and the World System* (University of Texas Press, 1991). Influential interpretation of the colonial economic system.

Hal Langfur, *The Forbidden Lands: Colonial Identity, Frontier Violence, and the Persistence of Brazil's Eastern Indians, 1750–1830* (Stanford University Press, 2006). Study of tensions between Portuguese and indigenous peoples in Minas Gerais.

Kenneth Maxwell, *Conflicts and Conspiracies: Brazil and Portugal, 1750–1808* (Routledge, 2004). Fundamental work on the transition from colony to independence.

Alida C. Metcalf, *Family and Frontier in Colonial Brazil: Santana de Parnaíba, 1580–1822* (University of Texas Press, 2005). Excellent study about wealth and land accumulation in rural São Paulo.

Alida C. Metcalf, *Go-betweens and the Colonization of Brazil, 1500–1600* (University of Texas Press, 2005). Role of intermediaries in the domination of indigenous peoples by Portuguese.

Shawn William Miller, *Fruitless Trees: Portuguese Conservation and Brazil's Colonial Timber* (Stanford University Press, 2000). Timber and lumber extraction policies in Brazilian forests under colonial rule.

Kirsten Schultz, *Tropical Versailles: Empire, Monarchy, and the Portuguese Royal Court in Rio de Janeiro, 1808–1821* (Routledge, 2001). Outstanding study of the move of the Portuguese court to Brazil.

Stuart B. Schwartz, *Sugar Plantations in the Formation of Brazilian Society: Bahia, 1550–1835* (Cambridge University Press, 1985). Comprehensive analysis of the Northeastern sugar civilization.

Laura de Mello e Souza, *The Devil and the Land of the Holy Cross: Witchcraft, Slavery, and Popular Religion in Colonial Brazil*. Translated by Diane Grosklaus Whitty (University of Texas Press, 2003). Witchcraft, religious life, and customs in eighteenth-century Brazil.

Empire (1822–1889)

B. J. Barickman, *A Bahian Counterpoint: Sugar, Tobacco, Cassava, and Slavery in the Recôncavo, 1780–1860* (Cambridge University Press, 1998). Integrative study of foodstuffs and their relationship to export and slavery.

Roderick J. Barman, *Brazil: The Forging of a Nation, 1798–1852* (Stanford University Press, 1988). Analysis of how Brazil remained unified after independence.

——, *Citizen Emperor: Pedro II of Brazil* (Cambridge University Press, 1999). Full-length biography of Pedro II's 60 years of rule.

Peter M. Beattie, *The Tribute of Blood: Army, Honor, Race, and Nation in Brazil, 1864–1945* (Duke University Press, 2000). The modernization of the Brazilian army and its role in nation building and notions of race.

Judy Bieber, *Power, Patronage and Political Violence: State Building on a Brazilian Frontier, 1822–1889* (University of Nebraska Press, 1999). Reinterpretation of nineteenth-century political power from the perspective of the outlying regions.

Emilia Viotti da Costa, *The Brazilian Empire: Myths and Histories* (University of Chicago Press, 1985). Enduring overall interpretation.

Maria Odila Silva Dias, *Power and Everyday Life: The Lives of Working Women in Nineteenth-century Brazil*. Translated by Ann Frost (Rutgers University Press, 1995). Study of slave and freedwomen in São Paulo.

Gilberto Freyre, *The Mansions and the Shanties: The Making of Modern Brazil* (University of California Press, 1986). Extension of his classical analysis (see under **Colony**) to the urban sector.

Richard Graham, *Patronage and Politics in Nineteenth-century Brazil* (Stanford University Press, 1990). Role of patronage networks in maintaining political stability in imperial Brazil.

Sandra Lauderdale Graham, *House and Street: The Domestic World of Servants and Masters in Nineteenth-century Rio de Janeiro* (Cambridge University Press, 1988). View of intimate family life in Rio during the era.

Thomas H. Holloway, *Policing Rio de Janeiro* (Stanford University Press, 1993). Important work on urban development and social control in the nineteenth-century capital.

Andrew J. Kirkendall, *Class Mates: Male Student Culture and the Making of a Political Class in Nineteenth-century Brazil* (University of Nebraska Press, 2002). Study of the education of lawyers and elite social networks.

Roger A. Kittelson, *The Practice of Politics in Postcolonial Brazil: Porto Alegre, 1845–1895* (University of Pittsburgh Press, 2005). Intriguing exploration of the unique patterns of Rio Grande do Sul's politics in the late Empire and transition to the Old Republic.

Hendrik Kraay, *Race, State, and Armed Forces in Independence-era Brazil, Bahia, 1790s–1840s* (Stanford University Press, 2001). The formation of army, race, and state in Bahia.

Cristina Magaldi, *Music in Imperial Rio de Janeiro: European Culture in a Tropical Milieu* (Scarecrow Press, 2004). Study of elite culture in nineteenth-century Rio de Janeiro.

David McCreery, *Frontier Goiás, 1822–1889* (Stanford University Press, 2006). Expansion of Brazil's far western frontier during the Empire.

Jeffrey D. Needell, *The Party of Order: The Conservatives, the State, and Slavery in the Brazilian Monarchy, 1831–1871* (Stanford University Press, 2006). Masterful study of political classes during the Empire.

Julyan G. Peard, *Race, Place, and Medicine: The Idea of the Tropics in Nineteenth-century Brazil* (Duke University Press, 1999). Development of tropical medicine in Bahia.

João José Reis, *Death Is a Festival: Funeral Rites and Rebellion in Nineteenth-century Brazil*. Translated by H. Sabrina Gledhill (University of North Carolina Press, 2003). Intriguing picture of the role of death in nineteenth-century Brazil.

Lilia Moritz Schwarcz, *The Emperor's Beard: Dom Pedro II and the Tropical Monarchy of Brazil* (Hill and Wang, 2004). Exploration of the rituals, icons, racial features, art, and politics of the emperor.

Stanley J. Stein, *Vassouras: A Brazilian Coffee County, 1850–1900* (Princeton University Press, 1985). Classic microstudy of nineteenth-century plantation life.

Adèle Toussaint-Samson, *A Parisian in Brazil: The Travel Account of a Frenchwoman in Nineteenth-century Rio de Janeiro*. Translated by Emma Toussaint; edited and introduced by June E. Hahner (Scholarly Resources, 2001). Travelogue describing slavery and social conditions in Brazil's capital.

Dave Treece, *Exiles, Allies, Rebels: Brazil's Indianist Movement, Indigenist Politics, and the Imperial Nation-state* (Greenwood Press, 2000). Colonial policies and literary representations of indigenous people.

Old Republic (1889–1930)

Todd A. Diacon, *Stringing Together a Nation: Cândido Mariano da Silva Rondon and the Construction of a Modern Brazil, 1906–1930* (Duke University Press, 2004). Thoroughly researched account of essential features of nation building—the telegraph system and land demarcation.

Todd A., *Millennium Vision, Capitalist Reality* (Duke University Press, 1991). Account of a farmers' revolt that threatened the land-holding structure.

Robert M. Levine, *Vale of Tears: Revisiting the Canudos Massacre in Northeastern Brazil, 1893–1897* (University of California Press, 1992). Examination of a popular revolt in the early years of the Republic.

Frank D. McCann, *Soldiers of the Pátria: A History of the Brazilian Army, 1889–1937* (Stanford University Press, 2004). Army, ideology, and revolutionary politics.

Teresa A. Meade, *"Civilizing" Rio: Reform and Resistance in a Brazilian City, 1889–1930* (Pennsylvania State University Press, 1997). An analysis of efforts to reform—and the resistance that came of such reforms—in Rio de Janeiro.

Jeffrey D. Needell, *A Tropical Belle Époque: Elite Culture and Society in Turn-of-the-century Rio de Janeiro* (Cambridge University Press, 1987). Superb study of the elite classes of Brazil's capital.

Steven Topik, *The Political Economy of the Brazilian State, 1889–1930* (University of Texas Press, 1987). Crucial to understanding the growing role of the state.

Vargas and an Experiment in Democracy (1930–1964)

John W. F. Dulles, *Carlos Lacerda, Brazilian Crusader*, 2 vols. (University of Texas Press, 1996). Profile of a key anti-Vargas figure who also played a central role in the political demise of Jânio Quadros and João Goulart.

Jens R. Hentschke, *Vargas and Brazil: New Perspectives* (Palgrave Macmillan, 2006). Reexamination of Vargas's legacy.

Stanley E. Hilton, *Brazil and the Great Powers, 1930–1939* (University of Texas Press, 1975). Background to Brazil's maneuvering before it joined the Allies in 1942.

Robert M. Levine, *Father of the Poor? Vargas and His Era* (Cambridge University Press, 1998). A study of President Getúlio Vargas.

Fernanda Morais, *Olga*, 4th ed. Translated by Ellen Watson (Grove Weidenfield, 1990). Best-selling account of one of the ugliest chapters of the Estado Nôvo, Vargas's delivery of Luís Carlos Prestes's wife to the Nazis.

Thomas E. Skidmore, *Politics in Brazil* (Oxford University Press, 1967). Overview that emphasizes the origins of the 1964 coup.

Daryl Williams, *Culture Wars in Brazil, the First Vargas Regime, 1930–1945* (Duke University Press, 2001). Revealing analysis of how Vargas's first government exploited cultural symbolism to strengthen its rule.

Military Government (1964–1985)

Archdiocese of São Paulo, *Torture in Brazil: A Shocking Report on the Pervasive Use of Torture by Brazilian Military Governments, 1964–1979*. Translated by Jaime Wright; edited with a new preface by Joan Dassin (University of Texas, Institute of Latin American Studies, 1985). Indispensable source on human rights violations by the military governments.

Martha Huggins, Mika Haritos-Tatouros, and Philip G. Zimbardo, *Violence Workers: Police Torturers and Murderers Reconstruct Brazilian Atrocities* (University of California Press, 2002). Intriguing study of police brutality in Brazil.

A. J. Langguth, *Hidden Terrors* (Pantheon Books, 1978). Documentation of U.S. government support for police operations in Brazil and other military dictatorships in Latin America.

Maria Helena Moreira Alves, *State and Opposition in Military Brazil* (University of Texas Press, 1985). Valuable analysis of the authoritarian bias in Brazilian politics of the 1960s and 1970s.

Kenneth P. Serbin, *Secret Dialogues: Church-state Relations, Torture, and Social Justice in Authoritarian Brazil* (University of Pittsburgh Press, 2000). Pioneering exploration of contact between the military rulers and the higher clergy.

Thomas E. Skidmore, *Politics of Military Rule in Brazil* (Oxford University Press, 1988). Analysis of the tension between democratization and authoritarian trends.

Anne-Marie Smith, *A Forced Agreement: Press Acquiescence to Censorship in Brazil* (University of Pittsburgh Press, 1997). Study of press censorship during the military regime.

Alfred Stepan, *The Military in Politics* (Princeton University Press, 1971). Still the indispensable source on the Brazilian military leading up to the 1964 coup.

Lawrence Weschler, *A Miracle, a Universe: Settling Accounts with Torturers* (University of Chicago Press, 1990). Gripping story of how human rights activists document torture by Brazilian military.

The New Democracy (1985 to the present)

Barry Ames, *The Deadlock of Democracy in Brazil* (University of Michigan Press, 2001). Detailed analysis of voting patterns of Brazil's national legislature.

Guianpaolo Baiocchi, ed., *Radicals in Power: The Workers' Party (PT) and Experiences of Urban Democracy in Brazil* (Zed Books, 2003). Close examination of the inner workings of the PT.

Fernando Henrique Cardoso, *The Accidental President of Brazil: A Memoir* (Public Affairs, 2006). Skillfully written first-person account of the trials of governing Brazil in the eight years before Lula.

Margaret E. Keck, *The Workers' Party and Democratization in Brazil* (Yale University Press, 1992). Study of the emergence of a dynamic new Labor party during the demise of the dictatorship.

Peter R. Kingstone and Timothy J. Power, *Democratic Brazil: Actors, Institutions, and Processes* (University of Pittsburgh Press, 2000). Examination of politics in post-military Brazil.

Scott Mainwaring, *Rethinking Party Systems in the Third Wave of Democratization: The Case of Brazil* (Stanford University Press, 1999). Illumination of the varied political alliances that followed the fall of the military regime.

Alfred P. Monteiro, *Brazilian Politics* (Cambridge University Press, 2005). Fine synthesis of contemporary politics.

Timothy J. Power, *The Political Right in Postauthoritarian Brazil: Elites, Institutions and Democracy* (Pennsylvania State University Press, 2000). Careful consideration of the civilian right in the context of the post-military era.

Alfred Stepan, ed., *Democratizing Brazil* (Oxford University Press, 1989). Chronicle of the transition to democracy.

Slavery and Abolition

Celia Maria Marinho de Azevedo, *Abolitionism in the United States and Brazil: A Comparative Perspective* (New York: Garland, 1995). Cross-national analysis of anti-slavery movements.

Laird W. Bergad, *Slavery and the Demographic and Economic History of Minas Gerais, Brazil, 1720–1888* (Cambridge University Press, 1999). Study of slavery in the mining district.

Kim D. Butler, *Freedoms Given, Freedoms Won: Afro-Brazilians in Post-Abolition São Paulo and Salvador* (Rutgers University Press, 1998). Examination of the different strategies that Afro-Brazilians employed to fight against racism.

Robert Edgar Conrad, *Children of God's Fire*, 2nd ed. (Pennsylvania State University Press, 1994). Excellent anthology of sources on Brazilian slavery.

——, *World of Sorrow: The African Slave Trade to Brazil* (Louisiana State University Press, 1986). Empathetic treatment of the human aspects of slave trafficking.

Zephyr L. Frank, *Dutra's World: Wealth and Family in Nineteenth-century Rio de Janeiro* (University of New Mexico Press, 2004). An economic analysis of slaveholding, wealth, and family.

Dale Torston Graden, *From Slavery to Freedom in Brazil: Bahia, 1835–1900* (University of New Mexico Press, 2006). Study of abolition in Brazil's largest Afro-Brazilian center.

Kathleen J. Higgins, *"Licentious Liberty" in a Brazilian Gold-mining Region: Slavery, Gender, and Social Control in Eighteenth-century Sabará, Minas Gerais* (Pennsylvania State University Press, 1999). Detailed examination of slavery and gender in a Brazilian mining town.

Mary C. Karasch, *Slave Life in Rio de Janeiro, 1808–1850* (Princeton University Press, 1987). Richly researched study using previously unknown sources on Brazilian slavery.

Elizabeth W. Kiddy, *Blacks of the Rosary: Memory and History in Minas Gerais, Brazil* (Pennsylvania State University Press, 2005). Early formation of Afro-Brazilian lay brotherhoods in the late colonial period.

Francisco Vidal Luna and Herbert S. Klein, *Slavery and the Economy of São Paulo, 1750–1850* (Stanford University Press, 2003). Study of economy and people of São Paulo during the critical transition from the traditional eighteenth-century colonial world to the modernizing world of the nineteenth century.

Nancy Naro, *A Slave's Place, a Master's World: Fashioning Dependency in Rural Brazil* (Continuum, 2000). The economics of slavery and the agency of agricultural workers in nineteenth-century rural Brazil.

Mieko Nishida, *Slavery and Identity: Ethnicity, Gender, and Race in Salvador, Brazil, 1808–1888* (Indiana University Press, 2003). Regional study of slavery in nineteenth-century Bahia.

Katia Mattoos de Queirós, *To Be a Slave in Brazil, 1550–1888* (Rutgers University Press, 1986). Imaginative reconstruction of Brazilian slavery's human dimension.

João José Reis, *Slave Rebellion in Brazil* (Johns Hopkins University Press, 1993). Picture of the Muslim religious impetus for slave revolt in Brazil.

Stuart B. Schwartz, *Slaves, Peasants, and Rebels: Reconsidering Brazilian Slavery* (University of Illinois Press, 1996). Collection of essays about the economics, politics, and culture of slavery.

Rebecca Scott, Seymour Drescher, Hebe Maria Mattos de Castro, George Reid Andrews, and Robert Levine, *The Abolition of Slavery and the Aftermath of Emancipation in Brazil* (Duke University Press, 1988). The legacy of slavery in Brazilian society.

Robert Brent Toplin, *The Abolition of Slavery in Brazil* (Anteneum, 1992). Study of the process of slave emancipation.

Race and Ethnicity

George Reid Andrews, *Blacks and Whites in São Paulo, Brazil, 1888–1988* (University of Wisconsin Press, 1991). One of the first empirically based studies of racism in the Brazilian workplace.

Roger Bastide, *The African Religions of Brazil: Toward a Sociology of the Interpenetration of Civilizations.* Translated by Helen Sebba (Johns Hopkins University Press, 1978). Still premier study of Afro-Brazilian religions.

G. Reginald Daniel, *Race and Multiraciality in Brazil and the United States* (Pennsylvania State University Press, 2006). Exposition of race and miscegenation in Brazil and the United States.

Jerry Davila, *Diploma of Whiteness: Race and Social Policy in Brazil, 1917–1945* (Duke University Press, 2003). Original analysis of Brazilian elites' thoughts about race in the twentieth century.

Carl N. Degler, *Neither Black nor White* (Macmillan, 1971). Analysis of the link between slavery and twentieth-century race relations.

Seth Garfield, *Indigenous Struggle at the Heart of Brazil: State Policy, Frontier Expansion, and the Xavante Indians, 1937–1988* (Duke University Press, 2001). Good discussion of the manner in which Brazilian government policy in the mid-twentieth century constrained the lives of an important Indian tribe.

D. Goldstein, *Laughter Out of Place: Race, Class, Violence, and Sexuality in a Rio Shantytown* (University of California Press, 2003). Empathetic exploration of a Rio *favela*.

Michael George Hanchard, *Orpheus and Power: The Movimento Negro of Rio de Janeiro and São Paulo, 1945–1988* (Princeton University Press, 1994). Insight into Afro-Brazilian–based social movements.

Rachel E. Harding, *A Refuge in Thunder: Candomblé and Alternative Spaces of Blackness* (Indiana University Press, 2003). Study of how Afro-Brazilians created alternative spaces for themselves in society.

David Hellwig, ed., *African-American Reflections on Brazil's Racial Paradise* (Temple University Press, 1992). Revealing survey of U.S. reactions to Brazilian race relations.

Hendrik Kraay, ed., *Afro-Brazilian Culture and Politics: Bahia, 1790–1990s* (M. E. Sharpe, 1998). An analysis of the intersection of culture, religion, and politics in the state of Bahia.

Jeffrey Lesser, *Welcoming the Undesirables* (University of California Press, 1995). Pioneering study of attitudes toward Jewish migration to Brazil.

——, *Negotiating National Identity: Immigrants, Minorities, and the Struggle for Ethnicity in Brazil* (Duke University Press, 1999). Analysis of race and identity formations of Syrian-Lebanese and Japanese immigrants and their descendants.

Jeffrey Lesser, *A Discontented Diaspora: Japanese Brazilians and the Meaning of Ethnic Militancy, 1960–1980* (Duke University Press, 2007). Exploration of how Brazilians understand Japanese-Brazilians' identities and their role in society.

Elisa Larkin Nascimento, *The Sorcery of Color: Identity, Race, and Gender in Brazil* (Temple University Press, 2007). Analysis of interactions of race and gender in Brazilian society.

Rebecca Reichmann, ed., *Race Relations in Contemporary Brazil: From Indifference to Equality* (Pennsylvania State University Press, 1999). Highly useful collection of papers on differing aspects of race in contemporary Brazil.

Livio Sansone, *Blackness without Ethnicity: Constructing Race in Brazil* (Palgrave Macmillan, 2003). An examination of race with deconstructions of racial terminology.

Lilia Moritz Schwarcz, *The Spectacle of the Races: Scientists, Institutions, and the Race Question in Brazil, 1870–1930*. Translated by Leland Guyer (Hill and Wang, 1999). Examination of the development of ideas about race within Brazilian scientific institutions.

Thomas E. Skidmore, *Black into White: Race and Nationality in Brazilian Thought* (Oxford University Press, 1974). Analysis of intellectual controversies over race in Brazilian thought between 1870 and 1945.

James Sweet, *Re-creating Africa: Culture, Kinship, and Religion in the African-Portuguese World, 1441–1770* (University of North Carolina Press, 2003). Ingeniously researched treatment of the records of African slaves in the Portuguese colonial world, developing a panoramic view of origins and locations.

Maya Talmon-Chvaicer, *The Hidden History of Capoeira: A Collision of Cultures in the Brazilian Battle Dance* (University of Texas Press, 2008). History and practice of the Afro-Brazilian martial arts.

Edward E. Telles, *Race in Another America: The Significance of Skin Color in Brazil* (Princeton University Press, 2004). Most comprehensive consideration of race relations in Brazil.

Frances Winddance Twine, *Racism in a Racial Democracy: The Maintenance of White Supremacy in Brazil* (Rutgers University Press, 1998). Examination of the discourse and practice of racism.

Economic, Environmental, and Social Issues—Historical and Current

Werner Baer, *The Brazilian Economy*, 6th ed. (Lynne Reiner Publications, 2008). Basic reference work.

Dain Edward Borges, *The Family in Bahia, Brazil, 1870–1945* (Stanford University Press, 1992). Study of social networks of elite families in Salvador, Bahia.

Teresa Pires do Rio Caldeira, *City of Walls: Crime, Segregation, and Citizenship in São Paulo* (University of California Press, 2000). Fear, crime, and social stratification in urban Brazil.

Donald V. Coes, *Macroeconomic Crises, Policies, and Growth in Brazil, 1964–90* (World Bank, 1995). Reliable guide to the ups and downs of stabilization policies in Brazil.

Warren Dean, *With Broadax and Firebrand: The Destruction of the Brazilian Atlantic Forest* (University of California Press, 1995). Detailed study of the devastation of the endangered Atlantic forest.

Winston Fritsh, *External Constraints on Economic Policy in Brazil, 1889–1930* (University of Pittsburgh Press, 1988). Discussion of the key role the external sector played in the Brazilian economy under the Old Republic.

Celso Furtado, *The Economic Growth of Brazil: A Survey from Colonial to Modern Times* (University of California Press, 1971). Benchmark interpretation of the fundamentals of the Brazilian economy from colonial times through the Old Republic.

Robert Gay, *Popular Organization and Democracy in Rio de Janeiro: A Tale of Two Favelas* (Temple University Press, 1994). Analysis of the political processes in two shantytowns.

Stephen Haber, ed., *How Latin America Fell Behind* (Stanford University Press, 1997). Innovative explanation of Brazil's nineteenth-century "lag," with an explicit comparison to Mexico.

Tobias Hecht, *At Home in the Street: Street Children of Northeast Brazil* (Cambridge University Press, 1998). Anthropological examination of the violent lives of street children in the Northeast.

Mercedes S. Hinton, *The State on the Streets: Police and Politics in Argentina and Brazil* (Lynne Reiner Publishers, 2006). Illuminating study on the vexing question of how street politics can be controlled.

Thomas H. Holloway, *Immigrants on the Land: Coffee and Society in São Paulo 1886–1934* (University of North Carolina Press, 1980). Good treatment of how Italian immigrants succeeded in building an asset base.

James Holston, *The Modernist City: An Anthropological Critique of Brasilia* (University of Chicago Press, 1989). Insightful analysis of the social cross-currents of life in the capital city.

——, *Insurgent Citizenship: Disjunctions of Democracy and Modernity in Brazil* (Princeton University Press, 2008). Anthropological study of popular participation in urban peripheries.

Wendy Hunter, *Eroding Military Influence in Brazil: Politicians against Soldiers* (University of North Carolina Press, 1997). Analysis of the declining role of the military after the end of dictatorship.

Lúcio Kowarick, ed., *Social Struggles and the City: The Case of São Paulo* (Monthly Review Press, 1994). Basic account of the fractioning of modern city life in Brazil.

Robert M. Levine and José Carlos Sebe Bom Meihy. *The Life and Death of Carolina Maria de Jesus* (University of New Mexico Press, 1995). The story of a woman's life in a *favela*.

Maureen O'Dougherty, *Consumption Intensified: The Politics of Middle-Class Daily Life in Brazil* (Duke University Press, 2002). Effects of inflation on the Brazilian middle class.

Darcy Ribeiro, *The Brazilian People: The Formation and Meaning of Brazil*. Translated from the Portuguese by Gregory Rabassa (University Press of Florida, 2000). Reflections on race relations and social conditions.

Eugene Ridings, *Business Interest Groups in Nineteenth-century Brazil* (Cambridge University Press, 1994). Economic history of imperial Brazil.

Nancy Scheper-Hughes, *Death without Weeping: The Violence of Everyday Life in Brazil* (University of California Press, 1982). Penetrating, still relevant, first-hand study of *favela* life in Recife.

Stanley J. Stein, *The Brazilian Cotton Manufacture* (Cambridge University Press, 1957). Classic work on Brazilian industrialization.

William Roderick Summerhill, *Order against Progress: Government, Foreign Investment, and Railroads in Brazil, 1854–1913* (Stanford University Press, 2003). Railroad policy, finance and expansion of transportation.

Donald E. Syvrud, *Foundations of Brazilian Economic Growth* (Hoover Institution Press, 1974). Still valuable as an evaluation of the military stabilization policies.

Barbara Weinstein, *The Amazon Rubber Boom, 1850–1920* (Stanford University Press, 1983). Good treatment of the economic expansion of an important export crop during the Empire and early Republic.

Angus Wright and Wendy Wolford, *To Inherit the Earth: The Landless Movement and the Struggle for a New Brazil* (Food First Books, 2003). Study of the landless peasants' movement in different parts of the country.

Culture, Religion, and Society—Historical and Current

Severino João Medeiros Albuquerque, *Tentative Transgressions: Homosexuality, AIDS, and the Theater in Brazil* (University of Wisconsin Press, 2004). Impact of HIV/AIDS on cultural productions.

Peter Beattie, *The Human Tradition in Modern Brazil* (Scholarly Resources, 2004). Edited collection featuring personalities from diverse sectors of Brazilian society.

Diana De G. Brown, *Umbanda, Religion and Politics in Urban Brazil*, 2nd ed. (Columbia University Press, 1994). Excellent study of the important phenomenon of urban *umbanda* and Afro-Brazilian religious networks.

John Burdick, *Looking for God in Brazil: The Progressive Catholic Church in Urban Brazil's Religious Arena* (University of California Press, 1993). Analysis of the grassroots progressive wing of the Catholic Church.

Stephanie Dennison and Lisa Shaw, *Popular Cinema in Brazil, 1930–2001* (Manchester University, 2004). History of mass appeal films.

Christopher Dunn, *Brutality Garden: Tropicália and the Emergence of a Brazilian Counterculture* (University of North Carolina Press, 2001). Sympathetic treatment of the musical and cultural movement of the 1960s and 1970s.

David William Foster, *Gender and Society in Contemporary Brazilian Cinema* (University of Texas Press, 1999). Representations of gender and sexuality in Brazilian film.

Rowan Ireland, *Kingdoms Come: Religion and Politics in Brazil* (University of Pittsburgh Press, 1991). Explains the intersection of these two phenomena.

Randal Johnson and Robert Stam, ed. *Brazilian Cinema* (Columbia University Press, 1995). A comprehensive overview.

Ruth Landes, *The City of Women*, 2nd edition, with an introduction by Sally Cole (University of New Mexico, 1994). American anthropologist's view of the role of Afro-Brazilian women in *candomblé* ceremonies based on research conducted in Bahia in the late 1930s.

Robert M. Levine and John J. Crocitti, *The Brazil Reader: History, Culture, Politics* (Duke University Press, 1999). Anthology of documents and articles about Brazil from colonial past to the present.

Tamara Elena Livingston-Isenhour and Thomas George Caracas Garcia, *Choro: A Social History of a Brazilian Popular Music* (Indiana University Press, 2005). Race, class, and nineteenth-century popular music.

Cecília Loreto Mariz, *Pentecostals and Christian Base Communities in Brazil* (Temple University Press, 1994). Study of conservative and progressive religious movements..

Bryan McCann, *Hello, Hello Brazil: Popular Music in the Making of Modern Brazil* (Duke University Press, 2004). Carefully researched analysis of the power of radio in forging popular musical forms.

Chris McGowan and Ricardo Pessanha, *The Brazilian Sound: Samba, Bossa Nova and the Popular Music of Brazil* (Temple University Press, 1998). A broad survey of Brazilian music.

Robin Nagle, *Claiming the Virgin: The Broken Promise of Liberation Theology in Brazil* (Routledge, 1997). A critique of liberation theology and its effects.

Charles A. Perrone and Christopher Dunn, eds., *Brazilian Popular Music and Globalization* (University of Florida Press, 2001). Exploration of Brazilian music and its international appeal.

Caetano Veloso, *Tropical Truth: A Story of Music and Revolution in Brazil*. Translated by Isabel de Sena; edited by Barbara Einzig (Alfred A. Knopf, 2002). Memoir of one of Brazil's most talented and lasting singers and composers.

Hermano Vianna, *The Mystery of Samba: Popular Music and National Identity* (University of North Carolina Press, 1999). Consideration of identity through music and culture.

Gender and Sexuality

Sonia E. Alvarez, *Engendering Democracy in Brazil: Women's Movements in Transition Politics* (Princeton University Press, 1990). Analysis of the emergence of a feminist movement in the new democracy.

Roderick J. Barman, *Princess Isabel of Brazil: Gender and Power in the Nineteenth Century* (Scholarly Resources, 2002). Biography of the heir to the Brazilian throne.

Susan K. Besse, *Restructuring Patriarchy: The Modernization of Gender Inequality in Brazil, 1914–1940* (University of North Carolina Press, 1996). Historical survey of shifting gender roles in Brazil in the early twentieth century.

Sueann Caulfield, *In Defense of Honor: Sexual Morality, Modernity, and Nation in Early-twentieth-century Brazil* (Duke University Press, 2000). Perceptive study of popular moral attitudes as reflected in court decisions.

Carol Ann Drogus, *Women, Religion, and Social Change in Brazil's Popular Church* (University of Notre Dame Press, 1997). Examination of progressive grassroots movement in the Catholic Church.

Sandra Lauderdale Graham, *Caetana Says No: Women's Stories from a Brazilian Slave Society* (Cambridge University Press, 2002). Outstanding study of the interplay of gender, race, and social hierarchy in nineteenth-century Brazil.

James N. Green, *Beyond Carnival: Male Homosexuality in Twentieth-century Brazil* (University of Chicago Press, 1999). Social history of male homosexuality in Rio de Janeiro and São Paulo.

June E. Hahner, *Emancipating the Female Sex: The Struggle for Women's Rights in Brazil, 1850–1940* (Duke University Press, 1990). Pioneering study of the development of the first feminist and suffragist movements in Brazil.

Don Kulick, *Travesti: Sex, Gender, and Culture among Brazilian Transgendered Prostitutes* (University of Chicago Press, 1998). Anthropological analysis of the constructions of Brazilian sexuality.

Linda Lewin, *Surprise Heirs*, vol. 1, *Illegitimacy, Patrimonial Rights, and Legal Nationalism in Luso-Brazilian Inheritance, 1750–1822*; vol. 2, *Illegitimacy, Inheritance Rights, and Public Power in the Formation of Imperial Brazil, 1822–1889* (Stanford University Press, 2003). Comprehensive research on family relations, inheritance, and gender in colonial and imperial Brazil.

Muriel Nazzari, *Disappearance of the Dowry: Women, Families, and Social Change in São Paulo, Brazil (1600–1900)* (Stanford University Press, 1991). Insightful study of the changing status and role of women.

Richard Parker, *Bodies, Pleasures and Passions: Sexual Culture in Contemporary Brazil* (Beacon Press, 1991). An analysis of Brazilian sexuality.

——, *Beneath the Equator: Cultures of Desire, Male Homosexuality, and Emerging Gay Communities in Brazil* (Routledge, 1999). Study of the growing visibility of gay men.

Cecília Macdowell Santos, *Women's Police Stations: Gender, Violence, and Justice in São Paulo, Brazil* (Palgrave, 2005). An examination of feminists, state, and domestic violence.

Labor

John French, *The Brazilian Workers' ABC: Class Conflict and Alliances in Modern São Paulo* (University of North Carolina Press, 1992). Analysis of labor relations, 1900–1953.

Biorn Maybury-Lewis, *The Politics of the Possible: The Brazilian Rural Workers' Trade Union Movement, 1964–1985* (Temple University Press, 1992). Study of the mobilization of rural workers during the military dictatorship.

Anthony W. Pereira, *The End of the Peasantry: The Rural Labor Movement in Northeast Brazil, 1961–1988* (University of Pittsburgh Press, 1997). Overview of rural labor demands during the military regime.

Salvador A. M. Sandoval, *Social Change and Labor Unrest in Brazil since 1945* (Westview Press, 1993). Study of state control over unions and labor militancy.

Barbara Weinstein, *For Social Peace in Brazil: Industrialists and the Remaking of the Working Class in São Paulo, 1920–1964* (University of North Carolina Press, 1996). Industrialists and social and labor policy in the nation's economic powerhouse.

Cliff Welch, *The Seed Was Planted: The São Paulo Roots of Brazil's Rural Labor Movement, 1924–1964* (Pennsylvania State University Press, 1999). Brazil's rural labor movement in the state with the country's most dynamic economy.

Joel Wolfe, *Working Women, Working Men: São Paulo and the Rise of Brazil's Industrial Working Class, 1900–1955* (Duke University Press, 1993). Study of the labor actions of textile and metal workers.

Brazil–U.S. Relations

Jan Knippers Black, *United States Penetration of Brazil* (University of Pennsylvania Press, 1977). Extensive analysis of U.S. covert and overt machinations in Brazil.

James N. Green, *"We Cannot Remain Silent"*: *Opposition to the Brazilian Military Dictatorship in the United States, 1964–85* (Duke University Press, 2009). Study of the emergence of a U.S. human rights movement revolving around torture in Brazil.

Mônica Hirst, *The United States and Brazil: A Long Road of Unmet Expectations* (Routledge, 2005). An overview of Brazil-U.S. relations since the 1980s.

Martha Huggins, *Political Policing: The United States and Latin America* (Duke University Press, 1998). Examination of the U.S. government's support of public security forces in Brazil and other Latin American countries.

Frank D. McCann Jr., *The Brazilian-American Alliance* (Princeton University Press, 1973). Excellent account of U.S.-Brazilian relations in the pre–World War II era.

Oxfam, *Finding the Moral Fiber: Why Reform Is Urgently Needed for a Fair Cotton Trade* (Oxfam, 2004). Well informed critique of the classic problem of U.S. protectionist policy (in this case, cotton) in the late twentieth century.

Steven Topik, *Trade and Gunboats: The United States and Brazil in the Age of Empire* (Stanford University Press, 1996). Examination of commercial treaties and pacts between the two countries.

W. Michael Weis, *Cold Warriors & Coups D'etat: Brazilian-American Relations, 1945–64* (University of New Mexico Press, 1993). Study of U.S. involvement in the overthrow of João Goulart.

INDEX